A World of Its Own

STUDIES IN RURAL CULTURE   •   JACK TEMPLE KIRBY, EDITOR

Matt Garcia

A World of Its Own

Race, Labor,
and Citrus
in the Making
of Greater
Los Angeles,
1900–1970

The University of North Carolina Press
Chapel Hill and London

© 2001 The University of North Carolina Press
All rights reserved

Designed by Heidi Perov
Set in Electra
by Tseng Information Systems, Inc.

Manufactured in the United States of America

The paper in this book meets the guidelines for permanence and durability
of the Committee on Production Guidelines for Book Longevity of the
Council on Library Resources.

Library of Congress Cataloging-in-Publication Data

Garcia, Matt.
   A world of its own: race, labor, and citrus in the making of Greater
   Los Angeles, 1900–1970 / Matt Garcia.
      p. cm. — (Studies in rural culture)
   Includes bibliographical references and index
   ISBN 0-8078-2658-8 (cloth: alk. paper)
   ISBN 0-8078-4983-9 (pbk.: alk. paper)
      1. Los Angeles Region (Calif.) — Ethnic relations.   2. Mexican
Americans — California — Los Angeles Region — Social conditions —
20th century.   3. Whites — California — Los Angeles Region — Social
conditions — 20th century.   4. Agricultural laborers — California —
Los Angeles Region — Social conditions — 20th century.   5. Citrus fruit
industry — Social aspects — California — Los Angeles Region — History —
20th century.   6. Los Angeles Region (Calif.) — Social conditions — 20th
century.   7. Los Angeles Region (Calif.) — Economic conditions — 20th
century.   8. Community development — California — Los Angeles Region —
History — 20th century.   9. Intercultural communication — California —
Los Angeles Region — History — 20th century.   I. Title.   II. Series.
F869.L89 A253   2002
305.8′009794′94 — dc21   2001035879

05 04 03 02 01   5 4 3 2 1

For my son,

 Mauricio Candelario,

  who is "beautiful like a rainbow . . ."

Contents

Illustrations

Maps

Acknowledgments

My esteemed advisor and friend, Vicki Ruiz, once explained to me that in Chicana/Chicano History, "the people drive the book." This book is no exception. I have learned the majority of what I know from the many people who dared to share their lives with me on tape, and it is those people whom I wish to thank first. Although too many to name here (see the bibliography for a complete list), I am most thankful to the many Paduanos, dance hall performers and patrons, packinghouse workers, citrus pickers, and civil rights organizers living throughout Southern California who all graciously gave their time and stories to me. Specifically, I wish to thank Candelario Mendoza, whose life has served as an inspiration to me and numerous other Chicanos and Mexican Americans who call the Pomona Valley their home. Gracias a todos.

I owe a tremendous debt of gratitude to the many educators and advisors who guided me through my education and research. I am grateful to the staff, faculty, and graduate students of the Psychology Clinic at the University of California at Berkeley, 1987–1991, where I was employed as a librarian, for giving me the confidence to imagine myself being a professor of anything. My professors at the Claremont Graduate School (which now goes by the name Claremont Graduate University) provided form and substance to this dream. As my opening sentence indicates, Vicki Ruiz served as a guiding light during the dark days of graduate school, and it is to her that I owe my deepest thanks. Vicki's dedication and sensitivity to students' needs is unparalleled in this profession, and I am grateful to have been one of the growing numbers of young scholars who has worked with her. Virtually all good things that have happened to me are attributable to Vicki's support, guidance, and friendship—thanks Vicki. The peripatetic, organic intellectual Mike Davis shared research, advice, and friendship during his years at the Claremont Colleges and has significantly influenced this book. Hal Barron served as my link to the world of agricultural history, providing insightful comments and helpful instruction throughout my graduate education. As well, Professors Janet Farrell Brodie, Robert Dawidoff, and Lourdes Arguelles all helped expand my knowledge of Southern California, Latina/Latino, and labor history during my days at Claremont.

Although I could not resist the urge to move back West, I do appreciate and value the support I received during the first five years of my career at the University of Illinois, Urbana-Champaign. I received helpful comments and criticism on two chapters from members of the History Workshop (aka, the Social History Group), especially: Jim Barrett, Kathy Oberdeck, Dan Littlefield, Cynthia Radding, Poshek Fu, Liz Pleck, Fred Hoxie, Fred Jaher, David Prochaska, Blair Kling, and Clare Crowston. Kathy Oberdeck also provided key comments on Chapter 6 in a much earlier and undeveloped form, and Fred Hoxie, Fred Jaher, and Dan Littlefield read the entire manuscript and gave me critical advice regarding revisions and publication matters. I also want to thank all my colleagues in the Latina/Latino Studies Program at the University of Illinois, especially Angharad Valdivia who provided helpful comments on Chapter 4 and copious amounts of support, friendship, and "sisterly" advice throughout my days in Illinois. Alejandro Lugo and Cameron McCarthy also provided brilliant insights into my treatment of the *colonia* in Chapter 2, and Alejandro inspired my analysis of the bracero program in Chapter 5. Finally, my attempt to shape my ideas into a professional and accessible book would not have been possible without the hard work of my research assistants at the University of Illinois: Eric Burin, Guisela Latorre, and Lilia Fernandez. Each one is a brilliant scholar in his/her own right, and I expect great things out of them in the near future.

My new home at the University of Oregon has been an extremely beautiful and productive space in which to work, made more so by my wonderful colleagues in Ethnic Studies and History. Peggy Pascoe, who had given me guidance from afar during the early stages of my career, has now become my pillar of support in Eugene. I thank the entire faculty in Ethnic Studies, past and present, who read my book manuscript and offered me many favorable and constructive comments. Also, Jeff Ostler, Jim Mohr, and Jeff Hanes of the History Department were exceptionally helpful in advising me on preparation of the final manuscript.

Institutional support for this book has come from many sources. A Claremont Graduate School Humanities Fellowship and Claremont Graduate School Dissertation Fellowship proved crucial during the early phases of this project. A Haynes Research Fellowship from The Huntington Library aided my research in their Southern California citrus archives. I have had a very supportive and productive relationship with the Smithsonian Institution. In 1994, I was part of the first Inter-University Program (IUP) for Latino Research, Graduate Training Seminar in Qualitative Methodology held in Washington, D.C. A year later I received a Smithsonian Dissertation Fellowship with the Museum of American History. My institutional mentor at the Smithsonian, Alicia González, provided me necessary guidance, instruction, and shelter during my summer in Washington, D.C., and she continued to be a dear friend and important advisor throughout the writing of the manuscript. I also appreciate the generous research support I received at the University of Illinois, Urbana-Champaign, including awards and fellowships from the UIUC Research Board, The Illinois Program for Research in the Humanities, The Center for Advanced Study, and the Scholars Travel Fund.

No less important has been the assistance from knowledgeable staff and faculty at the numerous libraries and archives I visited during the writing of this book. The staff at the Pomona Public Library, especially David Streeter, Susan Hutchinson, and Bruce Guter, had the confidence and trust in me to explore on my own the rich archives hidden in the bowels of Special Collections. Ginger Elliot at Claremont Heritage selflessly took time out of her busy schedule to retrieve important documents, photos, and books located in the organization's office. I appreciate the efforts of Jean Beckner at the Claremont Colleges' Honnold Library, whose persistence helped me eventually uncover the hidden history of The Friends of the Mexicans, among other crucial information. Dace Taube at the Regional History Center of the University of Southern California, Los Angeles, Linda Christianson and Arlene Andrew at La Verne City Hall, and Theresa Handley of the Ontario Museum of History provided me many important leads to documents and community groups that are discussed in the following pages. Additionally, I appreciate the assistance from the staff at the Bancroft Library, Stanford's Green Library, Upland Public Library, the Model Colony Room at the Ontario City Library, The Huntington Library, Van Pelt-Dietrich Library, Riverside Public Library, UCLA Special Collections, and the National Archives and the Archives of American Art in Washington, D.C. I am also fortunate to have had the services of Ada Arensdorf who transcribed important interviews, Patricia Mendez-Long who helped me with a few translations, and Tavo Olmos who reproduced most of the photos. Professor Mario García helped me avoid a long wait by graciously supplying a copy of Ignacio López's FBI file, and Fred Ross Jr. shared important memories and documents associated with his father's life.

I am privileged to have worked with the conscientious and professional editors at The University of North Carolina Press. Lewis Bateman was the first person to see the suitability of this book for the press and worked extremely hard in the early phases of the review process to get a fair and impartial review of my manuscript. Later, David Perry became a strong supporter of the project and saw it through to publication. I want to pen a special "thank you" to Jack Kirby, editor of the Studies in Rural Cultures Series, who not only wrote a very generous and constructive review, but also became my most steadfast advocate during the transition from one press editor to another. Thanks also to two anonymous reviewers whose comments helped me improve the book from its original manuscript form.

This journey could not have been completed without the support and, at times, sympathy of friends. Anthea Hartig, Margo McBane, and I (aka, the Citrus Study Group) shared important ideas and research experiences that improved all of our work. I thank my comrades at the Claremont Graduate School during those "golden years" of Vicki's reign: Marian Perales, Virginia Espino, Phil Castruita, Naomi Quiñonez, Emily Stoltzfus, Matthew Lasar, Lee Ann Meyer, John Lloyd, Matt Jordan, and Matt Reed. Torri Estrada, Julie Harder, Branko Perazich, Lisa Brown, Sue McNamara, Pete McNally, Nick Almendarez, and Julius Hewitt helped me stay sane by taking research and writing breaks with me to idyllic and not-so-idyllic destinations over the last seven years. Perla Batalla soothed my mind and invigorated my spirit with her sweet voice during my days in L.A. Along the way toward the book, a few new friends influenced my life in meaningful ways: specifically, Michael Willard, Joe Austin, and Rachel Buff who have helped me to discover the importance of generation and youth in my work. Still newer friends and colleagues read parts of the manuscript and offered useful suggestions, including: José Alamillo, Betsy Jameson, Mae Ngai, Jorge Huerta, Cindy Hahamovitch, Barbara Posadas, Hector González, Gabriela Arredondo, David Gutiérrez and Neil Foley.

This book has also been a very personal journey through the *colonias*, barrios, and neighborhoods inhabited by many generations and members of my family. My grandparents, although having very different relationships to the cultivation of citrus and the development of Southern California, equally shaped my perspectives on this history. I appreciate the love and support of my entire family, especially those of you who gave up your time to be interviewed. Thank you also to my mother and father, Janet and David Garcia, whose unusual union in the late 1960s produced a family that was in some ways years ahead of its time. Their guidance and love made all the difference during those years when I was not sure I was going to make it. My sister, Jacki, also provided much humor and encouragement during some rough moments for me over the last decade or so. Finally, I express my sincere love and appreciation to my wife, María Mendez, and my son, Mauricio Candelario, who have permitted me many leaves for professional duties. This book marks the end of a long struggle for all of us, and the beginning of a bright new future that includes a new baby, our daughter, Timotea de la Luz. ¡Adelante!

Matt Garcia

Abbreviations

AFL	American Federation of Labor
CAWIU	Cannery and Agricultural Workers Industrial Union
CCIH	California Commission of Immigration and Housing
CFGE	California Fruit Growers Exchange
CGS	Claremont Graduate School
CIO	Congress of Industrial Organizations
CSO	Community Service Organization
CUCOM	Confederación de Uniónes de Campesinos y Obreros Mexicanos
DIR	(California) Department of Industrial Relations
FEPC	Fair Employment Practices Committee
FHA	Federal Housing Administration
FSA	Farm Security Administration
HUD	Department of Housing and Urban Development
IAF	Industrial Areas Foundation
ICC	Intercultural Council of Claremont
INS	Immigration and Naturalization Service
IWW	Industrial Workers of the World
KKK	Ku Klux Klan
LACC	Los Angeles Chamber of Commerce
LAO	Latin American Organization
LAPD	Los Angeles Police Department
LULAC	League of United Latin American Citizens
MAM	Mexican American Movement
MOD	Mutual Orange Distributor
NAACP	National Association for the Advancement of Colored People
NLRB	National Labor Relations Board
POGA	Pasadena Orange Growers' Association
SGFLA	San Gabriel Farm Labor Association
SMSA	Standard Metropolitan Statistical Area
SRA	(California) State Relief Agency
UCAPAWA	United Cannery, Agricultural, Packing, and Allied Workers of America

UCLA	University of California at Los Angeles
UNESCO	United Nations Educational, Scientific, and Cultural Organization
USDA	United States Department of Agriculture
WASP	White Anglo-Saxon Protestant
WCTU	Woman's Christian Temperance Union
WPA	Works Projects Administration
YMCA	Young Men's Christian Association

A World of Its Own

Introduction

Driving westbound along Interstate 10 from Pomona to Los Angeles in Southern California, one cuts through the heart of what once was the richest agricultural land in the United States. On the south side of the freeway lie the grounds formerly occupied by walnut and deciduous fruit orchards and berry farms; to the north lie the interclimatic foothill "benches" and "fans" upon which growers once raised the most productive citrus groves in the nation. Today, however, the landscape is characterized by a seemingly endless string of suburban bedroom communities that become more densely populated and "urban" with each successive mile as one approaches downtown Los Angeles. Growing up in this area during the 1970s and 1980s, I watched the final stages of this transformation as strip malls replaced packinghouses and bulldozers uprooted citrus trees to make way for single-family homes. In 1976, my family moved into a new residential community in Upland where my friends and I played hide-and-go-seek among the wood frames and fiberglass of soon-to-be-built tract houses and staged lemon fights in the few groves that remained. For most residents, the receding line of citrus on the foothills represented progress and the promise of achieving the American dream of owning a home. By the early 1980s, most of the physical markers of the citrus industry had been wiped clean from the land.

As a child born of mixed heritage — my mother is Anglo and my father Mexican — I saw these changes from a slightly different perspective than most kids due to my unique relationship with the social and cultural geography that accompanied the development of citrus suburbs. Although both sides of my family have resided in Southern California for three generations and participated at various levels in the citrus economy, their experiences were neither similar nor equivalent in outcome. While my maternal grandfather worked as a data analysis supervisor for Sunkist in Ontario, providing my mother and her family with a middle-class standard of living, my father's family had a dramatically different experience. Born in a semi-rural *colonia* (colony) composed primarily of Mexican agricultural laborers, my father grew up in an unincorporated neighborhood that the local Spanish/English bilingual newspaper *El Espectador* referred to as "Tierra de Nadie" ("land of no one").[1] This title described the political situation of the community—the *colonia* resided at the crossroads of three cities (Claremont, Upland, and Montclair), and two counties (Los Angeles and San Bernardino)—but also captured the discrimination of white city and county officials who refused to provide the most basic city services such as sewer lines, garbage collection, postal delivery, paved roads, street lights, and police and fire protection. Indicative of the prejudice that characterized white attitudes toward Mexicans during the heyday of citrus, this segregation continued throughout my young life and provided evidence of the deep racial and class divisions that agricultural production engendered in the citrus belt prior to the 1970s. As I grew older, understanding the origins and legacies of these divisions became my passion. In the face of industrial and residential development that erased the physical reminders of this world, I sought to uncover the persistent social and cultural fissures still present within this society.

In this book I attempt to merge an analysis of community formation with the study of Chicano cultural development by focusing on the cultural history of the segregated citrus-growing area of the San Gabriel Valley from 1900 to 1970. Considered by many to be the key to Los Angeles's economic ascendancy prior to World War II, today these agricultural "belts" exist as understudied but integrated components in the region's historiography. Most historians focusing on Southern California emphasize the leadership of downtown magnets such as Harrison Grey Otis and the influence of the powerful Merchants and Manufacturers Association, but neglect the ways in which the expansion of citrus production during the 1920s created extraordinary wealth for predominantly white investors from the Midwest and East.[2] Their profits led to the growth of towns such as Pasadena, Glendora, Claremont, Ontario, and Riverside, and contributed to the establishment of a "polynuclear" suburban landscape that became the hallmark of Greater Los Angeles.[3] Promoted by the Los Angeles Chamber of Commerce as "the perishable fruit and vegetable garden of the United States," the agricultural "back country" of Los Angeles constituted an integral part of the metropolitan economy.[4]

The entire San Gabriel Valley, a region that geographically and culturally bleeds east from Los Angeles, encompasses numerous Mexican *colonias*. Unlike the industrial barrio of East Los Angeles, the *colonias* further east can be characterized by a mixed economy of agriculture and industry. Although farmers raised a variety of crops including grapes, walnuts, and olives, the cultivation of citrus defined the "citrus belt" of San Gabriel Valley. White growers preferred Mexican and Asian workers for manual labor positions in the groves and packinghouses for three important reasons: one, they were more easily exploited than white workers due to their perceived temporary employment status as alien, immigrant laborers; two, white growers and local authorities possessed privileges that allowed them to manipulate and control the movement of ethnoracial minorities; and three, white employers could segment the labor force by race, language, gender, generation, and citizenship, thereby reducing the chance of unionization. By the 1920s, Mexican workers became the exploited minority of choice because U.S. immigration policies did not restrict Mexican immigrants from entering the country as it did Asian workers. As citrus production increased and workers were needed for year-round positions, permanent worker settlements developed where many Mexican people raised families and "became Mexican American." This book focuses on these Mexican families and communities, and constitutes one of the first studies to examine the history of a suburban Mexican American population.

A focus on the suburbs constitutes an important contribution to the history of Mexican Americans in Southern California. Much of this historiography has stressed the urban experience of Mexican immigrants and their children, and the formation of barrios (urban Mexican communities) primarily in two places: "La Placita" near downtown Los Angeles and across the Los Angeles River in unincorporated East Los Angeles. In his important book *Becoming Mexican American: Ethnicity, Culture and Identity in Chicano Los Angeles, 1900–1945*, George Sánchez examines the cultural adaptations of Mexican Americans living in East Los Angeles prior to World War II. Rejecting the bipolar interpretation of immigrant culture used by both immigration and Chicano historians, Sánchez argues that a "hybrid" Chicano culture emerged that reflected the complexities of Mexican American urban life. This work builds upon the scholarship of Sánchez's predecessor and mentor, Albert Camarillo, whose book *Chicanos in a Changing Society* laid the foundations for modern Chicano history. Interpreting the impact of the structural and physical changes of Los Angeles on Chicanos, Camarillo invented the term "barrioization" to explain the movement and consolidation of Mexican people across the Los Angeles River. Camarillo used the concept not to define and delimit the boundaries of Mexican barrios, but rather to provide a model for understanding a complex and "changing society." Like Sánchez's concept of culture, the communities discussed in Camarillo's work are dynamic and expanding social spaces. Moreover, his focus on four barrios suggests the need for a more comparative approach to the study of Mexican American communities in Southern California.[5]

Only recently have Chicano historians begun to follow Camarillo's example and look beyond the neighborhoods of "La Placita" and East Los Angeles. Historian Gilbert González has been the most insightful critic of the urban bias in Chicano history and was the first scholar to offer a book-length history of Southern California *colonias*. In his book *Labor and Community: Mexican Citrus Worker Villages in a Southern California County, 1900–1950*, González examines the "quasi-independent" citrus worker villages in Orange County just south of Los Angeles. While González's book expands the scope of Southern California Chicano history, he does not produce a model that can easily be applied to the study of the San Gabriel Valley. Admitting that the citrus belt was "neither rural nor urban," as Carey McWilliams observed in his classic book *Southern California Country: An Island in the Land*, González nevertheless emphasizes the "rural character" of most Orange County settlements. His interpretation can be explained in part by the fact that Orange County ranchers grew Valencia oranges, which encouraged dispersed settlement and produced a "rural coloration," while inland growers raised Washington navels in "densely populated," "wealthier," and "urbanized" districts. These conditions, discussed in Chapter 1, resulted in differences that McWilliams called "almost imperceptible to an outsider, but very real nonetheless."[6]

In negotiating the "fragmented" and "polynucleated" landscape of Southern California, I have found the theories of Edward Soja, presented in his book *Postmodern Geographies: The Reassertion of Space in Critical Social Theory*, particularly useful.[7] Like Michel Foucault, Soja questions the privileged position of time and history in modern social theory and analysis. Space, to the extent that it is discussed by western Marxists and social scientists, has been reduced to a neutral or "dead" location where "history takes place" but has no critical impact on the course of human relations. Time, on the other hand, has been constructed as a continuum linking one group or human action to another in a series of events that constitutes an historical moment. For Soja, the preferencing of a linear temporal flow over spatial relations produces a one-dimensional rendering of capitalist societies that does not reflect the degree to which geography influences human interaction.

Like Soja, I begin with the assumption that landscapes are not "neutral" or blank sheets on which human history is written; rather, their form and process of creation often possess keys to understanding the type of social relations that exist within a given society. For example, in studying the San Gabriel Valley, a region that prior to World War II was as much an "agricultural" landscape as Orange County and the San Joaquin Valley, one is struck by the comparatively few violent conflicts between labor and capital. Moreover, of the strikes that did occur in the valley, most took place on strawberry farms or vineyards and not in the numerous orange and lemon groves that dominated the region. The reduced role of labor organizing and unions, however, should not detract from Mexican residents' constant, though less confrontational, challenges to the prejudice expressed by the dominant culture. The contrasts between the citrus belt and other agricultural areas in California have led me to ask the following questions: To what extent did the social and cultural geography of the San Gabriel–San Bernardino Valley mitigate worker activism? In what ways other than strikes did workers express their discontent? How did workers use the unique suburban geography of the San Gabriel–San Bernardino Valley to expand the space of their lives? And finally, to what extent did Mexican residents construct and maintain an alternative cultural geography to the mainstream that helped them endure and overcome discrimination and segregation?

Throughout the book, I employ what Soja describes as "an appropriate interpretive balance between space, time, and social being" in answering many of these questions. While virtually all historians and writers of various political persuasions and interpretations have conceded that Los Angeles exists as a network of suburban enclaves rather than a "traditional" city, few have demonstrated how this sprawling metropolis shaped "the formative spatiality of social life." In what follows, I explain how the formation of the citrus empire and its attendant worker settlements laid the foundations for the expanded and segregated landscape known as "Greater Los Angeles." While my act of imposing a restrictive boundary on this world (i.e., "Los Angeles County," or "the citrus belt") bares some of my own temporal and epistemological limitations and does not reflect the much more culturally and geographically diverse history of Southern California and its people, I nevertheless hope to contribute to the project of expanding the interpretation of Chicano community and cultural formation beyond a narrow focus on East Los Angeles and "La Placita." I have adopted Soja's theoretical model as a way of addressing the multidimensional aspects of this region, taking into account both geography (for example, the citrus belt) and history (for example, the process of cultural change and development) in interpreting twentieth-century culture in the San Gabriel–San Bernardino Valley. Moreover, I portray Mexican Americans as active agents in adapting to this expanded spatial geography by emphasizing their use of transportation and service industries in Los Angeles, as well as their creation and maintenance of information and social networks.

Expanding and refining the definition of Mexican American resistance constitutes the second goal of this book. Due to the predominantly working-class orientation of Mexican laborers living and working in the United States, much of Chicano history has centered on economic segmentation, exploitation, and labor activism, with the strike representing the ultimate act of resistance. Yet, as Antonio Gramsci argued, strikes or "wars of maneuver" represent flash points that cannot be properly understood without an investigation of employees' tangential "wars of position."[8] Responding to Marxists who understood the state's control of labor in strictly economic terms, Gramsci interpreted hegemony to be both economic *and* cultural domination that transcended the workplace and influenced all aspects of workers' lives. "Wars of position," therefore, represent the process of creating an alternative vision of human relations based primarily on cooperation rather than competition.

"Counter-hegemonic alliances" built through "wars of position" become rooted in the divisions drawn by the hegemonic processes of the state determined by the dominant culture. In the United States, these lines of demarcation have often been racial/cultural and gendered and have accentuated rather than deteriorated differences between whites and nonwhites, and men and women. For example, Chicana lemon packers were subject to three different forms of discrimination based on their gender, class, and ethnoracial background. While their situation may be interpreted as "layers of oppression," these women also possessed the ability to use one or a combination of their identities as a basis for counter-hegemonic alliances to improve the conditions of their lives. Forging temporary protest movements out of their common experiences as working-class, Mexican American women, these packers occasionally mobilized for wage increases and safer working conditions. Therefore, cultural affinity within nonwhite sectors and single-sexed workforces, particularly in a U.S. context, have contributed significantly to "wars of position" and consequently cannot be easily dismissed as corollary, concomitant, or inconsequential.

Ethnic studies scholars invested in merging a cultural studies mode of interpretation with a traditional political economy approach have begun to offer new definitions of working-class politics that situate identity as integral rather than peripheral and counter-productive to the formation of collective expressions of resistance. For example, in his book *Race Rebels*, Robin D. G. Kelley calls for a major redefinition of politics to include the "unorganized, clandestine, and evasive" expressions that have come to dominate minority responses to discrimination in the workplace. Akin to the "subalterns" of developing and third world nations discussed in the work of Gayatri Spivak and others, U.S. racial minorities often voiced their opposition to economic and social domination within *and* outside of "mainstream" political institutions and organizations.[9] Their image as interlopers in a labor market exclusively reserved for Euroamericans generated hostility among established unions and white working-class Americans. Moreover, their marginal status as nonwhites and occasionally noncitizens made issues of civil rights, racial equality, and citizenship as important subjects for redress as labor exploitation. Although Mexican citrus workers organized strikes and joined progressive unions whenever possible and necessary, more often these disfranchised, racialized, and segregated minorities challenged discriminatory conditions through an "infrapolitics" that transcended the workplace. Described by Kelley as the "daily confrontations, evasive actions, and stifled thoughts" of minority workers, "infrapolitics" over time had a cumulative effect on power relations in Southern California.[10]

Scholars invested in this new definition of working-class politics most frequently locate expressions of alternative cultural formation in the complex and occasionally contradictory arena of popular culture. The term popular culture is used throughout this book in opposition to exclusive and essentialist definitions of "culture" as elite art forms, artifacts, and representations. By popular culture, I refer to the expressions of working-class women and men that reflect their experiences and practices both within, and outside of, the workplace. As George Lipsitz explains in his book *Dangerous Crossroads: Popular Music, Postmodernism, and the Poetics of Place*, the exploitative and predatory nature of capitalist systems have become so pervasive in the twentieth century that oppressed communities of color have often waged critiques that are immanent rather than transcendent to the societies within which they reside. Countering the totalizing narratives of structuralists' interpretations, cultural studies scholars have demonstrated how aggrieved minorities have adapted to capitalist exploitation by incorporating strategies of resistance in their daily lives. For example, George Lipsitz explores the various ways in which oppressed ethnoracial minorities and women throughout the world have employed Gramsci's idea of a "war of position" (an effort to build a counter-hegemonic alliance) with cultural practices and performance rather than engage solely in a less effective "war of maneuver" (the effort to seize state power). Exercising a "strategic anti-essentialism" in their musical presentations, U.S. minority artists have turned popular stereotypes into instruments of affinity to forge multiracial coalitions and wage meaningful critiques of U.S. racism. Similarly, historians George Sánchez and Vicki Ruiz have demonstrated how young Mexican Americans' participation in, and reinterpretation of, mass culture produced an "ambivalent Americanism" among the children of Mexican immigrants and laid the foundations for the creation of a distinctive Chicano culture in Southern California.[11]

In *A World of Its Own*, I examine a full range of Mexican American protests, from the more traditional forms such as strikes, boycotts, and political organizing to the lesser studied though equally relevant artistic expressions of alternative cultural formation that rebuffed and/or critiqued prejudice and discrimination prevalent within Greater Los Angeles. By exploring their participation in two types of cultural institutions, "Little Theater" and dance halls, I demonstrate how young Mexican Americans used popular culture to improve intercultural relations among the many people living in, and moving to, the San Gabriel Valley. Although mediated by segregation, material inequality, and the influence of white patrons, Mexican American thespians at the Padua Hills Theatre and a culturally diverse body of young musicians and audiences at dance halls such as Rainbow Gardens and El Monte American Legion Stadium imagined a world where the possibilities of interethnic communication and shared spaces became a reality.

Shows at both venues affirmed the physical and cultural presence of Latinas/Latinos in North America and incorporated the influence of Mexican immigrants to this diverse group. In terms of the dance halls, Mexican artistic expression (re)established a foothold for *Latina/Latino* (as opposed to just Mexican or Mexican American) music that permitted Mexican American deejays to host Latin American music concerts in the citrus belt, featuring an ethnoracially diverse group of Latina/Latino performers, from Cuban-born mambo king Dàmaso Pérez Prado, to the Texas *conjunto/orquesta* band leader Beto Villa, to the local Chicano and Chicana rock 'n' roll sensations Ritchie Valens and Rosie Mendez-Hamlin (of "Rosie and the Originals" fame). As Américo Paredes and more recently Rubén Martínez, José David Saldívar, and Lisabeth Haas have argued, places such as the San Gabriel Valley and the entire Southwest represent a cultural area of "Greater Mexico/Greater Latin America" that transcends geopolitical boundaries. Mexican immigrants brought with them not only their labor, but also customs and entertainment interests that strengthened the cultural, economic, historical, and geographical ties to Mexico in particular and Latin America in general. Similarly, in spite of the control white proprietors exercised over Padua productions, the Mexican Players reminded Anglo patrons that Mexican migrants preceded Europeans in California.[12]

For most participants in these institutions, however, the political and social implications of their activities developed as a byproduct of their primary goal to participate in an emerging public culture shaped by American mass media and consumerism. By asserting basic rights of access to public space and markets, Mexican Americans dared to question the segregation that attempted to confine them to the *colonias*. In the many interviews I conducted, actors, musicians, deejays, and patrons rarely made distinctions between the desire to seek pleasure and the goal of ending discrimination; rather, most assumed the two to be intertwined since Mexican Americans (and all racialized minorities) had been systematically excluded from or segregated within theaters and dance halls patronized by Anglos. Consequently, the establishment of institutions like the Padua Hills Theatre, El Monte American Legion Stadium, and Rainbow Gardens constituted not only the formation of important public arenas where Mexicans could influence the "mainstream" culture of Southern California, but also "political" acts that sought to expand the space of Mexican American lives.[13]

In using oral interviews, I have developed a healthy tolerance for ambiguity and complexity since often these are the adjectives that best describe the lives and memories of my subjects. To be sure, I use documentary evidence to contextualize and interpret the experiences of Mexican Americans in the broader history of race relations in California and the United States; however, in making sense of their lives, I attempt to follow the advice of Robin D. G. Kelley, who encourages historians to see people "where they are rather than where we would like them to be."[14] Rather than sort out clear-cut "political" motivations from the incidental—even at the level of cultural politics—I examine what ethnic studies scholar Cameron McCarthy calls a "motif of possibility" in the various cultural expressions of Mexican Americans living in the citrus belt. As both historian Richard Johnson and ethnic studies scholar José David Saldívar have argued, subjective, but not necessarily conscious, acts of identification "includes the *possibility* . . . that some elements or impulses are subjectively active" (italics added). In other words, through their participation in institutions and events that articulate an identity separate from the dominant culture, minorities achieve a consciousness as political agents that may or may not be operationalized in future endeavors. The ability of minorities to "visualize a community" based on an alternative mode of human relations constitutes a "war of position" that, as Paul Gilroy has argued, transfigures society in *political* ways. By acknowledging the potential impact of minorities' involvement in cultural institutions like Padua Hills and the dance halls, I believe we arrive at a better understanding of the conflicted, but influential cultural politics of Mexican Americans.[15]

Some scholars have raised legitimate questions about this redefinition of politics. For example, David Stowe argues that without a consideration of the intentions of the people we study, historians run the risk of romanticizing their subjects and representing them in ways that they would neither recognize nor agree with.[16] While I am sympathetic to Stowe's call for truth-in-telling, I am also aware from the many hours of oral history I have conducted with performers, patrons, workers, and organizers that intentions and "political" motivations of participants vary dramatically. For example, among the many Paduanos I interviewed, some hesitated to classify their performances as "political" even as they explained that the Mexican Players had done much to improve race relations between Mexicans and whites in Southern California. Similarly, dance hall performers and patrons fondly recalled the rebellious acts of inter-racial dancing and dating, but were quick to qualify their experiences as "just having a good time." Still other participants at both the theater and the dance halls expressed a consciousness about the political significance of their acts and clearly articulated an anti-racist agenda. Through these interviews, I discovered the unique tensions experienced by historians using the methodology of oral history: our responsibility to interpret and contextualize peoples' lives within a historical period and a geographical setting sometimes conflicts with the ways in which interviewees themselves assign meaning to their endeavors. Consequently, rarely did clear, unambiguous intentions of historical participants, individually or collectively, emerge from these interviews.

Some individuals, of course, did articulate a strong, clear commitment to the realization of Mexican American civil rights. The life of Candelario Mendoza, whose narrative parallels and informs much of the history in this book, exemplifies the experience of many Mexican Americans who came of age during the 1930s and 1940s. An educator and civil rights leader in the Pomona Valley, "Cande" stood out as a vital narrator whose wellspring of knowledge I began to tap during my years as a graduate student at The Claremont Graduate School. In beginning our relationship, I fully expected to uncover the many rich stories of his involvement with the bilingual newspaper owner/editor Ignacio López; of his participation in the formation of a civil rights movement in Pomona; of his experience as the last president of the YMCA-sponsored Mexican American Movement; and of his long career as one of the first Mexican American school teachers and administrators in Southern California. I was less prepared, however, to learn of the many years he spent as the Spanish-speaking disc jockey for a local radio station; of his short stint as a performer at Padua Hills Theatre; of his athletic talents as a baseball player in the semiprofessional California Pacific Clay League; and of his long and colorful career as the emcee and music consultant for the Pomona dance hall, Rainbow Gardens. Although I initially approached Cande to find the roots of an organized and politicized Mexican American community in the citrus belt, my interviews with him taught me valuable lessons about the need to avoid compartmentalizing peoples' lives into rigid categories. I learned that Cande's reputation as an entertainer and local radio personality earned him the respect and support of local Mexican Americans and gave him the confidence to speak on behalf of the Mexican community in public forums. Moreover, his participation in these cultural institutions shaped his identity as a Mexican American political activist and strengthened communal bonds that were essential during periods of social conflict. Educated and upwardly mobile, Cande used his talents in the service of his community and has continued to defend the civil rights of Mexican and Latin American immigrants to the present.

Occasionally, Mexican American challenges to discrimination and segregation evoked a political response from white, upper middle-class citizens who sought to remedy the "Mexican problem" in their own "progressive" way. Although the term progressivism possesses many meanings, here it refers to the sympathetic, though often misguided, actions of white philanthropists and Americanization officials who invested their time and money to improve working and living conditions for Mexican Americans in Southern California. Inspired as much by a desire to project a compassionate self-image as by altruism, reformers constituted an "in-between element" that tried to mediate disputes among Mexican workers, citrus belt growers, and local and state governments. That these individuals displayed a condescending noblesse oblige attitude toward their mostly working-class, Mexican beneficiaries underscores some of the problems surrounding progressive reform during the early twentieth century, and suggests why these "good-doers" often fell short of the "intercultural understanding" they hoped to achieve with their Mexican neighbors.[17]

Like "progressivism," ethnoracial descriptors such as "white," "Anglo," "Euro-american," "Mexican," "black," and "Asian" are terms that tend to obfuscate and homogenize the various cultural groups that shaped Greater Los Angeles during this seventy-year period. As Neil Foley demonstrated in his book *The White Scourge*, people with diverse backgrounds and ancestry composed each of these communities and maintained cultural practices that fortified *and* challenged in-group cohesiveness and identity. Yet, despite their heterogeneity, each group maintained, and/or had imposed upon them, an identity that tended to locate them within a racial hierarchy that placed "whiteness" at the top. Frequently, those who could claim European ancestry made the most aggressive claims on "whiteness" and exercised the greatest influence over who received "white" status and who did not. For groups such as Mexicans, however, who claimed European, African, and American ancestry, other factors such as language, class, citizenship, and physical features (including, but not limited to, their skin-color) determined how society perceived them racially and shaped their access to "whiteness." Moreover, the historical period and place mattered in how ethnoracial minorities were labeled, as well as how these communities self-identified.

Given the fluid and complex history of racial identity formation in the West — one that, as many Asian American and Chicano scholars have pointed out, goes beyond the black-white dichotomy—I have chosen to be adaptable in my use of ethnoracial terms. In general, I use the terms and identities chosen by the people spoken or written in their particular period of time and try to highlight, whenever necessary, conflicts regarding these identities. I also provide evidence of internal divisions among groups, and explore the making and unmaking of racial identities as a way of exposing them for the social constructions that we have learned them to be. "Anglo," "white," and "Euroamerican" constitute just three of the most common and problematic identities used throughout the book. Admittedly, the use of the term Anglo to describe all whites of European descent is inaccurate given the ethnic diversity within this group, including Italians, Irish, and Germans, to name a few; nevertheless, this is the way many Mexicans and some "Euroamericans" identified this group. I use the term "Euroamerican" to clarify the origins (Europe) that were the primary basis for their identity, though I understand that many (if not most) Mexicans, African Americans, and Asian Americans could make a similar claim to such ancestry. Contradictions such as these highlight the problems of racial categorization and demonstrate how the "scourge" of whiteness has infected social relations in the United States throughout its history.[18]

Employing traditional and cultural politics, Mexican Americans of the citrus belt overcame labor exploitation, segregation, and racism to participate in the creation of Greater Los Angeles. Part I of *A World of Its Own* examines the physical and cultural formation of the citrus suburbs of Los Angeles and explores the Eurocentric and often racist underpinnings of this society. Chapter 1, entitled "The Ideal Country Life: The Development of Citrus Suburbs in Southern California," demonstrates the influence of Thomas Jefferson's agrarian ideal on the creation of the citrus belt and examines how white midwestern and eastern immigrants attempted to merge the best of farm life with the modern conveniences of urban life. That this "ideal country life" rested on the exploitation of Native American, Mexican, and Asian workers constitutes a major subject of this chapter as well as Chapter 2, entitled "The 'Colonia Complex' Revisited: Racial Hierarchies and Border Spaces in the Citrus Belt, 1917–1926." In both chapters, I expose the myth of the "ten-acre man" by exploring the discriminatory "system of employment" used by citrus ranchers. Chapter 2 also focuses on the struggles between Mexican immigrants and growers in shaping segregated community spaces Carey McWilliams called "the Colonia Complex."

In Chapter 3, entitled "Friends of the Mexicans?: Mexican Immigration and the Politics of Social Reform," and Chapter 4, "Just Put on that Padua Hills Smile: The Mexican Players and the Padua Hills Theatre, 1931–1974," I explore the subjects of immigration, social reform, and popular culture in Southern California. Chapter 3 examines how the battle over immigration played out among restrictionists, reformers, and growers during the 1920s and early 1930s, and focuses special attention on the relationship between Mexican immigrants and the Americanization organization, the Friends of the Mexicans. My focus on the history of the Padua Hills Theatre in Chapter 4 follows the development of intercultural relations into the post-Depression era. Pursuing the objective of "intercultural understanding" through entertainment, the theater helped maintain open lines of communication between white and Mexican residents in Southern California from 1931 until its closure in 1974.

Part II examines the post–World War II transformation of the citrus belt from a primarily agricultural economy to an industrial landscape distinguished by bedroom communities and single-family homes. Chapter 5, entitled "Citrus in the War Years: Gender, Citizenship, and Labor, 1940–1964," explores the emergence of a new "system of employment" during and after World War II dependent on the exploitation of Mexican contract laborers (*braceros*) in the fields and Mexican American women workers in the packinghouses. Building on the work of Vicki Ruiz, I explore the development of a "packinghouse culture" among Mexican women employees. This chapter also delineates the cleavages in Pomona Valley *colonias* between native residents and their *bracero* neighbors as they competed for jobs and social space. Many natives and longtime residents believed themselves to be a cut above the *braceros*, whom they viewed with suspicion and at times outright disdain.

In Chapter 6, entitled "Memories of El Monte: Dance Halls and Youth Culture in Greater Los Angeles, 1950–1974," I explore the other side of interracial, intraethnic, and gender relations in Southern California by focusing on the development of two multicultural dance halls in the citrus belt, Pomona's Rainbow Gardens and El Monte's American Legion Stadium. I demonstrate how Mexican Americans broke out of their marginalized communities to claim public space by staging and participating in dances featuring U.S., Latin American, and Mexican music for predominantly Mexican American audiences. These shows proved to be so successful that concert organizers like Cande Mendoza expanded their repertoires to cater to another disfranchised group in Southern California: youth. Hosting an eclectic mix of performers during the 1950s and early 1960s, the dance halls attracted culturally diverse audiences and created the potential for intercultural exchange across ethnic, racial, class, and gender lines. Dependent on radio, television, parkways and freeways, a multicultural youth culture developed within the dance halls that challenged established modes of race relations and dating.

The last chapter, *"Sol y Sombra*: The Limits of Intercultural Activism in Post-Citrus Greater Los Angeles," focuses on postwar political and community groups formed to combat segregation and discrimination in Southern California. The chapter focuses primarily on two organizations—the San Gabriel/San Bernardino Valley Unity Leagues and the Intercultural Council in Claremont —that presented two divergent models for intercultural organizing in greater Los Angeles. Organized by newspaper owner/editor Ignacio López, Industrial Areas Foundation representative Fred Ross, and activist/scholar Ruth Tuck, the Unity Leagues represented a bona fide civil rights movement that grew out of the struggles for racial equality among Mexicans and blacks throughout Los Angeles, San Bernardino, Riverside, and San Diego Counties. The Intercultural Council of Claremont (ICC), on the other hand, developed out of the Anglo-led social reform movements during the first half of the twentieth century. Composed of progressive-minded white residents, the ICC, beginning in 1948, improved the material conditions of Mexican Americans and promoted "intercultural living" through three specific programs: first, they provided Mexican Americans with low-interest loans to upgrade their dilapidated homes; second, they offered scholarships for higher education to local Mexican American youths; and third, they constructed an "experimental" intercultural community adjacent to the existing Arbol Verde *colonia* in Claremont. The struggles of both organizations demonstrate the promise and perils of multicultural reform efforts and the powerful and persistent influence of racism in twentieth-century social relations.

This book gets its title from a quote by Carey McWilliams, whose book *Southern California Country: An Island in the Land* serves as the original impetus for this project. Although I have made an effort to situate the history of Southern California in the broader history of the United States, as a native to the citrus belt I still value my home for the "exceptional" place that McWilliams understood it to be. In writing *A World of Its Own* I have attempted to combine the unabashed, passionate regionalism of McWilliams's work with the fluorescent histories of Mexican American struggle, creativity, and labor throughout the twentieth century. In this way, I hope to complement the most perceptive interpreter of Southern California culture and pay tribute to the friends and family whose labor made it possible for me to make this contribution.

Part One

This citrus belt complex of peoples,
institutions, and relationships has no
parallel in rural life in America and nothing
quite like it exists elsewhere in California. It
is neither town nor country, neither rural nor
urban. It is a world of its own.
—CAREY McWILLIAMS, *Southern California*
  Country: An Island on the Land

The Ideal Country Life
The Development of Citrus Suburbs in Southern California

Citrus fruit has always possessed a unique status among the many crops that make up California's vast agroecosystem. While wheat, cotton, and grapes have had their images tarnished by revelations of labor exploitation, grower vigilantes, and absentee landlords, citrus has usually escaped such criticism. Even today, the image of the orange evokes a vision of prosperity in abundance. Witness the opening monologue to the recent 1950s/noir genre film *L.A. Confidential* in which actor Danny DeVito uses the citrus groves as a metaphor for the wealth of Southern California. While flashing images of women swimming through a pool full of oranges, DeVito entices the American public to come to Los Angeles where "the orange grove stretches as far as the eye can see, there are jobs aplenty, and land is cheap."

Such depictions are consistent with those conceded by even the most strident critics of California agribusiness. Carey McWilliams, a prolific and insightful writer on the subject, acknowledged the seemingly impenetrable aura possessed by the orange tree and its grower when he wrote: "With its rich black-green shade, its evergreen foliage, and its romantic fragrance, it is the millionaire of all the trees of America. . . . The aristocrat of the orchards, it has, by a natural affinity drawn to it the rich and the well-born, creating a unique type of rural-urban aristocracy. There is no crop in the whole range of American agriculture the growing of which confers quite the same status that is associated with ownership of an orange grove."[1] In spite of his criticism of growers and their exploitation of minority laborers, McWilliams could not help but appreciate the citrus farms because "they have contributed as much, perhaps, as any single factor to the physical charm of the region."[2]

The image or "look" of citrus has contributed to the mystique surrounding the fruit. Numerous writers and scholars—Los Angeles boosters and debunkers alike—have identified the orange, and to a lesser extent the lemon and grapefruit, as "a symbol of California's call to civilized rural life."[3] Crate labels produced by the industry's marketing cooperative, Sunkist (the metonymic alias for the California Fruit Growers Exchange), perpetuated these images by integrating scenes of the California Spanish Missions with contemporary views of the linear citrus orchard. Through the "semiotics of selling," historian Douglas Sackman has argued, Sunkist recreated the nature of oranges to increase their consumption and sales throughout North America during the first half of the twentieth century.[4] Advertisements of the "sun kissed" orange came to represent a number of ideas, including health, wealth, and the achievement of the American dream.

These images, however, concealed more than they revealed. In an attempt to get behind "the orange curtain," this study focuses on the reality of citrus farming, in particular, the labor that produced the sweet fruit, idyllic landscape, and phenomenal profits. Although analyzing the "semiotics of selling" contributes to an overall understanding of the citrus industry, I am not concerned with the refashioning, repackaging, and re-presenting of citrus fruits by marketing agencies and advertisers. Rather, I am interested in the labor choices made by citrus ranchers, as well as the recommendations offered by citrus industry leaders, government officials, and community representatives. Integral to this project is a consideration of how labor transformed the "landscape"—both physically and culturally—of a region that experienced intensive citrus cultivation. Since citrus grew throughout California during the late nineteenth and early twentieth centuries, I have limited my survey to that portion of Southern California regarded as the "most highly developed and largest contiguous citrus area in the state."[5] This region, referred to by Carey McWilliams as "the citrus belt," stretched sixty miles eastward from Pasadena, through the San Gabriel and San Bernardino Valleys, to the town of Riverside.[6]

From the beginnings of the industry in the 1870s to the height of citrus production in the 1920s, industry and government literature depicted citrus ranching as an ideal occupation for eastern and midwestern investors. The warm, dry climate of Southern California, the availability of land, and the profitability of citriculture offered an attractive alternative to potential transplants nearing retirement, or those simply tired of cold weather and hard work. State and local government agencies, industry spokespeople, and the Southern Pacific Railroad Company produced pages and pages of promotional literature espousing the virtues of owning and operating a citrus farm in the Southland. For example, A. J. Cook, State Commissioner of Horticulture, published *California Citrus Culture* in 1913, a manual explaining to "the novice" the essential ingredients for a profitable citrus farm. Cook assured potential investors that a small orange grove of from ten to forty acres "[could] be cared for by its owner with very slight aid from others, and thus the greatest handicap in agriculture—inability to secure labor—is solved."[7] Moreover, Cook emphasized that the labor, "never too arduous and uniform the entire year through," promised health, vigor, happiness, and comfort "to the owner of a citrus grove that is properly located and well cared for."[8]

Promoters of citriculture often argued that citrus possessed a natural affinity for Southern California's environment. According to one writer, "the same amount of well-directed industry upon a small area of land will produce more return [here] than in almost any section of the United States." He attributed this condition to nature, suggesting that "the difference between this and many parts of our land is that [here] nature seems to work with man, and not against him."[9] Indeed, writers often projected the image of the yeoman farmer as the ideal citrus rancher and the foundation for a new and improved society in the far West.

Such visions conformed to the agrarian or pastoral myth associated with agricultural development in North America. Developed by Thomas Jefferson and Norman cartographer St. John de Crèvecœur in the eighteenth century, the agrarian philosophy rested on the idea that American society would expand indefinitely westward. Thomas Jefferson advocated the development of agrarian

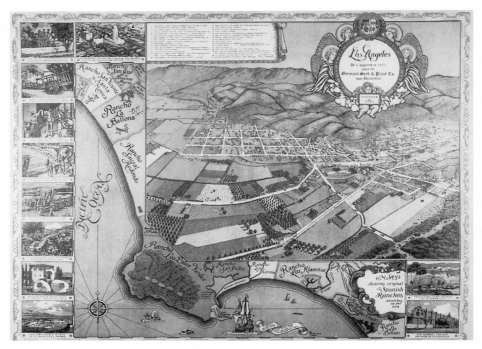

Map 1. Los Angeles, 1871. Images of an agrarian future are inlaid over the bygone era of the Spanish ranchos. (Courtesy of UCLA Special Collections)

communities because he believed that agriculture constituted the most vir-tuous of human endeavors and would strengthen the moral and democratic character of the nation. In his famous *Notes on Virginia*, Query XIX, Jefferson articulated this philosophy: "Is it best then that all our citizens should be em-ployed in its improvement, or that one half should be called off from that to exercise manufactures and handicraft arts for the other? Those who labour in the earth are the chosen people of God, if ever he had a chosen people, whose breasts he has made his peculiar deposit for substantial and genuine virtue."[10]

Jefferson acted upon this belief by prescribing a plan of orderly agricultural development in the frontier regions of his home state of Virginia. He advised that no more than ten people settle within a square mile, that primogeniture be abolished, and that education and government facilities be made conveniently accessible to all citizens. The Virginia legislature ultimately rejected Jefferson's original homestead plan, but his ideas significantly influenced land use patterns in the state and he successfully established one of the first public universities in the union.[11] Although regarded as utopian by critics, the philosophy developed into an "ideal" for Western conquest and settlement in the subsequent century.

In his classic study, *Virgin Land: The American West as Symbol and Myth*, Henry Nash Smith argues that Americans often idealized Jefferson's concept of the agrarian community without observing why he cherished the philosophy. On the most basic level, the agricultural settlement was universally recognized as the line separating civilization from savagery—the domestication of the "Wild West" and the creation of a "civilized" and "productive" society. Yet Jefferson valued the tight-knit, agrarian settlement not so much for what it contributed to the American economy, but rather for the guiding principles it provided Americans. Jefferson believed that the ideal agricultural communities promoted material equality and discouraged social stratification. Notwithstanding his narrow focus on white, landowning, male suffrage, Jefferson's key contribution to American political thought was his emphasis on the creation of a nation based on family farmers-proprietors who performed all of their own labor. He believed such investments would lead to a populace deeply committed to participatory democracy and the creation of institutions that protected their interests. The equitable distribution of land and the common purpose of farming suggested a process of horizontal or "even" development that Marx and his followers would later render as incompatible with a capitalist system. In fact, American settlement patterns during the nineteenth century contributed to the critique of Jefferson's philosophy as utopian. Ultimately, argues Smith, "the equalitarian overtones of this ideal were by no means acceptable to the country as a whole," and the "deeper belief in social stratification" prevailed.[12]

Americans' misinterpretation of the agrarian tradition generated important contradictions. The philosophy's implicit dependence on "nature" as the great equalizer conflicted with the notion of dominance inherent to capitalist societies. How could one adhere to the agrarian philosophy and accept social stratification if "labour in the earth" produced a more equalitarian society? This contradiction led Smith to conclude, "the capital difficulty of the American agrarian tradition is that it accepted the paired but contradictory ideas of nature and civilization as a general principle of historical and social interpretation."[13] Equally important (though not considered by Smith): What if the labor that produces this virtue is performed by someone other than the farmer? Indeed, as historian Jack Kirby argues, there is no place in Jeffersonian agrarianism for nonfamily labor, the likes of which came to be employed on American farms during the late nineteenth and twentieth centuries. Consequently, today we often speak of this tradition not as the "agrarian philosophy," but rather the "agrarian myth."[14]

Americans "resolved" the contradiction between nature and civilization by

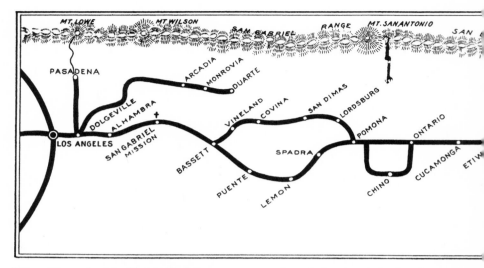

Map 2. The path of the "Inside Track," a vacation tour through the citrus belt offered by Southern Pacific Railroad. Published in *The Inside Track: The Way through the Wonderful Fruit and Flower Garden of Southern California*, 1907. (Courtesy of the Bancroft Library, University of California, Berkeley)

redefining the relationship of humans to the natural world. In *The Machine in the Garden: Technology and the Pastoral Ideal in America*, Leo Marx argues that prior to the industrial revolution, early capitalism in America developed vis-à-vis "geographic nature" rather than against social forms (such as feudalism), thus making "the relation between mankind and the physical environment . . . more than usually decisive." By the mid-nineteenth century, however, the predominance of technology produced yet another interpretation of the agrarian, or "pastoral" ideal. Rather than define nature strictly as external to human beings, Americans began to see technology, the natural world, and people as part of a universal nature. According to Marx, a "rhetoric of the technological sublime" assimilated technology into the natural world, while a "rhetoric of the nature sublime" "humanized" nature. By the end of the nineteenth century, Americans saw themselves sharing a common destiny—uniting technology and nature to "[create] a society in the image of a garden." [15]

Los Angeles boosters embraced the concept of the garden as an accurate depiction of Southern California. The Southern Pacific Railroad Company, a major landowner in California and the primary transporter of citrus fruits, used "garden" tours of the region to lure midwesterners and easterners westward. Advertising "the way through the wonderful fruit and flower garden of South-

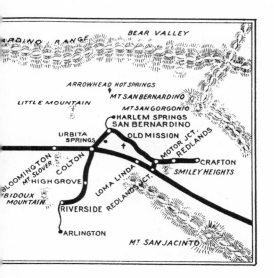

ern California," the company's tourist magazine *The Inside Track* characterized "citrus land" as one integrated landscape of cities, orchards, and mountains where residents lived in harmony with their environment. Tourists experienced a symphony of colors and aromas traveling eastward along the snow-clad peaks of Mount San Antonio, Mount San Bernardino, and Mount San Gorgonio. As the train coursed through the "orange belt" of the San Gabriel and San Bernardino Valleys, tourists witnessed the bright green of alfalfa fields and grape vineyards, the silver and gray of alluvial sands, the golden brown of mountain walls, and the sweet smell and deep green of orange groves. Passengers ended their trip in the archetypal citrus colony, Riverside, possessing "all the advantages of an unsurpassed rural district and a model city." [16]

Although Southern Pacific promotional writers advanced an idyllic image of the landscape, the trip reflected a pattern of economic, social, and cultural development unique to the region prior to World War II. Los Angeles depended heavily on agriculture and industry in its "hinterlands" as a foundation for its economy. In addition to oil, citrus formed, to quote historians Ronald Tobey and Charles Wetherell, "the engine" of a regional economy. Between 1899 and 1937, the multibillion-dollar citrus industry in Southern California grew at a rate unparalleled by any agricultural product in the world, and unequaled by most other industries in the region. In 1913, ranchers received almost $40 million in return on their investment, paying out approximately one-third of this total in transportation cost. By 1930, citrus growers in the five counties of Southern California—Los Angeles, Orange, Riverside, San Bernardino, and

Ventura—grossed a phenomenal $144.6 million. As a point of comparison, the area's combined manufacturing wages earned in the movies, oil, and aircraft industries totaled $196 million. Moreover, land under citrus cultivation in Southern California increased from 83,600 acres in 1903 to more than 329,700 in 1944. Although the initial investment required a substantial amount of money and patience (trees did not bear fruit of marketable quality until five years after planting), the payoff was potentially very high. For example, the owner of an average, fully productive, debt-free ten-acre grove in 1929 earned $2,800—four times the per capita income of Americans.[17]

Urban planners, geographers, and historians studying Los Angeles have commented on the unique structure of Southern California society. Dispersed economic development mitigated the formation of a city organized around a downtown district. Los Angeles's dependence on citrus and oil during its formative years significantly shaped what today many scholars regard as a "polynuclear" metropolis.[18] While oil drilling and refining spurred urban development south of Los Angeles towards San Pedro, the establishment of citrus cities throughout the San Gabriel Valley expanded the metropolis eastward.[19] In Los Angeles County, towns varying in size from Pasadena to Pomona and Ontario served as nuclei for local control and community development throughout the region. Although the California Fruit Growers Exchange (CFGE), the Los Angeles Chamber of Commerce, and the Southern Pacific Company influenced the expansion of the citrus industry from their offices based in Los Angeles, growers successfully organized local clubs, grower associations, water companies, and chambers of commerce that decentralized this agriculture-based economy. According to famous Los Angeles lover and historian Reyner Banham, this spatial arrangement resembled an "instant townscape" seventy square miles wide rather than a traditional city.[20]

In analyzing the roots of Los Angeles's postmodern geography, urban theorists and historians have debated its cause and effect. While most scholars interpret Los Angeles' development as haphazard and random, state and metropolitan officials, investors, and city boosters prior to World War II celebrated the settlement patterns and eclectic economy of Southern California. For example, in *Magnetic Los Angeles: Planning the Twentieth-Century Metropolis*, Greg Hise demonstrates that urban planners and real estate developers intentionally "planned dispersion of jobs, housing, and services" throughout the metropolitan landscape beginning in the 1920s. Similarly, historian Virginia Scharf called 1920s Los Angeles a "great, diffuse urban agglomeration" that "would prove to be the prototype for twentieth-century American cities."[21] Contrary to the city/suburb dichotomy subscribed to by traditional urban theorists, Los Angeles officials and investors embraced "suburbanization" as urbanization.

The Southern Pacific, CFGE, and real estate developers were not alone in their enthusiasm for Los Angeles' unique landscape. The Los Angeles Chamber of Commerce (LACC), the agency responsible for organizing the city's economic growth, acknowledged the importance of agriculture to the regional economy. The LACC aggressively promoted agricultural development in the county by publishing literature that compared the Southland to the most productive regions of the Mediterranean. In 1907, the agency strongly endorsed a bond issue that supported the construction of the L.A. Aqueduct and advocated the use of this water partly for the expansion of fruit and vegetable farms. Not exclusively committed to the growth of industry, the LACC pushed an agenda that balanced manufacturing with agriculture on a regional level. Beginning in 1888 and extending throughout the 1920s, the LACC published the booklet *Los Angeles: The City and County* in which author Harry Ellington Book outlined the various economic opportunities available to newcomers throughout the Southland. In his section on San Gabriel Valley, Book referred to the citrus belt as the "The Ideal Country Life" and appealed to a "back to the land" sentiment popular among Americans at the turn of the century. According to Book, "in no other section can an acre of land be made to yield products of so great value." Highlighting its unique blend of rural and urban characteristics he added, "here may be found beautiful rural homes, whose owners are within touch of social life, and enjoy the best features of the city and country combined." [22]

By 1918, the agency maintained a department entirely devoted to agriculture and allied industries. Headed by the indefatigable George Pigeon Clements, the department quickly grew into one of the most influential government agencies in California and the West, influencing farm operations from Fresno to the Mexican border. Clements believed that the prosperity of a great city or metropolis depended on its ability not only to feed itself, but also to dominate regional, and if possible, national markets. Southern California possessed an environment unusually endowed with rich agricultural land that allowed it to achieve these two objectives. In a 1924 article for the *Los Angeles Examiner*, Clements boasted that Los Angeles had become "the perishable fruit and vegetable garden of the United States" through the combination of water reclamation and a total use of "the most valuable acreage on the Western Hemisphere." "Los Angeles must depend upon the husbandman for her food," he wrote, "and every acre of ground must be made to bear its full burden to this end." Given the extensive agricultural development accomplished during the first two decades of the twentieth century, Clements assured readers that "there is no longer any back country; the city's sphere of influence has brought the so-called back country to constitute a part of itself."[23] During the 1920s and 1930s, Clements downplayed suburban/urban distinctions and made farming in Southern California the business of the LACC and the city. He took particular interest in the citrus industry, frequently speaking at local grower association conferences, coordinating meetings between ranchers, and representing their interests in Congress and the California State Assembly.

Government agencies interested in improving citrus yields and increasing profits also contributed to the success and importance of citrus in the first three decades of the twentieth century. The State Commission of Horticulture and the University of California invested in the industry by supporting scientific studies of geography and fruit. From the fruit-growing "boom" of the 1880s to the turn of the century, farmers used a costly process of trial and error to determine the most appropriate places to cultivate citrus. By 1910, geographers' surveys of the land eliminated much of the risk and helped the industry realize its full potential in the coastal portions of Southern California, particularly the Los Angeles basin. Studies conducted at the University of California's Citrus Experiment Station established in Riverside in 1913 revealed that the proximity of farms to mountains and foothills determined the type and quality of citrus. In Los Angeles County, the San Gabriel and San Bernardino mountains provided a necessary watershed and windbreak, as well as the right combination of soil and climate. Since most water runoff occurred below ground level in detrital cones, farmers planted citrus crops in the porous alluvial soils beneath the towering Sierra Madre range of the inland valley and along the slopes of the coastal mountains.

Climate was the principal environmental factor that made Southern California an ideal location for the commercial production of citrus fruits. Low-lying fog and cool breezes from the Pacific Ocean chilled the coastal plains and made frost a constant concern for farmers. Off the valley floor, foothills rose above the onshore flow of heavy, moist air providing warmer conditions more favorable to citrus. Higher up the mountain soil became too rocky for agriculture and the threat of frost increased during the chilly winter months. Consequently, farmers planted citrus fruits in thermal "belts" extending sixty to one hundred miles east from Los Angeles.[24] Researchers discovered that the hardiness of oranges, lemons, and grapefruits varied according to climate and soil types as one ascended from the valley floors. Ranchers planted oranges and grapefruits at lower levels because of their greater tolerance for cold weather, while frost-sensitive lemons grew at slightly higher elevations where mostly warmer air resided.

Among oranges, Valencias and Washington navels occupied different places in the citrus belt. Since Valencias possessed seeds and were used primarily for juice, farmers cared more about their quantity than quality. Consequently, ranchers grew Valencias near coastal ranges and further down the inland valleys. In the interior, a combination of dry desert breezes, low atmospheric moisture, and the threat of high-elevation frost produced oranges of higher sugar content with a deep reddish-orange hue. Farmers took advantage of such conditions by planting the seedless navel in these districts. Regarded as the sweetest eating-orange and the "autocrat of the price list," the navel thrived in a narrow belt that extended along the San Gabriel Valley's inner-mountain foothills from Pasadena to San Bernardino and Redlands.

Zones of agricultural production produced not only profits, but also an aesthetic quality to the landscape unparalleled by any other farming region in the United States. The variety of crops generated a diversity of textures and colors that impressed visitors and attracted investors and newcomers. Appreciating the "visible tokens of invisible soil and climatic variations," Carey McWilliams described a typical view of the San Gabriel Valley prior to World War II: "Alfalfa, grain, sugar beets, and other crops not injured by frost, are planted in the lowlands; farther up the slopes appear the belts of grapes and fruit crops, still higher, and usually in the form of a dark-green horseshoe curve around the rim of the valleys, is the orange belt; and, still higher on the slopes, are the zones of lemons and avocados."[25]

The physical landscape contributed substantially to the social organization of the citrus belt. In the coastal regions of Orange and Los Angeles Counties, Valencia groves predominated. Since the Valencia typically grew on large commercial farms that contributed to lower population density and fewer townships, a "rural coloration" characterized development in these areas. In the inland district of the Washington navels, however, growers engaged in more intensive farming. Ranchers raised navels in clusters since these oranges tended to be more sensitive to soil and climatic variations. Initially, the high-yielding ten-acre farm referred to by various promotional writers predominated in these areas, producing greater numbers of residents and more townships, including Pasadena, Monrovia, Duarte, Azusa, Glendora, Covina, San Dimas, Pomona, Claremont, Upland, and Ontario. Often, groves came right to the doorsteps of growers' homes.[26]

Since residential districts preceded or simultaneously developed with the groves, these communities exhibited an eclectic mix of urban and rural characteristics. Often, these "colonies" coalesced around the cultural and/or religious backgrounds of settlers. For example, in 1873, D. M. Berry of Indianapolis organized fifty families from his home state into the Indiana Colony of California. This group constituted the original members of the San Gabriel Orange Grove Association that founded Pasadena. Further east, members of the Church of the Brethren founded the town of Lordsburg (renamed La Verne), and Mormon missionaries organized the colony that became San Bernardino. Even "secular" colonies prided themselves on their high degree of homogeneity. Congregationalists in the town of Claremont tended to dictate the morals of that community, while city officials throughout the citrus belt enforced strict temperance laws. These culturally homogeneous communities eased the transition into a new environment for many migrants, and perpetuated the illusion that the small town of the Midwest and East could be recreated in Southern California.[27]

Investors found that by organizing into blocks, they could more easily control resources. Land purchases by groups rather than individuals allowed migrants to place more acreage under citrus cultivation, thereby transforming the environment more rapidly and radically. Strength in numbers also permitted them to form irrigation districts or companies that controlled local water resources. George Chaffey, for example, established the town of Ontario in 1882 by purchasing land, founding a colony, and organizing the San Antonio Water Company. Chaffey harnessed water flowing out of the San Antonio Canyon and built delivery systems that made the valley below blossom into one of the richest citrus- and grape-growing regions in California. His experiments in hydroelectric power provided Ontario all the amenities of a big city, including well-lit streets and eventually an electric car that carried residents from the citrus heights to downtown. In 1903, the U.S. government honored Ontario by selecting it as the standard of American Irrigation Colonies. Federal engineers constructed a miniaturized version of the "model colony" for exhibition at the St. Louis World's Fair held the following year.[28]

Ontario epitomized the social and spatial organization of most citrus belt towns. Distinguished by a strict adherence to a set of ideals determined by its founders, colonies reflected the combined influence of agrarian social theory and scientific management. In planning his colony, Chaffey followed four fundamental principles: "1) [equal] distribution of water to each [share]holder . . . irrespective of his distance from the source; 2) construct a main thoroughfare from one end of the settlement to the other and lay it out in such a way that it will be a thing of beauty forever; 3) provide a college for the agricultural education of the people of the colony and for the general education of their children;

and 4) secure the best possible class of settlers by a reversionary clause in the deeds to each allotment forbidding absolutely the sale of intoxicating liquor." [29] Seeking to set a new standard for agricultural communities, Chaffey subdivided the best land of his 2,500-acre tract into 10-acre lots, each one possessing a street or avenue frontage. Streets led directly to a town site comprised of 640 acres, one-half of which was deeded to trustees as a free endowment for the Chaffey Agricultural College.[30]

Chaffey's plan to place an imaginary grid upon the land and map out a complete vision of society reflected the Jeffersonian philosophy of settlement. Chaffey believed that through careful planning, he could promote republican and Christian values, educate citizens about advancements in agriculture, and elevate the general level of society. For Chaffey, success depended on access to government and education and the fair and equitable distribution of natural resources. The settlement of families on small, ten-acre farms ensured a manageable population density, while well-planned roads made downtown available to everyone. Last, the linearity of the community conformed to Victorian standards of beauty and attracted more investors to the town. Reyner Banham admired Ontario for initiating a pattern of "urban" development for greater Los Angeles. He wrote: "the general impression is that the citizens of Ontario built a 'garden city' and left out the 'city' part, urban homesteaders imposing their ideal of suburbs without *urbs* on the pattern of Greater Los Angeles almost before it had begun to take shape, a portent of the way the whole metropolis would grow." [31]

As David Roediger demonstrates in his book *Wages of Whiteness*, this "settler ideology" depended on racialized notions of land use that rationalized the dispossession of natural resources from Native Americans. During the early days of the republic, white imaginations of improvident Indians represented the polar opposite of Anglo-Saxon industriousness. As Anglo settlers moved into the West during the nineteenth century, Mexican or "Iberian/Spanish" settlers also served as a counterpoint to "hardworking whites." The settler ideology held that "lazy" Native Americans and Mexicans had failed to 'husband' or 'subdue' the resources God had provided and thus should forfeit these resources. Spanish missionization and Anglo campaigns to eradicate and marginalize California Indians reduced the size and strength of Native American opposition to settlement schemes. Rather than seeing native peoples as a threat to his vision, Chaffey perpetuated an American tradition dating back to the American Revolution by drawing upon the mythical/historical Native American male as a symbol of the new colonies' "independence." Chaffey christened his first colony Etiwanda in homage to an Indian Chief his uncle Benjamin knew in Canada,

and named Ontario after his former Canadian home, a name derived from
the Indian nation that inhabited the land prior to European settlement. These
names served as a magnet for Canadian and eastern white settlers, but also displaced the history of Southern California Gabrieleno Indians with references
to idealized and romantic visions of "noble savages" from the Northeast.[32]

More often "colonists" like Chaffey confronted mestizo and Californio
(elite, landholding Mexican) families that still occupied, if not owned, the land.
White migrants to California celebrated their "Iberian" predecessors for engag-
ing in agriculture and livestock raising, but faulted them for the modest scale of
their enterprises. Newcomers judged Californios' dependence on cattle raising
as a failure to realize the potential value of California land and a critical reason for their financial demise during the second half of the nineteenth century. Cattle raising symbolized "fixed wealth," while land ownership and development represented regenerative wealth that would escalate property values.
Contrary to the "pastoral" economies of the Spanish and Mexican era, Chaffey
envisioned a fully irrigated California, producing commercial fruits and vegetables that would integrate the state into a national and global economy.[33]

Native Americans and Californios, therefore, served as a foil to Chaffey's
foresight and ingenuity in the popular accounts and contemporary opinions of
Ontario history. As Chaffey biographer J. Alexander writes, upon Chaffey's first
visit to the "García Ranch" situated on the "Cucamonga Plain," he saw "lying
at his feet a colony settled by prosperous people setting a standard of comfort
formerly deemed unattainable by *ordinary people*, extracting a generous living
from a soil thought by generations of *Spanish proprietors* to be incapable of
settlement" [italics added]. In contradistinction to native and Mexican settlers
who had inhabited the region for hundreds of years prior to white settlement,
Chaffey himself reflected: "from the plateau at the foot of the mountain I obtained a bird's-eye view of the whole area I proposed to acquire, and while I
was standing there looking at it, I saw what Ontario was to and did become."
In an account that includes a trip down *"El Camino Real* — the Spanish King's
Highway of the Mission Era," Alexander reports that Chaffey "clinched on the
spot" a deal to buy 1,000 acres with water rights from the "easy-going" Portuguese seaman, Captain García.[34] According to Alexander, García had "dabbled
in irrigation in a small way," but relied primarily on sheep ranching as his main
source of income, a business commonly pursued by Californios, Portuguese,
and Basque immigrants prior to the settlement of citrus farmers. To whites,
these practices constituted a more wasteful use of land than cattle raising since
most saw goats and sheep as small, "scrubby" animals that possessed even less
market value than steer and cows.[35] Chaffey's land acquisition and subdivision

plans, therefore, represented the dawning of a new era in Southern California in which the random, "pre-capitalists" practices of Native Americans, Californios, and non-Anglo predecessors would be replaced by orderly, commercial agriculture.

The family run, ten-acre farm also served as a response to populism of the 1880s and 1890s. The inter-racial alliances and tenant class solidarity that characterized pre-1890s populism contrasted with Chaffey's vision of "whiteness" and agrarian democracy, and constituted a real, if distant, alternative to the "model colony." Chaffey's emphasis on the development of small, owner-operated, high-yielding farms eliminated the practice of tenant farming, and more importantly, sharecroppers themselves. By basing the colony on the equal distribution of land among financially independent, white property owners, poor whites and African Americans would not find a place in the community.[36]

Chaffey reflected the values prevalent among Americans as they approached the turn of the century. Unlike Jefferson, Chaffey saw his scheme as a money-making venture. Settlers received property not by rights of citizenship, but rather through investment. Second, Chaffey's love of engineering fueled his interest in the development of cities. Not merely an irrigationist, Chaffey sought ways of converting hydraulic energy into electricity on a massive scale. His success in providing electrical power to Ontario attracted the attention of federal, state, and local planners, and launched his career as an ingenious and revolutionary mercenary city planner. In 1882, Los Angeles officials hired Chaffey to organize the Los Angeles Electric Company, the electrical parent to the gigantic Los Angeles Gas and Electric Corporation. He made Los Angeles the first city in the United States, if not in the world, to be lighted exclusively by electricity. In 1885, the Victorian Irrigation Company wooed Chaffey away from Southern California to establish the town of Mildura in Australia.[37]

Uniting agriculture with technology to build better communities constituted an important organizing principal for city planners and investors in Southern California at the turn of the century. By World War I, communities throughout the citrus belt—from Pasadena, to Ontario, to Riverside and Redlands—enjoyed a higher standard of living than most Americans. Yet, citrus belt residents measured success not merely by the size of their bank accounts, but also by the predominance of luxuries and benefits not typically afforded to farming communities. Following the tenets of the City Beautiful Movement, investors and city planners believed that the construction of luxury hotels, banks, theaters, mansions, churches, and colleges served as a testament to the affluence of citriculture and the intelligence of the citrus grower. A. J. Cook expressed the belief held by many citrus growers when he wrote: "We all love and are ennobled by our environment where loveliness is dominant; and so it follows that citrus fruit growers will be generally marked by refinement and culture."[38]

Throughout the citrus belt, city elites "beautified" their cities with tree-lined streets and neighborhood parks. George Chaffey set the standard with his carefully designed Euclid Avenue, a double-drive, two-hundred-foot-wide boulevard marked out by four rows of eucalyptus, pepper, and palm trees with a strip in the center for trolley tracks. To advertise Ontario's irrigation system, Chaffey built a large fountain at the intersection of Euclid and the Pacific Electric and Southern Pacific railways that spouted water every time a passenger train passed through downtown. Similarly, Pasadena growers flaunted their wealth by constructing elaborate rococo-style mansions along Orange Grove Avenue near the heart of town. In Riverside, as early as 1895, residents boasted the highest per capita income in the United States.[39] To exhibit the community's affluence, city planners enforced zoning laws and implemented architectural design standards based on Mission Revival and Victorian styles. Between 1890 and 1930, citrus money transformed Riverside into one of the most ornate and lush built-environments in Southern California: the "English garden" meets the "desert oasis." The twin references of "Spanish" California and Victorian England, common among architecture throughout the region, served as "a visual sampling of power, of displaced wealth and command" unifying a narrative of conquest, past and present. Citrus belt residents celebrated the Spanish for subduing nature and native populations and saw themselves as the new Anglo-Saxon "conquistadores," remaking the Southern California environment into a productive and congenial landscape.[40]

The conditions of the "citriscape" stood in stark contrast to the state of agriculture across the rest of the United States. During the first two decades of the twentieth century, government officials, reformers, and commentators lamented the decline of the family farm in North America. Multi-acre, bonanza farms on cheap Western grasslands relied on machinery and inexpensive transportation to out-produce and out-price small farmers. Many filed for bankruptcy. Those who attempted to hold on found labor excruciatingly painful as competition increased the rate of production. Not surprisingly, children of these families grew up disliking rural life and committed themselves to the pursuit of nonagricultural work. Progressive reformers known as "Country-Lifers" organized a movement to address the needs of agrarian communities and attempted to forestall the flow of small farming families to overcrowded cities. President Theodore Roosevelt supported their efforts by organizing the Country Life Commission, but the appeal of rural life continued to wane.[41]

The displacement of families from agricultural lands also concerned a growing American eugenics movement that debated the effects of migration on the U.S. "racial stock." Most European and American eugenicists believed that humans inherited intelligence and talents, and that acquired characteristics could not be passed on to future generations through hereditary lines. Charles Darwin's cousin, Francis Galton, an English statistician, defined the dream of the movement when he wrote: "If a twentieth part of the cost and pains were spent in measures for the improvement of the human race that is spent on the improvement of the breed of horses and cattle, what a galaxy of genius might we not create."[42] Experimentation in botany and biology for the purpose of improving dairy and produce yields generated intense interest in the eugenics movement among American scientists. In 1906, the American Breeder's Association formed a Committee on Eugenics to study the heredity of the human race and to identify those blood lines that they believed would improve the American stock.

Composed of an eclectic group of scholars, including biologists, geneticists, geologists, and sociologists, this body of scientists deviated from Galton's vision in important ways. Luther Burbank, a California botanist who genetically engineered numerous "hybrid" plants, fruits, and vegetables, disputed the notion that acquired characteristics could not be passed to future generations. In his own treatise on the subject, *The Training of the Human Plant*, Burbank explained his understanding of the connection between environment and heredity as follows: "Environment is the architect of heredity; . . . acquired characters *are* transmitted . . . *all* characters which *are* transmitted have been acquired, not necessarily at once in a dynamic or visible form, but as an increasing latent force ready to appear as a tangible character when by long-continued natural or artificial repetition any specific tendency has become inherent, inbred, or 'fixed,' as we call it."[43] Burbank, therefore, advocated the Lamarckian theory that genetic traits, little by little, could be enhanced through good nurturance and constant attention to quality. At the other end of the spectrum, the most dominant American eugenicist, Charles Davenport, granted only token importance to the role of environment in determining a person's makeup, and expressed the belief that single genes determine such characteristics as laziness, musical ability, and creativity.[44] This diversity of opinion concerning the influence of environment on human evolution inspired private and public debates that transcended the narrow focus on "blood" and genes. In America, such debates peaked around World War I, argues Richard Hofstadter, when "[eugenics] had reached the dimensions of a fad."[45] The dramatic movement of people to and within the United States during this period influenced eugenicists to consider the impact of rural to urban migration on the future of America.

In 1916, the *California Citrograph* published the extracts of an article written by eugenicist O. F. Cook that perhaps articulates the principal concerns of many citrus families. Cook, a scientist with the U.S. Department of Agriculture, described the dilemma facing American society in general, and agricultural communities specifically:

> *If the time has really come for the consideration of practical eugenic measures, here is a place to begin, a subject worthy of the most careful study — how to rearrange our social and economic system so that more of the superior members of our race will stay on the land and raise families, instead of moving to the city and remaining unmarried or childless, or allowing their children to grow up in unfavorable urban environments that mean deterioration and extinction.*[46]

Cook sounded the concern that "the best of the rural populations" had been drawn to the city by modern luxuries and conveniences. Consequently, the most intelligent and productive members of American society abandoned "normal development" under an agrarian way of life. As Cook explained, "agriculture is not only the basis of our civilization in the mere economic sense of affording food to support our physical existence, but in a still more fundamental, biological sense. It is only in an agricultural state that the human individual attains a normal acquaintance with his environment and a full endowment of intellectual and social faculties of this [white] race."[47]

Cook prescribed two solutions to this dilemma. The immediate solution entailed the reversal of "the present tendency for the better families to be drawn to the city and facilitate the drafting of the others for urban duty."[48] He also advised against "eugenics regulations" such as sterilization, and claimed that "sanitary precautions" of the states "which are hygienic, but not eugenic" did not interfere with "the natural agencies" that would eliminate "undesirable lines of descent."[49] In other words, Cook espoused the belief that nonwhite people would eventually become extinct through natural selection.

For Cook and other proponents of "reverse migration," the call for "better families" to return to the farms did not mean an abandonment of the modern technologies that had lured these people to the city in the first place. Rather, the "enlightened eugenic standpoint," a Lamarkian strain endorsed by Burbank and other "liberal" eugenicists, required born-again horticulturists to harmonize agriculture with industry to create more productive farms and more tolerable living conditions for the farm families. California citrus growers fashioned themselves as the vanguard of these ideas and the purveyors of the most successful and civilized society in human history. The editor's introduction to

Cook's article makes this point explicit: "California is in a class by itself, without a peer. Here, the rural life has reached its highest development. The farm has no terrors, when combined with all the advantages of the cities. Good roads and public utilities have taken the sting out of rural life. The only noticeable difference between life on a farm or orchard in Southern California and that in the city is the difference in elbow room." [50]

In Southern California, a return to the farm did not require a choice between the luxuries of the city and the social and biological advantages of an agrarian life. Carey McWilliams would later describe the "typical citrus-belt town" as "really neither a town nor a city, but a suburban shopping district." [51] This model of agrarian development seemingly addressed liberal eugenicists' and Country-Lifers' concerns about rural decline by uniting Jefferson's homestead plans with modern technology.

Yet, much of what Los Angeles boosters, the LACC, the *Citrograph* writers and government officials celebrated as unique about the citrus belt was actually either an exaggeration or in a state of transition during the first two decades of the twentieth century. In spite of pronouncements that the average citrus farmer earned a handsome and sustainable profit margin by working his own land, many ranchers depended on some form of hired help from the beginning. In districts near the Sierra Madres, land had little value until large boulders and sediment were cleared from the soil. In Claremont, for example, the millionaire citrus rancher Lee Pitzer began his orange empire on thirty acres with the assistance of Sikh workers. He paid a team of between ten and fifteen Sikh men $25 to $50 per acre to haul away rocks "so heavy that they would break the wagons down." Sikh men also built canals, homes, and dormitories with the leftover rocks, and according to Upland rancher George H. Whitney, "[laid] out the groves" in the area. Another rancher, Paul Naftel, remembered that "quite a number of Japanese pick[ed] oranges when we first come [*sic*] out here [in 1910]." Russell Pitzer, cousin of Lee Pitzer, admitted to using "cheap" labor, but proudly asserted, "they were native Americans [white] . . . I never had any Japanese or Hindus [Sikh]." Although labor conditions varied from ranch to ranch, Chinese, Sikh, Japanese, Mexican, Filipino, and white workers labored in the citrus groves of the San Gabriel and San Bernardino Valleys. [52]

Prior to the war, most farms had not yet grown to unmanageable sizes and labor needs could be met with a mixed labor force of family and hired help. Many citrus farms consisted of between ten and thirty acres and were still in the "experimental" stage. Clifford Pitzer recalled that in 1903 his father "started the experiment [with] only two ten-acre pieces of citrus [land]." Five years later, Pitzer had "a nice producing grove and built a home on it." By 1917, Pitzer owned 175 acres of land from which he shipped approximately 300 boxes of fruit per year. The increase in production required Pitzer to employ farmhands, most of whom the packinghouse furnished.

Ranchers preferred to hire white workers to maintain the racial homogeneity of their communities, but low wages in agriculture across the nation discouraged many from seeking work on farms. In her book *The Fruits of Their Labor: Atlantic Coast Farmworkers and the Making of Migrant Poverty, 1870–1945*, Cindy Hahamovitch reveals that beginning in the 1870s, urban industrial wages rose while agricultural wages experienced a precipitous decline. According to Hahamovitch, mechanization of farm operations eliminated the need for year-round labor and made agricultural work primarily seasonal, migratory, and cheap. The nineteenth century trend toward a concentration of industrial production in cities also reduced the number of small industries in country towns where farmworkers formerly supplemented their incomes with part-time work. By the first decade of the twentieth century, these conditions produced poverty among Italian immigrant and black migrant farmworkers who accepted these jobs to avoid starvation.[53]

In the citrus belt, conditions differed from those extant on the Atlantic Coast or even in the nearby San Joaquin and Imperial Valleys. In his book *The Lie of the Land*, Don Mitchell argues that growers in the San Joaquin and Imperial Valleys kept wages and housing costs low by maintaining labor surpluses and keeping workers on the move.[54] Although labor migrancy occurred among workers in the Los Angeles basin, citrus laborers tended not to move around as much and often covered less territory when they did. Due to the unique geography and climate of the citrus belt, citrus growers grew a variety of fruit with harvest cycles that alternated throughout the year. J. B. Culbertson, the manager of the Limoneira citrus ranch in Santa Paula in Ventura County, noted that "the citrus grower has a different problem" than other farm owners. He continued, "his harvest season is almost continuous the year through and his other labor needs fit into the picking cycle to make possible steady, annual employment for much of his help."[55] In the San Gabriel and San Bernardino Valleys, Carey McWilliams observed that Mexican laborers "are not migratory workers, but settled residents of the areas in which they are employed (only 17% of the labor supply is non-resident)."[56] Claremont grower Russell Pitzer confirmed this observation, stating, "orchard work, such as picking, was done by people who lived here as far as possible." He added that limited labor migration between Los Angeles and Orange County districts covered bountiful navel and Valencia seasons.[57] The development of towns and local industry also diversified the economy in Southern California so that many laborers could find part-time work away from the orchards when harvest cycles dipped below their peak levels. No such opportunity existed for farmworkers in the rural districts of the Central Valley of California or the Atlantic Coast.

Although technology affected labor in the packinghouses with the addition of conveyor belts, forklifts, and fruit-washing machines, selective harvesting and marketing mitigated the impact of mechanization on the labor demands of the industry. Pickers chose fruit based on color and size and rarely "cleaned" a tree, since citrus fruit did not ripen after being picked. Asked whether mechanization would help solve labor "problems," Clifford Pitzer answered: "I don't see how they could ever pick lemons with mechanical harvesting of any type because . . . with lemons you are picking every six weeks the year around, and it is a very selective deal."[58] Growers felt compelled to employ a constant supply of pickers and packers to maintain a strict screening process and uphold the high standards advertised by the California Fruit Growers Exchange.

Citrus workers suffered the consequences of depressed agricultural wages since ranchers tended to value their workers according to the standards set by agriculture across the country, especially in California. Each year the state Chamber of Commerce gathered farm owners of various crops to discuss, among many issues, wage levels. Growers undertook such measures to prevent the creation of labor surpluses in high-paying districts and shortages on lower-paying farms. Agreements not to compete for labor depressed wages, ensured the presence of workers during harvests, and minimized conflict among growers.[59]

Comprehensive records of wages paid to citrus workers begin in the late 1910s and 1920s, a period in which packinghouses and local grower associations functioned as the main clearinghouse for labor. During the 1920s in western San Gabriel Valley, ranchers relied on the San Gabriel Farm Labor Association (SGFLA) to find and contract fruit pickers. The organization's board of directors, composed of the most prominent growers from various local exchanges, met regularly to establish wage rates, picking quotas, and hiring policies for the area. The SGFLA governing board divided workers by staggering wages per hour according to their seniority and the type of fruit picked: 36 cents for experienced orange pickers and 30 cents for inexperienced; 28 cents for all pickers of seedlings; and 25 cents for lemons.[60] Employers further complicated wage levels by varying the standards by which they paid their employees. As historian Gilbert González demonstrates, workers were rarely paid solely on the basis of hours worked. Rather, employers implemented several systems, including payment by boxes picked (a box equaled a full picker's canvas bag weighing fifty pounds); a straight day's salary for a nine-hour day; or a combination of a box rate with an hourly rate.[61]

Many growers' associations paid on a quality-quantity system whereby a picker earned a base wage and a bonus on boxes picked over a certain amount. Under this system, supervisors closely monitored the incoming boxes, looking for "defective" fruit. If, for example, more than 4 percent of the fruit was deemed defective, associations paid the picker only the base salary. Conversely, a picker who limited the amount of defective fruit in his box earned a "bonus" that could boost his per box rate by as much as 3 cents a box. Since base salaries often constituted a wage well below subsistence level, this system encouraged pickers to maintain an eye on the quality as much as the quantity of their pick. Additionally, some growers implemented a "season bonus system" whereby employers paid workers their weekly base salary, but waited until the end of the lemon, grapefruit, navel, or Valencia harvest to add up bonus totals. A 1921 *California Citrograph* article reported how the system worked: "at the end of the season a bonus is paid to all the men who are still with the crew, providing the quality of their work is satisfactory." [62] Growers used such payment methods to discourage laborers from seeking alternative employment during downturns in the picking cycles.

Wage levels also fluctuated according to the changing racial composition of citrus picking crews. In 1919, racially mixed, Mexican/white picking crews working for the SGFLA-affiliated Pasadena Orange Growers' Association (POGA) "averaged" $3.25 per day and earned a base salary of $19.50 for an eight-hour, six-day work week, though totals and hours varied according to the season. As Mexicans and Filipinos came to dominate the labor pool, growers lowered wages. By the 1923–1924 season, wage rates earned by picking "gangs" dropped to 25 cents per week, or approximately $30 biweekly before deductions for gloves and cash advances for living expenses. By 1928, growers denied Mexican and Filipino employees "advances" on their paychecks and lowered their wages to between $21 and $30 per every two weeks, an average that remained consistent during the Depression.[63]

Conditions of the labor market augmented racial prejudice to heighten race-consciousness among Southern Californians. The employment of Asian and Mexican workers in low-paying agricultural jobs simultaneously reinforced the "nonwhite" status of these immigrants, and perpetuated a dual labor system that restricted the mobility of ethnoracial minorities to higher-paying, skilled positions.[64] Consequently, as citrus production grew, so too did the numbers and importance of Mexican and Asian workers to the local agroeconomy. Upland grower and board member of the San Gabriel Valley Labor Associations, Wiley W. Mather, remembered: "We used to have some Hindus [Sikhs], we used to have men with turbans and there would be quite a mixture, Maylays [Filipinos] and of course a lot of Japanese people and Chinese and I remember lots of different people . . . different races, you know."[65] Census data from 1900 to 1930 reveals that "non-white" citrus belt populations including Chinese, Japanese, Indian, and "non-black others" increased apace with the expanding "white" population (see Tables 1 and 2 in Appendix). Mexican totals are much more difficult to come by because the U.S. Census Department did not institute a consistent method of counting them during this same period. Nevertheless, during the decades from 1910 to 1930 (the period of greatest emigration from Mexico to the United States up until that time), the total numbers of Mexican-born Mexicans in select citrus belt towns reveals similar if not more dramatic increases (see Table 3 in Appendix). Although Mexican and Asian populations represent just a small fraction of the total population during this period, statistics do not fully communicate the centrality of these workers to the local economy.

Rancher George Whitney recalled one Japanese immigrant in particular, Mr. Jigahara, who invented a tool crucial to the founding of citrus groves in the San Gabriel–San Bernardino Valley: "he invented the 'Jigahara Digger,' which is still used in getting boulders out of the ground because, as you know, the land around here is filled with those big round boulders!" Jigahara lived a solitary life on Whitney's ranch, converting an old cow barn into a little cottage where he maintained a "library with several hundred books" and wrote extensively in his native language. Although other Japanese immigrants regarded him as a well-known philosopher and poet, the white majority saw him as an enigmatic Buddhist "loner" who "hoed weeds" in exchange for his modest house.[66] Jigahara died in Upland largely forgotten by a white community whose success in agriculture depended on his genius.

Mexican workers also joined the labor force, immigrating to the area in significant numbers beginning around 1910. For example, Emilio Valadez arrived in Upland in 1907 as a *solo* (single Mexican male immigrant) railroad worker, but quickly found employment in the burgeoning citrus industry. Based on his mule-driving experience in Mexico, Valadez began as a teamster for local citrus rancher Charlie Ford. By 1916, he had earned enough money to liberate his wife and children from the tumult of the Mexican Revolution and brought them to Upland. As one of the first Mexicans in the area, Valadez ascended to the rank of foreman for another grove owner, Royal Miller, and built homes for many Mexican families who continued to come to the citrus belt.[67] The inroads of immigrants like Valadez and Jigahara laid the foundations for the growth and regeneration of Japanese and Mexican communities.

From the turn of the century until World War I, ranchers used white, minority, and family workers to address the labor needs of the citrus farm and to maintain the outward appearance of a new agrarian society. The beginning of hostilities in Europe in 1914, however, placed new pressures on the citrus industry that threatened to expose ranchers' growing dependence on nonwhite labor. Although the war benefited growers by cutting off competition from citrus producers in Europe, farmers had difficulty adjusting to these new demands due to transformations in the labor market. As war-related manufacturing and construction in and around Los Angeles developed, local white workers increasingly chose industry over agriculture. Moreover, the recruitment of white men for military service precipitated an acute labor shortage in the United States that agribusiness spokespeople labeled a "crisis" by 1918. These conditions generated discussions published in the *California Citrograph* that revealed racial and gender hierarchies prevalent within citrus communities.[68]

During the formative years of citrus farming, white women and children contributed significantly to the labor conducted on most Southern California farms. Women frequently picked and packaged citrus fruit for distribution, while young men helped their fathers till the soil and plant the trees. By the time of World War I, however, the Country Life Movement significantly transformed the role of women and children on citrus farms. A greater division of labor within the agrarian household confined the majority of women's activities to the cultivation of home and hearth and the education of children. Although white women continued to work in packinghouses, men believed their primary obligation was to the maintenance of the household economy. Rather than protest, many agrarian women embraced the separate sphere promoted by advocates of the Country Life Movement as one way to expand their freedom. Sole responsibility of the home granted women greater control over their own lives, while educational duties provided them leadership positions within the community.[69]

Growers regarded the creation of the Woman's Land Army to harvest agricultural crops as a temporary measure for the war, but not a permanent solution to the labor shortage problem.[70] The employment of women through the Woman's Land Service of Southern California and of high school–age boys through the Boys Working Reserve precipitated greater awareness of the hardships of agricultural work and prompted agrarian reformers to back fair wage standards, better working conditions, and strict child labor laws.[71] In addition, the citrus industry used prescriptive literature recommending child and women's labor to obscure from the public eye a growing dependency on foreign-born workers.[72] In the growers' culture, white women, especially growers' wives and daughters, belonged first and foremost to the domestic sphere.

White male citrus growers punctuated this point in 1919 when editors at the *California Citrograph* employed "Bungalow Mistress" Miss Peggy Jeans to write a regular column outlining the role of white women in the citrus belt. Entitled "At Home with the Citrus Grower," Jeans's columns explained the proper etiquette for women, defined the "instinctive" differences between the two sexes, and lauded the values and benefits of domesticity. According to Jeans, women of the citrus belt possessed just enough country in them to engage in horticulture, but neither the interest nor the instinct to manage a cash crop. Women were expected to tend to the garden surrounding their homes and cultivate a livable environment, as Jeans's first article demonstrates:

> *Even as the mistress of the house is responsible for its order and beauty within, so in many instances is she responsible for its exterior beauty. A man's garden is apt to be practical, with the emphasis on vegetables and produce; it is the woman that fusses with the flowers and makes her garden a place of beauty. The gardening instinct lives strongly in woman, — a survival perhaps from the days of savagery when man's contribution to the home was the spoil of the hunt; and his spouse was persuaded, — if necessary by his club, — to hoe the corn and raise the family garden. Or woman's fondness for her garden may be Eve's love for her first dress pattern.*[73]

Jeans's articles reflected the tenets of the Country Life Movement that also recommended women stay at home in order to educate young children. In a section of her regular page entitled "For the Little Folks," Jeans explored the interests of citrus belt youths and informed women on how to raise their children.[74]

Although some early twentieth century feminists believed that the Country Life Movement contributed a degree of autonomy and authority to farm-based women, the circumscribed roles of white women and children also conformed to the eugenicist's vision of a properly ordered society.[75] According to Cook, "little children not only do not need to be sent to school, but are much better off, educationally and otherwise, if allowed to stay at home."[76] Cook encouraged children not to go to school before the eighth or ninth year, and suggested that women provide their sons and daughters the necessary education and socialization to function in agrarian communities. Cook recommended that home education be conducted "out-of-doors" and stress the human accomplishments of domesticating plants and animals. Moreover, eugenicists, Country-Lifers, and citrus belt writers encouraged growers to employ their children, especially sons; however, such work experience prepared young men not for manual labor, but rather for the management of the farm. According to experts, farm work built character and intelligence in youths, but was not intended to develop an inexhaustible supply of labor.[77]

Restrictions on white women's roles, the limits placed on child labor, and the desire to create a painless society for the white family conflicted with the citrus ranchers' need for manual laborers. The preference of many single, white male workers for urban industrial jobs and the conscription of young men for World War I further hampered growers' ability to secure a dependable labor source. Many growers preferred to hire married men rather than single male workers.[78] In his 1919 address to the Lemon Men's Club, Charles C. Teague, owner of the Limoneira Ranch in Santa Paula and future president of the CFGE, expressed the prevailing belief among growers that "the man of family through necessity is more stable and dependable than the single man, and will not travel around so much seeking that which he may find."[79] J. B. Culbertson outlined the advantages of employing "the man of family," when he wrote:

> Taken as a class the married man is more dependable than his bachelor brother. He is more willing to do a full measure of work each day, . . . and is more disposed to apply the same principles of thrift and industry to his employer's interest that he would apply to his own. On the average he is an older man with more mature judgement and, given an opportunity to live in respectable quarters with good school facilities, steady employment and a wage that will enable him to save something above his living expenses, he is the ideal workman in agriculture.[80]

Married men represented the perfect model of social order in the citrus belt, and conformed to a society organized around the agrarian family.[81] Similarly, Paul Taylor, researching farm labor conditions in northeastern Colorado, found that sugar beet growers during the early 1920s established a resident supply of Mexican workers by appealing to Mexican families.[82]

Advocates for the employment of married men also believed that the responsibilities of family life made the worker less susceptible to the appeals of organized labor. The fear of strikes and labor protests constantly shaped the citrus growers' employment and managerial strategies. Such fears were not unfounded. Grassroots labor protest and union organizing took place in the citrus belt, especially during the second decade of the twentieth century, when radical labor unions such as the Industrial Workers of the World (IWW) aggressively sought to organize agricultural workers. During the 1917 picking season, Mexican and Sikh workers from Riverside to Claremont initiated a strike for a wage increase from 22 cents to 25 cents per hour, or $2.25 to $2.50 per week. Citrus growers complained about "the way in which the foreigners have been acting" and promised to replace them with "all Americans," but conceded defeat within a few days.[83]

Encouraged by their victory, workers again organized to challenge depressed citrus wages in 1919. This time, however, citrus growers were prepared. In March, the *California Citrograph* reported that a group of "alleged IWW and Russian Bolshevik agitators" operating out of the San Dimas Canyon in eastern Los Angeles County attempted to stage a strike. Labor leaders sent a formal letter to the Charter Oaks Citrus Association demanding an increase in wages from $3 to $4 a day, while organizers rallied workers in the groves of Azusa, Duarte, Monrovia, Upland, La Verne, Pomona, and Glendora.[84] An overwhelming response by white citrus belt residents stymied the organizing drive and successfully averted a strike through extralegal actions. The *Citrograph* writer reported:

> *The citrus communities have always been rather free from troubles of this character as the towns are made up largely of people who have an interest in the industry and who have homes and families there. . . . As a result of this feeling a party of about 400 residents of Covina, Azusa, Glendora, Charter Oak, La Verne and Claremont met in the Dequesne packing house at Charter Oak and decided to hire a truck, load the disturbers into it and carry them out of town. This plan was carried into effect and 31 were carried to the outskirts of Los Angeles, from whence they had come, and left there.*[85]

Citrus growers commonly exercised such vigilante-style tactics to snuff out labor organizing in the citrus belt. Carey McWilliams, while recalling another labor incident in Orange County in 1936, remembered his "astonishment in discovering how quickly social power could crystallize into an expression of arrogant brutality in these lovely, seemingly placid, outwardly Christian communities."[86]

Rather than eliminate "foreigners" from the workforce, citrus ranchers organized clubs to enforce their vision of society and to solve the "problems" facing the industry. *Citrograph* writers, for example, credited the American-Latin League with solving labor crises during World War I and "creat[ing] a better understanding between the employer and employee." Headed by influential citrus growers, the organization also included other employers of Mexican laborers in Southern California as well as an Argentine general manager, Dr. J. Z. Uriburu, who served as translator. The group resembled an employer's union and focused on issues other than wages, such as housing, health, and education to reach "a closer contact and more sympathetic relation generally with the aim of elevation and education of foreign labor."[87] Other clubs, like the all-male Lemon Men's Club, provided forums for citrus growers to share political, social, and economic objectives and forge "class collectivity."[88] V. V. LeRoy, secretary of the Claremont club, explained the virtues of forming such organizations when he wrote:

> *The farmer will not take the time enough from his work to keep an orga-*
> *nization alive and the politician well knows it, but the labor unions make*
> *themselves felt because they stick together. Politically the farmer is numer-*
> *ous enough to elect a large minority of legislators—generally he allows a*
> *small organized bunch of hangers on to select some failure of a lawyer for a*
> *candidate, and the farmer trots right up to the polls and votes for him. Why*
> *should the Citrus Grower organize Clubs? Because the Citrus Growers to*
> *my mind have the biggest men with the largest brain power among them,*
> *of any soil tiller in the world. Because in a large way, to save their industry*
> *from destruction, they have organized and successfully conducted the biggest*
> *and best marketing exchange in the world, and have held together; which is*
> *more than can be said of many farmers associations.*[89]

Citrus growers organized these clubs to oppose labor unions, but also to establish consensus on issues affecting the political, social, and economic life of the citrus belt. Furthermore, citrus growers depended on both the *California Citrograph* and local newspapers to report news and information, which ensured a spirit of cooperation and cohesiveness.

World War I initiated public discussions concerning labor shortages in the pages of the *Citrograph* and at the meetings of citrus clubs and associations that lasted throughout the 1920s. Citrus ranchers responded to the crisis as most other California farm owners did: they employed more nonwhite, immigrant laborers. Western farmers understood the "racial" implications of such practices, and shared public concerns about race mixing and a developing "race problem"; however, the expansion of markets and the inability to harvest crops adequately and in a timely fashion determined labor policies. Outside of citrus, agribusiness rationalized the dependence on Mexican and Asian laborers by claiming that workers were not permanent but seasonal, and thus temporary, employees.[90] Citrus ranchers could not make such claims. Since labor demands existed throughout the year, citrus industry spokespeople and advocates used racial (and to a lesser extent gendered) arguments about the character of foreign workers to justify labor practices, adjust to changes in public opinion, and influence popular thinking on race-related issues. As the number of laborers increased, ranchers attempted to marginalize non-European cultural influences through residential and educational segregation. Historian Gilbert González stated the practice of the citrus growers plainly when he wrote: "the industry divided minority and majority, at work, in residence, recreation, religion, education, and politics."[91]

Dependence on any hired help, particularly nonwhite labor, posed unique and important challenges to citrus belt communities. From the CFGE organ the *California Citrograph* to the Los Angeles Chamber of Commerce to the State Horticultural Office, citriculture advocates described citrus farming in Southern California as one of the highest forms of civilization—an "Ideal Country Life." Much of this had to do with the perception that one male farmer with perhaps nominal support from his wife and children could maintain a highly profitable farm and retire comfortably. While some ranchers began as lone "experimenters," many depended on some form of hired help to prepare the land and pick the crops. Stories of pioneer farmers risking everything they owned to begin citrus ranches obscure the role of Asian and Mexican workers in establishing the citrus industry in Southern California. Additionally, local and statewide government agencies provided crucial scientific support, while the California Fruit Growers Exchange handled marketing and pricing duties that substantially increased profits and production.

In spite of these realities, boosters and residents clung to an agrarian myth that served as the intellectual foundation of most citrus belt towns. Few acknowledged the contradictions raised by the employment of hired help: If "labor in the earth" inspires virtue, but someone other than the "farmer" performed the labor, who is then virtuous? Ranchers ignored this conundrum since profits, rhetoric, and material trappings shielded them from dealing with such questions. The employment of technology in the service of ranchers and the construction of a congenial and attractive landscape and built-environment placed cognitive distance between the farmer and what Raymond Williams has called "the curse of labour." The celebration of a balanced rural-urban development and of man's ability to manipulate nature served to extract this "curse" by concealing the existence of laborers: the thousands of Native American, Chinese, Sikh, Japanese, Filipino, and Mexican workers who figured prominently in the establishment and maintenance of the citrus industry from its inception in the 1880s to the boom years around World War I. In their "absence," citrus ranchers claimed exclusive credit for beginning a new agrarian society organized around citriculture.[92]

Increases in the number of semipermanent and permanent farmworkers in

Southern California during and after World War I threatened to reveal the existence of laborers and expose the agrarian ideal as a myth. The fact that most of these workers were nonwhite further complicated the situation since citrus belt residents valued the racial and cultural homogeneity of their communities. During the 1920s, growers and industry spokespeople responded by imposing racial and gender hierarchies in hiring that established Mexican male workers as the preferred laborers among the many racial minorities who worked the groves prior to World War I. New strategies of social control and segregation accompanied these decisions and precipitated debates within these communities over the treatment of workers. The continued growth of citrus townships attracted residents not directly involved in the citrus industry. These people, labeled the "inbetween element" by Carey McWilliams, occasionally expressed positions contrary to those held by ranchers. Finally, workers, as their settlements grew and their numbers expanded, refused to live according to the prescribed social conditions determined by the grower elite. The following chapter examines the changes in the racial makeup of labor populations, and explores the contests over control of public space and culture among growers, residents, and workers during the peak years of citrus production in Los Angeles County—the 1920s and 1930s.

*It would be misleading . . . to convey the
impression that the location of the colonias
was accidental or that it has been determined
by the natural play of social forces. On the
contrary, there is a sense in which it would
be accurate to say that the location of the
colonias has been carefully planned. Located
at just sufficiently inconvenient distances from
the parent community, it naturally became
most convenient to establish separate schools
and to minimize civic conveniences in the
satellite colonia.*
—CAREY McWILLIAMS, *North from Mexico*

The "Colonia Complex" Revisited

Racial Hierarchies and Border Spaces in the Citrus Belt, 1917–1926

In *Southern California Country: An Island on the Land,* Carey McWilliams
divides the "citrus land" of San Gabriel Valley into two primary groups: first,
"the 40,000 workers" who cultivated and harvested citrus crops; and second,
"the managerial elite" who ran the California Fruit Growers Exchange and "the
do-nothings who own the groves."[1] From his vantage point in 1946, McWilliams interpreted this social order to be a "whole system of employment . . .
perfectly designed to insulate workers from employers in every walk of life,
from the cradle to the grave, from the church to the saloon."[2]

While McWilliams's analysis provides a vivid and moving portrait of discrimination and segregation along racial and class lines, his vision presents a rather uncomplicated and straightforward breakdown of the cleavages within citrus belt society. Given the rapid growth of citrus towns and the development of services to accommodate this expanding regional economy, citrus growers found their influence over local government and culture challenged in the wake of World War I. By war's end, citrus communities had become a highly diversified economy with numerous competing interests. Doctors, lawyers, ministers, merchants, college professors, and teachers resettled in citrus towns not to engage in intensive farming, but rather to capitalize on the citrus aristocracy's need for services. McWilliams called these white midwestern and eastern transplants the "in-between element," and saw them as advocates of the "grower-exchange" view particularly during periods of social tension. Although they shared a belief in white racial superiority, their relationships with workers differed from those of the citrus growers and the California Fruit Growers Exchange. Contrary to McWilliams's characterization, the "in-between element" occasionally questioned the labor practices implemented by growers and the CFGE.

Similarly, farm labor was not an undifferentiated army of 40,000 workers, but rather bore the marks of ranch-by-ranch hiring practices, social policy, and the white majority's attitudes toward race, gender, and work during the first three decades of the twentieth century. McWilliams interpreted the workforce to be almost exclusively Mexican men, however, conditions before, during, and immediately following World War I reflected a diverse labor pool that included Native Americans, Chinese, Sikhs, Japanese, whites and Mexicans. Labor shortages precipitated discussions that resulted in grower preferences for Mexican labor, but the issue of race and its impact on citrus communities intensified during the 1920s and 1930s. The importation of Filipino, Jamaican, and Puerto Rican workers by some growers during the inter-war period extended debates regarding Mexican versus Asian (and to a lesser extent black) labor. Equally important, growers preferred not to hire white women and children, particularly wives and daughters; however, a racialized double standard developed for Mexican families. Starvation wages for pickers forced many Mexican women to seek employment in the packinghouses while children frequently joined their fathers in the groves as unpaid *"ratas"* (rats). Scurrying around the base of the tree, Mexican children gathered fallen and low-lying citrus that increased the fruit per box totals and produced larger paychecks for the patriarch of the family.

Finally, although McWilliams scarcely mentions the role of government in the formation of this "whole system," the state significantly influenced worker/

grower relations through the California Commission of Immigration and Housing (CCIH) in the Department of Industrial Relations (DIR). Formed by Governor Hiram Johnson in the wake of the Wheatland Riots of 1913 and in anticipation of increased immigration as a result of the opening of the Panama Canal,
this Progressive-Era institution grew into the most influential state agency affecting farm labor housing in California. Understanding that the search for
sanitary living conditions and work constituted an important first step in the
socialization of new immigrants, DIR presidents Simon J. Lubin and Catholic
archbishop Edward J. Hanna employed a cadre of field inspectors to enforce
the State Housing Law on California farms. Limited by only five full-time inspectors, however, the commission opted for a more cooperative approach to
reform. During the 1920s and 1930s, CCIH field inspector for Southern California, Leo Mott, and labor camp inspector Fred Rugg identified citrus ranchers
as the most progressive farm owners in California agribusiness, and worked
closely with many citrus associations to create model housing projects for farm
laborers. Although these projects received much attention from local media,
they concealed the agency's overall inability to affect the changes hoped for by
critics of farm labor practices. Far from remedying the problems, CCIH agents
endorsed the segregated housing projects of citrus ranchers and, thus, contributed to the structuring of inequality in the Southland.

This and the following chapter expand McWilliams's interpretation in two
fundamental ways. First, I explore how ranchers decided upon Mexican laborers as the preferred group for citrus work. Just as the discovery of ideal citrus
land moved from a process of trial-and-error to scientific study, hiring practices
also evolved from a haphazard, catch-as-catch-can process to an organized and
"informed" judgment. By the end of World War I a "system of employment"
took shape, influenced by government and industry officials. Like scientists'
studying geography and climate, these officials made recommendations regarding the hiring, housing, and education of workers based on "scientific" and observed theories of racial inferiority and superiority. Another factor—the desire
to repress labor activism and unionization—had a significant impact on these
discussions and played an equal part in defining employment options in the
citrus belt.[3]

Second, I examine inter- *and* intra-group differences among workers, growers, bureaucrats, and residents and highlight both worker and "in-between
element" resistance to the conditions of employment. Here it is necessary to
provide a definition of "resistance," for neither group substantially threatened
rancher hegemony with strikes and boycotts, nor did workers and residents
always agree with one another or amongst themselves as to objectives and strate-

gies. Public and private space—in particular the location of "home" and the conditions of life within the topospatial citrus *colonia*—served as the arena and subject of contests for power. In the following chapter, we will see how philanthropists, ministers, college professors, and "Americanization" officials objected to the material and social conditions within Mexican settlements and advocated various reforms including repatriation. Mexican families fought not only to improve conditions in the *colonia* through self-help and informal family and community networks, but also insisted upon shaping the social, cultural, and physical space of their homes independent of grower control.

My focus on community space as a site of conflict and resistance grows out of the significant body of scholarship produced by scholars invested in merging cultural studies with a political economy approach. Critical of labor historians whose focus on working-class resistance does not extend beyond the shop floor or union hall, historian Robin D. G. Kelley in his book *Race Rebels: Culture, Politics, and the Black Working Class* calls for an expanded definition of politics that emphasizes *why* rather than *how* people participate in grassroots social movements. Offering a more inclusive vision of labor history that includes struggles outside the workplace, Kelley argues, "politics comprises the many battles to roll back constraints and exercise some power over, or *create some space within*, the institutions and social relationships that dominate our lives" [italics added]. Likewise, ethnic studies scholar José David Saldívar, in his recent book *Border Matters: Remapping American Cultural Studies*, argues that the negotiation of "topospatial forms" and the "production of U.S.-Mexico border space" in a hostile and racist environment has been an integral part of life for all Mexicans/Mexican Americans living within the United States. Although the Treaty of Guadalupe Hidalgo granted Mexicans "white" racial status, in practice Mexican people have experienced segregation and discrimination as an ethnoracial group. Consequently, the lives of Mexican residents, like those of African Americans and Asian Americans, have been shaped by the process of defining and, wherever and whenever possible, expanding the space of their lives.[4]

The "Racial Fault Lines" in Citrus Labor

The dramatic expansion of citrus production forced upon townspeople important developmental questions about the future of the citrus belt. The growth of permanent worker colonies complicated the citrus aristocracy's goal of erasing the "curse of labor" from the landscape, and made considerations of the place of laborers a constant concern for growers. Moreover, the "racialized" nature of second-tier agricultural labor in a dual labor system ensured that workers would be both nonwhite and potentially volatile. These two threats struck directly at the heart of a citrus belt society that prided itself on its class and racial homogeneity.

Fearful of labor unions and aware of the potential for discontent among workers, citrus growers relied on various tactics to suppress labor protest and revolt throughout the first two decades of the twentieth century. Divide and conquer was among the most popular strategies, as Carey McWilliams notes in *Factories in the Fields.*[5] For example, prior to the 1920s in the citrus town of Upland, citrus growers employed Mexican, Japanese, and Sikh workers. According to one former Mexican worker, Baudelio Sandoval, local rancher Godfrey Andreas segregated employees by race at work and in residential camps. Sandoval recalled: "Japanese [lived] in a camp on 18th street. They made that camp for the Japanese. And 17th was for the Mexicans. . . . Afterwards, there was a Hindu camp on 14th street. . . . There were more Japanese than Hindus. There were 40 Hindus, but Japanese there were many, more than two hundred. Mexicans . . . were more or less around two hundred between those who lived on the ranches and those who lived in the [work] camps."[6] In the groves, growers also segregated workers along ethnoracial lines to prevent potential laborer solidarity. The employment of a diverse group of workers with their own customs and languages contributed to the segmentation of the workforce, and reduced the chances of labor organizing on and off the job.

Some growers refused to employ Mexican workers as foremen. As Sandoval remembered: "Mexicans picked their orchards. They had their foremen, Americans. Then, there were no Mexican foremen. For the moment, they were only American foremen . . . very mean." Other farm owners, such as the Ontario viticulturist Secundo Guasti, hired Spanish or Italian foremen whose language skills permitted them to communicate with Mexican workers and interpret conversations among the pickers in the fields.[7] However, the exclusion of Mexicans from foremen positions varied since some ranchers saw the advantage of maintaining a Mexican liaison between themselves and the large body of workers. For example, citrus foreman Iñez Campos of Claremont played the role of hiring agent (*rengachista*) and labor supervisor for the local grower James Blaisdell, but also served as a community leader in the nearby Arbol Verde *colonia* by communicating the concerns of Mexican parents to English-speaking schoolteachers. Although recognized as an influential entity within the *colonia*, Mexican residents viewed Campos with suspicion since he lived on the ranch in a home supplied by Blaisdell and implemented and defended the policies of his employer.[8]

The racial barriers in the groves carried over into community life. Outside of work, Mexican, Asian, and Sikh laborers found their movement and civil rights restricted by a Southern California brand of Jim Crowism that varied in severity from town to town. In Upland, for example, ethnoracial minorities were restricted from shopping anywhere but the market owned by Godfrey Andreas's friend, Mr. Klindt, and many store owners posted signs reading "Just-White-Trade-Only." According to Sandoval and delivery person John Bice, Japanese and Sikh workers tried to avoid shopping downtown by having their food imported; however, Mexicans consistently purchased their supplies in person from Klindt's market.[9]

Residents of Upland and Ontario traveled by trolley from the citrus heights down to the town center. As the trolley moved down the hill, Japanese at 18th street, Mexicans at 17th street, and Sikhs at 14th street could catch a ride in specially segregated cars monitored by local police. Andreas instructed officers to let his workers out at only two places: either the downtown district near Klindt's store, or their designated residential camps. After making their purchases, police and shopkeepers escorted Mexican, Japanese, and Sikh patrons back to the trolley and transported them directly to their respective camps. In neighboring citrus towns such as Ontario and La Verne, Mexican residents remembered that they shopped with fewer restrictions, but many recalled being peppered by white residents with racial epithets like "dirty greasers" and "spik." Former citrus worker Nick Fuentes recalled that in La Verne prior to World War II Mexicans were expected to step off the sidewalk and into the street when whites approached.[10]

Variations in the ethnic mix of the labor force and in the treatment of workers also depended on the size of farms and the amount of control ranchers had over the lives of their employees. On the large, plantation-size Leffingwell Ranch in nearby Whittier, Japanese, Mexican, and white laborers worked and lived in a self-contained universe that allowed ranch superintendent Dr. I. G. McBeth and packinghouse manager Mr. Henry A. Schuyler to observe the workers' every move. In addition to offices and laboratories for chemical and biological studies of fruit, soil, and trees, the sprawling ranch also included living facilities that segregated workers by race, class, and marital status.

In a 1918 tour of the plantation, *California Citrograph* writer and labor expert Archibald Shamel observed five separate living quarters for laborers. The "old clubhouse" housed white unmarried employees and provided numerous amenities to workers including a library so well stocked that it also served as a branch within the Los Angeles County system, and a large club room containing a piano, a Victrola, a billiard table, card tables, rocking chairs, pictures, and writing supplies. White workers ate in one large dining room, enjoyed access to a kitchen, showers, and a porch washroom, and shared spacious two-people sleeping rooms with two single beds and two lockers. The ranch charged $6.00 per week for these accommodations. Nearby, the "new clubhouse" provided the same luxuries in a slightly updated building for white unmarried heads of ranch departments including graduates of Agricultural Colleges conducting scientific studies sponsored by the United States Department of Agriculture (USDA) and the Citrus Experiment Station of the University of California. The superintendent and other married leaders of the ranch departments lived in attractive cottages surrounded by beautiful flower gardens, a park, and tennis courts kept in perfect condition for any white workers wishing to play. Ranch leaders often gathered in the "new clubhouse" to discuss work strategies and white employees used the facilities for dances and musical entertainment during the holidays.

Mexican and Japanese living conditions differed substantially from those offered to white workers. A "Mexican camp" consisting of one large dormitory located alongside a nearby canyon housed 45 to 125 employees who, according to Shamel, "[did] all of the ranch work except teaming." Mexican workers received sleeping quarters (but had to provide their own bedding), showering facilities, and meals prepared by a French cook. Similarly, Japanese packing-house employees lived in a separate dormitory with basic provisions, including showers and a plunge bath. Rather than hiring a chef, packinghouse manager Schuyler permitted Japanese workers to elect one of their members as cook for a six-month tenure with wages paid by the ranch. In spite of their inferior facilities and services, Mexican and Japanese workers paid $5.90 per week for these accommodations, just 10 cents less than what managers charged white workers for room and board.[11]

Although rigid segregation and labor segmentation prevailed in many citrus towns, this social order ultimately proved to be a temporary solution to the persistent "labor problem" of finding a tractable and dependable source of workers. Segregation required constant maintenance and the physical separation of the various ethnoracial groups. Some citrus ranches, such as the Limoneira Ranch in Santa Paula, successfully maintained structural inequalities by constructing a traditional company town.[12] Most citrus ranches, however, required cooperation among citrus growers, city officials, and town residents to maintain the racial hierarchies supported by white citrus belt residents. The social order of Upland, for example, depended on an agreement among all Euroamerican residents to keep Mexicans, Sikhs, and Japanese segregated and in a subordinate social position to whites. Citrus grower and camp owner Godfrey

Andreas maintained social harmony by holding barbecues for the townspeople and by directing worker business to Klindt's market, a shop Mexican employees called "the company store." The economic importance of Andreas's enterprise granted him political clout and resulted in his election to the California General Assembly.[13]

Public debates ensued over the suitability and potential threat of each group to the racial purity of white citrus belt society at grower meetings and in the pages of the *California Citrograph*. By World War I, the Native American population had dwindled to such lows that citrus growers no longer considered them a viable employment option and afforded them little attention in the debates.[14] Asian immigrants, on the other hand, constituted a group that posed a great potential for solving the labor problems and were used extensively prior to the 1920s. For example, in 1917, the *California Citrograph* editorialized: "One solution [to the labor shortage problem] that is meeting with a great deal of favor from farmers is the importation of Chinese or Filipinos, on a contract for some specified term." [15] Many citrus ranchers also employed Japanese and Sikh laborers.

Scholars such as Sucheng Chan, Ronald Takaki, Tomás Almaguer, Karen Leonard, and Valerie Matsumoto have contributed important studies of Chinese, Japanese, Sikh, and Filipino workers during the nineteenth and early twentieth century.[16] In her book, *Asian Americans: An Interpretive History*, Sucheng Chan argues that hostility against Asian immigrants may be divided into seven categories: prejudice, economic discrimination, political disenfranchisement, physical violence, immigration exclusion, social segregation, and incarceration.[17] Restrictive immigration legislation and vigilante violence tended to be the most aggressive expressions against Asian agricultural laborers and figured prominently in their limited use as citrus workers.

Chinese preceded all Asian immigrants to the San Gabriel and San Bernardino Valleys. According to Ontario viticulturist Ruth Milliken, Chinese rail workers arrived in the citrus belt during the 1880s with the extension of the railroad to Southern California. She recalled, "When they [Chinese rail workers] got through putting in the railroad, the Santa Fe, all these Chinese men had no place to go." Stranded without work in a hostile environment, these former railroad laborers formed "little Chinatowns" on the outskirts of citrus cities such as Cucamonga, Upland, San Bernardino, Riverside, and the rail town Spadra near Pomona. In San Bernardino, for example, a Chinatown formed in a place known as "Squaw Flats" where Native Americans had lived prior to 1880.[18]

Some Chinese immigrants sought work in the local vineyards and citrus groves, while others established truck farms on unclaimed land throughout the San Gabriel–San Bernardino Valley. Since many white farmers engaged in monocultural ventures for export, Chinese immigrants earned a subsistence income supplying vegetables to citrus town residents. Milliken recalled that 50 cents a week bought "soup vegetables": "Oh, occasionally Mama bought a little more but the first thing was soup vegetables; that would be a couple onions, couple of carrots, couple parsnips, couple turnips." Additionally, Chinese men found employment as cooks on citrus ranches and in local restaurants, or as laundry workers in the downtown districts of larger cities such as Pomona and Pasadena.[19]

The arrival of the Chinese occurred simultaneously with the rise of Anti-Chinese clubs intent on driving "coolie" labor from the state with acts of violence and anti-Asian immigration legislation. In Pomona, white residents organized a local unit of the Non-partisan Anti-Chinese League in 1886 to address the growing number of Chinese laundries that critics labeled disease-breeding "stench vats." Local nativists also opposed the Chinese presence on the grounds that "Chinamen . . . [took] the work that rightfully belong[ed] to the good, honest white men of Pomona City." A boycott against Chinese launderers, an ordinance, adopted in 1891, banning wash houses from the city (as opposed to the steam machine laundry run by white competitor Charles Lorbeer), and high licensing fees for nonresident laundry owners eventually forced many Chinese to close shop and take up truck farming or fruit picking in nearby orchards.[20] Similarly, in the depression year of 1893, a rash of anti-Chinese outbreaks occurred throughout the state. Euroamerican vigilantes invaded Chinatowns in the citrus towns of Pasadena, Redlands, Riverside, and San Bernardino, physically assaulting Chinese men and torching their ramshackle homes.[21] Attacks such as these and anti-Chinese legislation such as the Chinese Exclusion laws of 1882, 1888, and 1892 corresponded with downturns in the U.S. economy and reflected the tendency of white workers to blame Chinese immigrants for their woes.[22]

Many Chinese immigrants endured California nativism and continued to work into the twentieth century. Contrary to Carey McWilliams's claims that ritualized violence and discriminatory immigration laws drove the Chinese out of agricultural California after the 1880s, Sucheng Chan has discovered that in some rural areas such as the San Joaquin Valley, Chinese tenancy actually increased between 1890 and 1920.[23] Demonstrating the determination of many Chinese immigrants of this period, Andrew Kan, a resident of forty-four years, commented: "since I have lived and made money in this country, I should be able to become an American citizen."[24] In the citrus belt, Chinese immigrants demonstrated a similar interest in permanent settlement. For example, Ruth Milliken remembered that fellow viticulturist Mr. Thomas "kept the sixteen Chinese" who came to work for him in the 1880s until 1919. Milliken added, "They had worked for him for so many years, he just kept them on, but they were as slow as the itch . . . well, they were old, you know, awful [sic] old." [25] Unlike the Central Valley and urban districts such as Los Angeles, San Francisco, and Sacramento where Chinese immigrants established independent communities, the citrus towns maintained dispersed and dependent concentrations of Chinese workers. The growing labor demands of an expanding citrus economy forced white farmers to look for another source of laborers, since the Chinese population could not grow due to the Exclusion Acts. Consequently, Chinese workers were not so much driven out of Southern California as they were overwhelmed by the employment of immigrants who had yet to be identified as scapegoats and a "problem."

Japanese, on the other hand, increased their presence in the citrus belt during the early twentieth century and participated in farming throughout California. Whether as common laborers such as Jigahara, or as packinghouse workers such as those at the Leffingwell Ranch, Japanese immigrants arrived prepared and determined to establish themselves in the local economy. Many began as common laborers, but quickly ascended to the rank of independent farmer. According to historian Ronald Takaki, "by 1909, significantly, 6,000 Japanese had become farmers." [26]

A combination of factors led to their success in farming, particularly in California. The rise of industrialization and urbanization during the early twentieth century led to increased demands for fresh fruits and vegetables in cities. As with the early and relatively modest success of Chinese truck farmers, Japanese farmers filled niches in a booming Southern California economy dominated by citrus and oil production. Berries and truck vegetables became especially important crops to Japanese farmers. By 1910, they produced 70 percent of California's strawberries, and by 1940 they grew 95 percent of the state's beans and spring and summer celery, 67 percent of its tomatoes, and 40 percent of its fresh green peas. In fact, one of the most studied agricultural strikes in Southern California history, the 1933 El Monte Berry Strike by Mexican pickers, involved Japanese leaseholders. Japanese's gambles with "contract" farming seemingly paid off. By 1920, Japanese farmers claimed 458,056 California acres under their control.[27]

Their success caused a backlash, as white ranchers excoriated the Japanese for their ambition to own land, their methods of farming, and their cultural practices. For example, the author of a 1917 *Citrograph* article argued that "the

Asiatic element can not be assimilated," and disparaged Asians for their practice of tenant farming. The author reported:

California tenant communities [are] made up almost entirely of Asiatics or of peasants from those portions of Europe where life is sordid and the standards of living are low. These tenants have no interest in community needs. They maintain their racial indifference and aloofness. They are not a contribution to our political or social strength. They are willing and able to pay high rents, not because their methods of farming are better, though as a rule they are good farmers, but because they live more frugally than the American or the immigrant from Northern Europe. In other words, while Northern Europe is lifting the peasant farmers into a more independent and generous life, California is creating conditions which are in some cases worse than those of the European landlord peasant because the European had certain obligations founded on feudal customs and supported by public opinion which do not exist here.[28]

The author's reference to "the Asiatic element" reflected the common practice of whites to lump all Asian immigrants together; however, within the article, the author distinguished Japanese farmers as the greatest threat to agriculture in Southern California both in terms of their level of participation and their methods of farming.[29]

Aside from endangering the racial and class hierarchies, Japanese farmers also threatened the traditional gender divisions in citrus belt society. Although men dominated early immigration from Japan, many of the Issei sent for their wives or picture brides upon arrival in America. Consequently, unlike Chinese, Sikh, and later Filipino populations in California who were predominantly male and single, Japanese communities maintained a more equitable female/male sex ratio. The few population samples taken from the citrus belt bear this out. For example, the 1930 and 1940 census broke down male and female populations for Japanese and Chinese populations. In towns where census takers counted Chinese populations, the sex ratio was significantly skewed in favor of men; conversely, Japanese numbers demonstrate greater gender parity.[30] (See Table 4 in Appendix.)

Ronald Takaki and Valerie Matsumoto have demonstrated that among Issei and Nisei farming families, "husbands and wives worked side by side in the fields."[31] Men worked exclusively on the crop, while women divided their time into hatarite ita, or working, and asonderu, or keeping house. As Ronald Takaki explained, "often Issei women complained about their husbands being 'Meiji men': 'we worked from morning till night, blackened by the sun. My husband was a Meiji man; he didn't even glance at the house work or child care.'"[32] Divisions of labor provided a potential source of conflict, but underscored the importance of women's work to the maintenance of family life among Japanese immigrants living in California during this period.

White farmers ultimately sought to eliminate independent and ambitious Japanese farmers from the citrus belt with tactics similar to those used against the Chinese. In 1919, the Chamber of Commerce of the San Gabriel Valley held a special meeting of the board of directors in which leaders of the industry articulated their position regarding the "serious situation" of the "Japanese menace." The Chamber's president and Claremont grower Frank Wheeler reported:

> W. S. Rosecrans the Secretary of the County Farm Bureau was present and after lunch he laid before the Directors the serious situation facing this state and Los Angeles county in particular from the Japanese menace, there being over 120,000 Japs in this state at present and multiplying rapidly, the children born in this country (and therefore American Citizens) are sent back to Japan to be educated, and later return to U.S. more Jap than American. The Jap children here are gathered up in trucks and autoes [sic] and sent to Jap schools in this county, and Japs are fast crowding out the small farmer, by employing their own women and children.[33]

Opposition to Japanese immigration and land ownership had clear racial overtones, as commentators warned of fomenting a "race problem" by hiring Japanese workers, and citrus elites speculated about the "racial indifference" of Japanese immigrants to citrus belt society. Equally important, many citrus growers believed that the Japanese success in truck farming, if left unchecked, could challenge the economic superiority of white farms.

All of these concerns resulted in legislative acts that curtailed the Japanese influence on California society. Given Japan's rising military and economic power in the Pacific Rim during the early twentieth century, laws affecting Japanese immigration did not name them explicitly though legislators understood their intent. In 1907, Japan consented to the "Gentlemen's Agreement" whereby it agreed to control immigration by not issuing passports to laborers. In California, the state legislature attempted to minimize Japanese land ownership through a series of alien land laws, beginning with the 1913 Alien Land Act that declared unlawful the ownership of property by "aliens ineligible to citizenship." In 1923, California legislators strengthened the law with an amendment that forbade aliens ineligible for citizenship to "acquire, possess, enjoy, use, cultivate, occupy, and transfer real property."[34]

Although Sikhs and Filipinos mostly fell outside of these legislative restrictions, both of these groups found themselves the object of white racial antipathies reminiscent of that experienced by Chinese and Japanese immigrants. For example, in 1910, nativist residents in Claremont used Halloween as an excuse to intimidate a group of unwanted Sikh workers from the town. The local newspaper reported that the Sikh men, hired for a grading project, "failed to return to work after being terrorized by a group of 'unknowns.'"[35] East Indian immigrants were eventually barred from entering the United States by a clause in the 1917 Immigration Act that refused entry to all people living east of an imaginary line running from the Red Sea to the Ural Mountains. Filipinos, on the other hand, could not be excluded by immigration legislation since the Philippines remained a colonial possession of the United States until the Tydings-McDuffie Act granted the island nation its independence in 1934. Neither aliens nor citizens, Filipinos freely entered the mainland United States during the interwar period.[36]

Although a few growers enthusiastically endorsed their employment, most worried aloud about the effects Filipinos might have on citrus belt communities. After a decade of experimentation with Filipino and Mexican workers, George Clements, manager of the Agricultural Department for the Los Angeles Chamber of Commerce, reported to the Lemon Men's Club on October 2, 1929, that "the Filipino has not given general satisfaction—his susceptibility to disease has necessitated federal restrictions. The Mexican is our only recourse."[37] Later in his presentation, Clement explained the critical difference between Mexicans and Filipinos: "The Mexican is never a biological problem. He rarely marries out of his own people. A Mexican man never marries a white woman. Some white men marry Mexican girls. The Filipino is complicating matters here."[38]

Concerns of racial intermixing occasionally crystallized into anti-Filipino violence when Filipino men stepped outside their prescribed social roles as bachelor immigrant laborers. In 1930, an interracial party with Filipino men and "white female entertainers" at the Palm Beach Filipino Club in Watsonville, California, ignited several days of anti-Filipino rioting throughout the northern half of the state. The "fracas" began on January 21, 1930, when an "attacking mob of whites" ransacked a Filipino dormitory, killed one worker, and injured numerous others at a nearby lettuce ranch. Local judge, Honorable D. W. Rohrback, blamed Filipinos for the disturbance, stating: "Filipinos [come] to this country as little brown men attired like Solomon in all his glory, strutting like peacocks and endeavoring to attract the eyes of young American and Mexican girls, but ten years removed from a bolo and breechcloth."

News of the riots and the judge's remarks spread across California, influencing grower and resident opinions regarding the employment of Filipino agricultural workers.[39]

Given the fear of Filipino-white miscegenation and the belief that Mexican men practiced endogamy, farmers took steps to increase the flow of immigration across the U.S.-Mexico border. In 1917, farmers lobbied the United States Congress to suspend literacy tests and contract labor laws against Mexican agricultural workers. While it did not stop the practice of employing Asian laborers, it made it easier for citrus farm owners to hire Mexican workers. The editors of *The California Citrograph* soberly reported: "This is certainly a wise move on the part of the Government and ought to quiet the agitation for the importation of Filipinos." The writer continued, regretfully, "There must be something radically wrong about the labor conditions on the farms of this state. It ought not to be necessary to import laborers who are undesirable as citizens, and take the chance of developing a race problem."[40]

Removal of immigration restrictions for Mexicans contributed a "pull" factor to the massive migration of Mexican refugees. Between 1910 and 1920, approximately 10 percent of the Mexican population traveled to the United States to escape the uncertainty of the Mexican Revolution and earn wages that they hoped would sustain them during the conflict.[41] Extreme poverty, the nationalization of land ownership, and increased birth rates in Mexico forced many Mexicans to take advantage of the relaxed U.S. immigration policies and job opportunities in agriculture.[42] According to the United States census of 1920, 86,610 Mexicans resided in California, many of whom made their living in farm-related occupations.[43] An in-house study conducted by the California Fruit Growers Exchange in December 1919 ascertained that from 1914 to 1919, Mexicans employed in citrus orchards and packinghouses increased from 2,317 to 7,004, representing 30 percent of the industry's total employment.[44] By 1926, 10,000 Mexican pickers worked in Southern California citrus groves, and by 1940 approximately 22,000 Mexican men labored in the orchards, constituting nearly 100 percent of the picking force.[45] Approximately 11,000 Mexican women packed citrus fruit.[46]

Mexico's close proximity to California and the desire of many Mexican laborers to secure dependable employment informed grower preferences for Mexican workers; however, the ambiguity of Mexican racial status vis-à-vis Asian and black immigrants also influenced the thinking of citrus ranchers. In his book *Racial Fault Lines*, Tomás Almaguer argues that "the Mexicans' mixed European ancestry, romance language, Catholic religious practices, and familiar political-economic institutions elevated them above all other cultural groups

in the white man's eyes." [47] However, over a period of roughly fifty years, Euroamericans "racialized" elite Mexicans by appropriating their land and forcing
many into financial ruin. Stripped of their material possessions, Californios discovered that Euroamericans regarded them as "greasers," no different from the
majority of working-class mestizos in California. Although laws continued to
classify Mexicans as "white," in practice Euroamericans treated Mexicans as
second-class, nonwhite citizens. By 1900, Mexicans occupied a lower socioeconomic position in a dual labor system, working predominantly as manual
laborers for white-owned companies and farms.[48]

Often, an immigrant's complexion determined how he or she was treated.
According to historian George Sánchez, the United States Immigration Bureau
in Los Angeles labeled 82.9 percent of entering Mexicans as "dark (including
brown, brunette, olive, and ruddy)." Although recorded subjectively by immigration officials, the evidence suggests that the vast majority of Mexican immigrants entering Los Angeles were either mestizo or Indian. These findings
reflect the effects of the Mexican Revolution that tended to displace rural communities consisting of Indian and mestizo populations rather than urbanized
Spanish elites.[49]

The Spanish/Indian blood "mixture" of Mexicans—a combination as much
a social construction as a genetic configuration—was significant to agribusiness spokespeople and farmers interested in resolving the "labor problem" without fomenting a "race problem." Many growers regarded the vast number of
"half-civilized" Mexicans flowing across the U.S.-Mexico border as a source of
inexpensive labor that did not threaten the whiteness of the citrus belt as did
Asians, West Indians, or African Americans. The citrus industry in particular
supported a corps of investigators who studied the labor situation during the
interwar period and produced recommendations based on racialist arguments.
Two men, Archibald D. Shamel, a writer for the *California Citrograph*, and
George Hodgkin, director of the Industrial Relations Department of the CFGE,
published formal reports of labor conditions on citrus ranches across Southern California. Merging economic considerations with historically forged racial
hierarchies and emergent theories of racial difference, these men offered labor
recommendations that influenced farmer hiring and housing practices prior to
World War II.

Creating and Contesting Community Space in the Citrus Belt

Throughout the 1920s, industry-financed surveyors and *Citrograph* writers discussed and debated the role of Mexican laborers in the citrus belt. Writers

focused on three key issues: the employment of married Mexican men; the construction of adequate housing; and the education of Mexican women and children. Archibald Shamel initiated the citrus industry's obsession with race and labor in a *Citrograph* series entitled "Housing the Employes [*sic*] of California's Citrus Ranches" beginning in February 1918. In the series' first installment, Shamel expressed what would become the mantra for citrus spokespeople during the interwar period:

> *The writer, from his experience, has come to the conclusion that the Mexican laborers are human beings and that they respond to decent treatment as any other humans do. He has noticed that on these ranches where he is working, and where some intelligent effort is being made to provide decent houses and sometimes a little garden patch for the Mexican families, that the Mexican laborers are good workers, faithful to any trust that may be reposed in them, and anxious to make their families happy and comfortable.*[50]

Most industry leaders and *Citrograph* writers believed that Mexican men, if adequately cared for, would pledge their eternal allegiance to the citrus farm owner. Citrus growers at the 1919 Lemon Men's Club meeting reached consensus on this topic, as the *Citrograph* reported: "the Mexican laborer employed on the citrus ranches is very susceptible to kindness and consideration and . . . his loyalty to his employer's interest may be secured to a far greater extent by a friendly expression of interest than by any pecuniary advancement."[51] Citrus growers believed that Mexicans possessed less material ambitions than whites and could be satisfied simply by providing adequate living arrangements. As the editors of the *Citrograph* wrote: "The Mexican laborer, who has a comfortable little cottage in which he may maintain his family, is the contented man, and is less likely to be attracted by the blandishments of another 25 cents a day." Editors concluded, "In the final solution of the labor problem confronting the citrus orchardist, the proper housing of his employee will be found to have a very important bearing."[52]

Convinced of Shamel's findings, the California Fruit Growers Exchange established the Industrial Relations Department on April 1, 1920, for the study of employment, wages, housing, education, and other questions affecting workers in the citrus districts. The director, George B. Hodgkin, brought to his position credentials in scientific labor management, having earned a bachelors degree in economics and sociology from the University of California as well as serving as manager of the Labor Bureau of the Goodyear Tire and Rubber Company for two years. Hodgkin found that "employers, in general, no longer need riots or even laws resulting from riots to convince them that housing is a prerequisite to wholesome employment relations." Attempting to coordinate housing project construction with the needs of the farmer and the desires of the surrounding community, Hodgkin recommended "co-operation with public agencies," particularly those engaged in educational and health work.[53]

Hodgkin's recommendation to cooperate with "public agencies" was undoubtedly a reference to the California Department of Industrial Relations (DIR). Among the earliest advocates of scientific management, the DIR agents believed that providing workers with a sanitary and safe place to live could avert another Wheatland Riot. From 1914 to 1920, the DIR also maintained a separate division for Americanization, "authorized to cooperate with federal, state, local governmental, and private agencies in bringing to the immigrant the best opportunities for acquiring an education and obtaining citizenship."[54] Progressive governor Hiram Johnson appointed women reformers to the office primarily as token representatives, but middle-class and elite women in the California Progressive Party assumed control of the program to demonstrate the vitality and efficacy of the women's movement. Women reformers found a valuable advocate in DIR president Simon Lubin, who had earlier been inspired by renowned settlement workers Jane Addams and Frances Kellor. Genuinely supportive of women's involvement, Lubin convinced Johnson to choose widowed Los Angeles schoolteacher Mary Gibson as one of six women appointed to the division in 1913. Gibson drafted the California Home Teacher Act and worked with the Women's Legislative Council of California to ensure the bill's passage in the state legislature. In 1920, instruction for immigrants was subsumed into the state board of education, but women continued to be a force in Americanization programs, and the DIR's California Commission of Immigration and Housing (CCIH) maintained a vital interest in the assimilation and education of foreign workers.[55]

In theory, the CCIH had the authority to challenge the poor living conditions growers provided for their workers. According to the organization's bylaws, "the division [was] required to investigate the housing conditions of immigrants and working people, and [was] charged with supervision over the enforcement of the housing acts." Although the DIR did not have the authority to prosecute violators, "its agents [had] the power to enter private property, and to subpoena, administer oaths, take testimony, and mediate" to resolve disputes and, when necessary, turn over damaging evidence to "authorities charged with enforcement." In practice, however, CCIH executives instructed inspectors to avoid confrontations with ranchers. As the division's director Edward Brown advised Fred Rugg in 1926: "do not go into a camp and threaten the operator with arrest if his camp is not in conformity with the Camp Sanitation Act." Brown counseled Rugg, "wherever operators do not show any effort to cooperate with us in camp work, then is the time for you to commence legal actions."[56] Chief housing inspector and Southern California agent Leo Mott revealed the agency's philosophy in an address to the Americanization group, the "Friends of the Mexicans," in 1925: "since the inception of the Commission's work its housing activity has not only been confined to enforcing the State Housing Law, but the energies of the department have also been directed to the broader field of constructive work." "By that," Mott explained, "is meant the formulating of plans and the encouraging of, and assisting in, housing projects and better building programs that have been undertaken and developed in our state from time to time."[57]

While employers of seasonal labor in the expansive Central and Imperial Valleys challenged the mandate of CCIH agents, citrus growers conformed to the bureau's requirements. In 1920, citrus associations in Azusa, Claremont, Corona, Covina, Glendora, La Verne, San Dimas, Upland, and Whittier voluntarily embarked on housing projects that inspectors pointed to as models for California agribusiness to follow. "The big idea back [sic] of all these efforts," reported the Los Angeles Examiner, "is to make [Mexicans] so comfortable and contented that they will stay on in the model cottages through the season and through the year."[58] Citrus growers shouldered the expense of these projects, but the CCIH provided ranchers with information concerning recent innovations in industrial housing including inexpensive "ready-cut" or "factory built" homes by local construction companies. The CCIH championed the projects as evidence of their positive impact on labor housing conditions in the state, and credited these "few far-sighted men in the citrus industry [with] pioneer[ing] a movement to provide proper housing accommodations for their help close to the packing house."[59]

Local newspaper reporters interpreted these efforts as the "most intensive and highly scientific phase" of agriculture and lauded citrus growers for "join-[ing] hands with the social workers."[60] Hodgkin, however, rejected the connection between housing projects and philanthropy, plainly stating, "There is nothing philanthropic about it. . . . The employer's motive for going into social work," he asserted, "is neither narrow selfishness nor altruism, but enlightened self-interest, which means that what is good for the Mexican is good for the employer and good for the community." For Hodgkin, "housing employees means more than building shacks or putting up tents. It means modern houses with modern improvements, a community center, and last, but most important, *supervision*, or community organization. The community work is essentially educational work and is therefore a proper function of the schools [italics added]."[61]

Supervision began with the planners' careful attention to the spatial relations among workers in the camps. *Los Angeles Examiner* reporter Joseph Timmons observed, "the white laborer is not being overlooked," and reassured his readers that these workers received better quality homes than did Mexicans. Hodgkin identified five construction systems available to growers: adobe, wood frame, hollow tile, poured concrete, and ready-cut or "portable" construction. In Claremont, the local growers' association serving the El Camino and College Heights citrus companies opted for the less expensive, concrete homes for Mexican workers, while white employees lived in the more costly and better insulated wood frame bungalows. Growers segregated the small camp into exclusively "white" and "Mexican" blocks and afforded white workers more space than Mexican employees. Contractors constructed houses for white employees around a courtyard complete with walkways and lawns, while the Mexican homes were built in a straight line on the far western end of the camp. Although builders claimed that the concrete homes were "cooler in summer" and "warmer in the winter," Julia Salazar, a packinghouse worker and resident of the original Mexican colony, found this not to be the case: "[The houses] were not concrete blocks—they were just concrete, because I remember that during the cold weather we would have a little heater and the walls would weep or sweat." This made for very "wet" and unhealthy conditions within the homes, and, as Salazar recalled, "everybody would have a lot of problems with that." [62]

In La Verne, the local orange growers' association built cottages made of hollow tile and plaster that Mexican families rented for $10 a month. Workers also paid $1.25 for water and had a coin-operated gas line that delivered fuel to heating and stove units for a quarter. Mexican women circumvented the charge by collecting water from nearby sources and using wood to ignite old pot-belly stoves. Eventually, Mexican families learned how to subvert growers' attempts to collect money, as former picker Nick Fuentes remembered: "My mom found a little piece of steel about so long, real thin, but strong. Then the girls would poke the hole where you put the quarter and we'd get free gas [laughs]. Then the guy would come to collect and he'd get 50 cents or maybe a quarter. He would say, 'You people didn't use the gas.' We said, 'Well, we had a lot of wood!' We were stealing the gas and everybody was doing the same thing!" [63]

In addition to material concerns, Mexican workers experienced unprecedented interference in their daily lives from local educators and social workers interested in instilling white, Protestant values in Mexican immigrants. Historians Vicki L. Ruiz, Gilbert González, Gayle Gullett, Judith Raftery, and George Sánchez have contributed important studies of how school boards and settlement houses instituted Americanization programs for Mexican immigrants in the Southwest.[64] Working in conjunction with the DIR and school boards, white middle-class and elite women involved in these campaigns valued the experience it provided women reformers in state and local politics. Although several western states like California, Arizona, Oregon, and Washington enacted women's suffrage well ahead of the Nineteenth Amendment in 1920, many women progressives saw immigrant education as an opportunity to prove their interest in public affairs. Some women reformers believed they had a true affinity with immigrants since, like these new arrivals, they too were just beginning to gain full citizenship as equal voting members of society. Moreover, women, like Mary Gibson, believed Americanization was the appropriate vehicle for women to contribute to the improvement of their communities, for as she put it, "If they [women] carry through but half their far-reaching plans [for Americanization], the women of the country will have justified themselves and their claims to suffrage a hundred-fold."[65]

For Mexican residents, Americanization was as much an intrusion as a service due to the often ethnocentric and patronizing attitudes of many educators. Americanization workers accepted contemporary characterizations of Mexicans as "shiftless" and "thriftless," and approached their jobs with the intentions of saving American civilization from the influence of a degenerate race. Mary Gibson captured the attitude of many educators in a 1915 California *Outlook* article: "These [immigrant] families are with us and make up a definite part of our civilization—whether that part shall be valuable[,] or a menace to the body politic, rest[s] with us."[66] Unlike eugenicists, Americanization workers possessed the faith that Mexican immigrants could be adequately educated to overcome differences. "These people are *not* a hopeless proposition," asserted Amanda Mathews Chase, the first home teacher for the Americanization program in Los Angeles, "but they need education of a peculiar sort—education that shall be a disciplinary tonic—that shall give them standards—that amounts to evolution."[67] Through these California programs, Mexican women and children received enough education to perform proficiently in their low-skilled jobs. George Hodgkin approved of the curriculum, stating: "the sole object of building a labor camp is to provide a satisfactory supply of labor to do good work at the lowest possible cost."[68] Citrus ranchers embraced the programs since Americanization promised to serve their interest in establishing a permanent supply of tractable workers.

Although citrus belt residents and police immediately blamed Mexicans for any disturbances in the region, most believed Mexican people to be harmless. Tobias Larson, editor of the *Claremont Courier* newspaper, demonstrated the prevailing white attitude toward Mexicans when he described them as "strangers in a strange land, having little, wanting little, unacquainted with the language—yet they sing. Happiness or contentment is a state of mind."[69] Many researchers and writers believed Mexicans possessed a natural ability in the arts and reflected this in their home lives. Reporting on the La Verne citrus housing project, *Los Angeles Examiner* reporter Joseph Timmons observed that "little gardens of hollyhock and phlox brighten the place and the swarthy women and children swarming about the cottages plainly rest there in love of home." Hodgkin described Mexican people as "more interested in art and play than we [whites] are." He continued, "He [a Mexican man] wants music and dancing and a park in which he can meet and talk with his neighbors." Archibald Shamel also expressed this belief when he detected in Mexican people the tendency to improve their home surroundings "with flowers and music." Helen O'Brien, a Pomona College student studying the Mexican community in Claremont, commented: "In the school room, the children prove to be skillful in art and music, but seem to have difficulty in getting their education from the printed page."[70]

According to white observers, Mexicans' affinity for art, music, and "play," could divert workers from their primary roles as citrus farm laborers. "The chief enemy of the Mexican laborer is whiskey," wrote Shamel. He warned citrus ranchers to protect against the "outsider surreptitiously bringing American whiskey into the Mexican quarters."[71] Such "outsiders" threatened the peaceful and contented nature of the Mexican worker and jeopardized the order citrus owners so earnestly attempted to achieve on their citrus ranches. Shamel's views concerning Mexicans and liquor bespoke a general attitude toward Mexican people that characterized them as children with little control over their passions.

Architects of the grower-financed Mexican settlements emphasized the need for home-based education in which white teachers would "attempt to bring the home and the school closer together, and . . . to teach families practical home economics."[72] Families, and particularly women, were critical to Americanization programs. Pearl Ellis, a Covina schoolteacher and author of *Americanization Through Homemaking*, wrote, "Since the girls are potential mothers and homemakers, they will control, in a large measure, the destinies of their future families." Citrus growers regarded women as the keys to a contented and orderly household, and the first and most significant educators in children's lives, or as Ellis explained, "it is she who sounds the clarion call in the campaign for better homes."[73] Researchers believed that if women learned the tenets of Americanization, they could influence male workers and indoctrinate young children.

As Hodgkin argued: "The Mexican is reached most easily through his home and friends. If his family is well and happy, if his house is neat and clean, and his meals good . . . he will be pretty certain to think twice before uprooting himself."[74] As historian George Sánchez has demonstrated, Americanization programs often targeted women first for recruitment and education as a means to influencing the entire family.[75]

Americanization curricula attempted to mold Mexican residents into law-abiding, sanitary, and obedient members of the community. Educators expected Mexican people to develop a strong enough understanding of the American system to make them functional in citrus belt society, but not to acquire the intellectual tools to question their social positions. Expressing ideas typical of most Americanization programs, R. S. Vaile of the Riverside Experiment Station encouraged citrus ranch owners to institute "a well directed effort to educate the Mexican along the lines of American history and institutions, hygiene, sanitation, the English language, and Christian Democracy."[76] English language education became an especially important part of Americanization programs, as growers hoped to instruct workers on the job and understand and control their lines of communication. Dr. J. Z. Uriburu, general manager of the American-Latin League, believed that English-language education constituted the number one priority for the organization. According to Uriburu, "the only dividing line between the United States and the south [sic] is language."[77] George Hodgkin had these instructions for educators:

> Give them something they are interested in. . . . Instead of giving them such
> sentences as "See the red hen crossing the street," give them something about
> the business in which they derive their livelihood. Let the instructor draw
> a picture on the board of an orange tree and a man in front of it. A line
> such as "See the Mexican picking oranges," or "The man is picking oranges
> the right way." I believe that is the way to enlist his interest in education,
> Americanism and his business.[78]

With their focus on families, women, and children, Americanization programs mainly affected the development of future generations of Mexican Americans in the citrus belt. By design, citrus growers invested in housing and education projects not out of concern for the well-being of Mexican families, but rather for the long-term profit of their citrus business. At a time of incredible growth and profit in citrus farming, ranch owners believed that fostering an attitude of commitment and permanency among Mexican men and their families constituted the best strategy for ensuring their future.

Most Mexican workers shared an interest in establishing permanent residency and invested heavily in homesteads throughout the citrus belt. Econo-mist Paul Taylor, for example, expressed surprise when he discovered a high number of home-owning Mexican immigrants in the citrus belt "colonies" of Azusa, Claremont, Covina, El Monte, La Verne, La Puente, Pasadena, Po-mona, San Dimas, and Upland. "[They] will pay 300 to 500 [dollars] down on a home," Taylor noted, "when you think they haven't a cent." In spite of en-counters with discrimination and a lack of reliable social services, Taylor found: "over and over again, Mexican men have said [they] don't want their families to go back to Mexico." Similar conditions existed in the rural citrus-growing areas of Orange County, where Gilbert González also found homeownership a priority for Mexican families living and working in Valencia orchards.

Mexican residents, however, resisted growers' attempts to control their social and physical space by establishing independent citrus belt *colonias* (commu-nities) on their own terms where Mexican cultural practices flourished. Citrus town councils followed a general blueprint of segregation by restricting Mexi-can homeownership and settlement to undesirable or poor areas; however, variations in the quality of land, degree of urbanization, and county and city boundaries allowed some *colonias* to grow into large and complex communi-ties that exercised a significant amount of independence. As Gilbert González observed, residents maintained a network of social relations that span several miles and incorporated many *colonias*. While residents developed services and organizations in each *colonia* to meet their immediate needs and overcome the neglect of city and county governments, a "hub-satellite" pattern developed that made some settlements more central than others.[79]

Paul Taylor, in his 1927 unpublished field notes, bore witness to this unique development. Taylor found that while "a Mexican district" existed within, or alongside of, most citrus towns, some gained particular notoriety (or infamy) for their size and sense of community. In the relatively urban "Pomona district," for example, Taylor visited "200 families," but found that "deed restrictions . . . scattered" them along the southern and western fringes of the city, a condi-tion that led him to conclude, "Pomona hasn't a colony." In the rocky and in-hospitable terrain of Irwindale, however, Taylor encountered 2,000 Mexicans, ranging from the first to the third generation, who organized a *colonia* con-sisting of two churches (one Presbyterian, one Catholic), a Mexican mutual aid society (*mutualista*), and a locally owned store. Further west, the Mexican settlements of Hicks Camp and Medina Court in El Monte flourished into a "hub" for many Mexican immigrants working in local crops such as strawberries as well as nearby walnut and citrus groves located throughout the San Gabriel Valley. From 1922 to 1927, Mexican immigration infused a mixed Anglo, Japa-

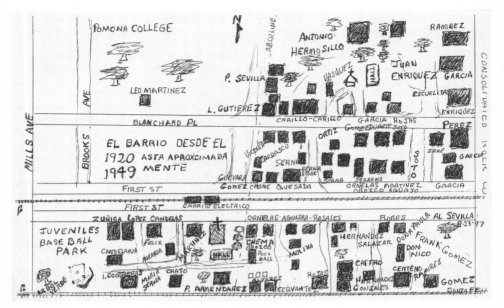

Map 3. Arbol Verde *colonia*, hand-drawn by longtime resident Alfonso Sevilla, 1997.
(Courtesy of Alfonso Sevilla)

nese, and Mexican community with new arrivals, increasing El Monte's Mexican population from 400 to 2,000. Like Irwindale, this "hub" settlement suffered from overcrowding and unsanitary conditions due to civic neglect, but also boasted Protestant and Catholic churches, sewing classes, mutual aid societies, and transportation networks to work sites that attracted many Mexicans from outlying areas. These and other nearby "hub" *colonias* provided necessary services to Mexicans living in dispersed "satellite" communities and allowed many to partake in an extended regional identity.

The following description of the Claremont *colonias* of Arbol Verde and La Colonia provides a detailed example of the pattern of Mexican community formation on a local level. In 1932, Helen O'Brien, a senior at Pomona College, conducted a study of the Mexican colony of Arbol Verde just east of the campus. Her thesis, entitled "The Mexican Colony: A Study of Cultural Change," reveals the degree to which citrus farm owners followed the recommendations for housing Mexican employees during the 1920s, and illustrates the independence and network-building of Mexicans living in two areas separated by geography, discrimination, and the social control of employers. Tinged with ethnocentricism, O'Brien's thesis nevertheless presents a useful vision of the "Colonia Complex," as named by McWilliams. Oral histories that I conducted with many of the residents of the Claremont *colonias* have helped me to sift through the biases of O'Brien's report.[80]

O'Brien observed that "the Mexican is economically (but not socially) a part of Claremont."[81] Living in the *colonia* known as "Arbol Verde" (Green Tree), Mexican residents found themselves spatially and culturally segregated from the center of Claremont community life. Mr. J. H. Brooks laid the groundwork for the colony in 1910 when he purchased and subdivided a tract straddling the Southern Pacific Railroad and Pacific Electric car tracks. Bisected by the Los Angeles and San Bernardino County line, the community was built directly in the path of a wash running out of the nearby San Bernardino Mountains. Hampered by rocky and barren soil and subject to occasional flooding, Brooks sold this undesirable land to Mexican immigrants who had arrived to replace Sikh and Japanese workers driven out of Claremont by white vigilantes.[82]

Although the owners of Claremont's El Camino and College Heights citrus groves invested in a housing project on the west side of town (known to Mexican residents as "West Barrio" or "La Colonia"), these structures failed to accommodate the numerous Mexican workers who migrated to the area.[83] Due to the diverse economy that developed in the region, Mexican workers also found jobs outside the citrus industry, namely as groundskeepers and manual laborers for the Claremont Colleges (at that time, Pomona College, Scripps College, and the Claremont Graduate School) or at the homes of upper-middle-class residents and merchants. In spite of the attempts by citrus growers to concentrate Mexican families in segregated work camps, Mexican residents constructed their own communities like Arbol Verde. These communities outside the grower-owned housing projects developed into the spiritual and cultural centers of Mexican immigrant life. Workers living in the company housing on the west side formed communal bonds of their own; however, because the development of religious and entertainment centers as well as "Mexican" markets occurred on the east side of Claremont, Arbol Verde became identified by most Mexicanos living in the area as the heart of both communities.

West Barrio residents frequently traveled to "East Barrio" (as Arbol Verde was alternatively called) for shopping, church services, and social functions. Mexican residents from both *colonias* constructed their own Catholic church, Sacred Heart, where Mexican people conducted semi-independent religious practices. Although the Archdiocese of Los Angeles often sent a priest out to the church to conduct services, some Mexican residents distrusted diocese representatives due to their harsh treatment of children and their prejudicial attitudes toward Mexicans. For example, Father Ramos of Lorain, a Spanish priest who frequently visited Sacred Heart, wrote that "All Mexicans are children, some of them are good children, some are bad children, a few of them are intelligent children, most of them are dull children; but all Mexicans are children. Never forget that."[84] Most Mexican residents never forgot the priest's attitude and restricted the diocese's access to the church, except for the celebration of mass every two weeks. Local women maintained the altar and often led prayers and ceremonies in the absence of a priest. Over time, however, Mexican residents accepted church officials at Sacred Heart on a full-time basis.[85]

Mexican residents also created local businesses to serve the Mexican communities of East and West Barrio. A market and local cooperative store known as Cooperativa (or "The Co-op") in Arbol Verde provided unique spices, vegetables, and cuts of meat necessary for making Mexican dishes. At The Co-op, residents could purchase items in bulk such as flour and corn to help stretch their incomes, while the friendly service in Spanish from local shopkeeper Mario Serna was a welcome departure from the discriminatory treatment Mexicans encountered at white-owned markets and company stores. More important, the store forged a strong communal bond among Mexican families living in the two communities who contributed labor and money to sustain it. Later, in the 1940s, Serna, a longtime resident of Arbol Verde, transformed part of his home into El Chisme (the gossip) market.[86] Both The Co-op and El Chisme served the material needs of the Mexican residents. They also functioned as community information centers where news from outside the *colonia* would arrive first and then quickly spread throughout the village. For example, Eusebia "Cheva" García recalled the fateful afternoon while working at The Co-op when she received the news of her fiancé's work-related accident. Cheva explained, "The foreman called to say that Salvador had lost his arm, and I had to go tell his family because The Co-op was the only place in the *colonia* with a phone."[87] In addition to frequenting the markets, Mexican men drank liquor and socialized at the local pool hall converted from a rooming house formerly owned by the El Camino Citrus packinghouse. Known as the "salon," Mexican men went to the tiny bar to discuss Mexican politics, listen to the latest *chisme*, and even create a little of their own.

Mexican parents, upset by the educational segregation of their children, sought to counteract the effects of Americanization by creating their own school. Interested in preserving Mexican culture and the Spanish language, local citrus foreman Iñez Campos, college groundskeeper and Arbol Verde resident Daniel Martínez Sr., and Pomona College student Juan Matute constructed the *colonia* school, "Leona Viscario."[88] After returning home from their segregated schools in Upland, Claremont, and Ontario each day, Mexican youths attended classes in the community. Younger children went from five to six o'clock in the evening and practiced reading and writing the Spanish language. From six to seven, older children met to study Mexican history and folk songs, or to write compositions in Spanish.[89] Occasionally, the teachers and parents organized plays based on Mexican history and culture that they performed before adult residents of both *colonias*.

The independence and organization demonstrated by the residents of Arbol Verde and La Colonia helped repel white efforts to control and manipulate Mexican worker communities. Although citrus growers hoped to place all local Mexican workers within one work camp on the west side of town, the diversity of the local economy, the number of Mexican families, and the determination of Mexican people to construct their own social space contributed to the creation of Arbol Verde. Moreover, Mexican residents maintained relations with friends and relatives throughout Southern California, forming a network that helped many Mexican families survive. Cheva García, like many other young Mexican women, earned money by working in a cannery close to her extended family.[90] As a teenager in the 1930s and 1940s, Cheva traveled the Pacific Electric "Red" Car to San Pedro where she worked in the Van de Kamp's Cannery and joined the ranks of many Mexican women who participated in a "cannery culture." During the week she lived in the San Pedro barrio with her grandmother and returned to Claremont on the weekends to be with her immediate family. Cheva's experience illustrates the mobility of many Mexican people who lived in one area but used public transportation and the assistance of relatives to overcome hard times.

Mexican residents also maintained ties with nearby settlements, occasionally coming together in hub *colonias* like Arbol Verde to organize social gatherings such as *jamaicas* (outdoor parties) and *tardeadas* (afternoon dances), religious events such as the staging of the *Pastorelas* (a re-creation of Mary and Joseph's search for shelter on Christmas Eve), patriotic celebrations such as Mexican Independence Day, and sporting competitions such as baseball games and handball tournaments. Candelario Mendoza, a resident of Pomona, remembered that each *colonia*, regardless of size, maintained a baseball team that competed in a regional "Mexican league" fully funded and staged by Mexican residents. Mendoza remembered: "Claremont had the 'Juveniles,' La Verne had the 'Merchants,' and Chino had a team as well . . . I was on the local Pomona team." [91] Mary Sevilla, a resident of Arbol Verde *colonia* and a supporter of the "Juveniles," recalled that mothers of the players organized baking contests and other fundraising events to buy equipment, while many women supported the team by traveling to their "away" games in other *colonias*. According to Sevilla, these efforts evolved into a *"Club de Damas"* (Women's Club) that, during and after World War II, became an important social and self-help network for local women (see Chapter 7).[92]

Located on the town's margins and in a less hospitable environment, Arbol Verde developed into the Mexican cultural center of Claremont largely through the collective efforts of residents in both *colonias* and the support of other nearby "satellite" settlements. Their commitment to the construction of a church, school, market, and pool hall for the benefit of Mexican people reflected not just the effects of white segregation, but also the will of Mexican residents to create cultural and physical space for themselves in the citrus belt. Moreover, the activities of the Mexican school Leona Viscario demonstrated Mexican parents' interest in reinforcing Spanish language and pride in Mexican culture. For Mexican workers, communities such as Arbol Verde constituted important social spaces where cultural practices and lifestyles could be dictated by parents and community elders.

As cohesive and self-reliant as these *colonias* needed to be, it would be a mistake to characterize them as communities free of tension and intraethnic conflict. The same population pressures that caused Mexican settlements to spill out into unregulated "no-man's lands" where Arbol Verde, the Irwindale *colonia*, and Hicks Camp and Medina Court took root, also occasionally created overcrowding and conflict among Mexican settlers during periods of economic stress. Paul Taylor, for example, detected a "smoldering resentment" between recently arrived "Texas Mexicans" and the "old men" of Hicks Camp. One "old-timer" told Taylor, "Los Tejanos son diablos" (the Texans are devils). This sentiment was partly due to the fierce competition that went on between the two groups for jobs in the nearby walnut groves during the off-season. Since most Mexican immigrants at this time passed through the El Paso/Cuidad Juárez border-crossing and stopped for months, if not years, in Texas before moving into the interior, it is likely that the label "Texas Mexicans" referred to immigrant Mexicans. The conflict, therefore, indicated not only divisions caused by immigration pressures and competition for jobs, but also a growing sense of privilege among Mexican settlers already inhabiting *colonias*. Many early settler families of Hicks Camp, some with second- and third-generation family members by the late 1920s, began to exhibit what Paul Taylor identified as "marks of Americanization" by investing in "American" cultural practices and coveting primary access to jobs, a privilege many assumed came with the rights of citizenship.

In spite of these occasional ruptures in intraethnic relations among community residents, the Mexican *colonia* remained the first, best, and last hope for newly arrived Mexicans migrating to the Southland. For example, Ben Quiros, a longtime resident of Hicks Camp, aided Mexican immigrants in need of housing by leasing part of his three and a half acres of property to new arrivals. Over time, this real estate enterprise became the primary source of income for this Mexican dairy worker and contributed to the expansion of the *colonia*, to the chagrin of local white residents. Although constrained somewhat by restrictive covenants and the complicity of white realtors who swore never "to put a Mexican family next to a Caucasian," Mexicans' willingness to settle in the margins of citrus belt towns brought the *colonia* to the doorstep of some white working-class neighborhoods by the mid-1920s. This condition upset white resident Mrs. Elmer Carfe, who, by 1927, now lived a block away from Hicks Camp. Carfe told Taylor in disgust, "I just hate to see those Mexicans pass my house." Similarly, "real estate men" in El Monte worried aloud about the expansion of the *colonia*, telling Taylor, "We don't want this to be considered as a Mexican town."[93]

For white citrus growers and residents, these independent *colonias* symbolized the failure to corral all Mexican workers into segregated camps and precipitated more drastic measures. Although the Jim Crow treatment of Mexicans varied from town to town, these communities expressed a Southern California brand of conservatism that combined Protestant righteousness with "American exceptionalism." According to one local historian, "the church had become as strong a symbol as the orange."[94] During the 1920s, Catholic Italians and Mexicans made up the majority of new immigrants to the Golden State. Responding to perceived threats to a Protestant society, two organizations gained a stronghold in Southern California: the Woman's Christian Temperance Union (WCTU) and the Ku Klux Klan (KKK). While the WCTU directed most of its activities at temperance law violators, Klansmen and Klanswomen acted in accordance with their support of prohibition *and* their racial antipathies toward Mexican people.[95]

A frustrated temperance movement in Southern California, particularly in Los Angeles County, contributed to the rise of the Ku Klux Klan in the San Gabriel Valley. Many white residents perceived the "fiery cross" as mightier than the "hatchet" and supported one of the largest KKK orders west of the Mississippi River.[96] Citrus belt Klaverns often held high profile, public ceremonies (called Klonklaves) and parades in which klanspeople burned crosses and prominently displayed placards reading "White Supremacy." At a Klonklave in Ontario on September 8, 1924, the KKK initiated 150 new candidates to the local order. According to newspaper reports, "Mounted klansmen, and several platoons of robed men and women" funneled into Chaffey High School stadium where a "huge fiery cross . . . visible from Upland to Ontario's business district" blazed until the midnight hour.[97]

A roster of the Pomona Valley Klan, containing each Klansman's name, occupation, and address, provides a glimpse into the profile of the typical Klan member in the citrus belt during the 1920s. Among the many jobs that appear, ranchers constituted approximately one-fourth of those listed, by far the most entries of any occupation on the list of 382 names. Law enforcement officials also frequently appeared on the list, including Pomona's police captain and La Verne's city marshall and deputy marshall.[98] The substantial representation of ranchers and law enforcement officials indicated where much of the power resided in the local Klan.

"New" Klan scholars have argued that the KKK of the 1920s did not bother ethnoracial minorities and concentrated most of their attention on enforcing temperance laws.[99] The goals of sobriety and social control of Mexican residents, however, were not mutually exclusive. Mexican distillers in the segregated *colonias* ran cantinas like "the salon" in Arbol Verde where Mexican men and an occasional white patron purchased home-brewed alcohol and hard liquor.[100] In the Mexican *colonia* in La Verne, for example, resident Nick Fuentes remembered drinking *pulque*, syrupy Mexican liquor made from the maguey plant, at the local pool hall.[101] Separated from the white community, Mexican business owners could violate temperance laws with relative impunity, but this provoked acts of vigilantism by the local KKK order.

According to one Mexican American eyewitness, the Klan in Ontario used intimidation to enforce residential segregation. Local resident Victor Murillo Ruiz remembered that in 1929 his father inquired about buying a house located outside the traditional Mexican *colonia*. When a white neighbor heard of his plans, he threatened Ruiz's brother: "If you're thinking of buying that house, you tell your dad he may buy it, but that house is going to be burned down the next day." Later, Ruiz recalled, the Klan terrorized his family: "I looked through the windows and I saw three cars with people with white hoods in them. . . . I can remember three men standing on the running board [holding on to] the car. . . . The people on the outside had torches. . . . I would look at them and hide; I thought they were ghosts. My mother . . . pulled me away from the window. She said, 'Don't do that. Those people don't like for you to look at them.'"[102] Ultimately, the Ruiz family chose not to purchase the house.

Typically, citrus belt Klan orders of the 1920s committed few if any acts of physical violence. Instead, most Klaverns relied on intimidation through impressive public parades and drive-by threats like the one experienced by the Ruiz family. Public KKK rituals and night-riding had a tremendous psychological impact on participants, viewers, and victims. For whites, Klan rallies affirmed a general belief in WASP exceptionalism, while for those who fell outside the fold of Klan beliefs, namely Mexicans, Jews, and Catholics, parades and psychological terror warned against challenging the social order. Moreover, Klan orders of the 1920s exhibited a high degree of anti-union rhetoric that appealed to local citrus ranchers and attracted them to the organization in greater numbers than any other occupation in the citrus belt. The popularity of the Klan represented the most extreme example of Euroamerican conservatism in Southern California.

Throughout the 1920s Mexicans continued to settle semiautonomous *colonias* on the margins of Southern California suburbs. These communities functioned as beachheads for Mexican immigration, providing a foundation for more families escaping the ravages of the Mexican Revolution. The imposition of an $8/head tax in 1917 and a $10 visa fee in 1924 forced many Mexican immigrants to forego formal border crossings and choose undocumented passage to the United States.[103] In spite of prohibitive charges at the border and a brief depression in 1921 and 1922, Mexicans came to the United States in search of economic stability and steady employment.

Citrus ranchers, nongrower community members, state and local government agencies, and Mexican residents engaged in a constant battle to shape what Carey McWilliams described as "the Colonia Complex": life and culture among the 150,000 to 200,000 Mexicans and Mexican Americans who made the citrus belt their home.[104] White communities formerly concerned about controlling a polyglot, multiracial pool of laborers, now worried that the decision to "Mexicanize" the workforce threatened their vision of Southern California based on Euroamerican transplants from the Midwest and East. Although ranchers still dominated local politics, by the 1920s the citrus belt had become the site of a diverse economy with a variety of interests that included churches, colleges, and community organizations. White residents not directly involved in citrus farming complemented *and* complicated efforts to control workers with their own ideas and efforts for how to deal with the Mexican presence. Frequently, these "good-doers" (as many Mexican residents called them) formed philanthropy and charity groups that espoused a strong interest in Americanizing Mexican immigrants and improving the standards of living in the *colonias*. However, increased national attention to the "Mexican problem" toward the end of the decade fractured white interests. As the 1920s drew to a close, Mexican immigrants found it more difficult to identify friends and foes among Euroamerican residents. In the following chapter, I examine the cleavages within the citrus belt, and expand McWilliams's binary worker/management interpretation to include community groups and government agencies that questioned the treatment of Mexican agricultural workers in Southern California.

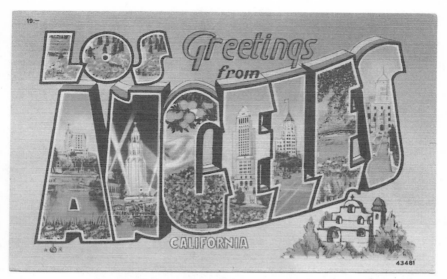

A typical postcard of Los Angeles, 1952. Gardens and citrus orchards are prominently represented among images of urbanity. The Spanish mission, a symbol of an eclipsed era, stands outside modern Los Angeles. (Personal collection of the author)

Citrus pickers in San Dimas, ca. 1930. (Courtesy of Pomona Public Library)

Citrus pickers in La Verne, ca. 1920. (Courtesy of Pomona Public Library)

Citrus pickers in La Verne, date unknown. (Courtesy of La Verne City Hall)

Mexican baseball team, La Verne, date unknown. (Courtesy of La Verne City Hall)

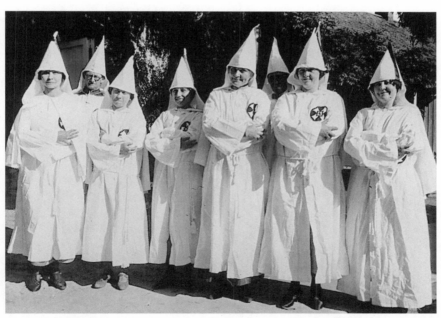

Ku Klux Klan members in Pomona, ca. 1922. (Courtesy of Pomona Public Library)

Ku Klux Klan Konklave in Pomona, ca. 1922. (Courtesy of Pomona Public Library, Frasher Collection)

An Americanization class at the Club House of La Habra Mexican *colonia*, 1921. (Courtesy of *California Citrograph*)

Escuela Mexicana ("Leona Viscario"), Pomona College Gymnasium Hall, Claremont, September 16, 1928. The author's grandmother, Cheva García, is the second child on the left, first row. Iñez Campos, local foreman and cofounder of the school, sits in the center (second row). (Courtesy of Claremont Heritage)

Escuela Mexicana ("Leona Viscario") Parade, Arbol Verde *colonia*, Claremont, 1928. The author's grandmother, Cheva García, is the first girl in row one. (Courtesy of Cheva García)

Sacred Heart Church, Arbol
Verde *colonia*, Claremont,
as published in the Pomona
College yearbook, *Metate*,
1947. (Courtesy of Honnold
Library)

An informal photo of Bess Garner and the Mexican Players taken in the fall of 1936.
(Courtesy of Pomona Public Library)

Padua Hills Theatre, Claremont, 1930s. (Courtesy of Pomona Public Library)

Paduana Manuela Huerta, dressed in the *huipil grande*, the traditional clothing of the Tehuantepec region of Mexico. (Courtesy of Pomona Public Library)

Paduanos Casilda Amador, Alfonso Gallardo, and Sara Macias strike a dramatic pose during the spring of 1935. (Courtesy of Pomona Public Library)

Paduana Rebecca (Camilla) Romo (Wolfe), center left, entertains guests at a postproduction *jamaica*, ca. 1936. Paduano Salvador Sánchez plays the guitar, while owner Herman Garner looks on from behind the trees. Paduanos Miguel Vera and Casilda Amador stand off to the right. (Courtesy of Pomona Public Library)

The dining room at the Padua Hills Theatre complex, ca. 1936. (Courtesy of Pomona Public Library)

When public-spirited citizens in the parent community have sought "to do something about the Mexican Problem," they have generally sought to impose a pattern on the colonia *from without. Establishing a clinic or reading-room or social center in the* colonia *has no doubt been helpful; but it has not changed, in the slightest degree, the relationship between parent and satellite community. In the face of this reality, it is indeed annoying to hear Anglo-Americans expatiate about the Mexicans' "inferiority complex" and to charge them with being clannish and withdrawn.*
—CAREY McWILLIAMS, *North from Mexico*

Friends of the Mexicans?
Mexican Immigration and the Politics of Social Reform

During the 1928 congressional hearings on the Box Bill, a proposal to extend immigration quotas to Mexico, the most vocal and powerful opponent of Mexican immigration East Texas congressman John C. Box remarked: "The character of the body of our citizenship will be lowered by scattering tens or hundreds of thousands more of these people [Mexicans] through some twenty or thirty states." Box chastised "sentimental" relief and charitable workers for taking too much pity on these immigrants. He complained: "Of whatever nationality or citizenship of the class of these people is composed, there are and have always been in every country those who would handle them in masses for purposes detrimental to the public good."[1] According to Box and the growing ranks of nativists like him, Congress, not charity houses or farm owners, should control this "social problem" and "not permit another race and color problem to erect its head by the slow processes of infiltration and differential fecundity."[2]

The influx of thousands of Mexican refugees as a result of the Mexican Revolution exposed western agriculture's dependence on Mexican labor. Eugenicists and journalists joined a growing chorus of critics who questioned why the Immigration Acts of 1917 and 1921 and the Johnson Act of 1924 placed quotas on immigration from southern and eastern Europe, the Far East, Africa, and the Middle East, but did nothing about the "hordes" of "Mexican Indians" that contributed to a "mixed-race problem" throughout the Southwest and the industrial belt of the Midwest. Labeled alternately as a "social problem," "biological problem," and "race problem," increased Mexican immigration during the 1920s drew the ire of nativists throughout the country and led to an endless string of congressional hearings.

Citrus growers fought the battle for unrestricted Mexican immigration on three fronts: at the national, state, and local levels. At the national level, citrus industry spokespeople found themselves conforming to an established agribusiness position that frequently deviated from the particular conditions present within the groves, yet advocated a policy—the retention of low-paid Mexican laborers—upon which all farm owners could agree. At the state level, citrus growers neutralized their greatest potential critic, the CCIH, by investing in housing projects for employees. As the debates intensified toward the end of the decade, the CCIH focused much of their attention on resolving the unsanitary labor camp conditions in the Central and Imperial Valleys and pointed to citrus worker camps as a model for agribusiness.[3]

At the local level, citrus growers faced opposition from a growing number of nongrower residents with alternative economic and social investments. These residents maintained little or no commitment to the employment of low-skilled Mexican workers and questioned the presence of a large nonwhite minority population in their midst. In spite of proclamations about the temporary and transient nature of Mexican workers made by agribusiness leaders, citrus belt residents knew that, in the case of Mexican citrus workers, Mexican immigrants established permanent homes and communities that required constant attention. As the size of *colonias* grew with the success of citrus and the development of a diverse economy, the interests of growers came into conflict with their goal of creating racially homogeneous communities. Growers argued that segregation quarantined the "social problem," but Mexican residents chose to live in spaces and in ways not prescribed by their employers. Some concerned white residents formed charities and educational organizations to improve the conditions of life within the *colonias*, while others preferred to eliminate "the problem" altogether and endorsed restrictive immigration legislation and the deportation of Mexican families.

In this chapter, I examine the myriad competing interests in the citrus belt concerning the "Mexican question." Just as the decision to "Mexicanize" the labor force and construct living quarters for Mexican families developed according to racialist understandings of the "Mexican character," during the late 1920s and early 1930s advocates for unrestricted Mexican immigration used the argument that Mexicans constituted a "docile" and "unambitious" race that posed little threat to the established order. Meanwhile, philanthropists and social workers, McWilliams's so-called "in-between element," conducted studies of conditions within the *colonias* and hosted regional conferences in order to reach an informed judgement. Many Progressive-Era women took the lead in these reform movements, imbued with what historian Peggy Pascoe has called "Victorian female moral authority." Embracing Americanization of immigrant mothers and children as "women's work," white middle-class women reformers saw themselves as uniquely qualified educators in a campaign to assimilate immigrants. Although they tended to be more sympathetic, their reliance on similar sources of information, their ethnocentric interpretations of "the problem," and sensitivity to economic failure ultimately led them to similar political conclusions as restrictionists.[4]

For Mexican residents, the close scrutiny of their lives forced many to be strategic in their opposition to racial discrimination, poor living conditions, and labor exploitation. Citrus growers, government officials, and industry leaders quickly mobilized against labor activism and effectively crushed strikes in the San Gabriel–San Bernardino Valley. However, as we will see in this and the following chapter, Mexican workers struck against weak links in the grower front, while some Mexican residents parlayed nongrower sympathy into critiques of white prejudice.

The Restriction Debate

In *Strangers in the Land: Patterns of American Nativism, 1860–1925*, immigration historian John Higham writes that "the immigration restriction laws of the early twenties . . . brought to culmination a legislative trend extending back to the 1880s." The Immigration Act of 1921 and the National Origins Act of 1924 imposed strict literacy requirements and established a stringent national-origins quota system that reduced the flow of immigrants from southern and eastern Europe and the Far East. According to Higham, such legislative restrictions pushed the limits of America's tolerance for "official coercion." "Further attempts to impose internal conformity," he argued, "would rest more completely in private hands."[5]

The absence of further restrictive immigration legislation after 1924 was not for a lack of trying on the part of nativists. Many Americans saw this legislation as incomplete since the restrictions did not apply to Mexican immigrants. One outspoken congressman, Albert H. Vestal of Indiana, questioned, "What is the use of closing the front door to keep out undesirables from Europe when you permit Mexicans to come in here by the back door by the thousands and thousands?"[6] Chair of the House Committee on Immigration and Naturalization, Albert Johnson, expressed similar frustration stating, "two years ago California came before this committee and stated herself in opposition to Chinese and Japanese exclusion; stated that they wanted to develop a great big white state in California, a white man's country; and now you come before us and want unlimited Mexican immigration." Johnson chastised employers of Mexicans, "What you want is a class of labor that will be sufficiently low type that they will not have the ambition or make any effort to become owners of any of your land." Challenging agribusiness's dependence on any nonwhite labor, Johnson concluded, "I cannot see the difference between Mexicans and Japanese and Chinese, except that the Japanese and Chinese are infinitely better."[7] In response to these criticisms, Texas congressman John C. Box pursued amendments in subsequent sessions of Congress to close loopholes in immigration legislation that resulted in the unrestricted flow of Mexican immigrants. Although Box and his allies ultimately failed in their attempts, congressional hearings led to a tightening of the U.S.-Mexican border and the intensification of the immigration debate during the interwar period.

Critics of U.S. immigration policy cited "biological" and "social" problems as their primary complaints against Mexicans. In 1928, *Saturday Evening Post* reporter Kenneth Roberts published a three-part series on Mexican immigration, outlining the various positions surrounding the debate. Among the "social problems," Roberts cited high rates of Mexican indigence and dependence on public services as one of the primary "social" costs of Mexican immigration. "Los Angeles, because of the liberality with which charity is dispensed there," he argued, "has become the goal of nearly all Mexicans in the United States who are able to indulge their fancies." Rather than addressing inadequate social services, school officials and health "experts" blamed the victims by complaining to Roberts that Mexicans lived in "squalid" communities that constituted blight on otherwise orderly and beautiful Los Angeles County neigh-borhoods. One informant of questionable credentials, University of California zoologist Samuel J. Holmes, made the criticism: "from the physical point of view, the Mexican is not exactly a public-health asset." "It is a tremendously serious thing," Holmes cautioned, "when we have people coming in our midst who know nothing about hygienic precautions and sanitation, the tendency for all diseases which are endemic among them to spread in our [white] popula-tion is very great." [8] As historian Neil Foley demonstrates in his book *The White Scourge*, such references to uncleanliness also functioned as "a euphemism for 'white' as well as an allusion to the eugenic maintenance of white 'racial hy-giene.'" Given Mexicans' perceived ethnoracial middle ground between Anglo Americans and African Americans, whites frequently separated light-skinned Mexicans from the mostly nonwhite ones with racial metaphors like "clean," "dirty," and "greaser." In addition, California officials often applied the term "Hispanic" or "Spanish" to the former as a way of distinguishing the racially pure from the contaminated. [9]

Indeed, restrictionists articulated these racial concerns through the fear of a "biological problem." Eugenicist Harry H. Laughlin, an official with the Car-negie Institution of Washington, spelled out the problem in his 1928 testimony before the House Committee on Immigration and Naturalization. Citing other "historical mistakes" such as "the introduction of negro slaves" and "oriental migration," Laughlin argued that the immigration of Mexican "colored races . . . principally Indian and Spanish, with occasionally a little mixture of black blood" represented the "sixth major racial problem in American history." He endorsed restrictive immigration legislation in the interest of "recruit[ing] our future human stock from immigrants of assimilable races, who will also improve our existing hereditary family stock qualities." [10] Another eugenicist, Princeton biologist Edwin Grant Conklin, criticized employers for feeding the American "melting pot" with "cheap labor," and asked the provocative question, "Do we want to bring about the mongrelization of America?" "The Mexicans," he cau-tioned, "are a race almost as distinct as the negro, especially the Indians, who form a very large component of that race."

Eugenicists' testimony reinforced racist attitudes toward Mexican immi-grants prevalent within American society. George Horace Lorimer, editor of the *Saturday Evening Post*, contemplated the end of white racial homogeneity on the West Coast when he editorialized: "It will prove a real catastrophe if a state with the remarkable natural resources and advantages of California allows an insoluble alien problem to become fastened upon it." [11] Bob Shuler, Los Ange-les Methodist minister and the spiritual leader of the local Ku Klux Klan, characterized Mexicans as "diseased of body, subnormal intellectually, and moral morons of the most hopeless type." "It is true," Shuler added, "that our civilization has swallowed and digested a good many nasty doses, but the gagging point has been about reached."[12]

Mainstream labor leaders mixed racism with job protectionist rhetoric, blaming Mexicans for the existence of a dual labor system in which Mexican immigrants' willingness to accept work for less pay suppressed wages and ultimately subverted labor organizing among American workers. They supported Mexican exclusion to protect wages and union solidarity, and to prevent Mexican workers from competing for positions they saw as white jobs. In testimony before Congress, American Federation of Labor representative William C. Hushings argued, "Americans can not compete with the Mexican standard of living or his wage rate, and so the American laborer is replaced by the Mexican just as the sheep ran the cattle from the grazing lands years ago." According to Hushings, Mexican "peons" descended from an inferior Indian "stock" whose "names and language are those of their conquerors, but their racial characteristics are unchanged." "Since the Spanish conquest," he added, "their lives have been a frenzied quest for frijoles and tortillas."[13] *Saturday Evening Post* writer Kenneth L. Roberts attributed Mexicans' desperate situation to a system of slavery in Mexico that produced "the most docile and gullible of all the immigrant arrivals that the United States has ever seen." Shaped by their "birthrights of laziness and dependence . . . inherited from [their] ancestors," Roberts concluded, "a new crop of ignorant, docile and sap-headed Mexicans come across the border each year" to accept "the lowest known prices" for their labor.[14]

Western agribusiness formed a potent and powerful lobby that supported the employment of Mexican farmworkers and almost single-handedly fought back restrictionists' calls for immigration quotas. Representatives took special aim at the charges that Mexicans constituted "cheap labor," whose employment displaced white workers willing and able to do similar jobs. Appearing before the Committee on Immigration and Naturalization in 1926, chairman of the Fresno County Chamber of Commerce and Central Valley viticulturist and cotton grower S. Parker Frisselle asserted, "We would prefer white agricultural labor." "But after a complete survey of all possibilities," reported Frisselle, "it seems that we have no choice . . . the Mexican seems to be our only available supply." Rather than challenge negative stereotypes of Mexicans, he agreed that the Mexican immigrant represented a "social problem," but argued, "he is a homer. . . . Like a pigeon he goes back to roost." Frisselle attempted to allay the committee's fears by assuring its members that,

We in California think we can handle that social problem. It is a serious
one. It comes into our schools, it comes into our cities, and it comes into our
whole civilization in California. We, gentlemen, are just as anxious as you
are not to build the civilization of California or any other western district
on a Mexican foundation. We take him because there is nothing else avail-
able . . . but . . . California believes that it can meet and handle the social
problem and develop agriculture at the same time.[15]

In spite of citrus farmers' need for year-round, permanent employees, citrus
industry spokespeople stood behind these statements and communicated the
agribusiness position to the public. Charles C. Teague, owner of the Limoneira Ranch in Ventura County, California, and president of the California
Fruit Growers Exchange, answered the serious charges waged by restrictionists.
Teague flatly rejected these "arguments of a sociological nature"; namely "that
they [Mexicans] are cheap labor," "that their presence in large numbers constitutes a menace to the Anglo-Saxon strain and dominance," and "that they
are of a lazy, thriftless class calculated to become a public charge." On the
contrary, he argued, "the great industries of the Southwest—agricultural, horticultural, viticultural, mining, stock raising, and so on—are to a very extent
dependent upon the Mexican labor which this law [the Box Bill] would bar
out." Teague toed the agribusiness line in arguing that many Mexicans engaged
only in temporary work and went back to Mexico after the harvest. "There is
little evidence," remarked Teague, "of a Mexican disposition to acquire land
and make permanent settlement." [16]

Agribusiness commonly made the claim that Mexicans constituted "birds
of passage" who migrated back-and-forth between Mexico and California, appearing and disappearing according to the rhythms of the harvest. Yet, as citrus
farmers and residents of the citrus belt understood, not all agricultural work
was seasonal. Consequently, comments from spokespeople representing citrus
districts drew attention to inconsistencies in the agribusiness position. For example, in the 1926 congressional hearings, Southern California citrus rancher
and LACC representative Charles P. Bayer testified that the "social problem"
had never become "serious"; however, in making his point, he revealed contradictions in the agribusiness argument. Bayer upheld the grower contention
that "[whites] will not do the work such as is required of Mexicans who do
this seasonal labor," but added, "I happen to be a citrus grower myself and we
use considerable Mexican labor, but that labor is used all the year round in
that particular industry." [17] Restrictionists also drew on testimony and letters
from residents and surveyors who suggested that many Mexican immigrants

were permanent rather than temporary workers. Complaining, "the Mexican is not a mere transient farm laborer," a group of white working-class Angelenos wrote to Box, "he [the Mexican worker] comes and stays and stays and stays."[18] Researchers sympathetic to the plight of Mexican workers corroborated such accounts. For example, Berkeley economist Paul Taylor made a similar observation during his visit to Orange County, California, in 1928 when he commented "few laborers come in from the outside," "the laborers are not highly migratory," and "a large percentage [of workers] maintain permanent homes in the county."[19] Even outside of the citrus belt, the claim that Mexican workers always traveled back to Mexico at the end of their seasonal jobs was without merit. In her study of Mexican agricultural workers in California, historian Camille Guerin-Gonzales found that "while most Mexican immigrants did return to their homeland at one time or another, forty to sixty percent settled in the United States permanently."[20]

Residents and surveyors of the citrus belt understood the fallacy of the agribusiness argument, given citrus growers' investment in employee housing and the growth of Mexican *colonias* on the margins of many Southern California suburbs. Carey McWilliams noted the frequency with which investigators like himself encountered Mexican settlements (he called "jim-towns" in reference to the Jim Crow–like conditions) when he wrote: "From Santa Barbara to San Diego, one can find these jim-towns, with their clusters of bizarre shacks, usually located in an out-of-the-way place on the outskirts of an established citrus-belt town."[21] The permanent status of these communities, however, did not negate the possibility of Mexican workers migrating for seasonal work. Eusebia Vásquez de Buriel, a resident of the Mexican *colonia* "Casa Blanca" in Riverside, California, remembered that many families supplemented their incomes by harvesting cotton, vegetables, and grapes in the San Joaquin or Coachella Valleys during a short "off-season" in citrus production spanning approximately four months during the late summer and early fall. *Colonia* residents, however, saw Riverside as their home and community, and invested time and money to establish a neighborhood church, Our Lady of Guadalupe Shrine. Vásquez de Buriel explained to historian Vicki Ruiz: "We worked real hard to have our church . . . the people were all poor, worse than we are now, but everything came up real nice, so we are very proud of . . . that church."[22]

In the navel-growing district of Claremont, labor in the El Camino and College Heights citrus groves began in December, reached its peak in May, and ended in October. During the 1920s, this eight-month schedule provided Arbol Verde and La Colonia residents with stable employment and sufficient income to invest in property. "The labor turnover among the Mexicans here is practically negligible," boasted the Claremont Citrus Association to Helen O'Brien in 1932, "for many of the pickers have been with us every season for the last ten years." Crews working for El Camino earned 35 cents per hour, while College Heights paid their pickers "by the piece." Under both systems, male employees earned an average of $3 per nine-hour day. Prior to the depression, some second-generation Mexican women tested the will of their parents by boxing fruit for 35 cents an hour in the College Heights packinghouse. The manager explained to O'Brien: "we were employing the Mexican girls in packing, for they proved to be very efficient; but many of the parents objected." "Now," he lamented, "there are only a few being employed."[23] Not until the late 1930s and 1940s did Mexican women dominate labor in the packinghouse. During the depression, some of these families used the four month hiatus from citrus work to join the migrant labor circuit that toured the Central Valley. Most Mexican families, however, maintained their homes in the citrus belt, leaving someone behind or depending on local kin and neighbors to watch over their property while they were away.

Mexican families took special pride in their homes, and invested what little money they earned into adequate living conditions. Reviewing the physical aspects of the Arbol Verde colony, Helen O'Brien noted: "Some of these houses reflect the artistic qualities of the Mexican and his ability to utilize existing material for ornamentation, for they are neatly trimmed with stone. Other houses, of the less energetic and poorer families, are made of scrap lumber, packing boxes, and adobe. But all of the houses, whether of the rich or poor, are brightened by the gay flowers so dear to the heart of the Mexican woman."[24]

O'Brien's opinions reflect common stereotypes about Mexicans; however, they also confirm the care and effort Mexican residents put into establishing their communities. A 1925 study of Arbol Verde, conducted by a local Americanization organization, found that of the 145 people living in twenty-one houses, most leased their land and had plans to return to Mexico. By 1932, however, local philanthropic and Americanization agents were surprised to find that the "little town" had "grown rapidly" in just seven years, more than doubling the number of residents to 300, and nearly tripling the number of homes to 60. "The Mexicans . . . did a good deal of subdividing themselves," a newspaper reported, "[selling] pieces of their lots to relatives and friends, and as a result the town resembles the dream of a jig-saw puzzle addict."[25]

The Armendarez family, one of the latecomers to the community, exemplified the kind of commitment many Mexican families had to home ownership. Arriving in 1941 from San Pedro, California, Carmen and Pedro Armendarez followed Carmen's sister and brother-in-law, Guadalupe and Daniel Martínez, to Arbol Verde, seeking agricultural jobs and a larger home for their growing family of ten. Carmen's daughter, Carmen, remembered, "[Mama] needed to raise $40 for the down payment; she used every cent she had saved from the walnut crop to buy her dream house." Although "small and *very* modest," the home "thrilled" Carmen's mother because, as Carmen explained, "she finally had a place [where] her children [could run] about freely without the restrictions imposed by the landlords in their previous homes."[26] "While many of the Mexicans interviewed have been residents of Arbol Verde for over ten years," commented O'Brien, "some of them tell a labor history which reveals continual moving before coming to Claremont." The common experience of constant migration prior to settling in the citrus belt made many Mexican families thankful for owning property.

CCIH agent Leo Mott encouraged this trend toward settlement, happily reporting, "Mexicans, by making small down payments, have acquired homes or ground on which to build homes, [and] they have rarely, if ever, failed to complete full payments and be vested with ownership." Of the Mexican families surveyed by the CCIH in 1925, Mott found that "ninety three percent of these people expressed a desire to own their own homes." The CCIH endorsed home ownership "because the owning of property will be of the greatest value in the Americanization of the Mexicans." Mott rationalized the agency's position by arguing, "a man will be loyal to the government which guarantees his property rights."[27]

Women played a critical role in cultivating home and hearth, working tirelessly against poverty and the environment to carve out a space for their families. Women rose at five or five-thirty, well before their children and husbands, to make tortillas, prepare breakfast, and fix lunches for the long day ahead. After the meal, men and their adolescent children departed for work in the groves while women continued with domestic chores. During the day, Helen O'Brien observed, "Arbol Verde is a woman's village." Women worked hard to maintain their community and homes by washing clothes, sweeping the altar of the Sacred Heart church, cooking meals, cleaning house, tending to their gardens, and rearing children. Civic neglect made sanitation a constant problem for many families and forced women to carry water in from an outside source to use in the community's few outdoor showers, bathtubs, and cleaning facilities. The barren and rocky soil, dry winds, and dust raised by the nearby rock crusher complicated work for many Mexican women. "Here it is too hot, too dry, too dirty!" complained one woman. "How can we keep our children clean? Where is the arroyo where we can wash and visit with our friends?"[28]

CCIH officials also expressed concern about the material conditions in Southern California *colonias*, but tended to blame Mexican people rather than poverty-level wages, segregation, and civic neglect. The increase in Mexican immigration to California during the 1920s concerned inspectors who encountered a growing number of unsanitary and substandard homes. In 1925, Leo Mott reported that Mexicans "number approximately 135,000 in our southern counties and of late there has been an unprecedented influx of them into our border states."[29] Although encouraged by the trend towards home ownership, CCIH inspectors found that the number of immigrants from Mexico began to saturate the low-skilled job market causing overcrowding in local *colonias*.

Surveying the Mexican citrus community of Casa Blanca on the east side of Riverside in 1924, Leo Mott discovered "deplorable" conditions that called for immediate reforms. Of the 181 houses inspected, Mott rated 141 "very bad," 38 "fair," and only 2 "good." He also declared 99 habitations "overcrowded," finding an average of 5.12 persons per house, or 3.24 per sleeping room. These conditions combined with poor ventilation and sanitation to create high levels of reportable diseases in the *colonia*, including measles, tuberculosis, and pneumonia. The situation so alarmed Mott that he called in his superior, executive director of the Immigration and Housing Division, R. W. Kearney, to make an appeal to "public-spirited" citizens to clean up the section. Kearney warned residents that if they did not follow the lead of other citrus towns that had recently built comfortable homes for Mexican employees, the city would receive the "skum [*sic*]" of the Mexican population in the state. Moreover, he cautioned, "these 'sore spots' are the breeding places of disease which is likely to spread beyond the Mexican population and infest the other sections of the city." "We must admit," Kearney concluded, "[the Mexicans] are here to stay, but whether we are to let them live here in unhealthy conditions and ruin the appearances of our cities depends on the people of this state."[30]

Mott and Kearney eventually persuaded Riverside officials to embark on an extensive cleanup of Casa Blanca, but the problems of poor sanitation and housing throughout Southern California continued to overwhelm the understaffed and over-worked CCIH and relief organizations. Reports from local charities increasingly complained about the volume of Mexican families seeking assistance and the severity of their conditions. A 1925 report to the CCIH observed that "the housing problem is a serious one wherever Mexican labor is employed." Although the report acknowledged improvements in home conditions and disease control as a result of efforts by DIR agents, county health officials, and charities, it also remarked that "[a]ll of this . . . demands enormous outlays of both public and private funds." For example, the Los Angeles County Outdoor Relief Division reported that Mexicans constituted 27.44

percent of their cases, while the Los Angeles Bureau of Charities claimed that Mexican families consumed at least half of their budget. One fatigued relief worker tried to place the situation in perspective: "Our problem is becoming so great with the Mexican family, who will never become good and efficient citizens, that it is impossible to work out a constructive program for the Mexican family who might become an asset to the community." "Due to the unemployment situation," the worker opined, "approximately 50 percent more time and money has been spent this year than last." These first-hand accounts led the unnamed author of the report to conclude: "The Mexican is not assimilable in the vast majority of cases, socially or politically. He is assimilable industrially for certain work if he does not enter in too great numbers."[31]

This growing sense of futility and frustration influenced the thinking of the CCIH leadership. The perceived limits to Mexican assimilation and the dramatic influx of Mexican immigrants led CCIH president, Catholic archbishop Edward J. Hanna of San Francisco, to alter the bureau's position regarding immigration from Mexico. Whereas previously the agency had unquestioningly pursued a policy of home improvement and Americanization for the promotion of immigrant assimilation, in 1926 Hanna expressed doubts in the CCIH's ability to achieve these goals. "Mexicans are doing our work and doing it well," the archbishop commented, "but there are thousands and thousands of them here illegally, against our laws, and over whom we have no control. . . . Any American having the future welfare of his country at heart, must agree that we could admit too many immigrants and that we could admit men lacking in mental and physical qualities that fathers of our citizens of the future should possess." Pursuant to this vision, Hanna urged Congress to "restrict Mexican immigration" and exclude those Mexicans that "create a labor camp problem and are of low mentality." In addition, he requested the support of the federal government to assist the CCIH in cleaning up labor camps and providing workers "conditions such that his children can grow into the fullness of American manhood." "Keep in mind," Hanna concluded, "that we need men but that we must not admit them in numbers that would make them a burden, and that the immigrant must have the qualities that transmitted to his children will give security to our civilization."[32]

In calling for restrictions to Mexican immigration, Hanna attempted to walk a middle ground between growers who preferred no regulation of the border and the public that increasingly favored an end to the flows of Mexican refugees. Hanna and CCIH agents took the position that enough Mexicans had entered the country to service adequately the needs of California agribusiness.

If allowed to do their jobs, CCIH agents could encourage home ownership and assimilation among these hardworking immigrants, and develop a settled and self-perpetuating pool of low-skilled laborers. Overcrowding in *colonias* was disrupting this plan, causing overflows into unregulated and unincorporated sections of Southern California counties, fomenting discontent among workers, and creating burdens for local relief agencies. Moreover, in criticizing the employment practices of growers, Hanna tempered his remarks by placing the blame for these conditions on Mexicans "of low mentality." Although they respected the hardworking ethos of most Mexicans, Hanna and his agents regarded Mexican immigrants as capable of limited assimilation, who, in "too great numbers," posed a threat to "our civilization."

Hanna's comments and new policy pleased no one, least of all Mexican residents in the United States. Interpreting the thinly veiled racism of his statements, Mexicans from all over the Southwest wrote into the CCIH with their complaints. A letter signed "The Catholic Mexicans of San Antonio, Texas" excoriated the archbishop for his comments, stating "if a Prelate of the Church of Christ does injure in such a vile manner the believers and adherents of Catholicism, we are not only surprised, but we consider this a scandal and we think that such action can only be instigated by a heart of stone and of egoism, considering that the Holy Church promulgates, in a most generous manner, sweet love to all human races." "You declare that in the prisons and the hospitals the percentage of Mexicans is preponderant," an anonymous writer from Houston wrote, "but you do not mention the large number of your own racial malefactors and felons." Comparing "a gringo" to the "infirm" and dirty race that Hanna believed Mexicans to be, the angry author recounted: "Do you think that your countrymen are any better? The other day, on the 7th of February a man of your race came to my house. He gorged himself with food and drink. He was one of your tramps. He was a gringo. But chili and frijoles were good enough for him. He ate like a dog."[33]

Another letter from a Mexican woman in Los Angeles angrily scolded Hanna, "it is almost incredible that a man like you, of a high grade of mentality, and holding such a distinguished post, should talk like an imbecile." The woman challenged Hanna's characterization of Mexicans as a burden on charity institutions, writing, "from our prosperous people, you derive more profits than the Mexican Government itself and from the poor crowd you squeeze out whatever you can in the churches." Hanna apparently complained that Mexicans required special attention in schools, to which the woman responded, "You call it 'low degree of mentality'—we call it 'no schools in faraway places.'" Unrepentant and unrelenting in her criticism of the archbishop, she concluded her letter with the declaration: "I am a Mexican woman [and] I give you what you deserve; forget me not."[34]

Mexicans' willingness to attack one of the few government agencies that advocated proper housing for Mexican laborers demonstrated the level of outrage and courage many of these immigrants possessed. However, part of the offense of Hanna's remarks revolved around his characterization of Mexicans as nonwhite, provoking some to voice their opposition in explicitly racialized terms. For example, the woman from Los Angeles chastised Hanna for not including Mexicans among the white race: "How about us being not of the white race? Will you call us yellow or black? You have here quite a number of black people. How about this most despised race of negro type? And still they are Americans. We are of the Indian origin. But we are of a stock which has not lost its superior qualifications, no matter whether in Indian or in Spanish blood."

Rather than challenging the myth of white superiority, some Mexicans chose to defend themselves by disparaging other minorities in racial terms. For example, the Catholic Mexicans of San Antonio began their letter of protest with the qualification, "We would not be surprised if, what you have stated, would refer to an Indian or to a Mussulman [sic], but your statements refer to Catholic Mexicans." Letters rarely revealed the true identities of the writers let alone their class status, but the quality of the writing suggested that most came from an educated, and therefore, lower-middle-class or middle-class background. As historians David Gutiérrez and Neil Foley have demonstrated, Mexicans not of the working classes often grasped for an illusive "white" status and maintained a tenuous "possessive investment in whiteness."[35] Consequently, middle-class Mexican Americans occasionally bought into Euroamerican-constructed racial hierarchies and perpetuated an elite Mexican racial prejudice toward Mexican Indians. Yet, as Helen O'Brien observed, working-class Mexicans of Arbol Verde took offense to the idea that Mexicans constituted primarily an Indian, and therefore, racially inferior group. One resident informed O'Brien, "we are Mexicans and that means Indian, not Spanish," while another young woman proudly asserted, "my mother can talk Indian!" These conflicting and somewhat contradictory statements about race notwithstanding, the efforts of Mexican residents to "define" Mexicans racially reflect the process of racialization that all Mexican and Mexican Americans, regardless of class status, confronted in the United States.

In the face of mounting restrictionist pressure, agribusiness stood firm in their support of open borders with Mexico and attempted to use racialized understandings of Mexican workers to their advantage. The Los Angeles Chamber of Commerce assumed a leadership role among employers of Mexican immigrants, gathering agribusiness and industry leaders to draft a formal response to the Box Bill and nativist legislation at the state level. In 1927, California agribusiness, under the auspices of the LACC, proclaimed their eternal vigilance against immigration quotas for Mexico, stating "the agricultural interests throughout the border and mountain states and the northwest group of states are a unit opposing this bill, realizing that it will interrupt and embarrass agricultural production throughout these states."[36] Moreover, foreseeing the conflict around the issue of foreign labor, George Clements promoted himself as a self-styled "expert" on labor relations and the Mexican character, borrowing generously from contemporary eugenic theories of racial inequalities to defend the agribusiness position. Colored by his own utilitarian and biased interpretations, Clements used these theories not as evidence of Mexican's unfitness to become citizens, but rather as proof that Mexicans constituted the least offensive and most malleable race of laborers available to employers. Although he, like Charles Teague, endorsed the politically expedient "birds of passage" theory whenever possible, Clements, as an Angeleno and frequent supporter of citrus rancher interests, understood the citrus grower preference for permanent, settled labor. Consequently, Clements defended ranchers' dependence on Mexican laborers by arguing that Mexicans were unlike other, more problematic races who had served (or threatened to serve) California agriculture. "Agricultural labor," Clements told his audiences, "is known as 'unskilled,' 'casual' labor and is not conducive to the United States standards of living, a type of labor to which the white man cannot adapt himself but which is of second nature to the Mexican or Indian."[37] Although he believed that "the oriental due to [his] crouching and bending habits" was also "fully adapted" to such work, Clements expressed a preference for Mexicans over Asians on racial grounds, arguing: "the cry that they [Mexicans] are a biological menace is without foundation. They are less a menace than our own negro, Filipino, the Japanese, or the Porto [sic] Rican negro."[38] Appealing to popular anti-black sentiments, Clements also compared Mexicans to African American and Puerto Rican migrants. He queried, "Should the Mexican be excluded, where would we go for our casual labor?" Clements answered his own question with a white vision of racial apocalypse:

> There is only one recourse—to outbid the south for the eastern negro and to import the Porto [sic] Rican negro or "Portuguese nigger." Of the former I need say nothing. By the use of the latter we are only increasing our already embarrassing negro problem. They are American citizens and cannot

be deported, more indigent than any alien labor that ever came to us and thus a greater social menace. They are less tractable. In coming, they are permanent. Biologically, they are a serious menace, particularly in California and the border states where we have so many dark skinned races and blends; since they are without the distinguishing features of the negro there is no protection. They are frequently red haired, blue eyed, freckled faced, thin nosed and thin lipped.[39]

Clements's aversion to "dark skinned races" reflected the tendency of whites to associate "blackness" with contamination and identify Africanism as the greatest threat to the "purity" of their own whiteness. Discounting the African influence on Mexico, Clements argued that Mexicans represented a Spanish/Indian hybrid whose racial characteristics were less menacing to American civilization than "the 32nd, 16th, 8th and Octoroon Negro." "It is questionable," Clements claimed, "whether this Mexican Indian blood in itself is not as acceptable or more acceptable than that which we have drawn to our bosoms from the north, the south and east of the Mediterranean which is triply tinted with Ethiopian, Semitic and Tartar blood."[40]

Clements, however, qualified his support of Mexican workers by narrowing the definition of the appropriate Mexican. "The so-called Mexican immigrant," he argued, "is . . . of two types—the cholo or hybrid of the great cities and the peon of strictly rural habits and Indian descent." Clements classified the "cholo or greaser class," as the "riff raff of the Mexican race," and the group most responsible for problems associated with Mexican immigrants in the United States. "They are the criminal Mexicans; they are worthless in labor and always a social problem; they are also chronic beggars, and sizzling with disease." Clements preferred the employment of Mexico's majority, the "peons," because, as he argued, "they are honest; they are generous to a fault; they are artistic, and as far as their light and knowledge will permit, seekers toward perfection; they have no idea of time or money or values as we know them; they are as primitive as we ourselves were 2,000 years ago; their hospitality knows no bounds." Their "years of servitude," he believed, had conditioned the immigrant from this group to "always [look] upon his employer as his padron [sic] and upon himself as a part of the establishment."[41]

Clements's race-based distinctions between appropriate and inappropriate Mexican immigrants reflected Victorian ideas about race and culture. As Peggy Pascoe demonstrates, doctors and scientists promoted theories of "scientific racism" that depended on a biologically determined concept of race, but such fine distinctions were lost on the public. "At least until the first decades of the twentieth century," Pascoe argues, "the concepts we call race and culture were fused in the popular mind, the differences between them only dimly perceived."[42] Similarly, Clements indiscriminately mixed history, culture, and physical features to forge a subjective and self-serving racial hierarchy that separated African Americans from Puerto Ricans, Mexicans from African Americans, and even Mexican "peons" from urbanized Mexican people. This final distinction reflected a popular belief in the pathology of urban socialization, particularly among Mexicans who many Euroamericans believed did not have the intellectual capacity and "civilized" background to negotiate the harshness of this environment. According to R. S. Vaile of the Riverside Experiment Station, the Mexican immigrant who emigrated directly to Los Angeles tended to get "his knowledge of the country and of civilization in general from the rabble of near-anarchists, or worse, [those] that congregate around such places as the Little Plaza."[43] Clements conveniently identified most Mexican people as "tribal Indians;" "as tribal and as pure in blood as our American Indian was when we first occupied America." Numbering over 13 million compared to the 1.5 million "cholos" Clements believed existed among the Mexican population, the "peon" Indian constituted the vast majority of Mexican immigrants to the United States.

Preference for the Mexican "peon" also reflected the attitudes and wishes of citrus growers who whole-heartedly endorsed Clements's vision of the appropriate Mexican worker. Rancho Sespe manager Howard F. Pressey believed "it is much better to allow [Mexicans] to develop along their own native and individual manners." He argued that because Mexicans "are primarily tribal," educators and reformers had to temper their expectations and enthusiasm for Americanization.[44] Growers worried about educational programs that cultivated the aspirations of Mexicans, which, in their minds, would destabilize the grower-worker or *patrón-peón* relationship. Clements tried to intervene on behalf of growers by offering the following advice: "we should in no way interfere with his religion, his politics or his ethics." He continued, "He [the Mexican immigrant] should be made to conform with the health and sanitation laws of the state, and observe the common usage laws of the state, and return to his own country better in pocket and physical health."[45]

Such attitudes reflected the tenets of welfare capitalism common among many employers during the 1920s. According to historian Lizabeth Cohen, among the Chicago manufacturers she studied, "progressive employers advocated providing for the welfare of their own workers to keep the state at bay."[46] Citrus growers' investment in housing projects may have placated the CCIH, but Americanization officials with the state board of education and charity workers affiliated with local churches frequently intervened in the social planning of citrus labor camps. Educators and social workers believed that Mexican assimilation was "*not* a hopeless proposition," and challenged the limited scope of community projects advanced by citrus industry spokespeople.[47] Welfare capitalists and self-styled labor experts like Clements resented progressive reformers' interventions and responded with harsh criticisms of charity houses and Americanization programs.

Clements frequently blamed local charities for offering Mexicans too much relief and causing the "pauperization of a splendid people." Responding to the complaints by Los Angeles charities that Mexicans constitute 68 percent of the cases handled in the county, Clements argued, "it seems to me that this itself is an indication that our social services should be investigated rather than the Mexican." According to Clements, Mexicans were not accustomed to such things such as windows, beds, and paved floors in Mexico, and should not be expected to adapt to these conditions in the United States. He complained, "you will force these free-breathing nature loving Mexican Indians into a domicile with closed windows and doors where he breathes vitiated air, and expect him to hold his health?" He criticized Protestant reformers in particular for trying to convert Mexican immigrants, stating "you take this free spirit of the wilds, a sun worshiper from antiquity, and demand that he be proselytized." "Religion is an intrinsic quality," he argued, "and once the premise is gone he has nothing to tie to." Ultimately, judged Clements, "that maudlin sentiment, open charity, and a loose purse are the undoing of these people since being tribal and having had one purse and one source of supply, they will accept as a natural sequence, and so depend upon anything that is proffered them."[48]

Charity groups responded to Clements, whose comments even he admitted had "received pretty rough treatment in the hands of the social service people."[49] Relief organizations countered with studies of their own. A 1926 report by the Home Mission Council analyzed the problems associated with Mexican immigration and offered an alternative, though equally unflattering and stereotypical, interpretation of the Mexican character. The report's author, Council chairman John McDowell, agreed with Clements to a point that Mexicans lacked "initiative": "In days of plenty, he buys silk shirts and a Victrola, later in a time of want to become a charge upon public charity." "For three hundred years," McDowell argued, "he has been a dependent and has been trained in the habits of dependence," a condition he attributed to "the kindness of the climate [of Mexico]." According to McDowell, Mexicans possessed a philosophy of "happy fatalism" that made them less difficult than African Americans or Puerto Ricans, and more appropriate for agricultural labor. As he claimed, "the Mexican is happy and satisfied with a living wage or better," while "the negro . . . is more of a trouble maker." [50]

McDowell objected to growers who took advantage of this "fatalism" by providing Mexican workers with inadequate, substandard housing. He challenged the CCIH and LACC contention that citrus ranchers had been leaders of their industry in creating employee housing, arguing that "they have built houses for them [Mexicans], but they are simply shells put up in the very slimsiest [*sic*] way." McDowell held that "shacks" built by Mexican immigrants "across the tracks" or "down the wash" were more typical of the conditions found in Mexican employee communities, and quoted the dismal prediction made by the Los Angeles County Health Records that "it will take at least a generation for the Mexicans to rise through the present stage of poor housing." These conditions went against the philosophy of the Home Mission Council, who believed that the home represented the foundational block in the construction of a healthy and ethical society. "Our civilization is established upon our homes," McDowell explained, "and if we are promoting any economic system which tends to destroy the home, we are drawing too heavily upon our bank account."

McDowell refuted Clements's contention that Mexicans constituted transient laborers with little interest in settling in the United States. He blamed employers for intentionally paying employees poor wages to "keep [Mexicans] as hungry as possible" and forcing many to engage in "tent migration" to survive. "There is a tendency," McDowell argued, "for workers to make themselves proficient in one crop and to establish a permanent home in some small town or city near such a crop." Based on his study of Mexican *colonias* in the citrus belt, he offered this alternative explanation of Mexican migrancy and settlement patterns:

> *After such a worker settles in a place like Uplands* [sic] *in California to work in the oranges, his family may for the first few seasons go so far as Fresno for the grapes and cotton, and to the Imperial Valley for the canteloupes* [sic]. *Gradually, however, as the members of the family grow, the children find temporary employment in the towns and villages, and every such tie makes it harder for the family to tumble itself into the Ford car, spin the crank, and whirl a couple of hundred miles away. So, the family tends to become stabilized and so colonies of agricultural workers have been built up in such places as Anaheim, Azusa, Santa Ana, Glendora, Uplands* [sic] *and Redlands in Southern California. . . . Always it must be borne in mind that the groups of a more migratory nature are largely made up of new recruits from Mexico.*

Finally, McDowell took special aim at George Clements in his critique of agri-business, turning the agricultural manager's logic against him. "Dr. Clements," he observed, "works out the theory that all industries in California are depen-dent upon agriculture. If this is true, most certainly it is true also that agriculture depends upon the Mexican. Into our coffers flow streams of silver and gold, and all of these streams flow through the brown hands of the Mexicans." Following his riddle to its logical conclusion, McDowell asked, "If we owe so much to the Mexican, how are we paying the debt?"[51]

Although varied in their motivations, most Progressive-Era reformers agreed with McDowell's criticism of ranchers, and became the foot soldiers in a battle to reform housing conditions in local *colonias*. Like McDowell, many believed that "the Mexican casual" had made a "real contribution to the wealth of the Southwest," and had earned the "right to demand that industry work out some plan whereby his residence shall be stabilized, and the permanency of his home shall be assured."[52] Middle-class and elite women took the lead in these orga-nizations, conducting Americanization seminars for Mexican women and in-viting speakers and holding conferences concerning the "Mexican problem." In the citrus belt, these organizations included the Women's Civic League and the Pasadena Settlement House in Pasadena, Friends of the Mexicans in Claremont, and the Women's Club in Riverside, which became radicalized in the wake of the 1924 CCIH survey of Casa Blanca *colonia*. Generally, reform-ers did not oppose ranchers' use of Mexican labor so long as sanitary condi-tions prevailed in Mexican immigrant communities (work camps and *colonias*), Mexican people stayed within their prescribed locations, and Mexicans did not "become community liabilities." In 1926, John McDowell concluded that Mexicans had become a "liability," but he maintained, "this does not mean . . . that it is impossible for them to become community assets, both economic and social."[53] This position, however, would be tested during the Great Depression.

The Depression and Mexican Repatriation

The onset of the Great Depression changed the tenor of the Mexican immi-gration debate and forced many groups to rethink their positions. In 1930, the Hoover administration blocked nativist attempts to pass the Harris Bill—legis-lation that singled out Mexicans for restriction—on the grounds that the law's prejudicial language would damage diplomatic relations with Mexico. The president's compromise, however, amounted to a moral victory for restriction-ists, since the administration initiated a tough new visa policy that essentially cut off Mexican immigration from the United States.[54] Nevertheless, nativists sought to expel Mexican immigrant families in light of the economic crisis, claiming that Mexicans were taking jobs reserved for white men. Additionally, county relief agencies continued to claim that Mexicans had become a public charge despite contradictory reports from the Los Angeles Department of Public Relations that Mexicans constituted only 16 percent of the county's case load in 1930, down from 21 percent in 1929.[55] In response, Southland newspapers and the Los Angeles Coordination of Unemployment Relief became the leading advocates for Mexican deportation. By 1931, the relief agencies' director, C. P. Visel, initiated a campaign to dismantle Mexican communities in Southern California, stating: "It would be a great relief to the unemployment situation if some method could be devised to scare these people out of our city." The Los Angeles Times sided with Visel, arguing: "In ridding ourselves of the criminally undesirable alien we will put an end to a large part of our crime and law enforcement problem, probably saving many good American lives and certainly millions of dollars for law enforcement against people who have no business in this country."[56]

Confronted by an organized and vocal opposition, ranchers depended on the Los Angeles Chamber of Commerce and the CFGE to muster a defense of their position. LACC president Kerr published an open letter directed at Mexican residents of the United States and the Mexican Consul, promising "fellow-citizens of Mexican origin" that they had "no cause for anxiety concerning the activities of the Bureau of Immigration."[57] Privately, however, George Clements prepared for the deportation of Mexican workers. "My own endeavor," he wrote in 1931, "is to try to convince the outside agricultural areas of the necessity of making provisions for these people twelve months in the year, [and] in creating a clearing house which will relieve the necessity for at least one-third of the present labor requirements through shunting this casual labor from district to district without loss of time to employer or employed." Now convinced that Mexican transience created a highly visible housing problem that was detrimental to the grower position, Clements became an advocate of Mexican settlement, stating: "As it is, one-third to one-half of the time of the Mexican casual is spent in looking for a job, and one-half of the money expended by the agricultural labor employment groups is spent in finding these Mexicans for employment."[58]

In an attempt to forestall the political tide moving against Mexicans and agribusiness, the California Citrograph and industry spokespeople challenged government efforts to impose quotas on Mexican immigration and rebuffed nativists' plans to expel Mexicans from the country. In 1930, the Citrograph editorialized: "To enact a Mexican exclusion bill now without the basis of facts or substitute corrective measure, would be to cripple the harvesting of California's crops for two or three years and disrupt the entire agricultural economic structure."[59] In another seemingly nonpolitical editorial entitled "Mexican Boy Won," *Citrograph* writers lauded young Pedro Espino as "the most worthy boy scout in the entire group of boy scout troops" in the Pomona Valley. Editors, however, politicized the piece when they concluded: "In fairness to southwestern agriculture and to the Mexican race itself the immigration quota restriction should not be made to apply to these people, at least until all of the facts are known." "When they are known," the editors concluded, "we rather doubt if fair minded men will feel that this proposed discriminatory law should be enacted."[60]

Despite intense lobbying by the LACC, the citrus industry, and other employers of Mexican laborers, the United States government moved from a policy of closed borders with Mexico to favoring forced repatriation of Mexicans living within the United States. Between March 23, 1931, and April 5, 1934, Los Angeles County relief agencies repatriated 13,332 Mexicans to Mexico.[61] An additional 3,492 Mexican men, women, and children left from San Bernardino and Riverside Counties, while approximately 2,000 Mexicans were shipped from Orange County.[62] In total, nearly 18,824 Mexicans and Mexican Americans repatriated to Mexico from the citrus-growing regions of Southern California.[63] Yet, in spite of this substantial exodus, the repatriations did not break up Mexican *colonias*, nor did it prevent citrus growers from continuing to employ Mexican workers. According to available published records, approximately 75,000 to 100,000 Mexican men, women, and children made the citrus belt their home between 1930 and 1940. According to the numbers listed above, in the worst-case scenario, repatriates constituted 25 percent of the total population of Mexican citrus belt residents.[64] Consequently, though the repatriations caused considerable disruption to *colonias*, Mexican families demonstrated incredible resiliency by choosing to stay in a very hostile environment (see Tables 5, 6, and 7 in Appendix).

Many citrus growers made it possible for Mexican workers to remain in the United States by continuing to offer them employment, and occasionally shielding immigrants from repatriation agents. For example, Charles C. Teague, owner of Limoneira Company in Ventura County and president of the CFGE, lobbied the Mexican consulate and U.S. government officials to exempt his Mexican employees from the repatriation and deportation drives.[65] Teague's actions reflected the attitude of many citrus growers who had become dependent on Mexican workers and had invested in housing projects for these employees. As the repatriation of Mexican workers and immigration restrictions began to take their toll on the citrus work force, concerned growers hired white Dust Bowl migrants and Filipino workers to round out their labor pool.[66] Throughout the 1930s, Mexican, Filipino, Okie, and Arkie citrus employees labored side-by-side in the citrus groves and packinghouses, yet lived in separate communities throughout the citrus belt.

"Enlightened self-interest" not altruism motivated growers to protect and defend Mexican workers against repatriation. During this period, the citrus industry used the crisis to freeze wages and exercise divide and conquer strategies by pitting Mexican, white, and Filipino workers against one another. For example, in the citrus belt town of La Verne, local newspapers reported the development of "An incipient race war between Mexicans and Filipinos . . . caused by rivalry between the two races over orange-picking jobs in the groves."[67] The newspaper also reported trouble between the two groups in neighboring Claremont, arguing that Mexicans had become "jealous of the inroads made by Filipinos." *Claremont Courier* editor Tobias Larson commented, "So it seems merely to be a case of survival of the fittest."

The depression and the Dust Bowl migration generated debate across a wide spectrum of citrus belt society. McWilliams's so-called "in-between element" of college professors, church organizers, and philanthropists adopted positions on issues surrounding the employment of Mexican immigrants that ran contrary to the thinking of citrus growers and the Fruit Growers Exchange. The history of the Friends of the Mexicans, a Pomona College–based organization, demonstrates the conflicts that emerged between farmers and townspeople in the citrus belt during this period. Organized in 1920 under the joint auspices of Pomona College and the Department of Elementary Education of the State Board of Public Instruction (the government agency that took over responsibility for Americanization programs from the California Department of Industrial Relations that same year), the Friends of the Mexicans held annual conferences each November in Claremont, California, which brought together "educators, social workers, agriculturalists and others." Early meetings concentrated on the subject of Americanization of Mexican women and children and the development of "good-will" between the United States and Mexico.[68] By the mid-1920s, however, organizers purported to address "practically all problems pertaining to our Spanish-speaking population."

Progressive women reformers figured prominently in the founding of the organization. Mrs. Grace C. Stanley, an Americanization specialist with the State Board of Public Instruction, conceived of the original idea to hold a regional conference in Southern California for teachers of Mexican children. James Batten, director of Regional Services at Pomona College, warmly received the plan and committed the college's resources to the conference. During the late 1920s, Batten established the Inter-American Foundation, an umbrella organization covering all activities directly related to improving Mexican-white relations including those of the Friends of the Mexicans. Ethel Richardson, head of the CCIH's Education Department served as co-director of the conference and a permanent member of the advisory board. Appointed to the Commission by Mary Gibson in 1917, Richardson used her connections in the California women's movement to attract numerous women educators to the conference, including Nora Sterry, principal of Macy Street School, a model Americanization program in Los Angeles; Helen A. Montegriffo, the executive secretary of the Catholic Welfare Bureau in Los Angeles; Christine Lofstedt, the president of the Adult Education Associaton of Southern California; and many local Americanization teachers working at the Chaffey Agricultural College and in nearby citrus camps. The advisory board of the Friends of the Mexicans frequently included more women than men and strove for gender balance among speakers at each conference. At the 1930 conference, delegates acknowledged their debt to women reformers by passing a resolution of bereavement over the death of Mary Gibson, whom organizers called "instrumental in starting the Friends of the Mexicans."[69]

Women reformers used Americanization as an example of the positive impact their recently won suffrage had on California society. Conferences like the Friends of the Mexicans provided white middle-class women a forum to voice their social agendas and identify white male allies in their goals of achieving political status. Arguing that Americanization was indispensable to the proper development of Southern California communities, women reformers made the case that such positions should no longer be regarded as volunteer but rather professional service. To increase the urgency of the matter, women progressives characterized the Mexican as an immigrant whose potential for becoming a "menace" or an "asset" rested in their hands. "Although the Mexican child is blessed with creative ability and a natural instinct for beauty, love of color and hand talents," argued conference delegate and advisory board member Grace Ruth Southwick, "we have not yet appreciated nor used these talents in vocational opportunities." Embracing a philosophy of education reminiscent of that advocated by Booker T. Washington, reformers endorsed the popular perception of Mexicans as primarily manual laborers with "hand talents" and sought to develop their "natural instincts" for agricultural labor in nearby citrus groves. Consequently, women reformers acquired clout in the community; however, their attitudes limited Mexican employment and social options and affirmed stereotypes of Mexican people.[70]

Conference planners invited speakers to address a wide range of topics, including "better housing, better sanitation, better school facilities and better understanding of the Mexican temperament and character."[71] Due to its popularity with a cross-section of Southern California's white population, including college professors, grade school teachers and administrators, and church missionaries, annual assemblies quickly grew from a modest one-day conference of 150 participants to a two-day regional event attended by more than 500 people in the mid-1920s. Headed by Batten and Richardson, the conference featured a diversity of speakers, including local elementary schoolteachers; Pomona College professors; progressive reformers like Mary Gibson; university researchers such as Emory Bogardus, Ernesto Galarza, and Paul Taylor; LACC agent George Clements; the *Los Angeles Times* owner Harry Chandler; CCIH officials Leo Mott and R. W. Kearney; and local Mexican consuls. The Claremont Congregational Church, in particular, played a crucial role in bringing the conference to Claremont. In Claremont's La Colonia citrus camp, women reformers, affiliated with the church, founded Su Casa, an organization that delivered hygiene and medical education to local Mexican residents and provided much of the "first-hand" knowledge and experience to Friends of the Mexican delegates in charge of the annual conference.[72]

Citrus growers received invitations, but conference participants consisted primarily of Americanization workers and Progressive-Era activists who often questioned the ranchers' housing standards for Mexican workers. During the first five years of Friends of the Mexicans, the organization supported "scientific investigations" into the "deplorable condition" of Mexican citrus belt settlements. By the 1925 conference, organizers proudly reported, "as a result of the conference movements have already begun to straighten up the Mexican Labor quarters of the Valley communities centering about Ontario, Pomona, and Claremont."[73] Interference in the management of citrus farms strained town and gown relations between Pomona College and growers; however, both parties remained cordial and cooperative throughout much of the 1920s. Just as growers did not control the Friends of the Mexicans' agenda, neither did participants critical of agribusiness impose their will on the conference. Consequently, although the conference placed a sharper focus on citrus industry labor practices, it did not disrupt the order most farmers had worked so hard to achieve.

Initially, Friends of the Mexicans catered to the social planning of the citrus grower, especially with their significant emphasis on Americanization programs. Most conferences stressed "the importance of conserving the cultural and artistic instincts of the Mexicans," and hosted performances of Mexican

folk songs and dances by children from Mexican schools throughout the Southland.[74] Discussion topics ranged from how to preserve the "artistic instincts" of
Mexican children to sessions concerning the "problem of the adolescent Mexican boy and girl." Educators used the event to discuss education strategies for
Mexican youths "who have glimpsed [at] our ideals, but are without the necessary mental initiative and moral stamina to put them into effect." They hoped
to expand and standardize Americanization programs on a regional level for,
as conference planners ultimately warned, "these Mexican boys and girls are
in imminent danger of becoming a menace to our citizenship unless all our
agencies co-operate in making effective in their lives the larger conception of
Americanism."[75]

The Mexican government sent representatives from the local consulate
whose comments often helped perpetuate negative stereotypes of Mexican immigrants. For example, Leandro Garza Leal, the Mexican consul of Los Angeles, addressed the conference in 1923 and delivered a decidedly middle-class
perspective on the "social problem" he believed both Mexico and the United
States shared. Leal stated:

> You have here in this country the same social problem, the same social
> strata, that we have in Mexico. There are the four hundred, the middle class,
> and then there are the lower classes, the ignorant and dirt. The real people
> are in the middle class. We have more or less the same thing in Mexico.
> There are the high classes and the poorer classes and sandwiched in between
> is the middle class. On this side of the line you are very well acquainted with
> our ignorance and dirt, and on our side of the line we are well acquainted
> with your divorcés and whiskey. What we need is to get the middle classes
> together.

Leal's opinions demonstrated the ambivalent attitude held by Mexican consuls
and the Mexican government toward Mexican immigrants in California. Although historians Francisco Balderrama and Raymond Rodríguez have documented the Mexican government's defense of Mexican workers against racism
and discrimination, some Mexican officials also regarded immigrants as "dirt"
deserving of little respect.[76] The deportations and repatriations of the early
1930s further challenged the Mexican consulate on their policy toward Mexicans in California. While their decision to aid in the repatriation of Mexican
immigrants could be seen as an attempt to make the best of a bad situation,
their control of Mexican labor protest in the golden state and their failure to
protect and accommodate repatriates in Mexico after their move demonstrates

that the Mexican government did not always serve the needs of their compatriots *afuera*.[77]

The issue of repatriation revealed the hypocrisy of the Mexican government and exposed an underlying rift between growers and townspeople in the citrus belt. Friends of the Mexicans, in particular, articulated the position of residents who approached the subject of Mexican immigration from a cultural, rather than an economic, standpoint. Townspeople viewed the presence of Mexican immigrants primarily as a cultural "problem," and not as a source of labor and economic stability. Therefore, as the United States' economy faltered during the late 1920s and workers across class and racial lines became unemployed, local white residents not directly involved in the citrus industry began to question growers' dependence on Mexican workers.

The first sign of trouble surfaced at the 1927 Friends of the Mexicans conference. The seventh annual meeting focused attention on the contributions of Mexican immigrants to the California economy and discussed proposed federal government plans to limit Mexican immigration through quotas. At the conclusion of the conference, participants passed a resolution recommending "a thorough study of the whole question [of Mexican immigration quotas]" and "intelligent and equitable legislation" by both the United States and Mexico.[78] Furthermore, the resolution stated its support "for the control of seasonal Mexican labor," and "for better housing of Mexican families."[79] Couched in careful and nonpartisan language, the resolutions, nevertheless, foreshadowed a shift away from Americanization and assimilation issues toward the support of Mexican expulsion and immigration quotas.

By 1929 the Friends of the Mexicans hosted an open debate on the value of the Mexican worker in the United States. The ninth annual conference began with speeches from two people with competing points of view: C. B. Moore, secretary of the Western Growers' Protective Association, and Nora Sterry, principal of Macy Street School in Los Angeles. Local newspapers reported that Moore's speech "reflected the opinion of the 'hard headed businessman' who feels that there is not sufficient labor for agriculture and who deplores the migration of Mexicans from agriculture districts to industrial centers." Moore argued that "more than 8,000 Mexicans" could be used in a variety of industries throughout the Southwest, and recommended that "a fair and impartial investigation of the Mexican labor situation" be conducted before the United States enacted any legislation limiting Mexican immigration.[80]

Nora Sterry, on the other hand, spoke in favor of restricting Mexican immigration based on the expense of employing, housing, and educating Mexican workers. Although a tireless advocate of Americanization, Sterry, like other principals during the late 1920s, developed strategies that preserved programs but also catered to the desire of school boards to limit costs. She asked "how in our civilization based on family life are we to try to teach the Mexican to maintain family standards and a home if he is to be compelled by the demands of seasonal labor to become a migratory laborer?" [81] The depression forced some local Mexicans to supplement their incomes by joining the pool of migratory laborers that traveled throughout California. Since this migration corresponded with the downturn in citrus production during the late summer and fall, the exact moment at which the school year began, concerned Americanization educators like Sterry worried that their efforts were being diluted and money wasted due to Mexican truancy. Similar to the attitudes of teachers and social workers, Sterry expressed frustration at the "slow" process of assimilation. Rather than fault the ethnocentric curriculum and a depressed economy, Sterry blamed the unmanaged flow of Mexican immigrants for the shortcomings of Americanization. Implicitly, Sterry also criticized farm owners whose labor policies encouraged immigration from Mexico.

The debate between Moore and Sterry demonstrated the divergent views of growers and educators and foreshadowed the direction of subsequent meetings as the depression took hold and public opinion forced the organization to take a stand against Mexican immigration. Conferences attempted to maintain a scholarly and impartial approach to the topic, inviting scholars such as Emory P. Bogardus in 1929 and Paul Taylor in 1930 to present sober, yet frequently contradicting interpretations of the situation. Increasingly, however, local town interests came to dominate the organization and moved the Friends of the Mexicans closer to an endorsement of quotas and repatriation. For townspeople living in the citrus belt, the expulsion of Mexican families made economic and social sense. As educators, many questioned the cost of running Americanization programs for Mexican youths and women. Since taxpayers, not individual growers, often financed segregated schools, many residents resented the Mexican presence. It made more economic sense, many argued, to halt immigration from Mexico and expel Mexican workers rather than continue to support Mexican education.[82]

Consequently, a conflicted Friends of the Mexicans ultimately chose to support the repatriation campaigns organized by the U.S. government and the Mexican consulate. On November 20, 1931, the *Claremont Courier* reported: "Deploring the tendency of individuals in this country to coerce Mexicans in returning to their homeland and at the same time recognizing that the return of so many Mexicans to Mexico is of great importance to citizens of both countries, the 11th Friends of the Mexicans conference, which closed here Saturday, went on record to advance all necessary aid and assistance to those Mexicans who decide to return to their own country." [83]

Although the conference attendees cast their decision as charity by "deploring" coercion and expressing their will to "aid" Mexican repatriates, their actions clearly articulated opposition to the presence of Mexican workers. The Friends of the Mexicans' support of repatriation represented an important departure from an agenda of Americanization and placed the organization in conflict with the interest of citrus growers dependent on Mexican labor. In the following years, the conferences continued to honor Mexican art and culture; however, the organization also contributed money and assistance to the repatriation of many Mexican and Mexican American families. Lecture topics became dominated by reviews of the repatriation process, including titles such as "Why 'That Mexican' Went Home," "Enroute with Mexican Repatriates," and "The Repatriated Mexican in His Own Country." [84] Moreover, the conference reported extensive cooperation among the Mexican government, U.S. immigration officials, and the Friends of the Mexicans to expedite the expulsion of Mexican residents.

The support of repatriation had three important effects on the Friends of the Mexicans and the community: first, it strained town and gown relations between citrus ranchers and Pomona College; second, it violated Mexican trust in local progressives; and last, it created the conditions for the collapse of the organization. Following the 1929 conference, growers and industry spokespeople withdrew their participation, thereby formally recognizing a schism that had already been well developed by the late 1920s. The break between Mexican families and the Friends of the Mexicans constituted the most significant and serious conflict for both groups. Prior to the 1931 meeting, Mexicans composed nearly one-third of the delegates and Mexican American schoolchildren regularly performed songs and folk dances at the conference. Although white conference attendees often exhibited paternalistic and condescending attitudes toward Mexicans, their fight for better housing and sanitation in the work camps and the *colonias* earned them the cooperation, if not the respect, of many Mexican immigrants. After the decision, however, an attitude of suspicion and distrust permeated relations between the organization and Pomona College, on the one hand, and Mexican residents on the other. Helen O'Brien, for example, detected a significant amount of hesitancy on the part of Arbol Verde residents to participate in her 1932 study. She reported: "such reluctance was greatly intensified in the Mexican group because of the situations arising out of racial differences and the fear of deportation." [85] Consequently, after 1931 local Mexican schoolchildren did not participate in the conference. Moreover, many parents, now fearful of forced repatriation, stopped sending their children to segregated schools.

Strained relations between Friends of the Mexicans and local Mexican families contributed to the demise of the organization and undermined the role of women reformers. In the years following the 1931 resolution, attendance dropped precipitously, going from a high of over 600 participants in 1931 to 300 in 1932. By 1933, interest and funding had fallen so far that the organization postponed the meeting until 1934. The *Claremont Courier* reported: "After carefully considering the matter, the advisory board has decided that as many of the Americanization and adult work teachers formerly interested are without positions due to this work being eliminated or reduced by our schools, it would be wise to postpone the next conference until November, 1934."[86] Ironically, Americanization educators employed by the state found their positions obsolete due to the government's emphasis on repatriation and Mexican families' refusal to send their children to segregated schools. Consequently, Friends of the Mexicans subverted its own position by deciding to assist the Mexican and U.S. governments in the repatriation of Mexican and Mexican American people. Although Friends of the Mexicans officials promised to regroup after the postponement, no evidence exists of the conference meeting in 1934 or anytime thereafter.

Made into scapegoats by politicians and journalists, exploited by employers, and turned aside by reformers, Mexicans mostly regarded the 1930s as a time to fight for themselves. Many joined unions and conducted strikes throughout Southern California in defense of a livable wage and a right to work. The 1933 El Monte Berry Strike, the 1933 Central Valley Cotton Strike, the 1934 Los Angeles Dairy Strike, and the 1936 Orange County Citrus Strike stand out as the most noteworthy campaigns that demonstrated to growers and local governments the labor organizing potential of Mexican workers.[87] Such strategies of resistance occasionally surfaced in the San Gabriel and Pomona Valley. In 1933, Ontario viticulturist Guasti used the depression as an excuse to slash wages from 35 cents to 10 cents an hour on his Don Lucas Ranch. Encouraged by the election of President Roosevelt and his New Deal policies, picker Enrique Vásquez gathered more than fifteen hundred of his fellow workers for a twelve-day strike. During the walkout, Vásquez consulted a federal mediator in San Bernardino who eventually intervened on behalf of the employees. Although wages did not return to their pre-depression levels, workers did win a ten-cent raise. The victory inspired a poem that Vásquez recounted in 1978:

Gentlemen, I'm going to tell you what happened on the ranch of the Lucas
A strike started on the first of September of 1933

All the people in the fields united together like brothers
We wanted an increase in salaries because everything is expensive and this
  is necessary

But the Lucas were Americans
They didn't listen to the poor Mexicans

They thought this was just a game
But three days later, they saw it was very serious

All the fellow workers got together in Cucamonga for the meetings
To reason out all their rights

In less than a week the news went around like lightening
Without wasting time Mr. Flores arrived to start the commission

That worked well for everybody.[88]

Citrus workers, some of whom worked for Guasti during the short off-season, tried to improve unfair wages in local groves, but organized citrus ranchers proved to be far too formidable. According to longtime Pomona resident Candelario Mendoza, growers stymied Mexican workers' attempts to unionize during the 1931 and 1932 seasons by hiring children like himself to break strikes. He recalled: "The orange pickers were just not getting enough money per box, and so the growers panicked and decided to hire anybody, and so they went out and hired children."[89] As breadwinners for their family after their father died suddenly in a construction accident in 1927, Mendoza and his brothers were forced by hunger to cross the picket lines with other desperate workers during the depression. Another Mexican citrus picker recounted his experience as a strikebreaker to Helen O'Brien in 1932:

The Mexicans decided to go on a strike because they wanted more money. But I told them it was more better not to. But they don't understand the Americans as I do, and one day they didn't work. But I went with some men to pick oranges. The other men think I'm a strikebreaker, and so they poison me. I had saved up over three thousand dollars, but I spent it all for doctor bills. Now I have no money, and I am not well enough to work. And so my step-son, he is very good to me and he pays my bills and gives me a house.[90]

In spite of activism by agricultural workers in other parts of the state, unionizing and strikes seemed relatively dormant in the citrus belt.[91] The clout of citrus grower clubs, the impact of social planning, and the depression conspired to control Mexican union building throughout the 1930s.

The success of Mexican laborers who appealed to federal mediators for assistance infuriated California growers and the LACC, provoking counter-maneuvers to regain full control of the industry. Following the negotiated settlements in the Ontario and Central Valley strikes in 1933, Clements responded by holding a meeting with growers in which he criticized the "National Administration [for] encouraging labor to expect more than agriculture can pay." The LACC Agricultural Department redoubled their efforts to quash labor organizing among workers by establishing closer ties to the county sheriff's office and the county Board of Supervisors. Writing to each of the supervisors in December 1933, Clements stressed the need to protect the citrus and avocado industry in particular given their importance to the Southern California economy. "We hope," entreated Clements, "that everything will be done by your Honorable Body to give adequate protection to the industry which has even in these depressed times been the greatest source of revenue that our country and state have depended upon." In 1935, Clements secretly supported growers in their efforts to organize the Associated Farmers, a vigilante group that pulled together agribusiness funds to fight agricultural labor unions. This organized front served its purpose the next year when sheriffs in Orange County used violence and harassment against Mexican workers to thwart a citrus strike throughout the district. Striking employees reported numerous violations committed by law enforcement authorities, but their complaints fell upon deaf ears as local newspapers portrayed strikers as dangerous "outsiders" and "agitators" "armed with knives." Despite appeals by the Mexican consulate for justice, law enforcement officials attacked workers with impunity and brought about a bloody and tragic end to the labor conflict. As the brutal suppression of the 1936 Citrus Strike in nearby Orange County demonstrated, the partnership among growers, local government, law enforcement, media, and the LACC spelled defeat for Mexican workers thinking of challenging grower hegemony in the citrus belt. Given the cohesiveness of the grower front, Mexicans in subsequent decades would have to devise other means of protesting the discrimination and exploitation inherent to this "whole system of employment."[92]

Citrus growers dictated wage levels and conditions on their farms throughout the 1930s, but their attempts to control worker communities mostly failed. Mexican families carved out a space in Southern California's cultural and physical landscape during this contentious decade, resisting grower social control and weathering the political storm of restrictionism and repatriation. Although citrus growers employed Filipino and white Dust Bowl migrant workers and experimented with Italian and German prisoners of war during World War II, Mexican workers continued to hold the majority of citrus jobs. In 1934, the independence of the Philippines led to the exclusion of Filipino workers. Moreover, as Southern California industrial jobs developed in preparation for the war, white Okies and Arkies and black migrants became the first agriculture-based workers to ascend to these new jobs and a new class level.[93] Consequently, Mexican workers proved to be the most dependable and consistent source of labor for the citrus grower.

During the late 1940s, citrus growers augmented their control of Mexican work conditions by tapping into the *bracero* program. Most *braceros* participated in more rural areas of California; however, some citrus growers used these temporary immigrant laborers to suppress wages. Although Mexican and Mexican American workers dominated citrus grove and packinghouse jobs throughout World War II, most failed to improve their material conditions due to the implementation of the *bracero* program. Occasionally, *braceros* defected from the formal program and integrated into the established and familiar environment of the citrus belt *colonia*. As we will see in Chapter 5, the importation of these contract workers led to conflicts among Mexican residents and highlighted the class, gender, and generational divisions within Southern California barrios.[94]

Bitter conflict between Mexican and white residents did not characterize all intercultural relations in the citrus belt. Although ranchers continued to exploit Mexican labor, the reform attitude among nongrower residents survived the repatriation drives and manifested itself in new ways. Friends of the Mexicans ended in 1934, but many of the white progressives who helped start the organization continued to question their relationship to their Mexican neighbors. A variety of impulses, from a fascination with Mexican culture, to an interest in religious conversion, to a desire to play a part in creating friendship between Mexico and the United States, motivated local church groups, college professors, and students to initiate new programs designed to remedy Mexican and white relations. As with pre-repatriation efforts, social reform during and after the depression drew much of its strength from white middle-class women who continued to search for female moral authority. Frequently, these intercultural exchanges affirmed racial hierarchies and race-based explanations of cultural differences even as they attempted to ameliorate racial tensions.

For *colonia* residents, the adversarial relationship with employers did not negate the possibility of "becoming Mexican American." As scholars Vicki Ruiz and George Sánchez have demonstrated, children of Mexican immigrants grew up in a world influenced by education and mass media that projected idealized images of American values. To argue that Mexicans fully embraced the lessons taught by Americanization workers would be inaccurate, for as Helen O'Brien found, the *colonia* complex she encountered was "a strange mixture of old and new." Mexican parents often detected the ethnocentricism and manipulation present in Americanization programs and limited educators' access to their children, but young Mexican Americans reacted favorably to mass culture such as music, clothing, and cosmetics that older generations could not easily control. Among the women of Arbol Verde, for example, grandmothers insisted that their granddaughters comb their hair back in one or two heavy braids and wear "the long-sleeved, high-necked, ankle-length dress." Adolescent girls, however, rejected such styles opting instead to wear bobbed hair and short skirts "in the latest American fashion." One young informant told O'Brien, "we are American in our tastes—just like you." The manifestations of generational differences demonstrated that as Mexican Americans came of age during the 1920s and 1930s, they began to adopt cultural forms unsanctioned by immigrant parents and grandparents.[95]

Such cultural transformation, however, did not take place in a vacuum. The political and economic conditions surrounding Mexican immigrants and their children colored their responses to mainstream U.S. culture and forced many to be opportunistic in their quest to "expand the space of their lives" in Southern California. In the three decades following the repatriation drives, Mexican Americans used traditional and nontraditional means to assert a "cultural citizenship" that simultaneously acknowledged their civil rights as American-born citizens and observed the historical and ongoing cultural significance of the Mexican presence in the Southwest.[96] Under pressure from a white majority that wished to negate or limit the influence of Mexican culture on Southland society, Mexican Americans' strategies for achieving equality and respect took a myriad of forms in a variety of arenas that will be the subject of the chapters that follow. Whether through protest and electoral politics or cultural expression, this group would redefine the Mexican "place" in Greater Los Angeles and reshape the cultural boundaries prescribed for them by white citrus growers and community groups.

The Padua Institute, located at the base of the Sierra Madre Mountains near Claremont, is another institution which works hard to keep the fantasy heritage alive. Here, in a beautiful setting, the lady from Des Moines can have lunch, see a Spanish or Mexican folk play, hear Mexican music, and purchase a "Mexican" gift from the Studio Gift Shop. . . . Harmless in many ways, these attempts to prettify the legend contrast most harshly with the actual behavior of the community toward persons of Mexican descent. To the younger generation of Mexicans, the fantasy heritage, and the institutions which keep it alive, are resented as still additional affronts to their dignity and sense of pride.
—CAREY MCWILLIAMS, *North from Mexico*

Just Put on That Padua Hills Smile
The Mexican Players and the Padua Hills Theatre, 1931–1974

Despite the trauma repatriation inflicted on Mexican communities, the campaigns failed to erase the influence of Mexicans in the development of a regional culture in Southern California. In addition to the historical markers such as the missions, ranchos, and street names that reminded all Angelenos of Spanish colonial and Mexican eras, live performances by and about Mexican people continued throughout the 1930s. Parades, pageants, and plays depicting Mexican culture and scenes from early California allowed many Anglos to indulge in a fantasy of conquest that reinforced the illusion of European superiority.

Map 4. This map appeared in many brochures advertising the Padua Hills Theatre to patrons throughout metropolitan Los Angeles. (From Deuel, *Mexican Serenade*, 1961)

Meanwhile, in the barrios and *colonias* throughout the Southland, Mexican people staged fiestas and vaudeville-style acts featuring Mexican folk dances and songs, comedy and historical dramas that connected local populations to a larger Spanish-language culture present throughout the American Southwest and Mexico. These performances served to unite Mexican immigrant communities during hard times and provided a forum for ideas about history, society, race, and national identity.

Traditionally, scholars have regarded these two forms of performance—California "pastoral pageants" and Mexican "ethnic theater"—as separate phenomena with their own distinct audiences and purposes. Live performances such as the Plaza Fiesta in downtown Los Angeles, the Mission Play at the San Gabriel Mission, or the Ramona Pageant in Hemet, California, featured all or mostly white casts and appealed to English-speaking, white audiences.[1] These performances typically portrayed Mexican people as genteel, pastoral, and god-fearing Catholics who rarely challenged Anglo American control of California. Often, white elites performed as Spanish conquistadores in an act of "imperial nostalgia" that Carey McWilliams wryly criticized as a search for an *"ersatz* weekend romance, evoking a past that never existed to cast some glamour on an equally unreal today."[2] Conversely, the ethnic theaters on Broadway Avenue in downtown Los Angeles, and the traveling *carpas* (tent shows) staged throughout the Southwest, offered Spanish-language entertainment that catered to an all-

Mexican audience. These shows frequently featured ribald humor and biting criticism on subjects such as repatriation, anti-immigrant politics, and segregation.[3]

California pastoral pageants and ethnic theater, however, did not represent the only Southern California performances spotlighting Mexican culture. The Padua Hills Theatre in Claremont featured Mexican-theme folk plays, romantic comedies, and historical dramas performed by young, local Mexican Americans. Begun as an "experiment" to save a dying community theater during the depression, the theater's troupe, the Mexican Players (or Paduanos as the performers called themselves), became one of the most celebrated collection of Mexican American artists in Southern California from 1931 to 1974. Hosting a repertoire of plays that included traditional and original songs and dialogue in Spanish, Padua Hills surprisingly drew a mostly English-speaking, white audience. After a short stint as a for-profit enterprise, proprietors Herman and Bess Garner successfully converted the theater into a nonprofit "institute" in 1936 with the expressed intent of forging "intercultural understanding" between European Americans and Mexicans. Inspired by the same impulses that created the Friends of the Mexicans, in time, Padua Hills exemplified a range of intercultural experiences between Mexican and white Americans in the twentieth century, and articulated many of the social conditions of this historical period.

In this chapter, I examine the impact of performance and art on intercultural relations through the history of the Padua Hills Theatre, the longest-running Mexican American theater in United States history. Although the Mexican Players did not challenge the status quo with political satire and criticism as did *carpa* and downtown ethnic theater performers, Paduanos and their managers influenced Mexican-white relations by initiating a dialogue between the two groups thought to be impossible at the time of its creation. Unlike other playhouses of the early twentieth century, the theater facilitated communication between Mexican performers and white audiences before, during, and after the plays. The Garners believed that such contact would lead to an appreciation of Mexican culture and people, and improve relations between Mexicans and whites at home and abroad.

Admittedly, the meaning of "intercultural understanding" varied widely among managers, performers, and audiences. Herman and Bess Garner, owners of Vortox, a local business that manufactured air filters for the modern internal combustion engine, and the most significant investors in the Padua Hills complex and residential development, enjoyed the greatest influence over the meaning and purpose of the theater. For Bess Garner who promoted the idea in numerous letters and pamphlets sent to donors and patrons of the theater, the concept grew out of her philanthropic work as a local reformer. A participant at the Friends of the Mexicans conference, Garner also founded a local community center in West barrio known as Su Casa where fellow reformers held hygiene classes and well-baby clinics for local Mexican families. Garner believed poor race relations began with a lack of familiarity between Mexicans and Euroamericans that led to stereotypes and unfair treatment of Mexicans. Carrying the progressive tradition into the 1930s and beyond, Bess Garner introduced patrons to the "beauty of Mexican culture" by highlighting early California history as well as the folk traditions of Mexico. That these images were far removed from the actual lives of Mexican Americans living and working locally mattered little to the Garners, for as they told their customers, the theater's primary goal was "to give [Anglo] people [an] opportunity for an intimate and friendly understanding of our Latin American neighbors." In this respect, the Garners hoped to improve patrons' impressions not only of local Mexican Americans but also of all peoples living south of the U.S.-Mexico border.[4]

Paduanos, on the other hand, expressed myriad interpretations of the meaning and significance of the theater, some of which qualified and/or expanded on those held by the Garners. Given the context of discrimination, segregation, and repatriation, many Paduanos valued the opportunity to perform in a public space rarely accessed by local Mexicans. The ability of performers to showcase their talents in front of Anglo audiences outside the *colonia* expanded the space of Mexican lives, and brought a greater number of whites in contact with their Mexican neighbors. Additionally, though the Garners and playwright Charles Dickinson often determined the content and "authenticity" of shows, many Paduanos were quick to acknowledge their influence over performances through improvisation on and off stage. In the most practical sense, Padua Hills provided many young Mexican Americans a job during the depression and an alternative to the back-breaking fieldwork in the nearby citrus groves.

Consequently, managers, audiences, and performers invested in the theater for various reasons that validated and articulated individual and occasionally group goals. Rather than diluting the influence of Padua Hills, the variety of interpretations suggests that the theater served many interests. This is not to imply, however, that all parties had equal access to power and that all agendas were addressed. As historian Peggy Pascoe has demonstrated in situations involving reformers and their clients, power dynamics were never equally balanced even when people on the receiving end of progressive reform exercised meaningful agency over their lives.[5] Nevertheless, the degree of influence the

Mexican Players enjoyed as performing artists ensured at least a "double articulation" that complicates the limited meaning attributed to the theater and its troupe by theater scholars.[6]

Chicano theater scholars, in particular, have dismissed the Mexican Players as disseminators of misinformation and have chosen to write them out of Mexican American theater history. Reflecting the influence of Chicano nationalism during the 1970s, Roberto J. Garza criticized Padua Hills for misrepresenting "the harsh realities of the oppressed Chicano population," and faulted the theater for not "captur[ing] and convey[ing] that *espiritu* of *La Raza* which was about to manifest itself."[7] More recent treatments of the theater have continued in a similar tact, depicting the Garners as unsympathetic and exploitative and the players as powerless and silent.[8] While these interpretations capture some of the intercultural dynamics present at Padua Hills, they also offer an overly simplistic and somewhat crude understanding of cultural representation and its effects. Similar to African American revisionists' interpretations of blackface minstrelsy described by Eric Lott in his book *Love and Theft*, these Chicano critics presume Mexican American subjugation at Padua Hills and offer a narrowly functionalist vision of cultural containment that denies the Paduanos any agency. Engagement with poststructuralist discourses and the dismantling of binary categories that suggest a "Mexican" and an "Anglo" perspective, allows for a more open interrogation of the theater's meaning, one that simultaneously recognizes Paduanos as co-creators, critics, and advocates of the Padua Hills Theatre "experiment."[9]

Adding to the complexity, audiences and critics registered their own interpretations that further complicated the definition of intercultural understanding at Padua Hills Theatre during its five decades of existence. While Padua Hills literature elicited the support of each patron "to become a partner in this movement for inter-American understanding and friendship," often reviews by white theater critics and letters from audience members to performers and managers contained condescending attitudes toward Mexican people that some Mexican Americans resented. Not surprisingly, such discrepancies between the intent and effect of performances demonstrate how consumers often help construct and reproduce white hegemony even (and perhaps especially) when performances are a part of "progressive" reform.[10]

The Making of the Mexican Players

The Padua Hills Theatre evolved out of a community and nation experiencing a "grassroots" revival in the performing arts. The "little theater" movement in the United States developed during a period of great change and cultural upheaval throughout the world. For Europeans, the advent of the little theater came earlier, during the 1890s; for Americans, this collective expression of culture appeared in 1911–1912, just prior to the First World War. In both cases, the movement symbolized an increased awareness among people everywhere of the dramatic arts for their communal, and often democratic, effects. For Americans, the emergence of this popular phenomenon occurred at a time when technology began to shape entertainment, as manifested in the rise of the phonograph, the nickelodeon, the radio, and eventually the movies. These great icons of mass culture significantly transformed American society, emphasizing the individual experience as opposed to a collective one. During the first three decades of the twentieth century, the little theater "experiment" in the United States represented a movement in which members of a community attempted to recapture the joy of producing entertainment, as well as observing it.

According to a contemporary writer of the period, the little theater represented a "center of experimentation." [11] Due to the meager budgets, theater productions reflected a strong emphasis on the craft of acting, as well as a more inventive use of playhouse resources, such as the stage, props, and lighting. In addition, most little theaters, almost by definition, operated as nonprofit, or low-profit, ventures. "Established from a love of drama, not from a love of gain," many of these performance centers eschewed commercialism in favor of accentuating the artistic value of the plays.[12] In addition, community theaters provided a place for local citizens to "experiment" in social relations and civic entertainment. Because local troupes, financiers, and audiences drew from a cross-section of the community, the performances were often less formal than other stage productions of the time, reflecting an off-stage affinity that existed between players and their observers.

By the 1930s, however, the little theater movement yielded to the economic and social pressures of the Great Depression. The collapse of global, national, and local economies forced players to concentrate on subsistence and survival, and compelled communities interested in live theater to abandon their idealistic notions of entertainment and its production. The refinement and commercialization of the motion picture industry, particularly the development of the "talkies," compounded the pressures against community theater by luring patrons to seek amusement in the movies. For many American little theaters these developments sounded a death knell.

Only a few managed to survive the crisis of the 1930s and successfully continued their productions into the post-depression era. The Padua Hills Theatre of Claremont was prominent among these enduring relics of community

drama, producing plays from 1930 to 1974. Created on the cusp of the movement, the Padua Hills Theatre inhabits a peculiar place in American theater
history. Not only did its tenure defy the historical generalization about little
theater, but the contents of its plays and the function of its performances also
represented a unique experience in the annals of American community playhouse productions.

Padua Hills Theatre is unique in many respects, including its genesis during
the Great Depression. Built in 1928 as part of a residential community restricted
to white ownership only, the ornate, mission-revival theater hosted productions
by a resident all-Caucasian troupe, the Claremont Community Players.[13] The
troupe adapted well-known European stage plays, occasionally sprinkling performances with the blackface characters popular in the United States during
the early decades of the twentieth century. Although patrons viewed this little
theater experiment as a refreshing and somewhat nostalgic alternative to Hollywood films, the Claremont Community Players Association ultimately suffered
the same fate as other theater troupes of this period. With the onset of the Great
Depression in 1929, the Claremont Players bounced from one financially difficult year to another. By the 1932–33 season, members of the all-white troupe
could no longer pay their dues and membership in the association declined
precipitously, leaving the Garners in possession of a $75,000 theater and no
actors to offer plays.

To their surprise, the solution to the theater's woes existed within the complex itself. In need of employees to perform other duties at the theater such as
cooking, serving, and cleaning, Bess Garner sought the help of local Mexican
youths living in nearby *colonias* like Arbol Verde. According to one account,
the Garners arrived at their decision during a dinner at a restaurant in Italy
where local boys and girls sang folk music while serving meals. Upon their return to Claremont, the couple hired Mexican Americans to perform the same
service at the theater's new dining room.[14]

The Garners saw these positions as an opportunity to reach out to young
Mexican Americans by providing them an alternative to agricultural labor. In
particular, Bess Garner regarded the theater as an extension of her reform
efforts, and often wrote of the theater as a place where Mexican youth attained
"self-help" and "practical and general training."[15] Although the Garners paid
the youths a minimum wage, they believed the pay was fair given that other
business owners hired Mexicans at wages below subsistence levels for jobs typically rejected by Caucasians. By employing Mexicans as waiters and waitresses,
the Garners believed they advanced a reform agenda while filling key positions
and saving money during a difficult time.

The Garners pursued many strategies in acquiring Mexican employees that resulted in a diverse group. "We came from varied backgrounds," Paduana Camilla Romo Wolfe remembered, adding: "some of our group were students at Pomona [College], and some were simply using [Padua] as a stepping stone to the real world without having any aspirations for the theater." [16] Many came from a segregated school for local Mexican students situated behind the Garner home on Indian Hill Avenue. Bess Garner maintained relations with local teachers to keep abreast of students with exceptional artistic ability, and often approached families in their homes to recruit young workers.[17]

Later, Garner sought young Mexican performers possessing formal training in song and dance. For example, she discovered the thirteen-year-old Casilda Amador at a Spanish dance performance in San Bernardino. "She saw me in a recital," remembered Amador, "and she went over and asked Mom and Dad if they would let me come up [to Padua Hills] on a Sunday." Initially, Amador's parents disapproved; however, Bess changed their minds by promising to house their daughter in her home while she performed at the theater.[18] Similarly, Camilla Romo arrived in Los Angeles to receive training as an opera soloist and performed at Padua on the weekends. Although an exception among a mostly working class troupe with limited formal education, some players, such as Juan Matute and Hilda Ramirez, developed a relationship with the theater's management through their affiliations as students at nearby Pomona College, the alma mater of both Bess Garner and the director, Charles Dickinson.[19]

The duties of the young Mexican employees included services such as waiting on tables, serving, cooking, cleaning, and gardening. Most significantly, these young men and women provided entertainment, which consisted primarily of Mexican folk songs during dinners and intermissions. In sponsoring these productions, the Garners hoped to expose the predominantly white audience to Mexican culture and to create an atmosphere that complemented the mission-style structure. These brief appearances quickly gained the popular acclaim of patrons attending the theater, providing them with a unique opportunity to witness and applaud the talents of local Mexican Americans.

The performances by Mexican laborers also impressed the theater management who saw in these young men and women a distinctive talent that should not be confined to the kitchen and the dining room. Therefore, on April 21 and 22, 1931, in an exclusive performance for the Claremont Community Players, the young Mexican performers presented a short, "colorful" production entitled *Noche Mexicana* (Mexican Night). The evening showcased the performing abilities of the Mexican employees, and earned them the approval of the white theater staff. They repeated the performance twice in the following month for the local Parent-Teacher's Association, again garnering favorable reviews.

The emergence of young Mexican men and women as artists, not merely employees, occurred at a critical moment in the little theater's history. The event also transformed the outlook of the Mexican people working at the facility, encouraging them to pursue in a public venue talents well known to their families and communities. According to Cheva García, a longtime resident of the Arbol Verde *colonia*, neighbors regularly held pageants and cultural performances where many of these fledgling artists lived. The community often produced festivals and ceremonies involving folkloric music and dance, either in response to Mexican holidays or in observance of religious days of obligation.[20] The Catholic Church of the Sacred Heart provided a source of inspiration for these activities and played a central role in introducing some white Catholics to the cultural richness of the barrio. In addition, local radio stations sought Mexican singers from the *colonias* to perform for the Mexican listening audience living and working throughout the region.[21]

Paduana Fernanda Cruz, hailing from the nearby Mexican barrio in Azusa, remembered getting her start as a performer at similar barrio celebrations. "My dad taught me to read in Spanish before I went to kindergarten and he loved poetry," she recalled, "and he would teach me all these Mexican things so that the committees that took care of celebrating the sixteenth of September [Mexican Independence Day] would always include me in their programs." Cruz's father and other citrus workers organized fiestas celebrating "Dieciseis de Septembre" and Mexico's victory over France ("Cinco de Mayo") that occasionally drew the interest of growers' wives. Noting the attendance of two women, Mrs. Vosenburg and Mrs. Chilburth, Cruz commented, "I assumed they were different [from most white people] because they seemed to be very interested in the Mexican community . . . and they always [had] a seat right in front wherever the festivities were." Vosenburg and Chilburth, both wives of prosperous citrus farmers, enjoined the support of another wealthy Southern Californian, Mrs. Doheney, to build a theater and health clinic for the Mexican community. Although inequalities remained, these shows established communication with key members of white society who occasionally adopted a reform attitude.[22]

Bess Garner recognized the marketability of her employees' talents and the value of exposing whites, both the prejudiced and the progressive, to the beauty of Mexican culture. She believed this chemistry presented the possibility of dispelling antipathies toward Mexican people while attracting large audiences. Moreover, the Mexican Players' emergence as capable stage performers suggested an eventual solution to the financial crisis of the theater: the production of plays exclusively by the Mexican Players. After a successful trial performance entitled *Serenata Mexicana* during the 1932 Los Angeles Summer Olympic Games, the Garners began to incorporate some of the Mexican plays into the regular repertoire of the Padua Hills Theatre.[23] By the 1932–33 season, the Garners were committed to the sole production of plays featuring the Mexican Players.[24]

From 1932 to 1936, the Mexican Players gained experience and confidence while their popularity with the local community grew. The Garners understood that the increased exposure of the Mexican Players would be necessary to ensure continued business at the theater. Therefore, Paduanos not only performed at Padua Hills, but also shared their talents with local crowds in department stores, clubs, and artists' gatherings. The players soon became goodwill ambassadors of the little Padua Hills enclave, helping to advertise the theater, and paving the way for their full-time ascendancy to the Padua Hills stage. Given that the theater was also part of a developing neighborhood in which the Garners and their investors hoped to sell lots for homes, the Paduanos' performances also helped promote an alluring, idyllic image of the community that enticed potential buyers.

By the 1935–36 season, the effects of the depression started to ease. Consequently, more people attended the productions of the Mexican Players, and many developed a great fondness for their work. That same year, the Garners instituted a postproduction party allowing the audience to stay and mingle with the players after the performances. These popular fiestas, called *jamaicas* in the warm months and *meriendas* during the cold season, facilitated an off-stage dialogue common to most little theaters. However, given the racial dynamics between Mexicans and whites in Southern California, these exchanges acquired new meaning in the eyes of the Garners. Describing the importance of the theater, Herman Garner wrote: "[Our] very important discovery was that many, many people who attended these lovely plays, even though they might previously have harbored some prejudices against our southern neighbors, went away with a new feeling of admiration and friendship. Even in a brief hour or two they had found and warmed to a contagious beauty by sharing the charm of these other lives."[25] Believing that visits to Padua Hills allayed or transformed prejudices held against Mexicans, management, critics, and audiences soon recognized the plays as much for their ability to create intercultural understanding, as for their entertainment value.

The Garners sought to capitalize on this "discovery" and openly expressed a desire to reverse the damage caused by the deportations and repatriations, as well as create better relations between Mexicans and Anglos. "Bess was an idealist," Paduana Camilla Romo Wolfe remembered, "[who] really cared and wanted to bring to the attention of the American folks the warm and beautiful heritage of the folklore of Mexico." According to Wolfe, Herman Garner shared this vision: "[He wanted] to clear the ignorance of most Americans [regarding] the culture and value of the Mexican American and Mexican, and I think, to a great extent, his efforts were very, very positive and effective." In addition to addressing Euroamerican ignorance about Mexico and its people, the Garners also saw the theater as an outlet for local Mexican Americans to showcase their talents. In the wake of the Friends of the Mexicans debacle, this cultural center represented an opportunity to establish trust with a new generation of Mexican Americans while simultaneously developing the artistic ability of Mexican youth. Influenced by the presence of famous local painters Millard Sheets and Milford Zornes, sculptor Albert Stewart, and art professors Jean and Arthur Ames, the players were exposed to some of the best known and most accomplished artists in Southern California. The Garners, therefore, envisioned the Padua Hills Theatre and the Mexican Players as the crown jewel in an art colony that united reform, art, and community development.

Once they established the theater complex and residential community around it, the Garners moved to secure the educational and intercultural goals of the Padua Hills Little Theatre. At the end of 1935, Garner and his associates formed and incorporated the Padua Institute, converting the business to a non-profit educational institution. The institute had three primary purposes: one, to expose the general public to Mexican culture through the performances of the Mexican Players; two, to provide local Mexican Americans education concerning music, dance, and the history of Mexico and California; and three, to contribute to the improvement of relations between the governments of Mexico and the United States. Toward this last end, the Garners hosted meetings of the Inter-American Foundation at the theater complex where guests from the United States and Latin America ate dinner and enjoyed entertainment by the Mexican Players. During World War II, the Garners saw the theater as part of an effort to unite the people of the Western Hemisphere against the Axis powers. In 1944, the Garners lent the Mexican Players to their friend and loyal patron, Walt Disney, who featured the troupe in *The Three Caballeros*, a film emphasizing hemispheric unity.[26]

In the years following its incorporation, however, the Padua Institute focused attention on the local level. Herman Garner served as the chairman of the institute's board of trustees, while Bess Garner, Millard Sheets, and local leaders from the Claremont Colleges and the surrounding communities filled the other seats. In spite of the varied talents and backgrounds of the players, the

Padua Institute stressed vocational training for Mexican Americans and advanced a philosophy of industrial education similar to that espoused by Booker T. Washington. Herman Garner explained the objectives of the institute as follows:

> Now the thing this brings to my mind is the training along various lines that Padua Institute should be giving to some of the Mexican youth of [this] part of the country. I wouldn't want, even if we could, to make highly trained scientists of them. But a little practical science mixed with good down to earth training in the fundamentals of gardening and landscaping would make wonderful careers, and useful too for a lot of boys, who otherwise are not likely to find any of the opportunities that surround them.[27]

Like the Friends of the Mexicans, the Padua Institute significantly underestimated the intellectual capacities of their Mexican American employees and encouraged them to pursue jobs traditionally offered to racial minorities. Although they appreciated the talents of the Paduanos, the trustees often made distinctions between their "natural" ability to perform and creative genius. Institute literature often lauded management for their foresight and ingenuity, and celebrated the initiative of the trustees.

The Plays

Pauline Deuel, the author of an institutional history of the theater, claims that Bess Garner and Charles Dickinson established most of the early themes and scripts for the Mexican Players.[28] An avid traveler and collector of Mexican crafts, Bess Garner often returned from Mexico with ideas that greatly influenced the shaping of the theater's future. She shared most of her experiences with her friend and fellow Pomona College graduate, Charles Dickinson, who served as the main director of the Mexican Players during the troupe's first fifteen years. His writing talents, ability to speak Spanish, and training in theater arts provided him the skills to mold Garner's stories and abstract concepts into coherent and entertaining plays.

Members of the early Mexican Players acknowledge the significant influence of Garner and Dickinson, but also maintain that the players had a hand in creating many of the plays. For example, Miguel Vera, an immigrant from the Mexican state of Guanajuato and a member of the original kitchen staff, introduced Dickinson to songs and dances that inspired Padua's most popular production, the Christmas play, Las Posadas.[29] According to Paduana Camilla Romo Wolfe, "Chuck Dickinson had a real understanding [of Mexican culture], although Miguel Vera was a wonderful, remarkable talent." She added, "He was a simple man with minimal education, but he did more for Padua than many a one with education far superior to his." In addition, guitarist Salvador Sánchez shared musical arrangements with Dickinson and his fellow players, while a small cadre of college-educated Paduanos, including Juan Matute and Hilda Ramirez, co-wrote scripts and directed plays with Dickinson.[30]

Paduanos also used improvisation to contribute to the uniqueness of Padua Hills productions. Dickinson employed an Italian style of theater known as commedia dell'arte that used stock characters and simple stories, but depended on impromptu and free-flowing dialogue from his actors to create variety in the plays. Paduana Fernanda Cruz always felt confident with this approach since Dickinson would sketch the plays beforehand, and leave much of the dialogue and acting to the players. "You would make up your own dialogue," she remembered, "so you never had stage fright because you knew more or less that when Ed Montaño finished saying this it was your turn to talk." Another player, Camilla Romo Wolfe, appreciated Dickinson for "[giving] us our lead." In her opinion, "that's what made Padua special, because [we acted] what we felt."[31]

During the formative years, Bess Garner invited Mexican, Mexican American, and Anglo artists to provide formal education for the fledgling players. The Mexican Players received visits from Mexican performers, such as Luz Maria Garces, Francisco Sánchez Flores, and Graciela Amador, who served as song and dance teachers. Señor Sánchez helped develop the play *Idolos Muertos? (Are the Idols Dead?)*, while Graciela Amador, a distant cousin of Paduana Casilda Amador Thoreson, arranged the special production *Aguila y Nopal (Eagle and Cactus)*. The dance and song instruction provided by these two artists made a long-lasting impression on the Mexican Players.

For plays focusing on early California, Bess Garner, Dickinson, and the players consulted descendents of Californio families who either remembered the ranchero era or shared family stories passed down through oral tradition. For example, Casilda Amador Thoreson recalled meeting former Padua Hills landowner and ex-ranchero, Don Ignacio Palomares: "He was already in his 90s, when he and Hilda [Ramirez-Jara] came up to Bess Garner. They thought [we should] use an early California dance, I guess it was 'The Varsoviana' and then we gradually started doing early California dances."[32] The "Early California Club," a group of descendents from Californio families, frequently met with the players to teach them popular nineteenth-century California songs and dances.

Occasionally, Bess Garner attempted to combine education with advertising by sending the troupe out on location to sites of historical significance. In 1934, the players went on a "pilgrimage" to California missions as part of the state-wide sesquicentennial commemoration of the death of the missions' founder, Father Junípero Serra. Traveling by car, the Paduanos attended several celebrations where they performed as a backdrop to the ceremonies. Many of the players kept notes on the trip, which the Garners later published as a pamphlet entitled, "The Pilgrimage Diary of Mexican Players of Padua Hills."[33] The following year, the players traveled by train to Northern California to take part in the dedication of Mission San Juan Bautista. While in the San Francisco Bay Area, the players performed at several venues, including the International House at the University of California in Berkeley.[34]

Although attention to authenticity became the hallmark of Padua Hills, Garner and Dickinson focused on aspects of Mexican and early California culture that avoided the social commentary prevalent in the performances of *carpa* and ethnic theater troupes. Padua scripts always passed through the hands of Herman Garner who screened against plays that conveyed a serious social message or dealt with controversial "love triangles."[35] Indeed, a main objective of the Garners was to divert Anglo attention away from impoverished conditions in the local *colonias* that might adversely affect white opinions of Mexicans. Bess wrote: "To the people in the United States, who know nothing of Mexico or have judged the country by the peon laborers brought to this country and now living for the most part segregated in colonies, the picture of Mexico presented at Padua Hills comes as nothing short of [a] revelation."[36] For Garner, the *colonia* was an embarrassment to local Mexicans and served only as a foil to what they had become with the help of Padua Hills.

Consequently, Dickinson stayed away from references to discrimination and segregation in the local community, and, with few exceptions, portrayed Mexicans and Mexican Americans in the past rather than in the present. Story lines depicting Californios adhered to contemporary histories that presented early California society as a pastoral and leisurely world. The Mexican Players' first plays, namely, *Serenata Mexicana* (*Mexican Serenade*), *Mi Rancho Bonito* (*My Beautiful Ranch*), and *Christmas at Mi Rancho Bonito*, reflect this romanticized vision of Mexican California dominant among Paduano performances. Such presentations avoided the harsh treatment of Native Americans before and after the collapse of the missions, and often stereotyped Mexicans as carefree, shiftless people, who spent most of their time singing and dancing. Although the intent was to create a deeper understanding of Mexicans here and abroad, the formula frequently skewed the image of Mexican culture, California history, or both, depending on the script. While some plays presented honest, accurate translations of Mexican traditions, others involved questionable portrayals of Mexican people, and many drastically altered legends and history.

The play, *Trovador Californiano*, provides one example of the historical inaccuracies and false perceptions present in many Padua productions. The drama focuses on the period of Mexican California history immediately following the "yanqui" conquest; issues of land ownership and Californio/Mexicano trust in American laws figure prominently in the story line. Manuel Dominguez, a young Mexican soldier, refuses to stay in California under American rule, despite being engaged to a beautiful Californiana, Carmela. According to Manuel, "California will be annexed to the American Union. I will not tolerate that act and I will not accept the new government. Tomorrow, I'm going to Mexico to serve under the Mexican government."

The women of the play, in contrast, trust the American government and believe that their land will be secure under United States law. Isabel Sepulveda, whose father has met with American officials, assures other Californianas that "California is in good hands." Led by Isabel, the women attempt to convince Carmela's fiancé to stay, but Manuel refuses and prepares to leave the following day. Before he can get away, however, American soldiers arrest Manuel, and jail him on suspicion of treason. Carmela prays for her future husband, while Isabel consults her father about Manuel's situation. In the end, Manuel gives in, and the Americans free him to go celebrate the annexation of California by the United States. The play closes with Manuel, Carmela, and the entire Californio/Mexicano community listening to the words of Isabel: "We rejoice in our new citizenship and for peace in our land. Let us all as good American citizens raise our right hands and swear loyalty." Everyone follows her directions, as the curtain comes down.

Trovador Californiano ignores the history of Mexican resistance in California, manifest in the battle of San Pasqual in 1846, and other uprisings during the U.S. occupation of California.[37] Although the play begins with the Californios expressing some uncertainty regarding the intentions of the United States government, the majority of the production concentrates on the persuasion and conversion of Manuel. Throughout the presentation, the play upholds the illusion that little or no opposition to U.S. imperialism existed, and that Californios, in general, favored statehood. To convey this message, the playwright appeals to gendered stereotypes of Mexican men as overly passionate subjects whose blind allegiance to Mexico and *la patria* prevents them from embracing U.S. rule. Conversely, Mexican women are afforded more authority and agency in the play, which constitutes a departure from the image of the submissive and somewhat exotic señorita made popular in films. Yet, the women's agency and intelligence serves to highlight the irrationality and immaturity of the Mexican men and suggests that Mexican women welcomed annexation to a "superior" civilization. For example, the play alludes to Isabel not only assisting in Manuel's freedom, but also facilitating his initial capture and encarceration. Lastly, the play attempts to erase a history of *mestizaje* among New Spanish and Mexican society by repeatedly asserting the Iberian origins of the Californio people, referring to them as "Spanish-Americans" rather than Mexican Americans.[38]

During World War II, an emphasis on women's roles increased as the U.S. military drafted Charles Dickinson and many male Paduanos for service.[39] Similar to industries affected by war mobilization, Padua Hills Theatre grew more dependent on women workers and provided many Paduanas greater influence on the plays. For example, Hilda Ramirez-Jara took over directorial duties in Dickinson's absence. To compensate for the lack of male players, she chose plays that featured primarily women characters, including scripts about Mexican women soldiers during the Mexican Revolution (*soldaderas*) and Mexican matriarchs (*Tehuanas*) in southern Mexico. Although Dickinson directed the plays *Adelita*, *Noches Poblanas*, *Juana, la Tehuana*, and *Marina* before his departure for the war in March 1943, these productions took on new importance during the mid-1940s when women dominated the ranks of the Mexican Players.[40]

The 1945 production of *Como Siempre (As Always)*, directed by Ramirez-Jara, demonstrates the thematic changes that took place during the war, as well as the ingenuity of Paduanas. The play explores the matriarchal society of Tehuantepec, a region on the west side of the Mexican isthmus in the state of Oaxaca. The story begins with a small group of young men, led by the main character, Pedro, attempting to serenade Don Anselmo's daughter, Elena. The widower Don Anselmo, however, does not approve of this, and turns the young romantic away from his daughter's window, much to the chagrin of Pedro and Elena. Elena, exercising her authority as a matriarch within her family, takes out her frustrations on her father's intransigence by confiscating his *mescal* (liquor), giving him an axe, and ordering him to cut wood. Pedro, meanwhile, retreats to devise a plan for winning over the favor of Don Anselmo.

Against the advice of his friends, who hold that marriage for men in Tehuantepec society equals slavery, Pedro insists that he marry Elena, who he says will break tradition and allow him to be the "boss" in his family. Doubting this scenario, his friends nevertheless help Pedro cut an immense amount of wood to present to Don Anselmo. Upon receiving the gift accompanied by a large bottle of mescal, Don Anselmo warms up to the notion of having another man around to chop wood, which would allow him to take more siestas. Don Anselmo agrees to the marriage of Pedro and Elena, and an elaborate Tehuantepec wedding ceremony ensues. After the wedding, however, Elena, continuing to assert her role as matriarch, presents her new husband with a wedding gift: a brand-new axe. The play ends with both Don Anselmo and Pedro chopping wood, and all the men saying "como siempre" (as always).

This play examines the renowned Mexican indigenous culture in Southern Mexico, made popular by Miguel Covarrubias, who documented *Tehuana* culture in his book *Mexico South: The Isthmus of Tehuantepec*, and by Frida Kahlo, who featured the elaborate clothing of Tehuantepec women in many of her paintings.[41] Although the story line features a significant amount of dialogue among men, the play contains many dances and songs by women players dressed in the stunning *huipil grande* (or *bida:niró*, in Zapotec), a beautiful headdress worn by *Tehuanas* that Bess Garner acquired on one of her trips to Mexico. The *tehuana* costumes, in particular, quickly became an audience favorite and were used repeatedly during the war years. The productions provided Paduanas the opportunity to depict Mexican women as leaders within their families and communities, and to place women at the center of the plays.

Borne of necessity, the focus and reliance on women also had the unintended consequence of empowering Paduanas such as Hilda Ramirez-Jara who not only directed many World War II–era plays, but also worked in the wardrobe department. Once the war ended, Charles Dickinson resumed directorial duties, an act by management that reflected postwar attitudes about the temporary role of women in the workforce. Nevertheless, Ramirez-Jara's stint as the theater's director provided her experience that served her later as the director of the popular Ramona Pageant in Hemet, California, following her career at Padua Hills. Another player, Casilda Amador Thoreson, became the lead hostess in the dining room and helped manage the theater until 1947, when she quit temporarily to marry Harold Thoreson. She recalled, "I was head of the dining room and the kitchen at one time until it was too much for me." Following the untimely death of her husband, Thoreson returned to the theater in 1951 to become membership chairperson and lead hostess. In 1958, Herman Garner chose her to write the *Padua Hills News Notes*, a monthly newsletter announcing performance schedules and background information regarding the cast that went out to patrons and donors of the theater. For Ramirez-Jara, Thoreson, and other Paduanas, the changes during World War II led to increased influence at Padua Hills.[42]

Yet, despite access to better jobs, the Mexican Players continued to produce plays using themes cultivated by Bess Garner and Charles Dickinson during the first decade of the troupe's existence. For example, Ramirez-Jara's 1945 pro-duction of *Como Siempre* grants women authority within the family, but also interprets *Tehuana* matriarchy much differently from the way men and women actually relate to one another in Tehuantepec. Traditionally, Tehuantepec men and women divide responsibilities, with each one respecting the other's role. Men perform the distinctively domestic sewing as well as artisan work while women control local politics and trade. Unlike their depiction in the play, women do not function as emasculating slave masters, driving men away from the institution of marriage. Moreover, while the play accurately depicts women as responsible breadwinners, their power seems somewhat subverted in the play by their inability to select their own marriage partners or to garner the respect of men. The portrayal of Mexican men as effeminate, lazy alcoholics and women as wedlock tyrants betrays the actual gender relations in Tehuantepec society and caters more to the prejudiced sensibilities of American audiences.[43]

The above plays demonstrate the general thematic nature of most Mexican Players productions. In spite of the Padua Institute's purported interest in edu-cating the public on Mexican culture, Dickinson and Garner included myths and partial truths in their plays that tended to entertain rather than enlighten Caucasian audiences. Often, the story line adhered to the popular notions of California and Mexican history, which reinforced white beliefs. For example, *Trovador Californiano*'s assertion that "Spanish-Americans" favored annexa-tion complemented non-Mexicans' perceptions of the conquest of California. Flyers advertised the play as "an authentic presentation of the colorful and romantic background of California History made beautiful and intriguing by to-days children of the old rancho."[44] The stunning costumes, elaborate set de-signs, and mission-style exterior of the theater contributed to the air of authen-ticity surrounding productions and legitimated the playwright's interpretations as an accurate portrayal of Mexican history and culture.

Although the Garners and Dickinson made specious claims to authenticity in the story lines of many plays, it would be a mistake to reduce Padua produc-tions to simple acts of counterfeit. Throughout the 1930s and 1940s, the Gar-ners made several trips to Mexico for costumes and stage props, and invested heavily in a wardrobe department that employed a small army of seamstresses to reproduce many of the garments worn in the plays. This attention to detail bespoke an overwhelming concern for the maintenance of an authentic and folk image of the Mexican Players and a sincere commitment to honoring what they perceived as the traditional cultures of Mexico and early California.

Such terms as "folk," "authentic," and "traditional," however, are socially constructed categories that reproduce race, class, and gender hierarchies and police the boundaries of modernism. Robin D. G. Kelley has offered the important insight that "folk" and "modern" are mutually dependent concepts that help maintain unstable systems of classification that often situate white, European, and "western" cultures in a superior position to non-European, nonwhite, "new world" cultures.[45] The use of the term "folk" to identify Mexico and its people signifies a preindustrial and rural existence that stands in stark contrast to the industrial and modern world represented by the United States. The inordinate amount of attention to rural settings and indigenous Mexican customs in the plays offered a narrow, and at times distorted, vision of life in Mexico that reinforced this dichotomy in the minds of audiences. The appreciation of Mexican culture expressed by the Garners and white patrons was largely a function of their ability to appropriate and represent it within a context that affirmed U.S. cultural hegemony in North America. Analogous to the "love and theft" discovered by Eric Lott in his explorations of white attitudes toward blackface minstrelsy during the nineteenth century, white investments in Mexican "folk" images at Padua Hills and similar institutions involved a simultaneous process of celebration and subordination that validated the existing racial and political order in Southern California and "Greater Mexico" during the early twentieth century.[46] Plays about contemporary Mexico featured noble, indigenous, and rural Mexicans that white audiences could admire, and even envy, but that ultimately were seen as too tradition-bound and antimodern to emulate. As for the "Spanish Californians" featured in plays such as *Trovador Californiano*, they represented a dignified and aristocratic culture that, nonetheless, gave way to a superior and industrious Anglo American culture in 1848. In either case, the popularity of Padua Hills reflected an ongoing process of negotiating a white racial and national identity that evoked the antinomic response of aversion to the backward and inferior Mexican on the one hand, and an infatuation with the antimodern and romantic Mexican on the other.

Regarded as an antidote to a modern world plagued by depressions and world wars, scenes of "old Mexico" and early California in plays and paintings of the period celebrated a simpler time and place, free of capitalist boom-bust cycles and global conflict.[47] Bess Garner set the stage for such interpretations in her writings and plays. In a rare moment of candor, Garner, in her 1937 book *Notes in the Margin*, published less than two decades from the heart of the Mexican Revolution, described Mexico as "a country struggling with its problems, problems we outsiders do not even understand, problems that are everywhere the price paid for progress." In spite of this admission, Bess remained dedicated to her depiction of Mexico as a tranquil, exotic place inhabited by a humble

people. She wrote: "I do not know what will happen in Mexico socially, politically, or economically. And I've written and am writing no book telling about
that. I have loved my excursions down the paths leading away from the main
road with its problems, back to the folk background, the cultural roots of the
people I find so dear."[48]

Committed to a vision of Mexicans as a people incompatible with the modern world, Bess Garner reflected a more general interpretation applied to "ethnic" people by white observers during the early twentieth century. For example,
Margaret Jacobs, in her book *Engendered Encounters*, explores the emergence
of "antimodern feminism" among Anglo women writers in the Southwest who
wanted to see in Native American art and culture an alternative to the chaos
of western cities. As well, European and Euroamerican fantasies of the "primitive," but noble past of African people contributed to the collection and exhibition of African and African American arts in Paris and New York during the
1920s and 1930s, while similar ideas about Mexican Indians informed Anglo
interest in Mexican and Latin American art during the 1930s and 1940s.[49] Although they constituted a break with the overtly racist and derogatory representations of ethnic people present within popular media and scholarship of
the period, white celebrations and re-presentations of non-European "folk" cultures perpetuated new stereotypes that often legitimated the subordination of
ethnic peoples to whites, and non-European countries to the United States.

Bess Garner's depictions of "Spanish California" (not "Mexican California")
were no less romantic and reflected a strong interest in preserving what she perceived as the dignified traditions of those that had preceded Anglos and other
Europeans into California. She published extensively on the topic, including
her book *Windows in an Old Adobe*, and raised money and lobbied public officials for the restoration and preservation of the homes of the original Californios.[50] Yet, for her, these Californio "windows" provided a view from which to
observe and celebrate the progress achieved by Euroamericans since the U.S.-
Mexican War. Celebrating these changes, Garner wrote: "The windows of this
house during their less than a hundred years have seen the days of the proud
Spaniards give way before the coming of the Anglo-Saxon pioneers. They have
looked on agricultural experiment and development. They have watched businesses, schools, churches, and cities rise where once the cattle and sheep of
Don Ygnacio grazed."[51] Garner's writing, therefore, gave voice to two seemingly
contradictory sentiments prominent among many Euroamericans during the
1930s and 1940s: a pride in the modern and industrial United States, tempered
by anxiety caused by global depression and world war.

Although scarce and difficult to come by, audience letters and critical reviews reflect these two attitudes. For example, in a letter to Paduana Micaela Velásquez on March 31, 1955, Esther Davis, a bookkeeper at a small manufacturing plant in Pasadena, wrote to thank "Senora Velásquez" and her colleagues for the "delightful and enjoyable experience" during her visit to the theater on her birthday. She wrote effusively about the "gay and friendly" nature of the Paduanos, and appreciated their "spontaneity and enthusiasm" while they serenaded Davis and her four friends during dinner. Providing testimony to the intercultural goals of the Padua Institute, Davis wrote: "you are certainly accomplishing your purpose, of deepening the friendship and understanding between our two countries, exceedingly well, and are particularly well-suited for the task, because you make people happy and when they are happy it is easy for them to love [sic]." Donald MacDonald of Benicia, California, also praised the Mexican Players, comparing the troupe favorably to the famous Mexican artists José Clement Orozco and Diego Rivera. Labeling all Mexican art "folk," MacDonald complimented the Paduanos for "[giving] expression to the people of Mexico and their hundreds of years of history." He continued, "[your art] is utterly devoid of insincerity and contriving commercialism, the hallmark of today's theater." Another longtime patron, Carl Spaulding of Long Beach, California, was so moved by his experiences at Padua Hills that he found it necessary to thank the Garners and the players as he prepared to leave California following the death of his wife. "Again," Spaulding wrote, "I want to express my thanks to you and your personnel for your many kindnesses to us. It was one of the highlights of our life in California."[52]

While such letters reveal patrons' sincere interest in, and even "love" for Mexican culture, they also reduce Mexico and its people to a foil for American progress and ingenuity. For Esther Davis, a visit to the theater transported her from a world of "dull and monotonous" work to a place and culture unfettered by the fast pace of modern civilization. Drawn to the play for its "freshness and simplicity," Davis compared the theater's depiction of Mexico and its people with her own life in the United States: "Here in America we tend to be overly sophisticated, and need to be reminded of the pleasure to be found in simple joys and emotions."[53] Meant as a compliment, Davis's comparison, nevertheless, demonstrates how plays upheld notions of American cultural chauvinism. For patrons who could afford to travel, a visit to Padua sometimes inspired trips to Mexico. For example, theater patron Marie Harrington wrote Bess Garner from Mexico to tell her that "[her] play was simply lifted right out of a section of any little town here and set down at Padua Hills." Although writing from Guanajuato, one of Mexico's largest and most modern cities, her preference for the rustic image of the countryside demonstrates the powerful appeal of this antimodernist tendency.[54] Similarly, Paduano Juan Matute recounted the story of another patron who traveled to Mexico "in her big limousine accompanied by a lady friend, a maid and chauffuer [*sic*]." "Before we knew it," he explained, "she was back and rather peeved at us because she did not find the Mexico she went to look for." When asked what she meant by this she informed Matute, "I like the Mexico you have here at Padua much better."[55] Oddly, many patrons preferred Padua Hills, a sanitized simulacrum of Mexico, to the real thing.

The antimodern appeal of Padua Hills reached its peak during World War II. In spite of the government's requests for people to ration gasoline and stay at home at night, Padua Hills Theatre experienced an increase in attendance as the conflict wore on. Herman Garner explained this surprising trend in his *Padua Hills News Notes*: "People are still coming to Padua from quite a distance. It seems as if the harder they work on defense work and related activities the more they need the relaxation and escape that a visit to Padua brings them. Someone told me the other day that it was as if she had spent a few hours in a different and lovelier world; that she went home feeling much refreshed and quite ready to do her bit for another week or two."[56] For Garner and some of his patrons, Padua Hills not only contributed the vital wartime service of uniting Mexicans and Euroamericans at home and abroad, but it also enabled local war industry workers to do their jobs more effectively by providing them respite from the rigors of the workplace.

Plays also perpetuated popular ideas about the "innate artistic instincts" of Mexicans that denied Paduanos proper recognition for their hard work and creativity. Instead, much of the credit went to the Garners and Charles Dickinson for their ability to mold raw and undisciplined talent into entertaining theater. Often, reviews of their performances combined the patronizing attitude of surprise with the belief that song and dance came "natural" to the players. Consequently, managers, critics, and audience members failed to acknowledge the diversity among them and confined the Mexican Players to a timeless and "authentic" identity.

Reviews by local reporters, letters from patrons, and publicity material written and distributed by Bess Garner reveal how most Caucasians regarded the acting and singing abilities of the Mexican Players. The following *Los Angeles Times* review epitomizes the white community's understanding of the productions:

> Out at the Little Theater in the Padua Hills, near Claremont, the other evening we saw a Mexican entertainment which was the most genuine thing

we've ever seen in the United States. It was all in Spanish, all presented by
Mexicans and all quite natural. They didn't act or speak for the audience.
They didn't seem to know there was an audience. They were just a group of
lively young Mexicans having a good time, and those who watched them
couldn't help having a good time too. . . . It is the most rapid-fire, sponta-
neous and natural thing of the kind we've ever seen.[57]

The terms "genuine," "authentic," and "natural" persisted throughout the many reviews written by observers. Bess Garner proudly shared such reviews with patrons when she wrote: "There is a simple, sincere quality of naive naturalness, spontaneity and gaiety to [the Mexican Players] that many such authorities as Gilmore Brown of the Pasadena Playhouse and Hallie Flanagain, head of the Federal Theatre Project agree has never been secured in any theatre in the United States."[58] Indeed, Garner explained the players' talent as "partly the instinct that all Mexican people seem to have for design and balance and partly . . . old timers' [sic] teach it to new ones just like young monkeys are taught to hang by the tail and chickens to pick up corn."[59] Although these reviews aimed to promote and praise the performances of the Mexican Players, they often denied the performers recognition as creative artists, and had the unfortunate effect of denigrating and belittling all Mexican people.

Off Stage and Behind the Scenes

Songs and dances may have been known to some of the Paduanos prior to their presentation on stage, but the roles and depictions of Mexican characters in the plays did not constitute an extension of their own lives. For the players, the musicals represented pure drama, and their performances, though they appeared "natural," did not portray their experiences away from the theater. When the audience came into contact with these same players during meals and post-production parties, they encountered people who seemed very similar to the characters they saw on stage. At these events, Paduanos remained in costume and were required to smile and greet the audience as part of their jobs.

In the Martínez family, a particular saying developed in relationship to this issue. Michele Martínez, cousin and niece to many of the performers, recalls a phrase she and her relatives used when forced to face adversity: "When times got hard, we used to say: 'just put on that Padua Hills smile!'"[60] According to Christina Pérez, a former Mexican Player, the smile was significant: "You had to smile a lot; that was one of the musts. You *had to* smile!"[61] These accounts reveal not only the performers' consciousness regarding their roles at Padua Hills, but also indicates that some players used acting as a mechanism to deal with difficult encounters and situations that arose while working at the theater.

Arguably, Padua Hills functioned like most theater in its ability to transport audiences to another time and/or place, an achievement testifying to the talent of the young Mexican actors. Yet, Padua also carried many other self-imposed burdens—including the education of its public and players—that raised expectations for the theater and set it apart from its peers. For example, during the 1940s, the Los Angeles school district encouraged its teachers to take students to matinee performances of the Mexican Players, and the Claremont Colleges ran Spanish-language summer seminars at the theater.[62] While theater managers and some patrons argued that this exposure softened Anglo prejudices against Mexicans, white attitudes of superiority remained intact and were often perceptible to the Paduanos. As Camilla Romo Wolfe explained, "We treated our [European] American friends as equals, even if they didn't treat us exactly as equals every time." She continued, "at least it was an affectionate type of patronizing, so we forgave them."[63] Immediately beyond the theater walls where improvement in intercultural relations perhaps mattered most, Padua seemed to have negligible effects on local race relations. For example, the persistence of racial restrictive covenants in new residential settlements, including Padua Hills, and segregation at local schools during the first three decades of the theater's existence illustrate the striking contradictions between the "intercultural understanding" pursued at the theater and the social realities of the Pomona Valley.

Most Paduanos learned to live with these contradictions and used the theater as a form of income to pursue educational and career goals.[64] For example, Paduana Fernanda Cruz traveled over fifty miles each way from the University of California at Los Angeles (UCLA) to earn money for school. She explained: "I would come from UCLA on the little red streetcar to home in Azusa. Then, my brother would drive me. I would go Saturday morning to Padua, and go back [to UCLA] on Sunday in the afternoon. My brother would pick me up, take me back to the streetcar and I would go back to school . . . I did that for about one semester."[65] Cruz also worked during the summer to supplement her income, and traveled to San Francisco with the troupe in 1935. Through hard work, she eventually earned a degree in Education and became a grade school teacher in her community. Similarly, Camilla Romo Wolfe traveled back and forth between Los Angeles and Claremont for lessons in operatic singing. "I lived in Claremont and commuted to Los Angeles," she remembered, "because all the Padua [women] players lived in what we called a dorm." Wolfe went on to become a popular singer during the 1940s, hosting her own nationally syndicated radio show on NBC.[66]

Dependent as some were on their Padua salaries, labor issues concerning low wages occasionally surfaced at the theater. "We were not completely comfortable [with our wages]," Wolfe remembered, "but that's not necessarily because we felt mistreated or underpaid." She explained: "it was just that we felt that our experiences and what we gave deserved some promotions at different times." Calling her salary "subminimal," she continued: "there were the usual mutterings about how we should have a raise, but nothing major." Although the Mexican Players essentially worked three shifts in one—serving meals, performing in the play, and entertaining at the postproduction fiesta—the players never received more than minimum wage for work in and around the dining room, and were not compensated for their participation in the plays.[67] When asked whether she thought she had been fairly paid, Padua Hills employee Rosa Torrez answered: "Ohhh, of course not [pause] . . . of course not. During that time [late 1940s], when I was a young girl, forty cents an hour."[68]

Trustees of the Padua Institute, on the other hand, regarded the Paduanos as beneficiaries of their goodwill and believed that the Garners' care and supervision adequately compensated the players. Assuming the role of noblesse oblige, the Garners took responsibility for the Paduanos' educational and theatrical advancement as well as their moral and physical well-being. To fulfill this role, the Garners provided living arrangements for the Mexican Players in need of housing. When asked whether she remembered what the Mexican Players received as payment, Irene Garner, Herman Garner's second wife and co-manager of the complex, answered: "No, [pause] . . . but of course they got their food, and many of them were housed." Women lived in a large dormitory attached to the Garner home, while men lived in cabins at the foot of Padua Hills.[69]

According to Paduano José O'Beso, the players had money deducted from their wages for room and board, while the housing for men amounted to little more than windowless, doorless shacks, with no running water or cooking facilities. "I never saw anything like it," O'Beso commented, adding "there were snakes and spiders inside . . . it was terrible." During the mid-forties, Paduanos paid $6.50 per month for these accommodations, and were required to use the bathroom and shower at Padua Hills. Given their meager salaries and housing discrimination in the local community, most Paduanos found it difficult to move away from the theater. "After the first two weeks," O'Beso recalled, "my salary was $18 dollars [laughs]!" Eventually, he made ends meet by confronting Herman Garner who agreed to pay him a little more for operating the gift shop.[70]

Paduanas faired better in their living accommodations, but came under greater surveillance by Bess Garner. The Garners discouraged dating among the players and tried to keep the men and women separate during times away from the theater. Occasionally, they permitted the Paduanos to go to the movies or skating together, but never without a chaperone. "I think Bess thought of herself as a [mother]," Camilla Romo Wolfe remembered, but added, "I can't say that we felt that way about it." Indeed, Bess's dedication of her book *Mexico: Notes in the Margin*, "to all my children, the blondes and brunettes" suggests that she thought of the Paduanos as family.[71] Wolfe's remarks, however, demonstrate that at least some of the Paduanos rejected this affiliation. Wolfe explained, "I think possibly we felt a little patronized by that thought . . . some of us anyway."[72] Casilda Amador Thoreson speculated that Bess Garner's longing for a daughter of her own (she had three sons) shaped her attitude toward the players. "[Bess] wanted so much to have a daughter," she remembered, "that she loved us like a mother and she felt responsible for us."[73] For those players, like Amador, who arrived at Padua Hills during their early teens, Garner's guidance provided a sense of stability; however, for more mature players, some of whom were in their early twenties, her attitude came across as infantilizing and overly sentimental.

Additionally, promotional literature occasionally bespoke a paternalistic attitude toward a racial minority, rather than the sentiments of a proud parent. For example, in a 1936 Padua Institute booklet, the Garners provided a glimpse at the way they perceived their Mexican beneficiaries:

> For children of Mexican parentage it has been an especially significant, a most wonderful experience, often a veritable turning point in their lives. Their simple minds, *sometimes tortured with the complexes of a minority group, have suddenly found for themselves an undreamed of background of romance and beauty! Why should they any longer be* apologetic *for their parents and grandparents? Their teachers have told us that this change of outlook has sometimes been little short of marvelous* [emphasis added].[74]

The words "surprise" and "wonder" also appeared often in the Garner's descriptions of the Mexican Players' accomplishments. Alluding to the successful subversion of parental authority, the Garners' patronizing sentiments reduced all Paduanos to the status of children and elevated themselves to the role of primary caretakers.

The benefits supposedly enjoyed by the Mexican Players may not have been as great as the Garners claimed. Although the exposure to theater and music provided valuable training to the Mexican youths, the performers never received official credit applicable toward a degree in the dramatic arts. Moreover, in spite of the Garners' connections with Hollywood stars and film industry moguls, they actively discouraged the movement of Paduanos from Padua Hills to radio or movies for fear of them becoming "too Hollywoodish."[75] Pervasive discrimination in the entertainment industry may have contributed to the Garner's thinking, for as José O'Beso remembered, "No matter how good [Mexican actors] were, they were not given opportunities in Hollywood."[76] For those that did succeed, such as Camilla Romo Wolfe, directors and producers expected them to fit into stereotypical roles. "They were forever trying to make me have an accent," Wolfe remembered, "and I just couldn't do it." "In fact," she reflected, "at this point, I would be indignant that I would be put into that stereotyped role, but [back then], reluctantly, I did it." Despite these challenges and limitations, Padua Hills still managed to spawn the first generation of "Mexican American" film actors and radio performers, including Camilla Romo Wolfe, Mauricio Jara, Natividad Vacio, and Manuel Diaz.[77]

The theater also demanded a significant amount of time from the players, which separated them from their communities and families, often during holidays. For example, José Alba Jr. recalled that the *Las Posadas* play ran ten days past Christmas. Reflecting on having to work through the holiday season, Alba commented: "I don't recall a good Christmas during my participation at the theater."[78] Ironically, the plays often separated Mexican youths from the very communities and families they supposedly represented on stage.

The life of Mexican Player Carlos Lícon demonstrates the bittersweet experience of one Mexican American artist who participated in the Padua experiment. Born March 16, 1929, in Los Angeles, Lícon's life began with much hardship. Fellow Paduana Casilda Amador Thoreson remembered that his parents died young, leaving his grandmother to raise him until she passed away during the early 1930s. By the late 1930s, Lícon lived in a Pasadena orphanage, where Bess Garner encountered him for the first time. Concerned for his well-being and fascinated by his ability to paint, she placed the Mexican youth in a home with an Anglo family living in the Padua Hills community. At the age of thirteen, Lícon joined the Mexican Players and enrolled at Claremont High School. In spite of his inauspicious beginnings, Lícon, it seemed, had finally stumbled upon good fortune.[79]

The Garner's intuition about Lícon's talent as an artist turned out to be well-founded. Lícon's skill and creativity as a painter drew the attention of Millard Sheets, who wrote about the young Mexican American artist in 1985: "From the beginning, Carlos reflected his ancient cultural heritage from Mexico. His superior feeling was reflected in his dancing, acting and painting, as he was born with a legacy of 3,000 years of cultural attainment in Mexico."[80] Influenced by the belief that Lícon possessed "natural" abilities, Sheets took the young artist under his wing and provided him with art supplies, studio space to work, and education to refine his skills. This exchange reached its peak in 1945 when Sheets appointed Lícon to be interpreter and assistant to famous Mexican painter Alfredo Ramos Martínez, on his Margaret Fowler Garden mural project at nearby Scripps College.[81] Lícon's exposure to Mexican art and his relationship with Sheets paid immediate dividends for the young artist. In 1948, at the age of nineteen, he won the coveted Scholastic Scholarship at the California State Fair art competition, an award that helped defray the cost of his education. Hailed as one of the emerging talents from the Claremont scene, Lícon's growth and development as a painter seemed boundless.[82]

Lícon's performances at Padua Hills Theatre introduced him to potential art patrons and reinforced his strong interest in Mexican culture. Not yet old enough for the draft, Carlos Lícon quickly became an audience favorite during World War II, always playing the role of the most animated male character in the play. His flair for performing seemingly mirrored his talents in painting, as many white patrons attributed his aptitude to the "natural" artistry of Mexican people. In fact, his lively performances more accurately reflected the influence of alcohol that would become a lifelong problem and his demise.[83]

Lícon listened to the bad advice of young adult players he associated with at the theater. Some players believed that liquor relaxed Lícon on stage, and therefore served the minor alcohol. This practice became a habit for Lícon and eventually led to a reprimand by the Garners during the 1940s. Herman Garner alluded to growing problems with Lícon in an April 28, 1944 News Notes, where he publicly chastised the Mexican youth for not coming directly to rehearsals from school even after the director, Hilda Ramirez-Jara, had sent for him. At one point in his early twenties, the problem became so severe that the Garners banned Lícon from the theater.[84]

Lícon's life took a tragic turn for the worse in the aftermath of his expulsion from Padua. In the years following his departure from the theater, Lícon's love of art constantly competed with his addiction to drugs and alcohol. "Honorably discharged" from the U.S. Navy even though he was caught smuggling narcotics from the Navy Children's Hospital in 1951, Lícon continued to traffic drugs to support his addiction. In 1960, Lícon landed in the California State Penitentiary in Vacaville, California, for a conviction on a narcotics-related charge. During the next seven years, he struggled through fits of depression, had a nervous breakdown, and attempted suicide. During this time, however, he pursued his talents as a painter and corresponded with Sheets, who often sold Lícon's work to interested art patrons. Released in 1967, Lícon renewed his efforts to establish himself as a fine artist. Once again, however, he was imprisoned on another narcotics charge in 1973 and remained incarcerated until 1976. Ultimately, his years of alcohol and drug addiction prematurely ended his career as an artist. After entering the hospital with a brain hemorrhage on June 26, 1982, he slipped into a coma and died on July 13, 1982.[85]

On an individual level, the stormy relationship between Lícon and the Padua Institute demonstrates the limitations of the well-intentioned assistance provided by the Garners and the trustees. Certainly much of the onus of Lícon's drug addiction and broken art career must be placed on the artist's own choices. Yet taken at their word, the Garners clearly reneged on their promise to oversee the proper development of each player. One might argue that placing Lícon at Padua Hills and focusing the spotlight on him at such an early age did him little good. As well, the Paduanos who served alcohol to Lícon bear much of the burden for his addiction, but the Garners' philosophy of relying on "old timers" to teach the "new ones," especially among men, may have contributed to his demise. Paduanos, in oral narratives, remember that the amount and type of supervision applied to young women and men varied. While the Garners exercised constant and even patronizing chaperonage of women, men often received their instruction from older players, a condition that reflected general biases toward the upbringing of boys and girls in society. The Garners' decision to ban Lícon from Padua Hills (by this time Irene Garner had replaced Bess as both manager and wife of Herman Garner) demonstrated the greatest abdication of responsibility by the family that introduced him to the community in the first place.

Stories such as Carlos Lícon's, however, need to be balanced against the many tales of kindness and dedication shared by Paduanos about the Garners to gain a more complete perspective of the history of the Padua Hills Theatre. The Garners' investment in the players' development, while less than perfect, constituted a "progressive" approach to race relations, particularly during the repatriation campaigns of the 1930s. In a time of immigrant scapegoating and persecution, Padua Hills offered an alternative vision in Mexican and white relations and extended and transformed the idea of "intercultural understanding" initiated by the Friends of the Mexicans a decade earlier. The theater demanded real sacrifices from the Garners, who committed much of their lives and money to this endeavor. Players remember Bess Garner, in particular, as a generous and friendly woman who never hesitated to help individual Paduanos in need of assistance. Fernanda Cruz, for example, recalled the crucial financial support Bess provided her during her last semester at UCLA. "Padua was very worth while," she remembered, "but really what saved me was being able to borrow two hundred dollars from Mrs. Garner because I didn't have to work at all and I could concentrate on what I was doing." She added, "I know that probably both of them helped quite a number of other people besides me, and [the theater] was a wonderful experience."[86]

Clearly, the Garners and their associates provided a unique service to the community in general, and the Mexican Players in particular. Without the presence of the Padua Hills Theatre, the Mexican Players may have never risen to the prominence they achieved from their beginning in 1931 to their disbanding in 1974. In that span of time, the players and the Garners established a special program that drew commendations from both public and private bodies, including local, state, and national government.[87] The tributes and acclaim for the theater and the Padua Institute, however, tend to reify the paternalistic relationship between the white community and the Mexican Players, while failing to recognize the valid artistry of the Mexican performers. For example, a 1973 official document designating May 20th through May 26th as Padua Week in Los Angeles County extends "its congratulations to the Padua Institute and to Mr. Garner," but neglects to honor the contributions of the Mexican Players. Similarly, the gaze of local historians and the Claremont community has focused on the Garners and the trustees.[88]

This is not to suggest that the Mexican community did not take pride in the contributions made to the theater by the Mexican Players. On the contrary, many of the local Mexican residents proudly remembered the players' performances and the significant influence the theater had on their lives. Juan Matute, a founding member of the Mexican Players, spoke on behalf of several Paduanos at a tribute dinner for Herman Garner in 1973 in which he lauded the achievements of the theater. Matute proudly claimed that the Padua Hills Theatre had raised the profile of local Mexicans and had become the "cradle of Mexican culture" in Southern California. Additionally, Matute expressed sincere appreciation for the efforts of Herman Garner who, he explained, "devoted hours, days and years of time and effort to carry on the work at Padua Institute."[89] Similarly, Camilla Romo Wolfe, a critic of the Garners at other times, conveyed her appreciation in a letter for this occasion. "Because of Mr. Garner's selfless dedication," she wrote, "I gained a deeper insight into my own Mexican heritage, and transmitted that to my children, and, through them — hopefully — to my children's children!" Indeed, Romo Wolfe expressed support for the Garner's strategy of intercultural understanding: "It would give me utmost pleasure personally to express my gratitude and admiration for someone who has for so many years so quietly achieved what is just now being initiated by those who seek better understanding between all Americans, from all ethnic backgrounds—what better way than to awaken a group into becoming a living artistic testimony to the beauty of its heritage?"[90]

Yet, despite these endorsements of the Padua experiment and the cheerful reunions that now occasionally occur, a palpable ambivalence exists among the former players when discussing the legacy of Padua Hills. Many retired players and barrio residents remember the generosity and kindness of the Garners, the joys and successes of the productions, and the many romantic relationships and close friendships that blossomed among the Paduanos working at the theater.[91] Others, however, also recall how hard they worked, how little they earned, and how Herman Garner mismanaged the theater and careers of the players. Some Paduanos have even refused to speak about the past or attend the reunions. One prominent former Mexican Player remembered Padua Hills as a "beautiful memory," but declined to be interviewed for fear of saying something that would "disturb" it.[92] Conversely, it was not uncommon for Paduanos who chose to voice their criticisms to also express a range of opinions that included sincere feelings of pride and satisfaction in their participation at the theater.

For many local Mexican Americans not involved with the theater, Padua Hills represented a dream concocted and maintained by the Garners and other reformers. In particular, the Claremont community, with its tradition in arts and education, tried to tackle the problem of prejudice by replacing demeaning and degrading representations of Mexicans with an equally essentialized and stereotypical vision of Mexican culture. For example, Crispin González, a ceramicist from Claremont's West Barrio, scorned the "pretty" and "nice" representations of Mexican people and culture projected in the plays at Padua Hills. His impressions of the theater demonstrate his disdain for such stereotypes: "Padua Hills, sad to say, was okay except that it more or less perpetuated stereotypes. You know. . . . 'That's the good Mexican—they sing and dance,' you know, that whole thing. It was nice. People used to come out from L.A. to have a nice dinner and see folk dancing and music. I thought it was great, you know. But, I thought let *them* do it. They were very pretty, and very nice, but I didn't relate to the whole thing."[93] Revealing of the opinions held by many local Mexican Americans, González's comments bear witness to the conflicting viewpoints extant within the community regarding Padua's legacy.

Balancing these perspectives has been a far more perilous task than I imagined when I first began this book. My articles and speeches about the theater have evoked numerous responses from the academic and Claremont communities, ranging from appreciation and curiosity to hostility and anger. Some academics have urged me to excoriate the Garners for their manipulation of the Mexican Players and their perpetuation of stereotypes, while a few have equated the "Padua Hills smile" with the "blackface" forced upon African American thespians such as Bert Williams during the first half of the twentieth century. At the other end of the spectrum, a few white residents and former Mexican Players have criticized what they see as my harsh treatment of the Garners, and suggest that my critical reading of the plays and management-player relations merely "emphasize [my] particular point of view."[94]

This debate (which I am certain will be stoked rather than extinguished by this book) gives credence to the wisdom recently imparted by historian Richard White, who, in his *Remembering Ahanagran*, argues, "History is the enemy of memory."[95] In speaking to many former players, managers, and patrons, I found that oral history accounts sometimes contradicted one another and conflicted with archival evidence in local libraries. In spite of claims to the contrary by Garner supporters (and a few local writers), Bess and Herman occasionally penned unflattering characterizations of Mexicans and displayed a paternalistic relationship toward the Mexican Players in letters and promotional materials. Careful not to confuse memory and history, I have used these "scraps" to construct a history of Padua Hills that challenges interpretations held by people who actually performed at the theater, attended the plays, or knew the Garners.[96]

Yet, I have also depended on the "memories" of participants and community residents to follow leads, understand experiences, and reach interpretations not evident in the documents. As White revealed, "there are regions of the past that only memory knows."[97] The difficulty has been negotiating the multiplicity of these remembrances as well as the discontinuities extant among Paduano accounts. Whom should I believe when stories contradict one another and documents do not resolve differences? How should I interpret the voluntary oaths of silence? And finally, how should I weigh comments spoken in retrospect? Instead of languishing in a poststructuralist haze, I have tried to find the place where history and memory meet to provide an interpretation that begins to appreciate the complex relationships that existed at the theater.

Rather than characterize the Paduanos as pawns in a game played by reformers to improve their own self-image, I prefer to see the Mexican Players as "strategic essentialists" who chose to emphasize their common Mexican roots and interest over their differences to attack more virulent forms of prejudice and attain personal goals.[98] Gayatri Spivak and, more recently, George Lipsitz have invoked the term "strategic essentialism" to describe individuals and groups who adopt essentialized identities as a means to achieving worthwhile, and often, political ends.[99] In the case of the Mexican Players, these young Mexican Americans seized upon the sympathy and curiosity of reformers to create a theater that provided them access to jobs and public space frequently denied to Mexicans living in Southern California. Many Paduanos used their experience to make money for college, avoid work in agriculture, acculturate to life after immigration from Mexico, or acquire communication skills that helped them achieve a degree of prosperity in their careers after their retirement from Padua.[100] In the process, managers and performers alike discovered the political potential of the theater as an organ for intercultural understanding. Admittedly, the Garners circumscribed much of its promise through their heavy-handed management and control of scripts; nevertheless, as Eric Lott argues, such acts of cultural appropriation are encoded with political conflicts and cultural contradictions that managers of such enterprises sought to repress. Distortions and historical inaccuracies notwithstanding, the introduction of Mexican performers to a mostly white audience constituted a radical departure from the standard practices of little theaters during this period, and created the potential for dialogue, albeit mediated, between two groups possessing unequal positions within society.[101] Access to white audiences and public space allowed Paduanos not only to disarm their detractors without confrontation and conflict but also to confidently state their presence within the region against the backdrop of anti-immigrant and anti-Mexican politics prevalent during the time of Padua's creation.

As some of the players' comments quoted above suggest, this access often required Paduanos to withhold their criticism of patrons and managers. Similar to others who have challenged racial prejudice in U.S. popular culture, most notably Jackie Robinson in Major League Baseball and Lena Horne, Dolores Del Rio, Ramón Navarro, and Lupe Velez in film, the Paduanos had to accommodate patronizing attitudes from white allies and audiences to accomplish their goals. Throughout the theater's history, Paduanos maintained "that Padua Hills' smile" in the face of adversity, and upheld an image that did not seriously threaten white spectators. While this approach catered to the desires of the Garners and masked the resentment that some Paduanos felt toward condescending patrons, the Mexican Players gained privileges unavailable to most Mexicans during that period. As we will see in later chapters, the experience for a select few also contributed to self-confidence and an ability to communicate with the Anglo community that came in handy during periods of interethnic conflict.[102]

For many outside observers, including Chicano theater scholars, the necessary accommodations practiced by the Mexican Players has rendered them unworthy of a place among the most celebrated Mexican American theater troupes in the United States.[103] I prefer to see their cooperation and accommodation as strategic and a reflection of the limitations placed on Mexican American performers of their era. Given the discrimination practiced against Mexicans, particularly in Southern California, the ability of the Paduanos to garner the favor of white audiences has to be seen as a significant step forward in the fight against anti-Mexican racism. Undoubtedly, by the 1950s and 1960s, this approach had outlived its usefulness, as a grassroots civil rights movement materialized in local *colonias* and a new generation of Mexican American thespians developed more radical forms of ethnic theater such as "El Teatro Campesino." In its heyday, however, the Padua Hills Theatre helped Mexican Americans expand the space of their lives beyond the confines of the *colonia*, and influenced the development of Southern California culture.

In the following chapters, I examine how Mexican Americans of the citrus belt utilized this newly claimed public space. Rather than continue with a temporary "strategic essentialism," a new generation of Mexican Americans participated in the creation of a post–World War II local culture that precipitated the emergence of a "Chicano" identity during the 1960s and 1970s. Through work, entertainment, and an assertion of their civil rights, Mexican Americans asserted themselves as equals to their Euroamerican peers, and laid the foundations for a more inclusive and multicultural Greater Los Angeles.

Part Two

*Oddly enough, [braceros'] contacts with the
local Mexican communities in California [have]
not been pleasant. Frequently they were told
by local Mexicans that they were "scabs,"
that they were being "used," that they were
working for lower wages than local labor
(which is not true), and that, ultimately, they
would remain here and take the jobs of
the local Mexicans.*
—CAREY MCWILLIAMS, *"They Saved the Crops"*

Citrus in the War Years
Gender, Citizenship, and Labor, 1940–1964

Despite the depression, citrus remained a profitable enterprise. Throughout
the 1930s the industry remained one of the foundations of the regional economy, evidenced by the extraordinary profits of ranch owners and the growth of
citrus farms. Growers' consistently pulled in revenues above $90 million annu-
ally through the 1930s, while land values and the number of acres under citrus
cultivation continued to expand. By 1939, citrus acreage in California exceeded
350,000 acres at an average price of $2,133 per acre. The mean size of parcels
topped fifty acres, reflecting the importance of large-scale operations, but small

farm investors kept the median size of lots to only seventeen acres. Consequently, unlike other agricultural investments, citrus withstood the tumultuous years of the depression and entered the World War II era in relatively good standing.[1]

Suppression of labor activism and the maintenance of depressed wages remained a defining aspect of the industry throughout the depression and contributed to the generous returns citrus growers received on their investments. While white farm owners survived and even prospered during the 1930s, the predominantly Mexican and Filipino workforce suffered the consequence of having to compete with poor, white Dust Bowl migrants for agricultural jobs. In spite of their contributions over the first three decades of the twentieth century, Mexican and Asian workers experienced the 1930s as a "decade of betrayal" when local, state, and federal officials called for their removal to Mexico and the Philippines. The majority of those that stayed and fought these injustices met an organized and impenetrable agribusiness front that increased its strength during the depression. Thanks to loopholes that excluded agricultural laborers from protection under the Wagner Act, striking citrus workers found little support for their causes from the National Labor Relations Board. Growers so successfully limited the strength of organized labor that by the late 1940s one former packinghouse worker observed: "Though the need for labor unions in the industry has been recognized by workers, labor leaders, the National Labor Relations Board, and many others, few workers are organized today."[2]

The failure to establish long-lasting unions remains one of the legacies of citrus in Southern California. Whereas unions such as CAWIU, CUCOM, UCAPAWA, and the Teamsters managed sustained union campaigns on Central and Imperial Valley farms and in California canneries throughout the 1930s, the 1936 Citrus Strike in Orange County proved to be an apogee rather than a starting point for further organization as, one by one, attempts by workers to increase wages were met with stolid defiance and repression from citrus growers. Particularly tight were the grower organizations in the San Gabriel and San Bernardino Valley who resisted challenges to their order in Corona, Riverside, Upland, and San Dimas in 1941 and 1942. In each town, workers struck for a living wage, but growers responded by replacing them with local youth. Often, ranch owners pitted Mexican Americans, Filipinos, Dust Bowl migrants, and Mexican immigrants against one another. In Corona in 1941, for example, hand-to-hand combat between angry strikers and strikebreaking Mexican immigrants along with junior college students resulted in the arrest of twenty-seven strikers and the abrupt end of the upstart CIO-affiliated Agricultural Workers Union. Similarly, in San Dimas, a strike engineered by Mexican pickers ended when Filipino workers chose not to accompany their fellow pickers on the picket lines, and growers obtained replacement workers from the United States Employment Service.[3]

The most serious blow to citrus workers came in the 1941 Lemon Strike in Santa Paula. Pickers and packers, organized as the AFL-affiliated Agricultural and Citrus Workers Union, Local 22342, confronted their employer and CFGE president Charles C. Teague to demand a modest increase in pay at the Ventura County Limoneira Company after a decade of low and static wages. Teague responded by evicting nearly 700 Mexican employees from the company-owned homes, replacing them with Okies and Arkies from the Central Valley. Determined workers set up a temporary camp in the city park they called "Teagueville," filed a complaint against Limoneira with the Fair Employment Practices Committee (FEPC), and sought relief from the California State Relief Agency (SRA) and the Farm Security Administration (FSA). Although these government organizations sympathized with the workers' plight, the strikers' status as agricultural laborers denied them collective bargaining rights and prevented the FEPC from negotiating a settlement to the conflict. The SRA provided funds and food to the beleaguered Mexican families, and the FSA offered strikers replacement housing. Such support, however, elicited charges of "collusion" from local growers and forced these agencies to limit their assistance. Demoralized by the lack of government support, labor leaders ended the strike on July 14th, five and a half months after walking off the job. The strike temporarily impeded the transport of Limoneira fruit to market, but Teague willingly sacrificed a few dollars to defeat the union. In a final insult to injury, humiliated and hungry Mexicans facing few job alternatives begrudgingly accepted Teague's invitation to replace Okie and Arkie workers at their old wages.[4]

The failed strike demonstrated that peaceful protest and ordinary labor tactics alone would not bring justice to citrus orchards and packinghouses. Rather, pickers and packers settled into a "long revolution" that grew more difficult as the war years progressed. With the outbreak of hostilities in Europe and the Pacific, the armed services drained local labor pools of young, able-bodied men for military duty. Those who were not drafted or called into service immediately found jobs in the burgeoning war industry located throughout Southern California. Although some Mexican American men benefited from the increased job opportunities, white Okie and Arkie men and women typically ascended to these well-paid, skilled positions ahead of their Mexican coworkers. Prejudicial employment practices and deficient education combined to place Mexican Americans at a distinct disadvantage. Moreover, as Cletus Daniel has demonstrated in his book *Chicano Workers and the Politics of Fairness*, the FEPC failed to defend Mexican Americans against discrimination in industrial jobs as they did African Americans.[5]

As Daniel correctly points out, the reason for FEPC's shortcomings can only be understood in the context of another wartime government program: the bilateral agreement between the United States and Mexico that brought 4.6 million Mexican contract workers to harvest U.S. crops from 1942 to 1964.[6] Although the committee's neglect of Chicano complaints can be blamed partly on its preoccupation with the plight of black workers, the dependence of southwest agribusiness on thousands of *braceros* (as Mexican contract workers were called) also factored into the equation. Fearing that revelations of discrimination against Mexican Americans would injure diplomatic relations with Mexico and lead to the discontinuance of the *bracero* program, President Franklin Delano Roosevelt chose to quash public hearings for Chicano workers. The decision foreshadowed future conflicts between Mexican Americans and Mexican nationals as growers implemented a new "system of employment" that engendered resentment among Mexican men, citizen and "temporary."

The new system also depended heavily on Mexican women whose employment in packinghouses replenished the depleted labor pool during wartime. Earlier restrictions against young women working in the packinghouses eased, as many Mexican families became increasingly dependent on wages earned by the entire family. Equally significant, the assimilative forces of mass culture and Americanization encouraged young women to partake in an "American lifestyle" that included working outside the home not only to support the family, but also to purchase the latest fashions or see the most recent American movie. The freedom associated with working in the packinghouse offset "Mexicanization" campaigns waged by parents and the Mexican consul and provided a new generation of Mexican American women the space to forge their own identities drawn from their home environment and the public world they now engaged. Moreover, their classification as "industrial" not "agricultural" labor provided them collective bargaining rights under the NLRB not enjoyed by pickers. Although unionization failed in the packinghouses as it did in the groves, for reasons that will be discussed below, women workers forged a "packinghouse culture" that empowered them to petition for pay raises and improvements in working conditions.[7]

This chapter explores how the gender and citizenship status of workers influenced the segmentation of the citrus labor market during and after World War II. The appearance of disadvantaged categories of labor such as women, *braceros*, and undocumented workers did not arise as *conjunctural* (i.e., entirely circumstantial) or *functional* (i.e., entirely determined) outgrowths of an accumulation process initiated by employers of agricultural labor. Rather, systems of inequality based on the citizenship, gender, and race of workers *parallel* a class system, and mutually constitute the subordinate and exploitative conditions of citrus (and consequently all agricultural) labor. As recent scholars of American citizenship have argued, agribusiness firms such as the citrus associations did not create the distinguishing statuses of citizenship, gender, or race, but rather seized upon them and transformed those characteristics to the organization's advantage.[8] Citrus growers preferred women for packinghouse labor and *braceros* or undocumented aliens for picking jobs due to their compromised positions in systems external to the workplace. For women, patriarchy within the family and the community constrained their choice of occupations: the dual role of wife and mother (or the expectation thereof) and their perceived status as the secondary wage earner limited their career options and gave employers license to pay women workers substandard wages. As Alice Kessler-Harris, Martha May, Teresa Amott, and Julie Matthaei have demonstrated, women have played a prominent role as "breadwinners" for their families and contributed to the U.S. workforce despite employer assumptions that their work is worth less. In addition, discrimination in public education adversely affected the ability of minority women to attain higher-paying jobs.[9] For *braceros* and especially *indocumentados*, noncitizen status placed them in a precarious relationship with their employers and the state whereby labor activism could result in dismissal from their jobs and expulsion from the country.

The reorganization of grower hiring priorities during World War II influenced intraethnic and gender relations within citrus *colonias*. Poor wages and a discriminatory work environment notwithstanding, the employment in packinghouses not only provided Mexican American women the opportunity to contribute to the family income (in some cases as the primary breadwinner), but also granted single women greater autonomy in choosing (or not choosing) a spouse. Sometimes these decisions included dating and marrying a Mexican national, providing him entry into the *colonia*. Mexican American men, on the other hand, looked upon *braceros* not as brothers from a distant homeland but rather as intruders who threatened to take their jobs, lower their wages, or steal away a potential love interest. For Mexican American soldiers returning from the front, the presence of "foreign" Mexicans in the *colonia* generated anxiety about the availability of Mexican women for courtship and raised feelings of resentment. Tension generated as a result of changing social interactions within the *colonia* occasionally erupted into violence as some Mexican American men took out their frustrations on *braceros*. That Mexican American men

and women sometimes regarded *braceros* differently in spite of cultural, lin-
guistic, and racial affinities demonstrates the significant impact of gender on
intraethnic relations and supports Paul Gilroy's contention that "gender is the
modality in which race is lived."[10]

The Citrus Packinghouse

Throughout the eastern portion of the San Gabriel Valley and the San Bernardino and Pomona Valleys, packinghouses played a critical role in finding and
hiring workers. Although some scholars have argued that growers and packinghouse management were independent of one another, owners of large ranches
often represented grower interests by sitting on packinghouse governing bodies.
Undoubtedly, smaller growers experienced less influence over their fruit as foremen dictated the modes of production in groves and packinghouses, but operations rarely deviated from the advice handed down by the governing board.[11]
Moreover, CFGE officials and scientific management experts used the Citrus
Institute and the *California Citrograph* to advise growers and packinghouse
managers on cost-saving measures and new labor policies. Consequently, although foremen hired and directed workers, these men carried out the decisions handed down a loose chain-of-command that traveled from the CFGE and
the owners of large ranches to the packinghouse management. The hierarchy
of power created an illusion that foremen worked autonomously, and therefore
absolved the growers, packinghouses, and the CFGE of any liability for accidents
on the job.[12]

Packinghouses maintained low wage standards for pickers and packers that
prevented competition for workers, minimized production costs, and placed
citrus jobs at the bottom of the labor market. Former La Verne citrus worker,
Modesto López, remembered: "people worked in citrus because they had to,
not because they liked it—nobody liked it." According to López and fellow
picker Frank Hernández, most Mexican workers regarded picking as a "low-
down job" and "were embarrassed to be pickers." Aside from the poor pay, fruit
picking was arduous work that involved heavy lifting and required great endur-
ance. Lemon pickers carted a forty-pound ladder into the groves each morning
and worked their way down the linear rows, filling a bag that eventually swelled
to seventy-five pounds. In the groves of La Verne where Hernández's father,
Manuel Ortega, served as foreman (or *mayordomo* as Mexican workers called
him), men were expected to reach a quota of one hundred boxes before they
could leave for the day. With each box equaling approximately one and a quarter bags, Hernández remembered, "we had to pick 100 boxes, but it was tough

to pick fifty." Lemons were particularly difficult since, unlike oranges that were sized and sorted in the packinghouse, employers expected pickers to measure the fruit on the tree before clipping it. Carrying rings, clippers, gloves, bags, and a ladder all rented from the foreman, workers complained of a "waste of motion" associated with sizing lemons that slowed the pace of work and caused many pickers to fall short of their quotas. In addition to the time-consuming mechanics of the job, pickers had to contend with careless grove owners who failed to prune their trees of sharp *espinas* (thorns) that tore at pickers' flesh as they reached into the foliage to pick the fruit. Workers also complained about ranchers who did not weed the work area between the trees. "In the winter," recalled Hernández, "the wet weeds would get our shoes wet and make us very cold." Conversely, during the summer pickers contended with extreme heat as temperatures in the San Gabriel Valley surpassed ninety degrees Fahrenheit for several days.[13]

Most men preferred packinghouse jobs to picking. "[Workers] in the packing-house," López recalled, "had it better than the guys outside." "But," he added, "it was hard to get a job in the packinghouse, especially for men."[14] Gender divisions of labor originated with traditional interpretations of field labor as "men's work." Early in the development of citrus, daughters and wives of growers provided many services to the farm. For example, Mary Naftel-Wheeler, who grew up on a Claremont citrus ranch, recalled: "I drove the tractor and the truck, irrigated, helped with the smudging when necessary, and cooked for the smudgers, and so did my mother." In spite of this work, Naftel-Wheeler regarded herself as her "father's tag-along helper" and never as a primary contributor to farm labor. According to Martin Weinberger, a former Claremont grower, "there were no [white] women that I know of that picked in the field; it was just too hard for them." Eleanor Forbes-Pierson, the wife of prominent Claremont grower Jack Forbes, concurred: "I don't think it would have occurred to a [white] woman to apply for a job on the ranch." She added, "Women at that time were probably only used in the packinghouse."[15]

Growers regarded packinghouse labor as "light" work, more suitable for women than men. Aside from the male foremen and supervisors, the few men employed at the packinghouse did a variety of odd jobs, including receiving, washing, and dumping fruit, as well as stacking and repairing boxes. By the 1930s, managers introduced automatic dumpers and more efficient conveyor belts that eliminated much of the heavy lifting and reduced the number of positions typically associated with men.[16] According to Glen Tompkins, a foreman at the College Heights Lemon House in Claremont, three conveyor belts carried lemons from washing machines to ninety or more women graders and packers waiting to sort, wrap, and pack the fruit. "If you had thirty women work-ing [on each conveyor belt]," Tompkins recalled, "you probably only had five or six men involved with them." [17]

Gender and ethnic divisions of labor significantly influenced wage differen-tials between men and women and between Anglos and Mexicans. As Vicki Ruiz demonstrates in her important study of cannery workers in California, em-ployers assigned women to routine tasks and passed them over for promotions when supervisory posts opened. Consequently, most women were paid accord-ing to a piece rate system, while white, male supervisors held positions that con-sisted of daily, weekly, or monthly wages.[18] Such conditions mirrored those in the citrus packinghouse. According to Glen Tompkins, only five employees at the College Heights Lemon House—all white men—earned enough money to pay income taxes in 1935: the manager received $3,200, the senior foreman re-ceive $2,800, and three division foreman received $1,200. Conversely, women packers were paid 35 cents per one thousand boxes and typically earned be-tween $3.25 and $3.50 a day.[19]

Prior to World War II, white women dominated the labor pool within pack-inghouses. When the war started, however, more Mexican women acquired grading and packing positions as white women took jobs in the war indus-try. "About the time that all these defense plants started coming out," Tomp-kins remembered, "that's when wages started going up and [Anglo women] didn't want to work in the packinghouse [anymore]." Packinghouse managers responded to the labor crisis by embarking on recruitment and training cam-paigns in nearby barrios and high schools. Julia Salazar, for example, began her career at the College Heights Lemon House in 1944. She recalled, "for a while it was all white ladies, and then I think it must have been during the war that they started hiring Mexican people. . . . The first [Mexican] girls who worked in the packinghouse told us, 'they're hiring in the packinghouse, why don't you go apply?'" She began as a part-time sample grader, but within the year advanced to the more prestigious and profitable position of packer along with a num-ber of high school girls recently trained to handle the seasonal "rush." By the close of the war, Mexican women comprised the majority of employees in the College Heights Lemon House, accounting for as many as 60 to 70 percent of the work force. In the groves, Mexican men made up approximately 70 to 80 percent of the pickers.[20]

Wages for packinghouse employees varied according to the job and the pack-inghouse. In 1918 at the San Dimas Lemon Association packinghouse—at the time considered the largest and most modern packing facility in the world— "lady graders" earned 20 cents per hour with a 10 percent bonus determined by the foreman. Packers earned a slightly higher base rate of 23 cents per hour and received a bonus according to how many boxes they packed beyond their quotas.[21] SGFLA packinghouses paid orange packers strictly by the box, offering a rate of 4½ cents for small oranges and 6¾ cents for larger oranges with a half-cent per box bonus. As with pickers, packinghouse managers lowered wages throughout the 1920s, though not without challenges from women employees. At the Covina Orange Growers Association in 1929, angry women packers questioned the board's decision to lower wages from 8 (small oranges) and 16 cents (large oranges) per box to 7 and 14 cents. The board responded by claiming a drop off in their productivity and compared their job performance and pay to that of other packinghouse workers in the citrus belt. Although packers disputed the association's claims, workers chose not to strike since Covina maintained the highest wages in the industry and jobs were becoming scarce. By the 1930s, most packers worked under a combined wage and piece rate system that guaranteed women a base salary but required them to reach a daily packing quota.

The increase in wages at the beginning of World War II forced packinghouse management to reconsider their labor practices. Rather than adjust wages upward to compete with industrial employers in the Los Angeles Basin, managers held the line by hiring young Mexican women. "When I started there [at the College Heights Lemon House] during the war," remembered Julia Salazar, "I made about 50 cents an hour." She continued, "when I left that place—and I was there 27 years on and off—I was only making $1.25 an hour."[22] Women also put in long, hard hours, especially during World War II. The elimination of Mediterranean and Asian citrus due to the war and the demands for fruit from soldiers and allies overseas increased production levels and forced packinghouse employees to extend their work hours. According to Salud ("Sally") Pérez, a packer at orange, grapefruit, and lemon houses in Upland, "in some of the places they worked only eight hours, but with us . . . once we worked a whole month even Sundays and Saturdays, ten hours without stopping." "Most of the time," she recalled, "we worked nine or ten hours."[23] Similarly, Salazar recalled: "We worked there at night, that's how much work we had. We would work nine hours and then we would come home and have dinner. Then we would go back and start at nine." In addition to long hours, packinghouse employees experienced extreme cold during the winter and sizzling temperatures during the summer. "Oh, [packinghouses] get very cold and in the summer they're very hot," Pérez remembered. "I don't know if at another packinghouse they [had] air for the packers, but in our place we [didn't]."[24]

Packing lemons and oranges was also tedious and strenuous labor. As Vicki

Ruiz notes in her book *Cannery Women, Cannery Lives*, cannery and packing-house managers maintained a strict policy of sex segregation within plants that delegated "heavy" work to men and "light" work to women, though such distinctions did not always hold true.[25] Although mechanization streamlined the workforce and made it possible to carry fruit to and from packers on conveyor belts, women still had to lift boxes within their own work space. Salud Pérez remembered, "We had a bench that we could lift [the box] up and roll it to the belt." "But," she added, "then we had to lift it up onto the belt and all that weight was very hard." Packers wrapped each piece of fruit with specially colored tissue paper carrying the brand name. Placing the fruit within boxes demanded great care and precision since employers required the brands to show between the wooden slats.[26] The packing of lemons and oranges also required different motions that influenced packers' ability to crossover from one packinghouse to another. According to Glen Tompkins, "the orange packer is a different packer all together than lemon packers." Employees had difficulty packing both fruits efficiently since oranges arrived to packers presorted, and the larger size of oranges taught women "wasteful" motions that slowed lemon packing and adversely influenced their pay. Tompkins recalled, "we would call [the orange packers] 'swing and sway with Sammy Kay [a famous 1940s big band leader]'" because they [would] get this swinging and swaying back and forth with their movement."[27] In the lemon house, graders working the conveyor belts had to separate and distribute four grades of lemons according to size and color as well as sort out diseased fruit and "culls" (fruit too small for market but useful for byproducts such as lemonade). Consequently, women working in the lemon packinghouse had to limit the amount of "swaying" in order to rapidly sort fruit as it came down the line. "For me it was hard," Salazar recalled, "because when they had the 'rush' it was one box right after another and you had to be sure not to mix them." Given the slight variations in lemon sizes, lemon packers scrutinized every piece of fruit before wrapping and packing it. "If they mixed," Salazar remembered, "they would have to stop the conveyor belt and the boys would have to come and sort them out."[28]

The fast pace of work and the presence of heavy equipment occasionally made the packinghouse a dangerous work environment. In spite of her years of experience, Julia Salazar made one mistake that produced severe consequences:

I lost my thumb there in the belt when I was a sample grader. The conveyor belt had rollers to make it run. At times the conveyor belt got stuck and sometimes I would pull it and get the lemons going again. That day, I had brand

new gloves and they are very hard when they are new. So, I went there, and
I tried to do it and part of my glove got stuck on the rollers and it took my
hand! The conveyor had been repaired not so long ago, and it had nails that
get the conveyor back together again, and one of those nails got my thumb.
I pulled it, but when I pulled it, one of those nails had already gotten the
inside of my thumb. I got the glove out, but I didn't know my thumb was
missing until I saw the blood. I was in shock.[29]

Salazar claimed, "It wasn't only me," adding "It was dangerous; they had a lot of dangerous things there!" She recounted numerous injuries, including a dock worker killed by a moving truck, a man who had his hand "skinned" and crushed by rollers, and a mechanic who had a fatal power saw accident in the machine room. Among fellow packers, she recalled two friends, Alejandrina Torres and Trini Hernández, who suffered hand injuries while working on the packing line. When Torres lost her finger, Salazar remembered, "she told them [that] as long as they gave her back her steady job, she wasn't going to sue, but I did!" According to Salazar, the packinghouse did not offer compensation to any of the victims of workplace injuries. "I hired a lawyer, and had about three thousand dollars left after [paying the lawyer]." She added, "it wasn't even worth my pain."

Despite the poor pay, long hours, and dangerous conditions, women packing-house workers took pride in their jobs and valued the relationships they made at work. For Julia Salazar, working at night during "the rush" provided a sense of camaraderie and excitement that took her mind away from her exhaustion. She recalled: "It was fun! We used to like to go there and see all the lights on the packinghouse and everything. The trucks coming to bring the fruit in [and] the boys filling all the box cars." Working on the packing lines allowed women to visit with one another and establish a pattern that became routine over time. "During the morning," Salazar recalled, "we would start talking and we would let time go by not knowing that the morning is when you could advance be-cause it was longer." "And then after lunch," she continued, "[I would say], 'oh no, I haven't even made my quota; oh, I gotta start picking it up,' and before you know it I would make more in the afternoon than in the morning!"[30] Women with teenaged children or large families also appreciated their positions since sisters, daughters, and occasionally sons held jobs in the packinghouse, provid-ing them the opportunity to maintain familial ties while earning money and contributing to the household income.

The packinghouse became a common ground for women of different gen-erations and backgrounds and served as a basis for what feminist scholars have identified as a "women's work culture": gender-specific concerns and aspirations forged through women's daily interactions on the packing line.[31] As a teenager working in the packinghouse, Lorraine Campos recalled: "they didn't pay very much, but it was a place that I really enjoyed while I was growing up." Campos appreciated "talking to different people and socializing" as well as the playful challenges her young cohorts made to senior packers: "We were the younger girls and we could beat the older ladies! We would be [ahead of them] on the conveyor belt, and we would be going real fast so that they wouldn't get anything to do. Well, it was good for them because they wouldn't be doing anything . . . That was fun!"[32]

During breaks young women visited with one another to talk about fashion, dating, and going out, while older women scrutinized their behavior and dress. "I used to like talking with Carmen Bañales [an older packer]," Campos remembered. "[She] used to scold us—not mad, but you know—because we were younger, and of course, we would go maybe with a short little skirt and she would say 'you're not suppose to be coming to work like this.'" Campos responded by grabbing Bañales for an impromptu dance. "She would say, 'you're going to knock me down,'" Campos explained, "and I would tell her, 'oh, just dance!'"[33] For some middle-aged, married veterans of the packing house, the presence of youth had a positive effect, as Julia Salazar recalled: "The young girls would come in, and the married women like me would feel kind of funny having them around us, you know, all crazy and dancing when they'd get a break. And then, I would look at some of [the dancing women], and some of them were even my age! It was fun."

Most packinghouse women of the 1940s and 1950s exhibited an independence that broke with traditional interpretations of Mexican womanhood. During the early 1940s, for example, Salud Pérez tested her father's will by playing the "American, male" sport of baseball in order to socialize with girlfriends and meet boys outside her home. She remembered:

> I used to like to play baseball so I formed a team. I got all the girls together and formed two teams. He [her future husband, Nicasio] came every afternoon when it was raining and he didn't work and he saw me there. There were about fourteen or sixteen girls. Out of all those girls he picked me (laughs). My mother had already gone, she had died—it was about five months—when I knew my husband. My father was by himself. . . . When I finished with my work with the kids and all, I went out to play ball. My father didn't know what I was doing playing ball . . . that I was also looking at the boys. My father didn't know that I had already met another boy

friend. I had one before [my husband]. It was a shock to [my father] that I wanted to get married and settle down because in my home my father always had his favorites and I felt left out. So then, [when] I met my husband and I loved him. . . . I said I won't let him go.[34]

Other women packers remained conservative in their behavior, but maintained autonomy when it came to decisions of courtship and marriage. "The Bañales sisters," Julia Salazar recalled, "were typical people from Mexico." She observed: "they used to go to work with sweaters even if it was warm. And if it got very hot, they would get a blouse that would go up to [the neck]. They wore a skirt and *medias* (knee-high stockings) . . . [and] never wore any socks or shoes like we used to. They had their hair combed back in a *chongito* (hairbun)." While their style of dress may not have attracted potential suitors, Carmen Bañales insisted that she and her sisters made a conscious decision never to marry: "We had no use to worry for a husband . . . or a son." As a young woman, Bañales remembered the anguish experienced by her mother when her brother would stay out late drinking at the pool hall after a hard day of work in the groves. "[Mother] used to bless the four corners of the house," she recalled, "and my father used to say, 'why are you scratching the walls? Your son is alright.'" The argument often led to a fight that had a profound impact on the girls' attitudes about marriage and child-rearing. Ultimately, all three women committed their lives to the packinghouse and the church and avoided men, whom Carmen Bañales regarded as "drunks."[35]

Among the former packinghouse employees I interviewed, many noted that a significant number of full-time packers at the College Heights Packinghouse chose not to get married. Observing this phenomenon, Julia Salazar commented, "one of the Guerreros, the Bañaleses, Catie [Aguayo], Helen [Ruiz], and Trini Hernández never got married." The unusually high number of single women working in the packinghouse concerned foreman Glen Tompkins. "It always worried me," Tompkins reflected, "because they were nice girls who worked up there in that packinghouse and they just never [found] anyone to marry them—about 5 or 6 of them." Tompkins blamed the situation on the "rowd[iness] of Mexican boys," while Julia Salazar attributed their marital status to personal preference. "They were attractive in their younger years," she explained, "[but] I guess they didn't care to get married." The decision to remain single represented an alternative lifestyle for women of that generation, particularly among Mexican families who saw marriage and kinship as a source of survival. Wage labor enabled packinghouse workers to make decisions not afforded to homemakers or daughters dependent on parental incomes. Having worked all her life in the packinghouse, Carmen Bañales never saw the need for a husband. "Why have one?" she stated rhetorically, "We worked all the time." For Carmen and her sisters, wage labor liberated them from the concerns and abuses some women experienced as wives and mothers.[36]

Since Mexican American women operatives held most but not all positions during and after World War II, intraethnic and interethnic relations developed among the workforce. For example, Carmen Bañales valued the variety of friends she made while working in the packinghouse. "We used to have lots of friends there," she remembered, "Americanos y Mexicanos, and . . . even *braceros!*"[37] "We never had any conflicts with the white women," Salazar remembered, "[though] at first, they [white women] used to think that the Mexican girls were not fast enough, but *they were* . . . I tell you, those packers from Pomona were real good!" Before the war, Mexican and white women took their breaks separately, and limited communication to the packinghouse floor. During and after the war, however, Salazar noticed a change in packinghouse race relations: "The Chicanas were [still] separate [from the white women], but they would make friends. There were some [white women] that were *gestudas* [angry-faced], and some that were real friendly. I remember one named 'Weenie.' We used to call her 'Weenie Bum.' She was real friendly with us. She was a packer and a grader."[38]

Although friendships such as these rarely transcended the workplace, they did lay the foundations for a distinct "packinghouse culture." Noting a similar phenomenon among cannery workers in California, Vicki Ruiz described this culture as "an intermingling of gender roles and assembly line conditions, family and peer socialization, and at times collective resistance and change."[39] Low wages, in particular, served as inspiration for interethnic solidarity among Mexican and white women employees. When asked whether white women got paid the same as Chicanas, Julia Salazar commented: "Oh yeah . . . Switzer [the head foreman] wasn't going to be making any [exceptions]!"

Constituting approximately 70 percent of the packinghouse workforce, women discovered strength in numbers. For example, senior women at the College Heights Lemon House initiated secret petitions calling for a 5-cent raise whenever earnings fell below subsistence levels. During the day, aggrieved packers surreptitiously signed on to the demands as the paper wound its way through the packing lines. Such organizing required great care, for as Salazar recalled: "We would pass a paper around for everybody to sign, but we would hide it! We wouldn't let Roy, or Switzer, or Glen [foremen] see it until we all had signed it. We made sure everybody signed it, because it's not fair that just two or three sign it and we get kicked out, you know. I am sure we would have."

At the end of the day, senior packers bypassed the plant foremen and took their requests straight to the "big manager." Management often conceded to their demands to avoid further unrest, but used a "good cop/bad cop" approach in an attempt to diffuse worker discontent while upholding the benevolent image of the association. Salazar explained: "Switzer would get us together, and the manager would start talking to us. He would say, 'I'll give you your five cents raise.' After he finished talking, Switzer would jump in and he would say, 'Now that he is through, I am going to give you your five cents worth of talking. I don't want anybody coming in at the last minute when the bell rings . . .' or whatever he wanted to make up just to have something to say."

Success inured packinghouse women to unfair criticisms heaped upon them by foremen whose job included discouraging labor activism while holding down wages. Salazar commented, "We didn't pay attention to him." She continued, "all we wanted was the other manager to approve our five cents that we worked for, [and] we were happy with that . . . (laugh) because [Switzer] couldn't take that away from us." [40]

In spite of their protection under the 1935 National Labor Relations Act (the NLRA, otherwise known as the Wagner Act), packinghouse employees failed to translate these modest accomplishments into a full-fledged labor movement. As Devra Weber demonstrates in her book *Dark Sweat, White Gold*, the Roosevelt Administration's failure to include agricultural laborers under this New Deal legislation led to unsuccessful challenges by the CIO to expand coverage to farm workers. [41] Additionally, however, AFL lawyers attempted to secure collective bargaining rights for cannery and packinghouse workers under section 7a of the NLRA by establishing them as "industrial workers." By 1937, the AFL won two landmark cases, one against the Sierra Madre–Lamanda Citrus Association and another against the North Whittier Heights Citrus Association that granted packinghouse workers "industrial labor" status. CFGE attorneys appealed the decisions of the National Labor Relations Board and the courts while Exchange lobbyists placed pressure on representatives in Congress to amend the Wagner Act. Union-busting provided the singular motivation of the CFGE, for as Ivan McDaniel the attorney for citrus employers stated, "producers must hold as fundamental that agricultural labor [packers as well as pickers] does not lend itself to unionization." [42]

The failure of agribusiness lobbyists and CFGE attorneys to reverse the court decisions created incentives for unions to take advantage of their legal victories and the momentum of the labor movement during the 1930s by initiating membership campaigns among citrus packinghouse workers. According to College Heights foreman Glen Tompkins, the culture that organizers encountered among packinghouse women differed from that of Los Angeles longshoremen. Tompkins recalled:

> One time they had a deal going on down at the harbor. They were trying to get the packinghouse to organize under [their] union. The guy came up and talked one night to the whole packing crew—oranges and lemons all. . . . Now, I'll say one thing first. The girls had pride in what they did. And this guy had nerve enough to say, 'down there at the harbor where we load boxes of oranges . . . , if we are hungry we pull an orange out of the box.' That killed it as quick as anything else. An orange packer had such pride that she did not want her box to have oranges taken out of it.[43]

For former packers, however, the fear of losing their jobs served as the primary obstacle to organizing unions. For example, Julia Salazar recalled the frustration she and her coworkers experienced when it came to pay raises and the attitudes of foremen: "They never volunteered to give us a raise. Switzer would say, 'if they don't ask for it, why bother to offer it.' We all got mad, but we never did anything. We were afraid, because we could lose our job, and at that time, it was hard to get a job."[44]

Many Mexican families also stood to lose their homes for challenging packinghouse employment policies. On some ranches, Mexican workers built their own homes, but employers often maintained control of their property. At Rancho Sespe in Ventura County, for example, the company furnished the grounds and the water for each lot, but deducted money from workers' monthly wages for lumber used to construct the house. "If a Mexican leaves the employment of the ranch before he pays the entire lumber bill," Archibald Shamel reported, "he loses his equity into the house." Consequently, losing one's job also meant losing both the home and the investment.[45] In other housing projects owned by the association or ranch, families could rent space only if enough members of the family held jobs as packers or pickers. As soon as workers struck, employers made it clear that they would replace them with other families willing to work.[46] After World War II, rising maintenance costs, the creation of temporary camps for *braceros*, and escalating land values prompted employers to sell off property formerly used for employee housing. As Mexican families purchased houses in and around their jobs in places like Arbol Verde, packinghouse associations sought other ways to discourage labor activism.

The division of the workforce into "temporary" and "permanent" employees also undercut the organizing strength of packinghouse workers. While most packinghouses typically employed over one hundred employees, employers classified a majority of them as "temporary" and "unskilled" workers who could be replaced on a foreman's whim.[47] "I worked seasonal," Lorraine Campos remembered, "but my mom worked full-time because my mom worked there for many, many years." "Seasonal" work, however, often constituted several months, especially in lemon houses where fruit arrived intermittently throughout the year. Consequently, employers maintained a skeleton crew that carried the burden of labor during the slow periods and increased the workforce whenever necessary by tapping a reliable source of semipermanent, family workers. Such arrangements subverted worker solidarity since only a few employees saw themselves as full-time workers. Noting a similar condition among California cannery workers, Vicki Ruiz found that, in 1938, women constituted 72.7 percent of the total labor pool among fruit and vegetable canning operatives, but a full 69.1 percent of these employees held expendable jobs that required no prior experience. Only 3.6 percent of the women employees held positions that required experience of one year or more.[48] Moreover, employers separated "temporary" laborers from experienced workers by placing them on different floors. "Upstairs was just seasonal," Campos recalled, "[but] my mom would work when they needed them to work all the time." She added, "They didn't have a lot of people downstairs, but just what they needed to send out stuff—maybe at the most fifteen people." By limiting contact between a handful of seasoned veterans and the majority of workers, employers reduced the chances of cross-generational and interdepartmental organizing.[49]

Ultimately, ranchers succeeded in squelching labor organizing in citrus packinghouses. Julia Salazar remembered, "There were never any unions." She added, "Everyone was afraid of Switzer [the head foreman]!" Intimidation played a significant role in reducing the chances of labor activism. Threats ranged from on the job harassment to organized vigilante tactics by the Associated Farmers, an anti-union organization heavily supported by the citrus industry and the Los Angeles Chamber of Commerce. On the packinghouse floor, foremen pestered contentious packers by closely inspecting their work habits. At the College Heights Lemon House, for example, packers paid for their successful petition of a 5 cents raise. "Switzer would come and stand where the lemons would come down," Salazar remembered, "and he would stand with his hands like this [hands on her hips] and grab [the packed lemons] and look at them." She added, "If they were not good enough, he would stop the belt and come and show every one of us."[50] Memories of failed strikes during the late 30s and early 40s in Orange, Los Angeles, and Ventura Counties also deterred workers from labor activism. In each of these labor disputes, the Associated Farmers, the Los Angeles Chamber of Commerce, and local law enforcement officials either perpetrated or sanctioned violence against strikers.[51]

The hiring of *braceros* as "temporary" laborers on packinghouse crews added yet another potential source of tension within citrus workforces and communities. Donato Busto, for example, began harvesting beets in Montana and northern California as a contract worker at the young age of 18 in 1942. In 1944, he acquired a contract in La Verne at the Mutual Orange Distributor (MOD) and Sunkist packinghouses. Initially, Bustos loaded trains with ice, but "later," he recalled, "I put fruit into the cars with belts or stack[ed] boxes in the ice room." Although Bustos occasionally picked oranges and lemons in nearby groves, packinghouse foremen became dependent on his services and expanded his duties to nailing lids, labeling, washing, and keeping track of packed boxes for women packers. "I worked nights and days," Bustos remembered, sometimes not leaving his job until three in the morning. Working long hours in close contact with women employees, Bustos eventually met his future wife on the job. In 1946, Donato and Alfonsa Bustos married. That same year Donato registered as a United States resident and terminated his contract with the Mexican government, but he continued to work in La Verne packinghouses through the 1940s and 1950s.[52]

Not all *braceros* experienced the success of Donato Bustos. For many Mexican contract workers, their temporary forays into the Southwest generated hostility and strong feelings of resentment among citrus *colonia* residents. Studying the reception of Mexican nationals by Mexican Americans in Glendora and Azusa, a surprised Carey McWilliams observed: "Oddly enough, [*braceros'*] contacts with the local Mexican communities in California had not been pleasant as many had been called 'scabs,' and 'locals' claimed the Nationals had come to take away their jobs."[53] For many Mexican Americans, *braceros* symbolized a threat to their jobs and their communities.

Intraethnic Conflict and the Bracero Program

Initiated in response to acute labor shortages in agriculture during World War II, the *bracero* program quickly developed into a cornerstone of citrus associations' new system of employment. In 1942 Mexico and the United States signed an agreement that brought thousands of temporary Mexican workers to harvest crops on farms throughout the West and Midwest. Although the governments planned to terminate the program once potential workers returned from the war front, U.S. agribusiness acquired an addiction for the low-cost foreign laborers. By the passage of a series of public laws, agribusiness lobbyists extended the contract system through 1964.[54]

The agreement had a particularly significant impact on agricultural labor in California. Although totals of contract workers varied according to the season and crop, California growers consistently attracted the highest number of *braceros* of all the states participating in the program. For example, among the twenty-four states involved between 1943 and 1947, California drew an average of 54 percent of the total *braceros* that came to the United States.[55] These numbers continued to grow in the postwar period, increasing to 456,000 by 1957, well above the wartime high of 76,184 in 1943. During the 1950s, Mexican nationals represented better than 10 percent of the total seasonal workers hired, but these figures masked many California growers' dependence on *bracero* labor. According to one contemporary observer, "in working certain crops in California . . . braceros represented more than 75 percent of the labor force."[56] *Citrograph* articles and studies of the citrus industry bear this out. "Of 4,203 brought into the country in 1942," a Berkeley researcher observed, "around 1,000 were transferred from sugar beet fields to pick oranges and lemons in the Fillmore (Ventura County), Whittier, Redlands, and Los Angeles districts." *Citrograph* authors confirmed the importance of the program to the industry, reporting that Mexican nationals performed 60 percent of all picking in 1945. By 1946, *braceros* constituted around 13,000 of the workforce in California citrus groves, or 80 percent of all pickers.[57]

According to the bilateral agreement, employers guaranteed Mexican nationals a wage of 30 cents per hour and were required to pay at or above the standard wage in a given region, a restriction adopted to prevent the replacement of local workers. In practice, *braceros* routinely earned less than what their contracts promised, but more than what they received for the same work in Mexico. For example, in the citrus orchards of Cucamonga, the prevailing wage averaged 70 cents per hour during the war years. By 1958, the hourly wage for Mexican American workers rose slightly to between 80 cents and $1, depending on the season, but employers often paid *braceros* between 10 and 15 cents less than their local coworkers. By the end of the season, local workers earned an average weekly gross income of $43.20 compared with $38.40 for *braceros*. Interviews with twenty-five *braceros* conducted by Claremont Graduate School student Daniel Martínez during the mid-1950s revealed that Mexican nationals worked at a piece rate instead of an hourly rate and did not earn the standard wages for local employees until late in the season. With deductions for room and board included, *braceros* stood to earn a net total of $20.10 per week in 1940. Although low by U.S. standards, earnings compared favorably to the average annual income of the typical worker in Mexico. During the same year, a Mexican laborer earned approximately 340 pesos per year, which amounted to roughly $40. Given the wide discrepancy between wages in Mexico and the

United States, Mexican nationals rarely complained of the exploitative conditions on California farms.[58]

In spite of better wages in the United States, *braceros* incurred many expenses that cut substantially into their profits. In particular, Mexican nationals resented the bribes or *mordida* (literally meaning "bite") many had to pay Mexican officials to be considered for the program. Although illegal under the formal agreement, standard practice dictated that potential *braceros* render between 150 and 300 pesos to agents in Mexico to initiate the process. Once they arrived, Mexican nationals had to purchase clothing and equipment and pay rent with the more expensive U.S. currency. *Braceros* living in the Cucamonga camp, for example, paid $12.50 per week for room and board, and had approximately 10 percent of their earnings deducted from each paycheck for nonoccupational insurance negotiated for them by the Mexican government. At the conclusion of their contracts, *braceros* could recoup some of this money, though the Mexican government required them to return to Mexico to collect their checks.[59]

Many *braceros* supported their families back in Mexico at a much lower cost than local Mexican American workers. During World War II, a Mexican national could support his entire family in Mexico with as little as $10 a month. Conversely, monthly expenditures for local Mexican Americans averaged $20 for rent, $13 for utilities, $10 for transportation, $10 for clothing, $10 for leisure time, $5 for medical care, and $10 for miscellaneous items. Moreover, increases in food prices during World War II pushed the monthly cost of maintaining a family of seven children from $40 at the beginning of the war to $80 by its end. The exorbitant cost of living also provided added incentive for married Mexican women to break with tradition and enter the workforce. Furthermore, Mexican nationals enjoyed the security of a guaranteed full-time job under the agreement while Mexican American workers could be laid off at a moment's notice.[60]

Wage differentials and unequal competition for jobs resulted in strong feelings of resentment toward *braceros* among Mexican American men. Interviewing local men from the Cucamonga barrio "Northtown" in 1957, Daniel Martínez found that a majority "strongly opposed the bracero program and any additional program of [its] type." Martínez observed, "[Mexican American men] felt that the braceros took jobs away from them, as well as lowered wages in the area, or at least kept them at the same level year after year."[61] Donato Bustos described the intraethnic tension, recalling that "[Mexican American men] didn't like us because we came to take the jobs away from them." Working alongside *braceros* in the La Verne orange groves, Frank Hernández recalled that Mexican Americans and Mexican nationals occasionally "tangled" over the best picking assignments and methods of picking. "Braceros were difficult," remembered Hernández, "because they picked it their way [and] they were not careful." He added, "braceros would get a bike and start picking before the sun came up." Angry Mexican American pickers objected to such behavior since early-rising *braceros* got to the highest-yielding trees first and made locals look lazy. Similarly, Julia Salazar commented that her husband, Roman, a foreman for the College Heights Lemon Association, routinely settled conflicts between Mexican Americans and *braceros* in the groves. "Once in awhile," Salazar recalled, "Roman would say that [a bracero] would get irritated because the one from here [Mexican American] would be telling him that he was [picking] wrong." Occasionally, fights erupted into violent confrontations. "Sometimes [braceros] would pull out knives!," Salazar recalled. She added, "my brother-in-law, Cuco, told Roman that one time [a *bracero*] even chased him with a knife because he was backing the one from here [a Mexican American]."[62]

Former *bracero* Donato Bustos, however, objected to characterizations of Mexican contract workers as a burden on the Mexican American community. "We made the wages go up," Bustos asserted, "because when I started in Redlands picking oranges, they paid us 6 cents a box." Unable to pay their rent, Bustos and his fellow *braceros* initiated a strike to improve wages for all workers in the groves. He recalled:

> I picked twenty-eight boxes the first day [and] I couldn't pay my rent! And then, pretty soon we started a strike. . . . One day we didn't want to pick, they took us to the grove and we didn't pick. We went out of the grove and told the other guys [Mexican Americans] to go out to raise the price. They [said they] didn't want to walk out because of the Depression and they wouldn't give us our jobs [back] and this and that. . . . So, we told the driver to take us to the camp and he [a Mexican American] didn't want to. So we walked all day to the camp.[63]

Despite the lack of solidarity among Mexican Americans and Mexican nationals, the *bracero* strike forced the local growers association to boost the rate per box to 14 cents by the end of the 1943 navel season. Although such a strike made some employers question the use of potentially militant *braceros*, for the most part, wage differentials between Mexican nationals and locals encouraged many growers to continue supporting the program.[64]

Bustos also claimed that Mexican Americans, not *braceros*, initiated most intraethnic conflict between the two groups. "[Mexican Americans] didn't like [*braceros*] because they were outsiders," he recalled. "Braceros usually went out in a group," Bustos added, "because otherwise . . . sometimes they beat us."[65] The doctor for the Cucamonga and San Antonio *bracero* camps, Walter W. Wood, reported that during the height of the program, he treated from eight to ten *braceros* weekly for injuries received in fights with locals. Work conditions informed much of the intraethnic conflict; however, contemporary observers also noted another source of tension: competition for Mexican American female companions in the local *colonias*. Citing the report of local judge William B. Hutton, Daniel Martínez summarized, "during the period from 1944 to 1946 eight to twelve men, braceros and locals, appeared before the Cucamonga District Court every Monday morning on knifing or shooting charges resulting from friction over local girls or employment."[66] This conflict became particularly acute after World War II when Mexican American male populations increased with the return of soldiers.

Conditions of life and labor in the *colonia* and the structure of the *bracero* program also contributed to the tension. The fluidity of *braceros'* lives, traveling back and forth between Mexico and the United States, raised Mexican American suspicions about the intentions of Mexican nationals. For example, Alfonsa Bustos commented that initially her family did not like her dating Donato because, as she explained, "they thought he was going to take me to Mexico." Alfonsa put their fears to rest by informing Donato that she would not live in Mexico under any circumstances. Others worried that Mexican nationals courted Mexican American women for sexual gratification and casual relationships that lasted only as long as their contracts. For example, the Mexican and U.S. governments inadvertently intervened in many interpersonal relationships when the program temporarily withdrew Mexican nationals at the end of World War II. Although lacking a precise number, Martínez reported, "many of these local girls were left with children," a situation, he claimed, outraged their families and confirmed Mexican American misgivings about *braceros*.[67]

Many Mexican American parents objected to marriages between Mexican nationals and their Mexican American daughters because they believed that *braceros* entered into such unions for the sole purpose of attaining U.S. citizenship. Such marriages of convenience concerned Julia Salazar, who commented: "Some [Mexican American women] would not be so lucky. They would find out that [their *bracero* husbands] were married in Mexico and all [*braceros*] wanted was to get their visas or whatever."[68] Martínez found similar attitudes among seven Mexican American women who married or had lived with Mexican contract workers in Cucamonga's Northtown barrio. "All seven," he reported, "shared the opinion that the braceros were just opportunists seeking a way to remain in the United States and marriage was the easiest way for them to gain this end." One woman who failed to give her name reported that she had had three children with a *bracero* as his common law wife. Despite having eventually married, the couple was separated when the U.S. government deported her husband once he finished his contract. She then spent her life savings on lawyers to prove that they had, in fact, married and that he should be allowed to return to the United States. After two months of living with the family, her husband left them for a high-paying job in downtown Los Angeles. Although she attained a court order requiring him to pay child support, at the time of the interview the woman had not received any money from her estranged husband for over six months.[69]

Selling work clothes to *braceros* for the local retailer Miller's Outpost and hosting weekend dances at local ballrooms during the 1950s, Candelario Mendoza witnessed exchanges between Mexican contract workers and Mexican American women. He explained: "[*Braceros*] would talk to some of the chavalas (young Mexican American women) that they used to see around the barrio here, and I think that was part of the animosity. The fact that they were wooing some of the available gals—perhaps already involved with somebody else or someone was looking at them—and these guys [*braceros*] were pretty glib."[70]

According to Mendoza, Mexican American men resented Mexican nationals since *braceros* performed their "verbal love-making" in Spanish, an ability that many acculturated locals no longer possessed. Julia Salazar concurred, recalling "at dances, [Mexican American men and *braceros*] used to fight." Many conflicts began when *braceros* approached wives and girlfriends of Mexican American men for a whirl on the dance floor. "Some of the men from here don't like just anyone to go get [their] wife and pull her out to dance," Salazar commented. She added, "[*braceros*] thought anybody could dance, you know, with anybody here." For Salazar and other married local women, "braceros were too forward; they thought they were a gift to women from god!"[71]

Often, however, romance between *braceros* and Mexican American women did not result in the tragic endings feared by parents of Mexican American youth. Julia Salazar and Candelario Mendoza recalled a number of these marriages that survived the initial culture shock and stood the test of time. Donato Bustos, for example, respected the wishes of his fiancée, Alfonsa, to remain in the United States, and "skipped" his contract to start a new life. Soon after their wedding, the Bustos rented a house for Alfonsa's entire family. Eventually, the couple purchased a house in the La Verne barrio where they have lived since 1945.

The relative autonomy of a new generation of Mexican American women provided them the freedom to make their own decisions about whom they should and should not date. When asked whether women from the barrios courted *braceros*, Mendoza commented "oh yeah . . . I think love supersedes almost any obstacles!"[72] Donato Bustos concurred, recalling that some wives of servicemen began dating *braceros* in their husband's absence. "When they were left alone," he recalled, "they got with *braceros*."[73] As Douglas Monroy has argued, employment "facilitated greater freedom of activity and more assertiveness in the family for Mexicanas." Similarly, Vicki Ruiz and Mary Odem have demonstrated how employment provided Mexican American women the means and confidence to participate in an expanding consumer culture that included public entertainment.[74]

Daniel Martínez observed that such intraethnic/intercultural courtship came at a high price, remarking that often, women who dated or married Mexican nationals "were ostracized by the community as well as by their families." Women with children who had been abandoned by *braceros* received particularly harsh treatment at the hands of local residents. In need of a job to support their families, some of these women sought employment as prostitutes in bars designated for Mexican nationals. Bar owners took advantage of their situation, for as one proprietor explained, "Since they have become outcasts in the community for associating with *braceros*, this is the only type of work they can find." The bar owner tried to justify his actions, explaining that "the *braceros* would look for [women] anyway so why not provide them with the companions in a place where they could not get into trouble with the locals and at the same time be protected from being 'rolled' (robbed and beaten while under the influence of alcohol)?" The proprietor saw his business as a service to "the nicer girls from the community" since *braceros* would not be as inclined to seek them out for dates when they had plenty of opportunities to meet "outcasts" in the bar. The prevalence of prostitution within these drinking establishments, however, influenced the attitudes of many locals who questioned the morality of any Mexican American woman seen publicly with a Mexican national.[75]

In spite of attempts to keep locals and Mexican nationals separate, conflicts often came to a head in the vice-ridden bar districts located in areas adjacent to *bracero* camps and Mexican American *colonias*. In Cucamonga's Northtown, for example, business from young, local men, some Mexican American women, and Mexican nationals supported six bars that provided a lively nightlife on the weekends.[76] Captain Mayer of the San Bernardino County Sheriff's Department and Cucamonga constable Oscar Raven reported a consistent escalation of crime and violence in the area since World War II, attributing most of the problems to unemployment, prostitution, and juvenile delinquency. Neither official, however, felt inclined to remedy the situation, since both believed "there is very little that can be done until the residents themselves try to do something about it." Quite often, law enforcement authorities were slow to respond to conflicts due to their distance from these outlying areas and a pervasive attitude of apathy and neglect. Cucamonga's Judge Hutton reflected the true feelings of many local officials when he explained, "[I] personally do not think that the residents of Northtown know the meaning of the word morals; otherwise they would try to clean up their own mess." Managers and doctors in charge of *bracero* camps occasionally exhibited similar prejudices and were equally disinclined to intervene during moments of social conflict. For example, Doctor Baro, a physician serving a camp in Irwindale allegedly told Daniel Martínez that he believed very little could be done to solve the problems associated with Mexican nationals since "all the braceros have an I.Q. of a one year old."[77]

Intraethnic tension between Mexican Americans and Mexican nationals reached a boiling point on April 19, 1952, when four Mexican American youths murdered Ricardo Mancilla Gómez, a *bracero* employed in the Cucamonga area. The tragic death of the twenty-two-year-old Gómez typified a season of growing violence in which one other Mexican national, Magdaleno Cornejo, had been killed and several others beaten. Reported as an "assassination" in the Pomona Valley newspaper *El Espectador*, the "cold blooded" killing disturbed Ignacio "Nacho" López, a local defender of Mexican American civil rights and co-owner of the Spanish-language weekly. Lamenting that Gómez's death had come "at the hands of brothers of the same race," López editorialized that if such murders continued, "El México de Afuera" (México of the Exterior) will exterminate the "México de Adentro" (México of the Interior). He blamed the mistreatment of *braceros* (whom he called "ambassadors in overalls") on the moral deprivation of young Mexican American *valientes* (bullies) corrupted by ignorance, vice, and the spiritual decay of a country living in the shadow of the atomic bomb attacks on Hiroshima and Nagasaki, Japan. According to López, a government capable of killing millions with a single bomb shared some of the responsibility for creating "a morbid psychosis in society at large."[78]

Reports that Gómez's underage assailants — Manuel Fierro, Frank Mendoza, Felix Montoya, and Sabiel Mayo — had been smoking marijuana and drinking at the Cucamonga cantina "La Cita" re-ignited moral panic over juvenile delinquency among minority youth. Sharing the concerns of a generation of educated Mexican Americans who came of age just prior to World War II, López worried that many young Mexican men had forsaken education for a lifestyle of "hoodlumism." During the 1940s, López became an outspoken critic of zootsuiters whom he regarded as "pachuco miscreants" that inspired prejudicial attitudes among Anglos toward all Mexican Americans.[79] Yet, unlike the Los Angeles County Sheriff's Department who attributed the problem of Mexican American juvenile delinquency to the "inherent vicious[ness]" of all Mexicans, López believed that the roots of "El Pachuquismo" were "deeply entrenched in the economic and social discrimination practices inflicted on minorities by the dominant groups of our nation." Consequently, although Mexican American critics like López blamed youth for the violence against *braceros*, they identified the larger societal problems of racism and warfare rather than the biological proclivities of the Mexican race as the origin of such delinquency.[80]

In response to the murder, Mexican consuls Salvador Duhart of Los Angeles and Roberto Urrea of San Bernardino immediately withdrew 178 Mexican contract workers from Cucamonga and announced the suspension of the *bracero* programs throughout the Pomona Valley. Acknowledging that the murder was not an isolated incident but rather part of a larger trend, Duhart expressed outrage at the "repeated abuses against our braceros that have been the motive [for the suspension]." Deliveries of workers, they concluded, would not resume until all possible measures had been taken to correct the problem of violence against Mexican nationals.[81] In all, Mexico recalled over 500 contract workers from the Southern California Farmers Association, the primary distributor of *braceros* in the Pomona Valley. Many *braceros* expressed their support of the consulate's decision in a letter signed by 123 coworkers of Ricardo Gómez asking for the immediate termination of their contracts.[82]

The Mexican government's actions precipitated a community-wide conversation held at the local elementary school that revealed many of the social and economic tensions created by the *bracero* program. Not surprisingly, local ranchers expressed their disappointment over the loss of Mexican contract laborers and promised to exercise their political influence to bring about the reinstatement of the program for the Pomona Valley. Mexican Americans were less unified in their response to Mexico's actions since defining "the community interest" had become a complicated matter in the ten years leading up to the crisis. The Southern California Farmers Association encouraged the marginalization of Mexican nationals by placing work camps on the outskirts of towns near Mexican American *colonias*. Some Mexican American merchants and business owners took advantage of this arrangement by setting up shops and establishing bars that catered mainly to the Mexican contract workers. Although *bracero* patronage benefited a few middle-class Mexican *comerciantes*, the working-class majority of Mexican Americans opposed the program on the grounds that the presence of Mexican nationals created unfair competition in the workplace and inspired violence and vice in their community.[83]

Siding with the majority, López became the mouthpiece for aggrieved Cucamonga residents. Affixing blame to contracting agents, government officials, and local bar owners for the crisis, López also reported that the meeting produced a "plan of action" that prescribed a tentative solution to the intraethnic violence. A majority of the 150 participants expressed a desire for camp managers and law enforcement officials to enforce the separation of young Mexican American men and *braceros* upon the return of Mexican nationals. In spite of strong objections to the program, López conceded its eventual reinstatement given the significant political influence of ranchers. Instead, López saved his harshest criticism for profit-driven bar owners who, he explained, "have let loose a plague on the good citizens of Cucamonga." Alarmed by escalating violence in the bar districts of Northtown, López and other meeting participants called for a unified community movement to clean up Cucamonga by making it more difficult for irresponsible proprietors to acquire liquor licenses. López argued that only pressure from concerned citizens could alter the ethics of bar owners whom he called "ostriches hiding their heads in the corrupt sand."[84]

By early August 1952, growers successfully petitioned for the return of the *braceros* to the Pomona Valley. Between April and August, López and local leaders joined together to produce a list of seven recommendations that encompassed the complete concerns of Northtown residents. In his weekly column "Marginal," López offered the following suggestions to returning Mexican nationals: they should dedicate themselves completely to their work; they should avoid, as much as possible, bar fights; they should respect the private property and dignity of locals; they should avoid personal friction that could lead to tragedy; they should establish cordial relations with local families and all their members; they should always demand employment conditions and salaries equal to that of domestic workers; and they should avoid displacing local workers in their jobs. Following up on his initial concerns of juvenile delinquency, López also issued a separate warning to parents and young people about the spread of alcoholism among youth in Cucamonga.

The list went beyond the blame game previously played by López and local leaders to confront the larger social and economic problems associated with the *bracero* program. In particular the last two suggestions addressed the issue of job competition and the program's negative impact on wages and job security for local Mexican Americans. López, despite his middle-class background, shared the concerns of working-class Mexican Americans. He supported the AFL and

CIO's opposition to the bilateral agreement and questioned why Mexico, with its rich agricultural lands, could not develop a program to sustain rural life in the Mexican countryside. Anticipating observations made by current scholars on the subject, López further argued that the *bracero* program prompted "illegal immigration" by creating an "obsession" among all Mexicans to "cross the Rio Bravo" for work.[85] In another editorial he likened the conflict of the "Mexican brothers" (*braceros* and Mexican Americans) to the biblical story of Cain and Abel. Coming down squarely on the side of local laborers, López pointedly argued, "field workers of this country must have primacy over those other elements—even in the sad case when these elements are of our same race and language."[86]

Aimed at Mexican nationals, López's recommendations sought to curb *bracero* behavior while marking the domain of Mexican Americans, particularly the social spaces occupied by men. The language of López's editorials positioned Mexican nationals as eternal outsiders whose place in society could be accepted only after their acquiescence to rights and privileges that belong first and foremost to Mexican Americans. Moreover, requests for *braceros* to respect the dignity, personal property, and families of locals allude to the *braceros'* marginality. Given that most physical assaults had been perpetrated against, not by *braceros*, and that theft did not constitute a major source of tension between the two groups, such vague references left much room for interpretation. For example, one could speculate that the coded message communicated to Mexican nationals by López meant that Mexican American men assumed ownership and privileges over "their" women just as they assumed access to "their" jobs. Furthermore, his recommendation that *braceros* "dedicate themselves completely to their work" conveyed the hope that Mexican nationals would remain singularly focused on their jobs and not seek diversions with local women in *colonia* bars and pool halls, and at public dances.

Ultimately, community efforts to revise the *bracero* program and clean up vice districts garnered only symbolic reforms from local law enforcement officials and ranchers. In the wake of the Gómez tragedy, Cucamonga sheriff Charles Jones promised to reduce disorder in Northtown, while the contracting agency, the Agricultural Association of Southern California, assigned a new camp director, Ray Orton, to oversee improvements and foster better public relations with the community. Orton addressed Mexican American concerns that *braceros* would be used to replace local workers by stating, "in the first place it is prohibited by the terms of the signed agreement, and in the second, this was not the intention of local ranchers." Nevertheless, many Cucamonga residents interviewed by Daniel Martínez in 1957 continued to cite wage differences between Mexican nationals and local workers and blamed the *bracero* program for the loss of jobs and a steady decline in pay.[87] Moreover, the problems of violence continued to simmer in bars and pool halls throughout the region. In 1957, for example, a group of Mexican American men stripped and robbed *bracero* Pedro Carrillo in Pomona after offering him a ride back to his camp located in Montclair. Three years later, another bar fight in Cucamonga between three Mexican American men and a Mexican national resulted in the murder of *bracero* José Gómez Trejo.[88] Although these occasional robberies, beatings, and killings of *baceros* hardly constituted a pattern, such incidents are indicative of simmering resentments and tensions as the program entered its third decade of operation.

The citrus growers' postwar system of employment received a fatal blow on December 31, 1964, when civil rights advocates and labor organizations turned public opinion strongly against the *bracero* program and forced Congress to formally end Mexican contract labor in the United States. By that time, however, growers had discovered a new source of labor impervious to fluctuations in international relations: undocumented Mexican labor. As López had observed in 1952, the *bracero* program contributed to the expansion of immigration flows from Mexico during the postwar period. Between 1940 and 1943, the U.S. Immigration and Naturalization Service (INS) reported apprehending an annual average of 7,023 undocumented migrants; but that number rose rapidly to 29,176 in 1944. Three years later, apprehensions reached nearly 200,000, prompting INS officials to declare a war on immigration from Mexico in the form of "Operation Wetback."[89] In spite of aggressive policing at the border and neighborhood sweeps in Mexican American neighborhoods, undocumented immigrants continued to come to the United States enticed by agribusiness employers. According to labor activist and immigration scholar Ernesto Galarza, growers regarded *indocumentados* not only as an alternative source of labor to *braceros* but also as more skilled workers than their fellow Mexican nationals. Galarza explained:

> *Braceros found the Wetbacks as anxious to please as they were willing to endure. From among them the employer selected the more able workers for tasks requiring skill, such as irrigating and truck driving. They became differentiated from the common run of illegals, serving in specialized operations and becoming* stable, regular *employees. The employer would make unusual efforts to keep them and to arrange for their return if by chance they were picked up by the Border Patrol. (emphasis added)*[90]

Referred to as "specials" by employers, these undocumented laborers rose above the status of *bracero* or "stoop laborer" to become essential members of the agricultural labor force. Daniel Martínez noted this same trend in the Pomona Valley when he discovered that "many farmers preferred 'wetbacks' to locals *or* braceros mainly because the wetbacks worked twice as hard for half the pay." [91]

Indocumentados presented agricultural employers with several advantages over *braceros*. Unlike Mexican contract workers whose limited work certifications required them to be replaced at regular intervals, undocumented workers could remain in their positions as long as employers wished them to stay. The longer job tenure allowed *indocumentados* to acquire skills that elevated them above the average farmworker and made them indispensable to many ranchers. Indeed, such advantages inspired many *braceros* simply to "skip" their contracts and become undocumented workers. [92]

Equally important, the ideology and practice of citizenship pursued by labor and civil rights groups inadvertently laid the foundations for the post-*bracero* labor system. Civil rights leaders like Ignacio López and labor organizations like the AFL and CIO forged a unified front against the Mexican contract system by calling for rights and privileges for citizens of the United States. Although demands for citizenship rights helped end the *bracero* program, they also drew the line of membership around a national community that accentuated the differences between members and nonmembers. This line of inclusion/exclusion cut at right angles against potential class and ethnic solidarity, and ultimately helped increase the vulnerability of those at the bottom of the community: initially *braceros*, and eventually undocumented workers. Uneven economic development between Mexico and the United States and the lack of entitlements for noncitizen workers under the welfare state denied *indocumentados* a "safety net" and forced many to seek low-paid agricultural jobs typically reserved for *braceros* and resident Mexican workers. Furthermore, in spite of achieving skills that garnered pay raises for citizen workers, the political vulnerability of undocumented laborers (for example, fear of deportation) prevented them from either petitioning for state regulation or pursuing collective bargaining with their employers. Presented with few alternatives, undocumented workers toiled silently, remaining active in the U.S. workforce at high levels of productivity in order to survive. [93]

Transformations in the regional economy, however, mitigated the extent to which this post-*bracero* system of employment affected citrus ranching in Greater Los Angeles. As the scholarship of Richard Lillard and, more recently, Mike Davis demonstrates, during the 1950s and 1960s Los Angeles County supervisors and real estate developers transformed the "garden metropolis" into one continuous suburban jungle linked together by ribbons of freeways.[94] Witnessing the transformation firsthand, Daniel Martínez noted that discussions of how Mexican Americans could reclaim citrus jobs from *braceros* and *indocumentados* had largely become irrelevant by the late 1950s since many of the groves in the San Gabriel Valley had given way to housing subdivisions. In Los Angeles County alone, between 1936 and 1956 the total acreage of orange ranches dropped from 45,000 to only 18,000. In 1958, the Agricultural Department of the Los Angeles Chamber of Commerce reported that, since the peak year of 1942, 145,949 acres or 54 percent of agricultural land in the Los Angeles metropolitan area had been plowed under for housing projects, while the Regional Planning Commission of Los Angeles County predicted the loss of an additional 11,000 acres over each of the next twenty years to the postwar population boom.[95]

Although these transformations had an immediate impact on pickers, packinghouse employees also experienced job relocation or early retirement. As developers uprooted citrus groves throughout the Los Angeles basin, packinghouses consolidated operations in houses further east and north where citrus continued to form the basis of local economies. For example, during the mid-1950s, Julia Salazar recalled that College Heights Packinghouse began to handle fruit that had formerly been packed at smaller houses west of Claremont. By 1971, however, suburbanization had significantly encroached upon the Claremont area, forcing Sunkist to close College Heights and consolidate packing operations at larger packinghouses in Corona and Arlington (Riverside). "They had closed and they were sending the girls out," Salazar remembered. She continued, "Cencha got to go to Arlington, but I didn't; I went to Covina to work up there."[96] Relocation broke up the networks established among packers and undermined the job security many workers had cultivated over several years. For Salazar and Campos, the move made packinghouse work less convenient and more expensive, as both now had to commute long distances to their jobs. Consequently, both pursued other positions outside the citrus industry.[97]

Wage labor helped break down some of the bonds of the familial oligarchy for many Mexican American women who came of age between the Great Depression and the postwar period. By contributing to the family income, women gained some control over their own lives and claimed privileges and public space formerly restricted to men. After World War II, for example, the practice of chaperonage declined as employed women now "[went] out with the girls" to dances where they met young men.[98] In terms of dating, women's insistence on choosing their own partners occasionally produced conflict within the *colonias*, but more often it led to a vibrant social life among young Mexican Americans. The participation of women at public events influenced some entrepreneurs to create entertainment options that appealed to men *and* women. Seeking to take advantage of these young consumers, some business-minded residents began dances in downtown ballrooms and auditoriums throughout the citrus belt as an alternative to the bar districts. Set within an expanding, multicultural, suburban environment, these dances facilitated the emergence of intercultural exchange and broke down some of the barriers between white and minority youths in Southern California. In the following chapter, I explore the history of two citrus belt dance halls, Pomona's Rainbow Gardens and El Monte American Legion Stadium that characterized the kind of cultural convergence and exchange extant among a new generation of Angelenos.

Memories of El Monte

Dance Halls and Youth Culture in Greater Los Angeles, 1950–1974

With great anticipation, the staff at Rainbow Gardens, Pomona's famed dance palace, prepared for another night of ballroom dancing in 1950. This evening's dance, however, differed substantially from any other function held by the club since its opening in the mid-1940s. For one, concerts usually occurred only on the weekends at Rainbow; this event was happening on a Wednesday. Second, and perhaps most noticeable, this evening's attraction drew Mexican Americans, not the white patrons who usually frequented the establishment.

"You're gonna lose your shirt," cautioned the wary owner, Gertie Thomas, to a young, confident local disc jockey, Candelario Mendoza.[1] Mendoza, who had taken over a regional Mexican radio program in August 1949, understood the potential of hosting Latin American music concerts in the Pomona Valley. Spinning the latest Mexican, Cuban, Puerto Rican, and Mexican American tunes from 5:00 A.M. to 7:00 A.M., Mendoza developed a loyal listening audience from among the many Mexican citrus workers and their families laboring in the groves extending east from Los Angeles. As a former *rata* (a name given to children who picked citrus) and a resident of the barrio, he had a genuine connection to the community. Moreover, as a radio personality "connected" to performers and their managers, he knew that many Latin American *orquestas* and Mexican American *conjunto* bands frequently passed through Southern California.

Still, Gertie and Ray Thomas, owners and operators of Rainbow Gardens, had little confidence that a mid-week dance could make a profit. Fearing imminent failure, the Thomases opened only one of three bars, scheduled just one security guard and a few waitresses, and permitted Mendoza to use the facilities without charge. Mendoza graciously accepted their gift and proceeded to advertise the event on his radio program.

As a large crowd of Mexican Americans began to gather in front of the door, Gertie Thomas immediately realized she had underestimated both the number of Mexican people living in Pomona Valley and the drawing power of Latin American music.[2] Beto Villa, the popular *Tejano* bandleader, Rainbow's first Latin American act, drew over 750 people that evening. Frantically, Gertie Thomas called in all available employees to work while Mendoza served as emcee. Admitting later her error, Gertie Thomas told Mendoza, "How can this be? Who is this guy that you are bringing? He must be the greatest around. I cannot even get that many people to come in and see Les Brown, Harry James, or even Count Basie on a Saturday night."[3] A new era for Latin American music had begun in the San Gabriel Valley.

The emergence of Rainbow Gardens as a venue for Latin American music represented the beginnings of a re-negotiation of public space in Southern California during the 1950s. Consisting primarily of Mexican Americans and whites, but also African Americans and Asian Americans/Pacific Islanders, Southland communities engaged in a degree of intercultural communication that increased over time. In this chapter I evaluate this evolutionary process through the interethnic history of two dance halls: Pomona's Rainbow Gardens and El Monte's American Legion Stadium. Following the leads of Steven Loza and George Lipsitz, I treat music and dance of the 1950s and 1960s as cultural forms that expressed much of the intercultural conflict, exchange, and convergence prevalent in Southern California society.[4] To their studies I hope to contribute an understanding of the geographic, aesthetic, and cultural importance of the dance halls in the creation of this predominantly youth-oriented culture.

The emergence of a culturally hybridized music and dance culture depended on the unique "multi-nucleated" physical and cultural geography of Greater Los Angeles. As suburbanization reshaped the citrus belt during the postwar period, the construction of parkways and freeways, residential segregation, and the popularity of radio and television continued to transform the spatial relations among an expanding population of Angelenos. While physical, economic, and social structures of inequality segregated Mexican Americans and other racialized minorities, their historical presence, employment, and resistance provided the potential for a transformation in Southland race relations. The parkways and freeways, for example, destroyed and divided existing barrios toward the urban core. As Eric Avila and Raúl Homero Villa have demonstrated, however, many Chicana/Chicano artists and writers regarded the freeway as a polysemic structure that has often been a canvas for critical art or a means to get beyond the barrio, even as it has been a wall dividing communities.[5] For Mexican Americans living beyond the urban barrios but within the orbit of metropolitan Los Angeles, the freeways and parkways reinforced old links between them and communities formerly accessible primarily by the interurban railway. Their determination to claim equal access to public space, their manipulation of Greater Los Angeles's unique physical and cultural geography, and their preservation of distinctive cultural forms contributed to the ongoing social development of Southern California.

Demographic and economic changes during the 1950s also influenced the creation of multiethnic and multiracial dance halls. The postwar "baby boom" produced a youth market that forced business owners to focus their attention on forms of entertainment that catered to these new consumers. Although occupational and social inequalities continued to divide youths along racial, class, and gender lines, the relative prosperity of the 1950s provided a new generation of Angelenos the opportunity to break out of their segregated worlds for an evening and share in a public culture influenced by young people. In these marginal spaces emerged a multiracial youth culture that challenged the accepted social relations in Greater Los Angeles.

Although spontaneous music and dance events occurred throughout Southern California in church halls, local armory auditoriums, and high school gymnasiums, a few men and women involved in the burgeoning music industry invested in night clubs and ballrooms and promoted regular weekly dances in "civic" buildings. These institutions, to name just a few, included Los Angeles's Palladium and Zenda Ballroom, East LA's Paramount Ballroom, Long Beach Municipal Auditorium, Fullerton's Rhythm Room, San Bernardino's Orange Show and Valley Ballroom, El Monte's American Legion Stadium, and Pomona's Rainbow Gardens.[6] I have chosen to focus on the last two establishments, Rainbow Gardens and the American Legion Stadium, as a vehicle for analyzing musical importation and hybridization in Greater Los Angeles because their stories represent the kind of cultural transference, transformation, and creation that took place in the Los Angeles suburbs (or "hinterlands") between World War II and the student movements of the late 1960s.

Rainbow Gardens

Prior to 1950, Rainbow Gardens had an established reputation as one of the few premier venues for big band music in Southern California. Euroamerican bandleaders and personalities such as Harry James, Les Brown, Perry Como, Lou Costello, and Pat O'Brien performed frequently at Rainbow Gardens. In addition, although rarely a black or brown face appeared in the audience, the great Count Basie transcended barriers of racial discrimination and exhibited his talents as one of the most revered bandleaders of the period. Latinos, although experiencing a significant musical renaissance of their own, did not appear at Rainbow Gardens as either audience members, or performers.[7] In fact, when asked whether Mexican Americans attended Rainbow Gardens' dances in the 1940s, Cande Mendoza commented: "Oh, no. Absolutely not. In fact, and I hesitate to say this, but I think that even before then a Mexican American had to be *extremely* well dressed and not even look too much like a Mexican in order to get into Rainbow Gardens on a Saturday night [with the white bands]. It just was one of those things. It was a sign of our times, at that time, when discrimination was still there."[8]

In spite of this discrimination, Latin American music from both sides of the border emanated throughout the *colonias* and work camps of the citrus belt via radio. Corresponding with the least valuable airtime, and coincidentally, with the time many Mexican agricultural laborers went to work, Mexican disc jockeys inhabited the early morning hours of predominantly English-language radio stations with Latin American music programs. This allowed many Mexican Americans to stay abreast of the various trends in Latin American music emanating from Mexico, Cuba, Puerto Rico, New York, and the American Southwest. Exposure to folk, *conjunto*, *norteño*, and *orquesta* music established continuity with the past, while familiarizing local populations with contemporary Latin American music played throughout the Americas.[9]

For Mexican workers, the music helped prepare them for a day of strenuous labor. By singing many of the songs on the job, some continued the music on their own after the radio stations had returned to their English-language, big band format. "We used to sing until somebody would come out and tell us to shut up," commented Alvino Aguilera. Paco Castellano, a former La Verne picker, remembered: "we would have two or three singers in the orchards so when one tired, the other would take his place. We had to have fun. Otherwise the work would get too monotonous."[10]

Outside of work, the exposure to Latin American music inspired the formation of many local bands, dance clubs, and theater groups. In addition to Claremont's more formal Padua Hills Theatre, designed primarily to entertain white audiences with Mexican folkloric performances, Mexican Americans also participated in various grassroots cultural events and dances held within the barrios of Pomona Valley. Paco Castellano, a performer both at Padua Hills and in his own band, stated, "there were bands and groups everywhere."[11]

Many Mexican Americans of the citrus belt recognized Cande Mendoza as the central figure in promoting this music. Like Paco Castellano and many other local Mexican youths, he too had worked briefly at Padua Hills. His presence on the radio, however, made Mendoza a household name in the *colonias* throughout the San Gabriel and Pomona Valleys. And, as Pomona's first Mexican elementary schoolteacher by day, people came to know Cande Mendoza not as a distant radio personality, but rather as an approachable role model for the community.

Soon after Beto Villa's appearance at Rainbow Gardens, Gertie and Ray Thomas made Mendoza the permanent music consultant, booking manager, and emcee at the club. This role added substantially to his fame, and extended his influence over a broader range of music and geography. As the appeal of big band styles waned in the late 1940s and audiences began to shrink, the Thomases voluntarily handed over the operations to Mendoza in hopes of boosting business. Although Mendoza mixed Anglo acts with Latin American bands, once Mexican Americans began to frequent the club, whites ceased to patronize Rainbow Gardens. According to Cande Mendoza, "[Latin American] music should have had a cross-cultural appeal," especially since many Latin American recording artists garnered Anglo favor through their exposure on the national weekly radio show "The Lucky Strike Hit Parade."[12]

Mendoza later reflected on Rainbow Garden's incarnation as a predominantly Latino Club: "I don't think the Anglo population knew or cared about Rainbow Gardens. They ignored it, but didn't fight it."[13] The Thomases' "careful" handling of the business probably had much to do with its marginal acceptance into the community. For example, in order to avoid any reasons for public opposition, the Thomases employed an army of predawn workers to clean up within a radius of several blocks of the ballroom's downtown location. Such "rituals" successfully averted any problems with a white-run city government.

Within Rainbow Gardens, Cande Mendoza earnestly worked to establish the club as one of Southern California's premier ballrooms for Latin American music. Notable entertainers and musicians such as Beto Villa, María Victoria, Luis Arcaráz, Ray Touzet, Lola Beltrán, Tito Puente, Tín Tan, and Dámaso Pérez Prado made Rainbow a major stopping place in their touring schedules during the 1950s and 1960s. Located on the route between Los Angeles and Las Vegas, many of these performers found Pomona to be a convenient and profitable venue for their music. According to Mendoza, consistency of quality acts made the club successful.

Each Saturday night, Mexican American patrons came from all over Southern California for a memorable night of dance and entertainment. Rainbow Gardens maintained a "classy" image by enforcing a dress code that required a coat and tie for men and a gown or nice dress for women. Once inside, patrons sat at tables with specially arranged centerpieces, complete with full restaurant services. Rainbow's interior curtains throughout the ballroom made for perfect acoustics, while murals of tropical settings provided an appropriate ambience. On Sundays, Mendoza also hosted a less formal, but well-attended *tardeada*, or afternoon dance, which usually featured a local band or mariachi group.

During these functions, Mendoza served as the emcee, showman, and general greeter for the club. As patrons gathered and familiar faces appeared, Cande announced their presence, making them immediately feel at home. Typically, Saturday nights featured the headline act for an opening and closing set, interspersed with a local intermission band from the Pomona Valley. While most featured acts consisted of the twelve- to fourteen-piece *orquesta* bands, intermission bands often were much smaller and represented the more working-class genre of music known as *conjunto*. Consequently, a trip to Rainbow Gardens on Saturday nights exposed patrons to a full range of Latin American music: small, local working-class bands, to large, internationally known *orquestas*.[14]

Among the international recording stars appearing at Rainbow Gardens, audiences had their favorites. Cuban-born, Mexico City based artist Dámaso Pérez Prado always filled the ballroom to capacity. His hit "Cherry Pink and

Apple-blossom White," which topped the charts of the Lucky Strike Hit Parade on April 30, 1955, made him a familiar bandleader to most Mexican Americans.[15] Initially, however, Gertie Thomas questioned the marketability of this famous recording star. "Who in the hell is Pérez Prado?" demanded Gertie Thomas to Cande Mendoza, the first time Prado visited Pomona. Mendoza answered, "Well, he's a bandleader, why?" Thomas responded, "Well, the reason I'm calling you is that he wants twelve hundred dollars to play one night. Who in the hell does he think he is, Jesus Christ?" After some convincing, Mendoza managed to get Prado the money. His concert was such a success that, as Mendoza remembers, "the next time Prado was over, she didn't have to call me."[16]

Latin American bands and performers from New York to Mexico City appealed to Rainbow Gardens audiences. Aside from Pérez Prado, Mexico's Luis Arcaráz and his band often drew large crowds. Occasionally, Arcaráz would combine his talents with the voice of María Victoria, one of Mexico's glamorous film stars. Mexican cinematic heroes such as Tín Tan and Javier Solis also performed, backed by fourteen-piece orchestras. In addition, Puerto Rican and Cuban performers from New York such as Machito, Tito Rodríguez, and Tito Puente often played at Rainbow Gardens. Looking back, Cande Mendoza remembers, "Rainbow Gardens got quality acts that for today's clubs would be impossible to get."[17]

Although Mendoza began his tenure at Rainbow Gardens as a champion of the Latin American big band sound, he also recognized the generational cleavages within the Latino community. In response to the growing popularity of rock 'n' roll in the mid-1950s, Mendoza began Friday night dances at Rainbow Gardens to accommodate large numbers of Mexican American teens interested in the "new" music. As with his big band shows, Mendoza successfully attracted notable recording stars in the business, including Little Richard and a young, Mexican American rock 'n' roller, Ritchie Valens.

Inspired by Valens and other Los Angeles bands, many local Mexican American youths formed rock 'n' roll groups to emulate their heroes, play music, and create homespun sounds. Mendoza encouraged such experimentation by providing young Mexican American rock 'n' roll acts a venue for their performances. Whether on his afternoon radio program for teens that began in the mid-1950s, or his Friday night dances at Rainbow Gardens, Mendoza's support of their music contributed to the formation of the "Eastside Sound" made popular by groups such as Thee Midniters, Tierra, El Chicano, Malo, and Los Lobos. Pomona Valley bands such as The Velveteens, Ronnie and the Casuals, and the Rainbow Gardens house band The Mixtures recorded many local hits, while drawing substantial audiences at clubs throughout Southern California.

The emergence of rock 'n' roll represented an important change in the direction of Mexican American/Chicano music. Although young people of the late 1950s and early 1960s shared an appreciation for mambo, *conjunto*, and *orquesta*, many viewed these forms as the music of their parents. According to Jerry Castellano, a veteran of the music scene and founding member of two Pomona bands, The Velveteens and The Royals, "we appreciated it [Latin American music], but we were into another bag."[18] For him and his peers, Mexican music occupied a space on the kitchen table in the form of a transistor radio. "Like any other person, all [Mexican] families did this—the father would get up early and eat breakfast before going to work, and the wife would get up and make breakfast for him—and they had a little radio with a *soft* Mexican station on so it wouldn't wake up the kids. That was the only time we heard Mexican music. . . . But, it wasn't the "in" thing to listen to Mexican music, because Mexican [or Spanish] was a second language."[19]

In addition to the language barriers, generational gaps also played a part in separating young Chicanos from music of a previous generation. For example, although Pérez Prado's popularity reached its highest level in the mid-1950s across a very diverse audience, a young, new generation of Latinos with a growing interest in rock 'n' roll mostly regarded him as an elder icon of the Latin American big band scene.[20] Jerry Castellano explains his generation's impressions of Prado:

> *Everybody had their own taste, but mainly all the groups—the Latin groups and the big band groups—they were much older, much much older than us. Pérez Prado, when he was popular, he wasn't a young man. He was already—and I'm guessing—he was already mid-30s or 40s already. And the reason for this was because it took so long for them to get exposure. You know, T.V. wasn't in that much, and you couldn't get into radio [Latin American musicians on English-speaking radio]. It was very difficult to get the word out. So they had to travel a lot to get exposure.*

Rainbow Gardens served as an important venue for bands such as Prado's, and helped disseminate and popularize the music among the Mexican population of Southern California. However, for a younger generation of Mexican Americans (many second and third generation), raised, if not born in a predominantly English-speaking, mass culture–based, multicultural society, this music did not have the same appeal. These youths increasingly validated artists' fame with their appearances on mainstream radio stations and television programs, while Rainbow Gardens' Saturday night dances and entertainers became associated with an older crowd.

For Castellano and other young aspiring rock 'n' rollers, generational as well as ethnic/racial affinity represented an equally important factor in encouraging young Mexican Americans to take up music as an expression of their culture. For example, Castellano recalls the importance of seeing Ricky Nelson weekly: "We grew up with him on T.V. We grew up with him as a little boy, growing, and playing. And I remember every time he sang or played, it was like 'if he can do it, so can we!'"[21] Such enthusiasm translated into increased record sales for rock 'n' roll artists and encouraged record companies to focus more attention on the emerging youth market. When Ricky Nelson's 1958 hit "Poor Little Fool" unseated Pérez Prado's "Patricia" for the number one spot on the Top 100, it represented just one example of a move on the part of the greater listening public to rock 'n' roll oriented music during the late 1950s.[22]

Many Chicanos acknowledged the African American origins of rock 'n' roll, and identified black artists as the inspiration for much of their own musical experimentation. For young Mexican American musicians who had also experienced the pain of discrimination and segregation, the success of African American artists inspired Chicanos to express themselves musically, and to engage in an industry that held remote but not impossible possibilities for acceptance and achievement. The success of Ritchie Valens, a local artist from Pacoima in the San Fernando Valley, galvanized other Mexican American youths. As Castellano remembered: "Especially when we saw someone like Ritchie Valens make it to the top. Wow! That means that we can do it; we can do it. . . . Chicanos that made it!"[23]

Although Valens had the good fortune of succeeding on a national level early in his career, the rock 'n' roll music culture of Southern California mostly developed in the dance halls and small auditoriums throughout the Southland. Music groups, whose proliferation easily surpassed the number of recording companies willing to sign them, depended mostly on exposure at local venues such as Rainbow Gardens. Due to his commitment to satisfying the varied musical tastes of Mexican/Mexican American patrons, Cande Mendoza, by the mid-1950s, filled Rainbow's weekend schedule with rock 'n' roll on Fridays, Latin American *orquesta* and *conjunto* on Saturdays, and the *tardeadas* on Sunday afternoons.

Architects and planners, however, designed venues like Rainbow Gardens primarily for big band dances that catered to a more intimate ballroom experience.[24] As Paul Gilroy and other cultural historians have demonstrated, music and live performance possesses a mimetic quality that produces a dialectical image making/affirming relationship between performers and their audiences.[25] An exchange of ideas regarding the "look" of the music resulted in the formation of a particular style or fashion that reflected the ambience and mood of the "swing" era. The decor and acoustics complemented the big band musical aesthetic and inspired patrons to dress in their finest attire. In addition, the dress, demeanor, and formal presentation style of the performers evoked from their audiences an attitude and behavior that reflected the refined image of big band music.

Rising interest among youth in rock 'n' roll necessitated a correlative aesthetical shift in the ways in which people experienced popular music during the 1950s. While Cande Mendoza adjusted his focus to incorporate rock 'n' roll music into the Rainbow Gardens weekend repertoire, the change did not (and could not) include spatial and structural alterations in the physical appearance of the building, inside and out. In spite of the many rock 'n' roll concerts held at the dance hall, the aesthetics of Rainbow Gardens reflected the tastes of an older generation, which firmly established its reputation as a venue for Latin American big band music.

El Monte's American Legion Stadium

El Monte's American Legion Stadium, on the other hand, reflected the aesthetics of an emerging rock 'n' roll culture. Built prior to the 1932 Olympics, the developers constructed this multipurpose structure with the idea of hosting major sporting events and conventions to accommodate the mostly working-class communities of the San Gabriel Valley. In its early days, Legion Stadium hosted the wrestling matches for the 1932 Olympics held in Los Angeles, and later became the sight of roller derby matches for the Los Angeles team, the Thunderbirds. In addition, as an American Legion hall, the armed services used the facility for benefits, reunions, and meetings for local veterans and service people. Moreover, the auditorium maintained an open invitation to organizations interested in using the stadium. Regardless of the event, the functions held there inevitably reflected the blue-collar image of the people who lived nearby and used the hall.

An assortment of economic, geographic, social, cultural, and political preconditions contributed to El Monte's development as a venue for rock 'n' roll music. The formation of rock 'n' roll bands and the creation of new music represented youthful attempts at imitating the popular images presented on television and in magazines (for example, Ricky Nelson and Elvis), mimicking African American rhythm and blues sounds emanating from the radio, and achieving a degree of local celebrity and respect. For many promoters, record company representatives, and disc jockeys, economic reasons propelled their involvement. Radio personalities gained popularity as interest in the music increased, while a nascent recording industry began to realize the profitability of the emerging youth market in terms of record and concert ticket sales. At times they exploited young artists, causing distrust among performers and promoters of rock 'n' roll music. Initially, however, competition between bands, recording companies, and disc jockeys helped nurture the rock 'n' roll music scene.

Regardless of their motivations, all involved agreed that live performances contributed to the promotion of rock 'n' roll. Many of the potential consumers of this music, however, represented "underage" teens who could not attend many concerts because of a Los Angeles city ordinance that restricted gatherings of people under the age of eighteen. Therefore, although many promoters and local disc jockeys wanted to host local concerts in the city of Los Angeles, this law often prohibited even the performers of this music from participating due to their underage status.[26]

The spatial dimensions of Greater Los Angeles and the less restrictive laws of Los Angeles County created the potential for the development of a dance hall culture in the Southland. Art Laboe, a noted local radio disc jockey, record producer, and concert promoter, stated simply, "Concerts started at El Monte because the laws were different in the county than they were in the city [of Los Angeles]."[27] In particular, rules restricting underage gatherings did not exist in the county, which permitted Laboe and other disc jockeys and promoters to host rock 'n' roll shows for teenagers. Similarly, relaxed county legislation also benefited other venues situated in Los Angeles's hinterlands, including Rainbow Gardens and the Long Beach Municipal Auditorium; the latter competed with Legion Stadium in size and reputation.

Angelenos' experience of life in Greater Los Angeles—a network of suburbs connected by parkways and freeways—encouraged young people to drive from their homes to county dance hall sites. Although young people may have lived in a particular neighborhood segregated by race and class, the common experience of listening to music broadcast across the Southland on KRLA and other radio stations prefigured the interethnic popularity of the halls. Located approximately fifteen miles east of downtown Los Angeles and accessible by the main traffic arteries in the region, El Monte drew a diverse clientele from all ends of the Southland. Recalling the racial and class composition of audiences, Art Laboe commented: "White kids from Beverly Hills, black kids from Compton, and local Chicano kids used to come out to our shows every weekend."[28]

The commute gave rise to an emergent car culture. Inheriting or borrowing the cars of their parents, young people altered or "customized" their vehicles and formed car clubs. According to one faithful El Monte patron, Richard

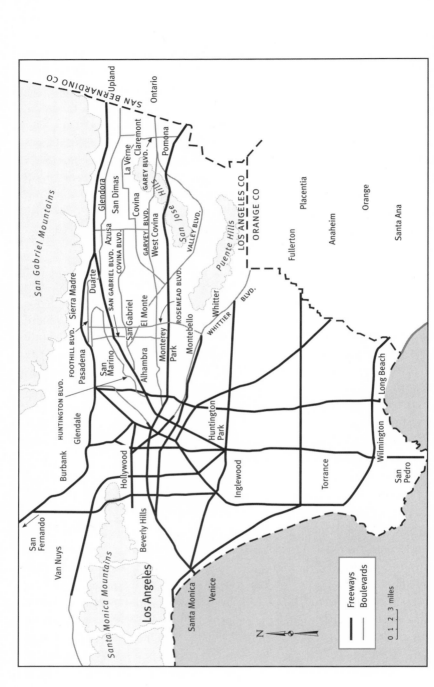

Map 5. This map shows the proposed plan of the Los Angeles Freeway system, implemented with minor additions in 1941. (Adapted from Brodsly, *L. A. Freeway*, 1981.)

Rodríguez, "lowriders were early fifties, and everybody was lowriding." To lower their cars, teens would heat the suspension springs underneath their wheel base or load their trunks with sand or cement bags. For those who owned their own vehicles, elaborate modifications were possible. Many invested in expensive chrome "spinners" or hubs and whitewall tires that they illuminated by affixing semi-truck lights to the fenders and skirts of their cars. These truck "reflectors" came in amber, blue, orange, and red, allowing individuals to vary colors, which gave each car its unique look. Often, lowriders played music from *within* their cars as a way to prepare for the night's entertainment. As Rodríguez remembered, "you had your record player that was made by Craig. The actual 45rpm record inside the car! If you hit a bump in the street, there went the record." [29]

In addition to the cars, clothes shaped the world of the teen dance halls. Unlike Rainbow Gardens, which maintained a dress code, El Monte American Legion Stadium allowed young patrons to wear whatever they desired. This condition led to an eclectic, nonconformist fashion at El Monte, indicative of the cultural diversity extant in rock 'n' roll audiences. Khaki pants and a "Sir Guy" brand, Pendelton-style, plaid shirt were particularly common among many local Chicanos, while Chicanas frequently wore a short-sleeved blouse with a tight-fitting, short, pegged skirt, usually cut about six inches above the knee. According to El Monte patron Marta Maestas, women also wore white, flat shoes known as "bunnies." Maestas remembered, "you wore them with socks." She added, "If you were 'bad,' you pulled them up; if you weren't you kept them down." [30] These fashion statements expressed subtle acts of rebellion on the part of Mexican American youths who consciously broke with the "classy" suit and gown look of their parents. [31]

The multiethnic composition of El Monte's audiences affected teen fashion as many white, Mexican American, black, and Asian/Pacific Islander youths shared styles and influenced one another. Often, the varying styles led to the development of "fads." For example, Jerry Castellano recalled adopting the "collegiate" look of a cardigan-style, lettermen's sweater worn by many white teens as a way of distinguishing himself from other Chicanos. [32] Richard Rodríguez remembered, "the black guys—those guys would *dress* all the time! Those guys wore suits or sports coats." [33] Many African American men dressed in suits that imitated the look of popular black performers such as Don Julian, Brenton Woods, and Richard Berry. Wearing tailored suits trimmed with velvet or satin along the sleeves and lapels, audiences adapted these fashions to their material means and aesthetical tastes to create the "Continental" look: "that would be narrow lapels, narrow pant legs, [and] Continental pockets meaning . . . kind of your western cut. But, it was a tapered pant or slack." [34] These fashions would make their way back to the stage as performers tried to adapt to the changing tastes of their audiences. White performers such as Fabian and Jerry Lee Lewis simultaneously influenced and incorporated changes in fashion by contributing their own regional tastes in clothing and appropriating styles worn by audiences. Occasionally, clothing fads informed the themes of songs, as represented in Hank Ballard's tune "Continental Walk." Similarly, the car culture inspired many songs such as Thee Midniters' "Whittier Blvd," or for a later generation, WAR's classic 1975 hit "Lowrider." [35]

The performing groups and their music best represented the degree of intercultural exchange and ethnic/racial diversity present at rock 'n' roll shows. Several bands consisted of musicians from a variety of cultural backgrounds including African American, Mexican, white, and Asian/Pacific Islander. The intermixing facilitated a blending of cultural influences within a musical genre already distinguished by its hybridized origins of African American rhythm and blues, jazz, gospel, and white country and rockabilly. [36] Created within the context of the ethnically diverse environment of Southern California dance halls, music emerging from this scene possessed a broad-based, cross-cultural appeal, which facilitated understanding among the racially diverse audience. Recalling how music affected his life, and the lives of people of his generation, Jerry Castellano remembered: "The music of the fifties kind of helped because everybody got into it. . . . the blacks were popular entertainers, the whites were popular entertainers. . . . It helped bring generations—not generations—but cultures together and understand. We took that same road, and we tried to do the same thing as far as bringing people together. That's all we did in our music." [37] Following these tenets, Castellano recalled adding a Jewish pianist with a "classical" background into his group, The Royals, as much for his musical contributions as for the message it delivered to audiences. "We did not want to keep it just a Chicano band." [38]

Such was the case with Rainbow Gardens' house band, The Mixtures. The self-conscious, iconographic title of the group epitomized the intentions of many bands and artists who sought to reflect the multicultural world of Southern California's dance halls. Led by Mexican American pianist Steve Mendoza and African American saxophonist Delbert Franklin, the group also included a Chicano drummer (Eddie de Robles), a Puerto Rican bass player (Zag Soto), a black horn player (Autry Johnson), a white guitarist (Dan Pollock), and an American Indian/West Indian percussionist (Johnny Wells). The band saw their diversity as an asset and tried to highlight the uniqueness of their multiracial composition, as Delbert Franklin explained: "We started as The Playboys, and then I would say about sixty or sixty-one we became The Mixtures. We changed the name because we looked around and we were all mixed so [we thought], 'why not be called The Mixtures?'"³⁹

Playing on a local radio station in Oxnard, California, The Mixtures caught the ear of Hollywood restaurant owner Eddie Davis who had begun to dabble in producing and managing teen rock 'n' roll bands. Drawn to the group initially by their talent, Davis believed their diversity would contribute to their success. Davis recalled, "I remember [Steve] Mendoza asking me if there was a chance that they could do anything in the future because they were racially mixed. In those days you remember, blacks and whites did not mix, period." According to Dan Pollock, Davis was particularly intrigued by the ability of white teens like himself who could play R&B: "Eddie booked us because he thought it was unique that we were playing this sound . . . and that there *were* white people in [the band]!" Pollock added, "[Davis] thought—two birds with one stone, he could break this thing out—you know, have this mixed band, this mixed act get over where others had feared to tread."⁴⁰

Connected to some of the most popular disc jockeys in Southern California such as Dick Moreland, Wink Martindale, and Bob Eubanks, Davis quickly found work for the band on radio and television stations, as well as in local dance halls and concert auditoriums. Southern California's most popular rock 'n' roll radio station, KRLA, featured the group regularly during their all-night shows, while Cande Mendoza contracted The Mixtures for Friday night dances.⁴¹ According to Franklin, the band appealed to the racially diverse audience at the club: "Rainbow Gardens is a good way to put it because that's what it became, a rainbow garden."⁴² Later, Davis arranged for the group to appear on a Saturday afternoon dance show, "Parade of Hits," hosted by African American announcer Larry McCormick on the local television station, KCOP, Channel 13. On Saturday nights, the band traveled throughout the Southland, playing at a few of the many dance halls in Southern California, including El Monte American Legion Stadium.

Eddie Davis took pride in being "the first guy to put out a record with a racially mixed group" and fondly remembered the local popularity of The Mixtures. Yet, for all their success, the group never achieved national fame, a fact that disappointed "The Godfather of the East L.A. Sound."

"I tried and tried to promote them nationally," Davis lamented, "[but] I could never get The Mixtures out of Southern California." Franklin shared these feelings, stating: "I wouldn't say we were the first Southern California band, [but] we opened the doors, not just for mixed bands, you know, but for [all] bands." Famously known as the "good luck band" within the dance hall circuit, many successful performers such as Lou Rawls, Barry White, Bobby Riddell, The Rivingtons, and The Beach Boys began their careers either singing in front of The Mixtures, or opening for them on Friday nights. Although their diversity helped them gain work, Franklin believed it also prevented them from gaining access to lucrative recording deals. "We didn't get recording deals," Franklin remembered, "[partly] 'cause the record companies were afraid even though they saw what we were doing." For Pollock, racism was the crucial factor in restricting the growth of the band's popularity:

> [Our diversity] held us back. [It] held us back because you gotta remember that . . . the greater LA area was still a rather prejudiced area. Albeit . . . it was more progressive than say, Mississippi, but it was still . . . less than ten years from the time where black people couldn't even stay in hotels in Los Angeles. They had to go to the Dunbar [a hotel for African Americans] or find people's homes to stay . . . I mean, excellent performers . . . all the greatest guys in the world would come through. They couldn't . . . get a room, until Nat King Cole finally bought a house in the Hollywood Hills and broke the color barrier. It was headlines! It takes a while for that assimilation see, and these were still very prejudiced times here in Southern California.[43]

For record executives who invested in the "exotic" appeal of all-African American bands or the "novelty" of all-white bands playing "black music," The Mixtures did not fit their narrow definitions of a marketable group. Commenting on the effectiveness of their intercultural message, Pollock explained that although "the guys were all together on this thing," he also believed that Davis "bit off more than he could chew." Davis's own assessment of his strategy to highlight the multiethnic composition of the band confirmed Pollock's impressions, admitting that "I was very naïve and I never knew anything about prejudice."[44]

Despite never achieving national fame, The Mixtures possessed an "aural and visual" appeal that garnered favor from Southern California's diverse audiences and radio personalities.[45] That The Mixtures gained popularity as a live band but never as recording artists also suggests the importance of place in the formation of Los Angeles's interethnic music culture. Although many teens respected the "commercial" success of Ritchie Valens or Ricky Nelson, Southern California bands could also achieve a degree of fame from their live performances. Noting the unique qualities possessed by The Mixtures on their only record album (not surprisingly, a live album recorded at Rainbow Gardens), Dick Moreland wrote, "California has discovered them [The Mixtures] to be the most exciting act which has ever provided in-person entertainment in their area."[46] Although disc jockeys and promoters often used such hyperbole to sell records and tickets and increase their own popularity, the emphasis on the live or "in-person" quality of the band accurately states the significant connection between audience and performer, and music and dance, that made the dance halls the center of an emerging youth culture. Moreover, it demonstrates the relatively egalitarian or democratic nature of musical production during this period. Although recording deals only came to precious few bands, aspiring musicians could seek affirmation and acceptance outside the recording industry in the dance halls.

For women performers who appeared on stage less frequently and in fewer numbers than men, the dance hall held more remote promise for recognition and respect. The career of Rosalie Mendez Hamlin, or "Rosie" of the group Rosie and the Originals, provides insight into the unique experiences of women in this male-dominated industry. Early in her career, Hamlin's participation in an emerging music and dance hall culture proved to be her salvation. Born in Alaska to an Anglo father and a Mexican mother, Hamlin moved to San Diego as a teenager, where her parents began to have marital problems. After a period of great upheaval that, in her words became "physical," Hamlin ran away to live with her Aunt Soccoro and Uncle Frank. There, she cultivated her talents as a piano player and singer. According to Hamlin, "music was a way to not lose it, you know, because you don't understand why grown-ups are doing all this fighting and breaking up." When her single "Angel Baby" hit big in 1962, Hamlin moved to Los Angeles to join the dance hall circuit. Once she arrived, she found a diverse group of veteran male performers who supported her professional development. Hamlin recalled, "I was put on stage with a lot of well seasoned entertainers that I respected a whole lot and they kind of raised me and taught me a lot about music." She added, "it became like a family and it was really good because I no longer really had any family, I was sort of just traveling around a lot and it was wonderful to have that support and influence." Relying on a surrogate family that included popular performers such as Richard Berry, Johnny Otis, and Don Julian, Hamlin became one of the few women to gain popularity in the Los Angeles music scene.

The nurture and guidance of veteran musicians, however, did not make Hamlin immune to the discrimination experienced by women in this industry. According to Hamlin, women in rock 'n' roll bands performed as either background singers with little visibility, or as lead singers restricted to singing only. Although her hit single "Angel Baby" earned her an elite place among women performers, she resented some of the restrictions placed on her as a woman musician. Hamlin explained:

> *Usually, in those days, if you were a female singer, you were the front per-*
> *son . . . and you didn't get back there and play. It was not kosher—it wasn't*
> *cool [for women to play instruments]. It was like you should stand up there*
> *and look cute, you know. That's what it was. There's a lot of women that*
> *played instruments, but usually you saw them up front. . . . [or] A lot of*
> *times women would not do any front work, they'd just be up there and sing*
> *and then disappear discretely, and the band leader, like Ike of Ike and Tina*
> *Turner, would be the one that was the important person.*[47]

Even during the mid-1960s, when Hamlin had established herself as one of the few successful women performers in Southern California, she experienced discrimination from concert promoters who denied her equal rehearsal time before shows and rescheduled her appearances to accommodate the whims of younger, male performers. Hamlin explained, "I would just tolerate it, you know, because it was really a man's business."

For women who attended the shows, the dance hall was a place that could evoke both curiosity and fear. Marta Maestas, for example, remembered being "more scared than curious" when she attended concerts at El Monte as a fourteen-year-old in 1954, but also called the experience "the time of [her] life." Although many things contributed to her feelings of "edginess," including sneaking out with her girlfriends, the vastness of the stadium, and the occasional drinking and fighting in the parking lot, the "raw, sexual energy" present in the music and the dance hall figured prominently in her reminiscence of El Monte. "It scared me," she remembered, "because I did not know how to react even though it was all around me there." She added, "the music was much more sexual and I was not attracted to the softer, pop stuff. I was obviously attracted to the sexual energy." Maestas dealt with these tensions by confining this energy to the dance floor, where she maintained more liberal rules about touching. Maestas explained: "There was an invisible line that you didn't cross with me. It was o.k. when you were dancing. It wasn't, but I made it that way so I could deal with it [the sexual energy]."[48]

Frequently, passions kindled on the dance floor spilled over into the parking lot where distinctions between "good" and "bad" touching became more difficult to maintain. An encounter with a sexually active girlfriend and an overzealous boyfriend ultimately persuaded Maestas to stop going to El Monte American Legion Stadium. She explained: "A lot of stuff happened outside. We [Maestas and her boyfriend, Henry] went back to the car. My friend Joanne and Henry's friend weren't just necking—they were actually getting ready to have sex. And I'd never seen anything like that, and it scared the hell out of me.

[Henry] wanted to do the same thing and I told him, 'No way! You're out of your mind!' I made him take me home and I wouldn't go with him anymore."[49]

Although other youths chose freely to engage in sexual relations outside of the stadium, women often received unwanted advances from male peers influenced by the environment of the dance hall. Remembering the pressures that many women felt, Maestas asserted, "a lot of that was brought on by the music." While popular songs such as Hank Ballard's "Sexy Ways" and "Let's Go Again (Where We Went Last Night)" conveyed the sexual freedom of the times, it also encouraged men to expect such sexual favors from all women they encountered at the shows.

Other musicians, however, wrote song lyrics that emphasized romantic encounters and sincere feelings of love. Reflecting on the music of the period and the primary inspiration behind her songs, Hamlin commented, "It was all based around a love theme." "[It was] probably because of our age," she added, "experiencing what's new, like puppy love that turned into romance that, you know, later became marriage."[50]

Romance within multiethnic dance halls often led to interethnic/interracial dating and provided youths the unique opportunity to challenge racial prejudices in Southern California. A tradition of cooperation in multicultural communities and multiethnic organizations such as the Community Service Organization competed with discriminatory attitudes to shape the larger society's response to intercultural mixing at rock 'n roll shows.[51] Prejudices against intercultural courtship and dating, particularly between nonblacks and African Americans, persisted in the minds of many parents of the 1950s. Richard Rodríguez remembered his experience living in Duarte during the early fifties: "You see, back in the fifties, if you dated a black girl, your parents would probably move out of the area. If you were even seen walking with a black girl, [and you were] Mexican, your old man would probably take a switch to you."[52] Living next to African American families in a community segregated because of racial restrictions in housing, Rodríguez recalled: "[my parents] rented a house to black people, [but] I was not allowed to date a black girl. My mother didn't want it, my uncles and aunts didn't want it . . . And it was like I better not do this."[53]

The experience of growing up in a racially mixed community, however, provided a basis of familiarity that presented the potential for breaking down color and cultural barriers. Through exposure to multiethnic music and contact with a racially diverse audience in the dance halls, a new generation realized some of this potential. As Rodríguez recalled: "When I went to El Monte, I felt that I could date anybody I wanted to; I could dance with anybody I wanted to. But,

I was a little shy yet at El Monte because I was trying to understand the crowd, and why the girls would dance with black guys, and nobody's fighting over it."[54] Eventually, such interethnic mixing on the dance floors and in the parking lots broke down youths' ambivalence toward intercultural romance. According to Marta Maestas, "that was a time when, in the outside world, [interracial dating] was unacceptable." Reflecting on her experience during the mid-fifties at El Monte, Maestas recalled: "It was Latina women with a black man. It was black girls with Latino boys. But, it was kind of an easy mix. I didn't feel the same kind of barriers then as I did in the late sixties." Similarly, during the late 1950s, Rodríguez remembered seeing "more blacks dating white girls and Chicana girls." He added, "Every now and then you might see a white man with a black girl or a white man with a Mexican girl, or vice versa. . . . El Monte was a melting pot!"[55]

Political decisions and demographic realities in Southern California suburbs facilitated the blossoming of intercultural cooperation among youths in the 1950s. The combination of a growing youth population and the failure of the educational infrastructure to address such growth led to a high degree of race and class mixing in local schools. For example, in the heart of the San Gabriel Valley, the cities of Monrovia, Arcadia, and Duarte maintained just one high school for the three townships. Arcadia contained a white affluent and middle-class population, while Monrovia and Duarte had a cross-section of black, white, and Mexican working-class families. Although this clash of cultures initially resulted in conflict, administrators, out of necessity, actively sought ways of facilitating understanding and tolerance by holding "get-acquainted dances" and naming the school mascot the "M.A.D. Wildcats" [Monrovia, Arcadia, and Duarte].[56]

Music and dance served as a bridge between cultures and helped to ameliorate racial tensions on Southland campuses. Playing at a high school function in Pasadena, Jerry Castellano recalled how music forged a link between him and a mostly white audience: "We went thinking we were going to be playing to a lot of Latinos. Wrong! They were all white. So we thought, "what are we going to do, what are we going to play?" So we decided we'll mix it up. We'll play their music, and we'll throw in ours once in a while. And, as it turned out, we played our own stuff and they loved it!"[57]

Although Castellano and other Mexican Americans played a hybridized music composed of a variety of cultural influences, many still acknowledged distinctions between mainstream rock 'n' roll and "their" music. Much of this can be attributed to the regional development of a unique "Eastside Sound" characterized by the presence of Mexican/Latin American influences. Although African American rhythm and blues formed the basis of this music, Chicanos had their own variation of R&B. Mexican teens emphasized a more "intense" rhythmic pattern. According to Castellano, "we didn't use a bass player; we used rhythm guitar."[58] In addition, many Southern California groups incorporated a brass section, particularly a saxophone, into their bands. "We always had a saxophone, a rhythm section, and a brass section. It was part of the make up of our music," commented Castellano.[59] Moreover, these bands maintained contact with their audiences throughout a show so that patrons could often call out to the performers, "play that song, or we want to do this dance."[60] This made for a particularly "raw" or "primitive" quality, in which audiences' hoots and hollers figured prominently in the Southern California musical aesthetic.[61] Audience "contributions" were recorded on many albums such as The Mixtures' "Stompin' At the Rainbow," or the more popular hits of the period such as Thee Midniters' "Whittier Blvd." and Handsome Jim Balcolm's "Corrido Rock."

The popularity of the latter song (which also served as El Monte's theme song) demonstrates the important influence of Mexican/Latin American rhythms on Southern California bands and the acceptance of this music by a multiethnic community. Although the traditional *corrido* typically contains words and a distinguishable rhyme scheme, rock musicians probably used the title "corrido" not as a literal description of the song, but rather as a reference to the Latin American origins of its musical arrangement.[62] "Corrido Rock" contains all of the above-mentioned influences, such as a strong rhythmic guitar beat with a saxophone lead that harkens back to a previous generation. This dance hall "standard" represents an adaptation of the instrumental music enjoyed by a mostly Mexican American audience at places like Rainbow Gardens on a Saturday night. Moreover, the recording of this song by a white artist exemplifies the cross-cultural appeal of this music.

Music from a previous generation, however, was not as remote as the separation of these two worlds might suggest. For example, Latin American big band venues continued serving adult audiences through the 1960s. At Rainbow Gardens, where rock 'n' roll and Latin American big band "shared" the stage, though on different nights, teens could keep up with the popular trends in Latin American music. In addition, youths commonly began their musical education at home. Jerry Castellano recalled: "I learned [music] from [home] . . . My dad taught me or my uncle had taught me. They were all Mexican chords. Then I used them in rock 'n' roll and then as the years went by, I learned the seventh chord. . . . the jazz chords. . . . But, they all came from the Mexican chords that my dad used."[63]

The experience of performing in church, and at family and community functions also shaped the tastes and attitudes of many young musical artists. María Elena Adams-González, for example, recalls how she got her start in music by singing at the Fiesta held every year in the Arbol Verde *colonia* in Claremont: "It was right next to grandma's [house] at the hall of the Sacred Heart Church in the community. Cecilia [her younger sister] and I would sing every year there."[64] "Discovered" by Frank Zappa who lived in the Pomona Valley during the late 1950s and early 1960s, Adams-González went on to perform with the popular local band Ronnie and the Casuals, and later recorded and performed as a solo artist under the name "Gina Terry."

Frequently, the origins of artists' music and the inspiration for their participation conflicted with the emerging "commercial" mentality of the industry. Ultimately, record producers and promoters came to dominate the rock 'n' roll scene and soured many musicians' interest in pursuing a professional career in popular music. For example, Adams-González remembers singing for pleasure and to express her culture and feelings through song; however, "when Frank [Zappa] heard me for the first time at the Ontario Music Center, all I remember is him telling me he saw dollar signs."[65] Although Adams-González mentioned, "Frank was a very nice man," she did not view her talents as a vehicle to fame and fortune. After a short teen career, recording and performing at local venues, Adams-González chose to leave the profession and pursue music in less commercial venues.[66]

Similarly, Jerry Castellano remembered: "we didn't do it for money. It was something else to do, to stay out of drugs, to stay out of trouble."[67] For Castellano and his partners, forming a band represented another option for gathering with friends. Their popularity, however, attracted an agent, who imposed a new mode of relating to their music and to one another: "When the agent came in, he did get us a lot more interest, and bookings, and stuff like that. But, what we later found out was that he was doing it for his own purposes. Things were beginning to happen, like little small arguments between us because of him. . . . To make a long story short, he took over the whole thing and we had no say so in it anymore."[68] Despite achieving some local success, Castellano and two original members eventually broke off from their first band The Velveteens and formed new groups.

Many young performers who pursued a career in music found the industry dominated by self-interested recording executives and predatory music promoters who often bilked artists out of profits generated by their songs. Frequently artists would record original material and send it to a recording company for consideration. Often, the band or artist would never receive a reply; however, the music, or some portion of it would manifest itself in the sounds of groups already signed by the label.[69] Even those artists who secured contracts with recording companies did not always profit from their creative endeavors. For example, Rosie Hamlin signed an illegal contract with Highland Records in 1960 that paid her only a penny per record for her hit "Angel Baby." Although the song became a mega-hit and propelled her career, Hamlin earned few royalties on the song until she had the original contract invalidated and won a copyright infringement lawsuit in 1988.[70]

By the early 1970s, a small number of large recording companies bought out many of the over 400 local recording labels of the 1950s and significantly consolidated the industry. This consolidation resulted in a concomitant concentration of varied musical expressions into the music of select groups and artists. Although musicians such as Jerry Castellano and Rosie Hamlin continued to perform and create music, access to radio airwaves and dance hall stages became increasingly difficult. Radio stations and recording companies interested primarily in increasing their market share attempted to ensure their profits by channeling their resources into the promotion of particular artists or supergroups.[71] These decisions transformed the complexion of rock 'n' roll as the number of bands and the interest in live performances at small, intimate venues waned toward the end of the 60s and the early 70s.

The world of the dance halls and the message of the music also changed as a result of the social, political, and economic turmoil of the period. In addition to the Vietnam War and its dramatic effects on teenaged populations, material inequalities and persistent social injustice contributed to a fracturing of Southern California society. As the 1950s boom economy slowed and industries began to relocate in right-to-work states, black and Latino communities were the first to be hurt by growing unemployment.[72] Although the intercultural mingling at places like El Monte's American Legion Stadium and Rainbow Gardens familiarized blacks, Latinos, Asians, and whites with one another, it also tended to accent the growing material inequalities among Southern California's residents. Moreover, as rebellions developed in Latino and black communities in response to the deepening economic and social crises, whites tended to recoil from the intercultural understanding of another age, back to their secure white, middle-class neighborhoods. The construction of new schools and the further development of homeowners' associations, which supported de facto segregation along racial and class lines, facilitated such retrenchment.[73] With the "refinement" of commercial radio and the promotion of particular popular music stars and supergroups, the local music scene lost its appeal for many teens, including blacks and Latinos.

By the early 1960s, the mambo craze that swept the United States in the 1950s had subsided, thus reducing Saturday night audiences at Rainbow Gardens. Although the Pomona dance hall remained a viable and profitable business, both the Thomases and Cande Mendoza chose to leave the music business. Gertie and Ray Thomas retired, while Mendoza, inspired by his early activities in community organizing and journalism, pursued a successful career in education and politics.[74] In 1963 the Thomases sold Rainbow to the owners of Virginia's, another Latin American venue operating in downtown Los Angeles. Somewhat mysteriously, the facility burned down the following year, never to be rebuilt.

El Monte's American Legion Stadium continued to host dances through the 1960s on the strength of rock 'n' roll's popularity. Initially, as the industry grew, so did El Monte's stature among fans. Toward the end of the 1960s, however, changes in both the music business and society made El Monte a less suitable place for live shows. Even Richard Rodríguez acknowledged that something had changed midway through the 1960s. In a recent retrospective article he commented: "The shows inside the place reflected the changes going on outside. Stabbings, beatings, and riots were commonplace. Rival gangs fought each other as the music provided them with a soundtrack."[75] Ultimately, promoters moved performances elsewhere as laws changed and demographic, geographic, and economic circumstances reshaped the location of entertainment. El Monte's American Legion Stadium was destroyed in 1974.

Compilation albums of that period, retrospective collections recently assembled, reunions such as the annual "Memories of El Monte" show, and the many "oldies" radio stations throughout the Southland preserve some of the memories of the musical culture extant in Greater Los Angeles between the end of World War II and the tumult of the 1960s. The evolution from exclusively white big band ballrooms of the 1940s, to predominantly Latino clubs in the 1950s, to multiethnic teen music dance halls in the 1950s and 1960s demonstrated the degree to which public space opened for a greater number of Southern California residents and cultural influences after World War II. Although material inequalities and persistent racial/ethnic prejudice continued to shape social relations throughout this period, people of diverse cultural backgrounds were able to discover some common ground in the music culture and dance halls.

The creation of such places required a respect for, or at least tacit acceptance of, predominantly non-Euroamerican based music by a larger, white-dominated society. The market for Latin American music concerts and recordings provided Mexican Americans a cultural foothold and a sense of belonging in U.S. society. Equally important, it presented the potential for Latin American culture to influence and transform dominant culture *and* public space by making both more receptive to non-Euroamerican influences.

Eventually, mambo and other forms of Latin American music garnered favor from a predominantly white listening audience in the United States.[76] This popularity, however, did not dramatically alter white perceptions of Latinos within their immediate surroundings, nor did it inspire them to reconceptualize and reorganize public space. As the above history suggests, whites may have listened to the music, but places like Rainbow Gardens on a Saturday night remained mostly Latino.

The creation of shared, multiethnic public spaces, and cross-fertilization among various cultures in music depended on a new generation of Angelenos. Although de facto segregation and material inequalities persisted, young people of various cultural backgrounds voluntarily chose to enter the multicultural environment of the dance halls and enjoyed the culturally hybridized sounds of Southern California rock 'n' roll. Shaped by radio, television, and freeways, the "postmodern" social geography of Greater Los Angeles facilitated the convergence of Southland youths in places like El Monte's Legion Stadium.

Finally, the intentional mixing of cultural forms, the use of symbolic iconography, and the incorporation of environmental influences in the music and dance hall culture of the 1950s and 1960s suggest that many youths had more on their minds than just "good time" rock 'n' roll. The music and experiences of these teens represent what Paul Gilroy calls a "politics of transfiguration." Communicating through nontraditional means, using nonlinguistic mediums such as rhythms, body motion, and fashion, these youths projected "an alternative body of cultural and political expression that considers the world critically from the point of view of its emancipatory transformation."[77] Although their exchanges were often restricted to the dance halls, youths, nevertheless, quieted the dissenting voices implanted in their heads by a larger society to forge relationships across racial, ethnic, and class lines. Moreover, performers successfully transcended divisions in society to create a hybridized music influenced by the many cultures present throughout Greater Los Angeles. The intentional blending of musical forms; the purposeful cultural diversity in bands such as The Mixtures; the cross-cultural exchanges that took place on the dance floors among African Americans, Asian Americans/Pacific Islanders, whites, and Latinos; and the sharing of fads and fashions across ethnic/racial lines all provide evidence of this alternative vision of human relations considered by these young Angelenos.

The blossoming of institutions like Rainbow Gardens, El Monte American Legion Stadium, and Padua Hills Theatre in the "hinterlands" of the metropolis forces a reassessment of the center-periphery analyses of cultural development that cast cities as beacons of enlightenment and creativity.[78] In Greater Los Angeles, progressive and creative cultural forces did not always emanate from the city; rather, the incorporation of suburban settlements into the metropolitan orbit allowed entertainment centers to shape Southern California culture. Indeed, in the case of Legion Stadium, cross-cultural exchange and hybridization in popular music occurred on the "Eastside" because the city maintained ancient laws restricting the congregation of youth and the LAPD aggressively policed "race mixing" at rock 'n' roll concerts within their jurisdiction.

The post–World War II citrus belt also served as an important location for experiments in nonwhite-white coalition politics. During the 1940s and 1950s, a group of young Mexican Americans, led by newspaper owner and editor Ignacio López, drew on the support of African Americans and white, working-class activists and scholars to achieve civil rights for minorities living on the fringes of this expanding metropolis. These second- and third-generation Mexican Americans organized political groups known as "Unity Leagues" that predated the important Community Service Organization of East Los Angeles, and used López's *El Espectador* to aggressively fight racial discrimination throughout the valley. Their efforts placed pressure on many white, middle-class and elite community leaders to address the problem of residential segregation, and led to the formation of "intercultural" communities during the 1960s and 1970s. In the following chapter, I explore the successes and failures of intercultural political organizing as suburbanization redefined the place and space of minorities in Southern California after World War II.

Candelario Mendoza during his days as a deejay for Ontario radio station, KPMO. (Courtesy of Candelario Mendoza)

Rainbow Gardens, Pomona, ca. 1950s. (Courtesy of Candelario Mendoza)

Big band leader Les Brown stands aside for a comedian during one of his shows at Rainbow Gardens, Pomona, ca. 1950s. (Courtesy of Candelario Mendoza)

Beto Villa and his singing duo, Carmen y Laura, join Cande on stage for a photo during their 1950 performance. (Courtesy of Candelario Mendoza)

Legendary "mambo king" Dámaso Pérez Prado with Candelario Mendoza during a show at Rainbow Gardens, ca. 1950s. (Courtesy of Candelario Mendoza)

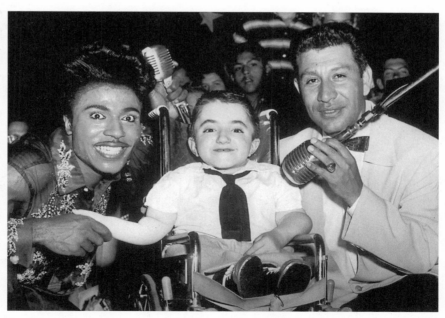

Candelario Mendoza hosts a rock 'n' roll benefit for disabled children with Little Richard at Rainbow Gardens, ca. 1961. (Courtesy of Candelario Mendoza)

Promotional photograph of The Mixtures, ca. 1962. (Courtesy of Candelario Mendoza)

Rosie Mendez-Hamlin and Noah Tafoya of Rosie and the Originals, ca. 1961. This photo along with the story of the song, "Angel Baby," appears in the Rock and Roll Hall of Fame in Cleveland, Ohio. (Courtesy of Rosie Mendez-Hamlin)

A typical weekend crowd at El Monte's American Legion Stadium in the late 1950s. Disk jockey, concert promoter, and emcee Art Laboe stands in the foreground. (Courtesy of Original Sound Record Company, Inc.)

College Heights Orange and Lemon Association Packing House, Claremont, ca. 1920s. (Courtesy of Pomona Public Library)

Interior of College Heights Orange and Lemon Association Packing House, Claremont, ca. 1920s. (Courtesy of Pomona Public Library)

College Heights Packing House crew, May 4, 1949. (Courtesy of Claremont Heritage)

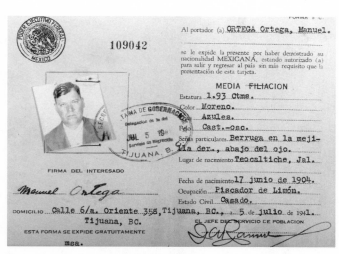

Temporary worker papers for Manuel Ortega Ortega, 1941. Ortega himself eventually became a foreman of *braceros* in the La Verne citrus orchards. (Courtesy of La Verne City Hall)

The newly completed Intercultural Council housing project in Arbol Verde *colonia*, Claremont, early 1950s. (Courtesy of Claremont Heritage)

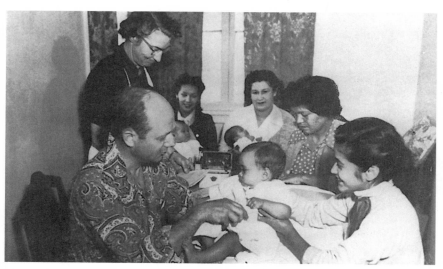

The Well-Baby Clinic in the Arbol Verde *colonia*, Claremont, Calif., 1950s. (Courtesy of Claremont Heritage)

As the grove-owners have relinquished the reins of power and have not been succeeded by their sons, all sorts of civic positions have been filled by outsiders. Occasionally the service clubs of the district, largely made up of this newer element, have asserted themselves, on minor issues, in a manner not sanctioned by the older generation. This tendency is likely to become more pronounced in the future as the grove-owners, already divested of many of the functions ordinarily associated with ownership, are removed by death. Seemingly impervious to social change, Citrus Land has finally begun to respond to new movements of thought and opinion.
—CAREY MCWILLIAMS, *Southern California: An Island on the Land*

Sol y Sombra

The Limits of Intercultural Activism in Post-Citrus Greater Los Angeles

Although citrus growers and local politicians continued to support policies and employment patterns that separated Mexicans and whites and undercut the economic and social mobility of Mexican Americans, during the 1940s and 1950s some Angelenos began to question discrimination in public spaces. Dance halls, Padua Hills Theatre, schools, and the armed services provided sites for intercultural encounters and inspired limited cooperation among a multicultural populace. In particular, "spaces of pleasure" like Rainbow Gardens and Padua Hills reinforced bonds of fellowship among Mexican Americans and illuminated the possibilities of coalitions among minorities and progressive whites, even as they revealed the potential conflicts across race, class, and gender lines.[1] While their efforts were far from perfect and complete, Mexican American, African American, and white activists separately and collectively organized. Their attempts to transform the idea of "intercultural understanding" into action on a broad and far-reaching level manifested a sincere desire to address prejudice in Southern California. Their shortcomings, on the other hand, exposed the limits of symbolic integration, the continuation of material inequalities, and the persistence of racial stereotypes.

This chapter highlights the efforts of community groups and individuals who struggled to remedy discriminatory conditions for Mexican Americans and African Americans living throughout the Southland. As with other historians researching the period between World War II and the Chicano Movement, my focus will *not* be comprehensive, but rather will discuss specific organizations and people committed to particular goals.[2] Often Mexican Americans involved in these organizations represented an educated and/or middle-class sector of the community, which did not necessarily speak for the entire Mexican American populace. Although their message resonated with most Mexican Americans during this period, their leadership also illuminated class differences that reflected internal divisions among a diverse Mexican American community.

The participation of whites in struggles against discrimination and segregation provides a nuanced understanding of intercultural relations during the 1940s and 1950s. Before World War II, many Euroamericans in the citrus belt believed in the racial superiority of whites; however, opinions varied. The Friends of the Mexicans, Su Casa, and other white "good-doers" not formally associated with the citrus industry frequently assisted their Mexican neighbors. Although these organizations at times reinforced stereotypes and often sought to influence Mexicans and Mexican Americans, they also generated greater interest in Mexican culture both at home and abroad. As the history of Padua Hills Theatre illustrated, sometimes these interactions led to unintended consequences. Progressive-minded whites and shrewd Mexican Americans recognized the potential of such interactions and began to use these connections to address the unequal and unfair conditions affecting racial minorities in Southern California.

College professors and community and labor organizers often took leadership roles in these struggles for equality. This "newer element" as Carey McWilliams called them, shed public light on the problem of segregation and discrimination through their writings and activism, and engaged in projects that challenged the social order of a previous generation. Among Mexican Americans, Ignacio "Nacho" López mobilized residents by criticizing government officials and local business owners in the pages of his bilingual newspaper *El Espectador*. His passionate defense of African American and Mexican American civil rights in the San Bernardino, Pomona, and San Gabriel valleys not only galvanized African Americans and young, second-generation Mexican Americans, but also appealed to whites committed to the goal of social justice. Ruth Tuck, a professor at the University of Redlands and author of the 1946 book *Not With the Fist*, and Fred Ross, an organizer affiliated with Saul Alinsky's Chicago-based organization, the Industrial Areas Foundation (IAF), were two grassroots organizers who united with López and the Mexican and African American communities to fight segregation in education, public facilities, and housing. Organized in multiracial political groups called "Unity Leagues," these activists fought discrimination, registered minority voters, and ran minority candidates for public office in San Diego, Riverside, San Bernardino, and the Pomona Valley. This movement also rallied middle-class reformers such as Claremont Graduate School professor Dr. W. Henry Cooke, and Congregational church activists, Harland Hogue and Ruth Ordway, who founded the Intercultural Council of Claremont (ICC) in 1948 to increase racial integration in Southern California. Primarily composed of Anglos, the ICC created the first multiracial neighborhood in the citrus belt and offered financial support to Mexican Americans for home renovations, postsecondary education, and health care.

Activists' attention to the problem of residential segregation and discrimination in public facilities reveals structural and physical changes in the citrus belt after World War II. The industrialization and suburbanization of the Southland during the 1940s and 1950s transformed the role of Mexican American workers, white agricultural laborers, and the citrus industry in Southern California. For example, Gilbert González has documented the industrialization of Orange County during the late 1940s with the construction of a General Electric plant, Oranco Steel, a clothing factory, and other heavy and light manufacturing companies.[3] The citrus belt of Los Angeles and adjoining San Bernardino counties underwent a similar transformation with the construction of Kaiser Steel in Fontana, General Electric in Ontario, the Western Electric Guided Missiles Plant (later renamed General Dynamics) in Pomona, and a variety of other industrial companies radiating out from Los Angeles.[4]

The creation of these new industries had two primary effects on the citrus belt: it provided higher paying industrial-style jobs to local residents and eroded the ideal conditions for cultivating citrus. White citrus industry workers found opportunities in the burgeoning war industry of Southern California and abandoned the picking and packing jobs that originally drew them out of the Dust Bowl. Many Mexican American men and women also integrated into the new industrial labor force though at entry level positions that showed little promise for the upward occupational mobility experienced by white workers.[5] Discrimination in hiring and promotions, and the adverse effects of a segregated school system, prevented most Mexican American industrial workers from attaining secure, highly skilled, well-paying positions.[6]

The other consequence of these structural changes—the undermining of citrus production in San Gabriel, Pomona, and San Bernardino Valleys—happened over a period of three decades, roughly from the end of World War II to 1970.[7] Industrialization of the citrus belt created the need for more housing for employees flocking to Los Angeles suburbs. This process generated a boom in development and escalated land values throughout the region. At the close of the war, nefarious housing contractors secured Federal Housing Administration loans to construct "quick-buck . . . tract housing and sub-divisions."[8] Between the end of World War II and the 1970s, citrus growers discovered that they could make more money selling their land to developers than they could raising citrus fruit. Those who did not recognize this potential or who resisted selling their property eventually succumbed to environmental pressures caused by the rapid settlement of the citrus belt. The construction of freeways, houses, and industrial plants contributed to a worsening air pollution problem that deteriorated the quality of citrus produced in the Los Angeles basin.[9] Consequently, by 1970, developers had transformed the garden metropolis of Greater Los Angeles into a network of industrial and residential suburbs.[10]

The transformation from a predominantly agrarian-based economy to an industrial-based one, however, weakened the social control of citrus growers and permitted greater mobility for Mexican Americans. Assuming a significant position in the evolving cultural and physical landscape of the new Southern California, Mexican Americans and African Americans asserted themselves as citizens with rights and access to public space equal to that of Euroamericans. Moreover, some progressive-minded whites championed the goal of racial equality and created institutions that they thought would help correct the effects of past discrimination. The collaboration of Mexican Americans and whites in such organizations as the Unity Leagues and the Intercultural Council were not the first of their kind; however, they marked an important episode in the evolution of a regional Mexican American civil rights movement and a significant example of intercultural cooperation.[11]

World War II itself had a significant effect on intercultural relations between Mexican Americans and whites. As many Chicano scholars have pointed out, the war against fascism raised the consciousness of many Americans concerning discrimination and prejudice on the home front, and motivated some to engaged in civil rights struggles.[12] Recently, however, George J. Sánchez questioned Chicano scholars' interpretation of World War II as a "watershed" and challenged the idea that "returning servicemen for the first time fought for their rights as citizens." Sánchez argues that "much of the cultural identity and sense of self of the Mexican American second generation was already shaped before the war." Using the YMCA-sponsored youth group Mexican American Movement (MAM) as an example, Sánchez claims to have revised this long-held assumption on the part of Chicano scholars.

Both interpretations have merit. Certainly, the Paduanos and the many citrus belt workers who chose to weather the repatriation drives demonstrated a desire to remain in the United States. For example, in 1932 Helen O'Brien acknowledged that children and young adults of the Arbol Verde *colonia* showed significant signs of acculturation, and had become invested in American cultural life. According to O'Brien, "changes seem to have taken place along age lines," causing "the problem . . . not only of adjustment to a culture foreign to his [Mexican immigrant], but one of maintaining peace and harmony in the home."[13] Entitled "The Mexican Colony: A Study of Cultural Change," O'Brien's thesis confirms Sánchez's interpretation that the "rise of the second generation" contributed significantly to a "Mexican American" consciousness before the war.[14]

This, however, does not negate the impact of World War II on Mexican American political consciousness and activism. The correlation between the creation of post–World War II grassroots political organizations such as the Community Service Organization (CSO), the Unity Leagues, and the Latin American Organization (LAO) and the return of veterans from the war cannot be understated. In the brief period between 1945 and 1950, Mexican Americans, through these groups, helped Mexican candidates get elected to local and regional government bodies, desegregated schools in Southern California with the *Mendez v. Westminster* case, and registered numerous Mexican American voters.[15] These changes not only signaled more activity on the part of Mexican Americans, but also greater willingness on the part of some whites to redress discriminatory laws. As Candelario Mendoza, the last president of MAM and a World War II veteran, communicated to me in an oral history, "things changed" as a result of the war, which gave him the confidence to be "a little more assertive" in demanding his civil rights during the late 1940s.[16]

Post–World War II organizing and the prewar "rise of the second generation," therefore, should not be seen as mutually exclusive developments in Mexican

American political and social consciousness. MAM—a mostly male, regional organization with an educated cadre of Mexican American youths—contributed to the formation of a postwar Mexican American civil rights movement. However, historians must account for the noticeable "change" in the social climate after World War II and the significant political advancements made by minority and white activists during this period. The following examination of Mexican American, African American, and white cooperation in the name of civil rights elucidates some of the important transformations that took place in intercultural relations before, during, and after World War II.

Ignacio López, El Espectador, and the Creation of a Civil Rights Movement

The efforts of journalist and community organizer Ignacio Lutero López exemplified the push for civil rights by Mexican Americans between the depression and the student movements of the 1960s. Born on March 19, 1908, in Guadalajara, Mexico, López immigrated with his parents to the United States as an infant. After residing in El Paso for ten years, his family moved to Pomona, California, where he lived for the rest of his life. The son of a Protestant minister, López did not share the experience of his Mexican American peers harvesting citrus fruit in the local orchards. Rather, he had the uncommon fortune of attending Pomona High School. Following his graduation in 1927, López studied at Chaffey Junior College for two years before entering Pomona College, where he received a Bachelor of Arts degree in 1931.[17]

In 1933, López married for the first time and began the Spanish-language newspaper *El Espectador*.[18] During the early years of its existence, *El Espectador* functioned primarily as a newspaper for Mexican residents, providing information that did not appear in the English-language newspapers such as Ontario's *Daily Report*, La Verne's *Leader*, and Pomona's *Progress Bulletin*.[19] López and his first wife, Beatriz, published *El Espectador* every Friday and charged the nominal fee of 3 cents per copy. Local Mexican residents depended on the newspaper to communicate and receive important information concerning *mutualista* meetings, dances, and news pertaining to the *colonias*, thereby strengthening the community bonds among Mexican families living and working in the citrus belt. By the mid-1930s, the masthead of *El Espectador* read: "distributed every Friday morning in all Spanish speaking homes in Pomona, Alta Loma, Chino, Cucamonga, Upland, Ontario, Guasti, Etiwanda, Claremont, San Dimas, La Verne, Spadra, Mira Loma, Fontana, and Decles."[20]

As *El Espectador* increased its readership and covered a wider area of the

Southland during the 1930s, López bore witness to acts of violence and discrimination against Mexican Americans that inspired him to expand the definition and purpose of the newspaper. Translated as the "the spectator" or "the witness," *El Espectador* gravitated toward the latter as López committed himself to reporting violations of Mexican American civil rights in addition to the news of community gatherings and social events. By 1937, López aggressively reported stories of discrimination against Mexican Americans, and voiced his opinion through an occasional editorial. For example, in an article entitled "Pedimos Justicia" (We Demand Justice), López called for an investigation into the police beating of a young Mexican American, Antonio Camacho. According to police statements, officers apprehended the drunken youth as a suspect in an assault charge. In the process of arresting Camacho and his friend, Ontario police officers beat the Mexican American youth and then placed him in a jail cell overnight without tending to his wounds. Outraged by this offense, López castigated the Ontario police department and city officials. López proclaimed "*El Espectador* the only Mexican organization of this district and the defender of all Mexicans," and argued, "police never have the right to beat anyone, unless that person resists arrest."[21] In addition to putting public pressure on the police department through the newspaper, López helped resolve the matter by visiting with Ontario town officials and demanding immediate attention to the crisis. The following day the judge announced that a case of mistaken identity had occurred and he ordered the release of Camacho and his friend with apologies to his family and the Mexican American community.

The effectiveness of this campaign inspired López to pursue a civil rights agenda in his newspaper from 1937 to its final publication in 1961. A friend and fellow Mexican American journalist, Eugenio "Eno" Nogueras, provided López helpful advice on how to improve *El Espectador*. Nogueras published his own Spanish-language newspaper *El Sol* in San Bernardino, and occasionally wrote guest editorials concerning Mexican American civil rights for *El Espectador* under the heading "Sol y Sombra" (Sunshine and Shadow).[22] In 1938, Beatriz and Ignacio López employed a local Mexican American lawyer, José M. Ibañez, to write a column entitled "La Ley" (The Law), in which he gave professional advice on legal battles common to most Mexican American residents. These changes instituted a more aggressive political agenda for *El Espectador*, which López characterized as "not a combative newspaper," but one that "is vigilant about reason and justice."[23]

While pursuing an activist agenda, López also attempted to reach out to women and a new generation of Mexican American youth. In 1937, he added a section specifically "for her" ("por ella") entitled "Belleza Femenina" ("Feminine Beauty") in which an unidentified author offered beauty tips to Mexican American women. López assumed women's disinterest in politics and primarily addressed issues of etiquette, diet, and cosmetics. The articles warned of the "dangers of makeup," and prescribed the conservative combination of a "proper diet, correct posture, and regular exercise" for women interested in improving their beauty.[24] This advice articulated an older generation's concern for the modernization of women, especially younger women increasingly exposed to ethnic-specific advertisement strategies by cosmetic companies.[25]

López demonstrated both conservative and progressive attitudes toward Mexican American youth in his newspaper. Frequently, he castigated "zoot-suit gangs" and blamed them for the negative stereotypes of Mexican people.[26] According to López, "they have aroused the ire and contempt of our countrymen with their hoodlumism of which an uninformed public blames all Mexicans." López, however, balanced his criticism by stating, "we also know the social and economic failings of our democracy that have bred these young culprits."[27] In 1938, he added the section "Our Youth in the Schools (and News)" to *El Espectador* for the purpose of controlling the spread of "hoodlumism" and developing a sense of citizenship and responsibility among Mexican American youth.

Seeking to empower the most accomplished Mexican American youths in the community, López reached out to two Mexican American high school students for editorial assistance: Candelario Mendoza of Pomona High School, and Rosemary Rodríguez, editor-in-chief of the school newspaper for Bonita High School in La Verne. Mendoza remembered jumping at the chance to work with López, whom he "admired . . . because he was a Pomona College graduate, [was] extremely erudite, and [had] a vision that was way ahead of its time."[28] Rather than require Mexican American youths to read and write in Spanish, a language discouraged by schoolteachers and therefore spoken mostly at home, López acknowledged the effects of Americanization on Mexican American youths and endorsed English-language education as an avenue for Mexican Americans to succeed in U.S. society. "Our Youth in the Schools," therefore, was published entirely in English.[29]

The page included news about high school sports, dances, plays, and a column by Mendoza entitled "And So It Goes." Through this column, Mendoza articulated the vision of a young, educated, second-generation Mexican American. He encouraged youths to attend school, to aspire to go to college, and to avoid the use of drugs and alcohol. Mendoza offered advice to Mexican American youths on how to overcome generational differences with their parents. In an article, entitled "Are We To Obey Regardless," he acknowledged that "We of the younger generation are beginning to stand up on our feet and fight for our rights." "So," he counseled Mexican American youth, "live according to the present trend of life, but at the same time weigh the experience of the 'old folks,' then use your own sane judgement."[30]

Under the direction of López, *El Espectador* inspired Mexican Americans of various generations to fight for civil rights, while articulating a particular vision of Mexican American cultural empowerment. During the 1930s and 1940s, López wrote editorials and served in positions, such as the Spanish liaison to the Office of War Information, that defined his political philosophy and informed his strategies for social change. Both he and Eno Nogueras expressed the belief that most Mexican Americans experienced discrimination because of their own acquiescence to domination. Nogueras, for example, characterized Mexicans living in the United States as "innocently asleep in a dream of listlessness and unconcern."[31] Similarly, López excoriated Mexican American voters for not participating in a 1940 mayoral and city council election in Chino, California. Only 149 of the 350 registered Mexican voters cast their ballots, prompting López to write, "[The Mexican] People must be awakened from lethargy."[32] López believe that full participation in U.S. society and government provided Mexican Americans the best option for relief from discrimination. Following his own advice, in 1937 he passed up a lucrative job with the Department of Education in Mexico, and instead became a naturalized U.S. citizen on September 21, 1938.

López's educational background and middle-class status afforded him a special position from which he could easily castigate Mexican residents for their reluctance to vote. For example, Victor Murillo Ruiz, owner of a market in Ontario's Mexican *colonia*, remembered the Lópezes being slightly better off than other neighborhood families. Ruiz recalled, "Of course . . . their father had money to send them to school."[33] López, however, applied his relative wealth and education to assisting the Mexican American community. As a young man, López would use his local influence and money to rent the high school auditorium for Mexican Americans to perform Christmas plays. Ruiz remembered, "Everybody got a little bag of peanuts and an apple and a couple candies." His generosity and leadership qualities gained him many loyal friends and much authority within citrus belt society.

López often used his influence to shape Mexican American opinions, and to criticize Euroamerican prejudice in Southern California. In 1943, the so-called "zootsuit riots" in Los Angeles provided López an opportunity to articulate his vision of race relations in the Southland. Following six days of violence against Mexican youths by white U.S. sailors, First Lady Eleanor Roosevelt blamed the disturbances on a history of "undemocratic discrimination and segregation practiced by the Anglo-Americans on the Hispanic-Americans." Numerous white-owned newspapers, including the *Los Angeles Times*, criticized Mrs. Roosevelt for her interpretation, calling it "untrue" and "dangerous." In an article entitled "Wooing in the Dark," López delivered a spirited defense of the First Lady and outlined his impressions of Southern California society. He wrote: "Race discrimination against the Mexican minority of the Southwest has and is being practiced. The attitude of race superiority by our Anglo-American 'brothers' is not limited to individuals and private organizations but is the established policy of many of the cities of Southern California." [34]

López strategically published "Wooing in the Dark" in English to communicate a Mexican point of view to Euroamericans, and to participate in the public debates surrounding the race riots. Moreover, he challenged white liberals supportive of Roosevelt's Good Neighbor Policy to remember the home front. He concluded: "If charity begins at home—good neighboring must begin in our own back yard." [35]

López attempted to move between two worlds, the Mexican *colonia* and local government, in order to forge coalitions that would help improve the position of Mexican Americans. Although he criticized most Caucasians for possessing attitudes of racial superiority, he recognized important allies who could help facilitate the shared goal of equality. Throughout his career he forged significant relationships with many white liberals, and occasionally allowed them to publish English-language editorials and articles in *El Espectador*. These allies included professors at citrus belt colleges like the University of Redlands, University of California at Riverside, and the Claremont Colleges;[36] elected officials in the Democratic Party; progressive journalists and activists like Carey McWilliams;[37] and local and national labor leaders. Throughout the late 1930s and early 1940s, López maintained membership in just two organizations: the all-white Ontario Kiwanis Club, and the all-Mexican *mutualista*, Sociedades Progresista.[38] In addition, he advocated work within the system, and held positions with the Office of War Information from 1941 to 1942.[39] While employed by the government, López relinquished editorial duties to his friend Eno Nogueras and left the general business of the newspaper to his wife, Beatriz.

López simultaneously promoted integration and resistance, and saw himself as the torchbearer in the fight to defend Mexican American civil rights. His leadership inspired a new cadre of Mexican American activists, and contributed to a decade of improvement in Mexican American and white relations in the citrus belt of the San Gabriel, San Bernardino, and Pomona Valleys. López succeeded in mobilizing Mexican Americans in Ontario and surrounding citrus belt communities on many fronts, including battles to desegregate movie theaters, elementary schools, and public pools.[40] These public challenges to Jim Crow laws garnered the support of many white residents who occasionally joined in boycotts of businesses accused of discriminating against Mexican Americans. For example, the normally conservative *Ontario Daily Report* endorsed the campaign against Upland's Grove Theater, which segregated Mexican Americans to seats in the front row of the movie house. After a month-long boycott observed by Mexican Americans and whites, the theater's owner was forced to rescind his segregationist policy. Signaling an embrace of the struggle by the white press, on March 3, 1939, the *Ontario Daily Report* announced: "No Discrimination Pledge: Mexican Organizations Win in Controversy over 'Jim Crow' Seat in Movie Theatres."[41]

Whites supported the movement for Mexican American civil rights during the late 1930s and early 1940s for many reasons. Some sincerely supported the struggle for equality and justice, and had forged meaningful alliances with Ignacio López in hopes of furthering a general liberal agenda in the citrus belt. López had also won over many white allies by promoting an aggressive, but disciplined Mexican American civil rights movement. His emphasis on education and civic responsibility appealed to many whites who feared the alternative of marauding "zootsuiters" popularized by the Southern California media.[42]

Most important, the fear of reprisal by Mexican American customers and voters motivated many business owners and elected officials to back the movement. Within the small towns of the suburban citrus belt, Mexican American communities constituted a substantial percentage of the population, and therefore, possessed considerably more clout than urban minorities such as African Americans and Mexican Americans in Los Angeles. During the late 1930s, many Mexican Americans began to see the potential power of manipulating the unusual demographic and geographic composition of the citrus belt to their advantage. For example, López published a 1937 editorial by F. Moreno, in which the author stated:

> In the [San Gabriel] Valley which extends from the city of El Monte to Guasti, there exist 16 to 18 strong Mexican communities where close to 50 to 55 clubs, lodges, unions, societies and ordinary commissions function. These represent 80% of the total Mexican population which lives in the already mentioned valley . . . If one takes these facts into consideration, nobody would escape the transcendental effect of a confederation of societies, where representation of all societies in each town was united. . . . What would be the strengths and the benefits that a confederation of societies would report to its members?[43]

As Mexican Americans of the citrus belt organized and united they began to recognize the potential of their vote, while whites realized the cost of discrimination.

By the middle and late 1940s, Mexican Americans living in the San Gabriel and San Bernardino Valleys participated in local elections, protested against segregation, and forced many discriminatory businesspeople and government officials to respect the power of an organized Mexican American community. This movement crystallized into a broad political coalition known as the Unity Leagues, consisting of Mexican American business owners, college students, community leaders, war veterans, and white allies. In some areas, Mexicans collaborated with the Asian American and African American community leaders.[44] Although World War II temporarily diverted attention away from Mexican American civil rights during the mid-1940s, it also served as a catalyst to a more aggressive movement after the war and contributed to the determination of Unity League members. For example, Cande Mendoza remembered his attitude after returning from the war front as he tried for the second time to secure a teaching job in Pomona. He recalled:

> I said, "Here I am, I'm back again!" [laughs] And, you know this time I was a little more assertive I guess, because I said to myself, "My gosh, I went into World War II, and I was overseas for two years, and served with George Patton's third army as an infantryman attached to a tank and battalion, and . . . if they tell me they are not going to give me the job this time, they're going to find the activist in me coming out." [laughs] So, things had changed by that time, and they did give me a job.[45]

Mendoza quickly applied this sense of entitlement to fair and equal treatment to political action in the Unity Leagues. In 1946, Mendoza collaborated with López to form the first of these organizations in Pomona. He remembered: "Ignacio López and I started a group in Pomona called the Pomona Unity League, which we called "pul"—P.U.L—and I was sort of the executive secretary. . . . [The group consisted of] young people that just got back from the service, and gals. We went through registration for voting, and that helped."[46]

Among early Anglo supporters of this movement, Fred Ross, a field director for the American Council on Race Relations, lent his time and organizing skills to the formation of eight Unity Leagues. Ross had originally been sent to San Bernardino Valley during the mid-1940s to investigate the local Ku Klux Klan who had allegedly burned to death black civil rights activist O'Day Short and his family on Christmas Day, 1945.[47] Upon his arrival, Ross contacted Ruth Tuck, a sociologist at the University of Redlands and a friend of Ignacio López.

After an introduction from Tuck in 1946, Ross became fast friends with López, and the two took numerous trips throughout the Mexican American and African American communities, sharing ideas about organizing and building interracial coalitions. Ross's activities upset Council directors in Chicago who expected Ross to survey and report back his findings, but not to engage in political organizing. Ross's actions, however, caught the attention of Saul Alinsky, the founder of the Industrial Areas Foundation, an organization committed to empowering minority and unrepresented working-class communities to demand social justice, enfranchisement, and better education and civil services. Alinsky championed the work of Ross and eventually recruited him to serve as one of his West Coast representatives.[48] Following IAF-style strategies, López and Ross organized fifty young Mexican American men and women and founded Unity Leagues in towns throughout the citrus belt, including prominent orders in Pomona, Chino, Ontario, San Bernardino, and Redlands. In areas such as Riverside and San Diego, where Mexicans shared community space with blacks and Asian Americans, the Unity Leagues were multiracial organizations that sought common causes across racial and ethnic lines.[49]

Mexican American collaboration with African Americans and Asian Americans represented a novel approach to civil rights organizing during this period. For example, the League of United Latin American Citizens (LULAC) and the G. I. Forum, two Texas-based organizations, claimed a "white" identity and fought to protect privileges granted to U.S. citizens, but not to end racial discrimination and segregation. "While these organizations and their middle-class Mexican American leaders sought equality based on their constitutional rights as U.S. citizens," historian Neil Foley argues, "increasingly they came to the realization that race—specifically, being White—mattered far more than U.S. citizenship in the course of everyday life." The construction of a "Latin American" or "Spanish American" identity placed them further from their Mexican origins, and thus allowed some to escape the discrimination directed at recently arrived Mexican immigrants who bore the brunt of Euroamerican racism toward Mexicans. Many Mexicans knew the benefits of "whiteness" and "whitening" (blanquemiento) before arriving in the United States, but the U.S. racial hierarchy encouraged lighter-skinned Mexicans to make a "Faustian Pact with whiteness" and deny their African and indigenous ancestry.[50]

Mexican American members of the Unity Leagues, on the other hand, found in African Americans, Asian Americans, and progressive whites allies for an antiracist movement. Although more research is necessary, archives reveal that Mexican Americans worked with African Americans in particular as collaborators and co-creators in these civil rights organizations. For example, in the

Riverside *colonia*, Casa Blanca, Mexicans composed 90 percent, blacks 8 percent, and Japanese Americans the remainder of the total population of about 3,500, but members of the local Unity League maintained a slate of officers consisting of three African Americans and four Mexican Americans. Belen Reyes, a Mexican American woman, was the first president, while an African American, J. R. Riggins, served as the vice-president. As one of their first protests, the league joined with the local NAACP to present an ordinance to the Riverside City Council demanding the elimination of "White Trade Only" signs from all places of business. Building on this success, Belen Reyes demanded and won equal bussing services to public schools for Mexican American and African American children, and lobbied local politicians to support the removal of local Jim Crow laws. These actions stand as a testament to the antiracist vision of the Unity Leagues and suggest that Mexican Americans within these organizations felt an affinity with African Americans. Rather than base their demands for equality on claims of being "white," Mexican American Unity Leaguers embraced a nonwhite identity and fought for the eradication of all forms of racial discrimination in Southern California.

Although the Unity Leagues spoke out on a number of issues, from police brutality to segregation, the main goal of the organization was to register minority voters and organize local political campaigns for minority candidates.[51] Despite the minority status of Mexican Americans in Southern California towns, Unity League organizers believed an active Mexican electorate could function as a swing vote in close elections, and in areas of higher concentrations, allow minority candidates to capture a city council seat. "In this Southern California region," Ross explained, "it is particularly significant that although the largest Mexican American concentration—roughly 175,000—is in the city of L.A., the group is scattered throughout the entire area and constitutes from 12 to 25 percent of the population of most towns."[52] These demographic distributions may have limited Mexican American and minority empowerment in urban Los Angeles, where they constituted a smaller proportion of the city's total population; however, their relatively higher percentage of suburban populations granted them more clout at election time. For example, in an eight-day period in 1946, Ross and López registered 265 African American and Mexican American voters in Casa Blanca, nearly quadrupling the number of eligible minority voters. Although far from a majority, the Unity League voting block demanded to meet with the dueling city council candidates, Hare and Rothgaeber, to secure a promise to end segregation in local businesses. Hare's support of the Unity League combined with Rothgaeber's refusal to meet with the group translated into a victory for Hare and the Unity League's first taste of influence in local politics.[53]

Later that year, Unity Leagues in Chino and Ontario supported two Mexican Americans seeking elected city council seats: Andrés Morales (Chino) and Herman Moraga (Ontario). League members held fund-raising dances, solicited monetary and organizational support from Mexican American social groups and mutual aid societies (such as Sociedades Progresista), and pooled money collected by all Unity Leagues to finance these two campaigns.

These strategies proved to be effective on election day. In Chino, Morales won a seat on the city council making him the first Mexican American to be elected to such a position in California since the nineteenth century.[54] In Ontario, Moraga narrowly missed winning a council seat, placing a close third behind two white candidates. Like other movements orchestrated by López, the Unity League campaigns focused on minority empowerment, but also appealed to sympathetic whites. In Chino, where the Mexican American population was large but did not exceed 35 percent of the total electorate (the percentage needed to gain a seat), Morales depended on the additional support of white voters to win a position on the council. In Ontario, Moraga garnered the support of many prominent whites, which forced two opponents backed by organized labor, Robert Miller and Buel C. Autry, to resort to political fraud. The two candidates distributed handbills accusing Moraga of considering a bribe in exchange for removing himself from the race. Their tactics failed. After a close election, *The Ontario Daily Report* proclaimed: "Our prediction that the candidates, Miller and Autry feared Herman Moraga was borne out by the total. Their strength lay in the very precincts where Mr. Moraga polled his largest vote and in practically all cases he led these men. It will also be noted that Herman Moraga's unexpected strength in the precincts where people of his racial background do not predominate, was a fine vote of confidence and approval."[55]

Success in these elections inspired Unity League members to focus on new issues and other campaigns. Unfortunately, the victory in Chino marked a fleeting moment in Mexican American enfranchisement rather than the beginnings of political integration in the Pomona Valley. In subsequent years, the Unity Leagues tried to emulate their accomplishments in the fight for fair employment in California (Proposition 11), the Chino School Board elections, and the 1948 city council elections in Upland and Chino, all to no avail. López, ever the tireless organizer, drew criticism from Mexican Americans who feared a white backlash to the rapid push for integration.[56] López admonished his critics from the editorial page of *El Espectador*, and backed the younger generation of Mexican Americans who wanted to continue the movement. Yet even the younger members became discouraged by the defeats and began to focus on their own lives.[57] Disappointed by the failure to follow up on Morales's victory, Cande Mendoza remembered: "[After that] we didn't accomplish a heck of a lot, but we probably got a few people to register. . . . We were all young people; most of us not married. I think the moment that we married, and started raising our own families and so on, and trying to bring in some bread and butter to the table, our group disintegrated."[58]

The failure of councilperson Andrés Morales to address the needs of Mexican Americans in Chino further disillusioned López and Unity League members. The issue of fair and integrated housing provided the lightning rod that divided López and Morales and drew the Mexican American community into an internecine struggle that sapped the energy of the civil rights movement.

The fight over fair housing in the Pomona Valley began well before Morales's ascendancy to Chino's city council. In 1942, the federal government offered to subsidize the replacement of substandard dwellings with new, improved homes. Municipal governments interested in acquiring the funds had to submit a project proposal in order to be considered for the program. Acknowledging the potential economic benefits and the need for better housing in their town, the Ontario city council took up the issue for consideration during the spring of 1942.

Since much of the dilapidated housing stock was in the Mexican American districts of the town, the program, if enacted in Ontario, promised to assist Mexican Americans more than whites. Consequently, Mayor Taylor M. Peterson and city councilperson Sam Richards opposed the idea of submitting a project proposal on the grounds that it would primarily help Mexican Americans. Richards argued, "If such destruction [of 'Mexican slums'] were done, the homes would be occupied only by Mexicans, and for that reason [I] oppose the program."[59] Mayor Peterson supported this argument, and helped swing the council vote against submitting a proposal.

López, infuriated by this action, expressed his displeasure in the pages of *El Espectador* and organized a campaign to oust Richards and Peterson from their elected positions. Focusing on Mexican American voters, López organized a "Voters' Club" that rallied against the two men. Although unsuccessful, the campaign contributed to the larger Mexican American civil rights movement, and brought the issue of fair housing to the forefront for citrus belt communities.

Throughout the 1940s, the federal government maintained programs to improve housing stock in the United States. López advocated the participation of citrus belt towns in these programs, adding to this agenda the goal of integration. Grower housing projects and racial restrictive covenants had forced most nonwhite minorities, including Mexican Americans, into segregated communities with inferior and inadequate facilities. For López, improvement of structures, fair housing, and the ballot box constituted the keys to constructing a more equal and just society in Southern California. López articulated this position in one of his editorials when he wrote: "It is not the anglo-saxon who will reap the repercussions of . . . segregation . . . it will be those of us who have yet to understand that the only way to end discrimination and segregation is for us to integrate fully into society . . . making us part of the community and not trying to live in an exclusive world reserved only for ourselves." [60] Consequently, when the Unity Leagues helped Morales get elected in 1946, López anticipated the resumption of the 1942 battle over fair housing, this time with the support of a supposed ally on the city council.

Andrés Morales, however, proved to be anything but cooperative on this issue. Initially, López and the Chino City Council seemed to be in agreement when the issue to submit a project proposal came up for reconsideration in 1949. This time, Washington was offering more money ($20,000) for the construction of 150 to 200 new low-cost houses. The council started the process of application by ordering a census in Chino. López advised the Mexican American community to cooperate and directed a suggestion at Morales when he wrote, "local Mexican-American leaders [should] be alert so that the new housing project will not be built in a location which will only perpetuate the existing segregated state of Mexican housing." [61] Whether López's pressure adversely affected Morales and the City Council cannot be ascertained from existing records. Whatever the impulse, Morales and the rest of the Chino council members surprised the Mexican American community by voting not to submit a proposal. López, angered by what he interpreted to be Morales's betrayal, angrily commented, "we have bred a buzzard who has attacked our eyes." [62]

As in 1942, López rallied the Mexican American community, this time with the objective of salvaging the proposal. The overwhelming response from the community countered Morales's claim that Mexican Americans lacked enthusiasm for the project. The pro-housing coalition of Mexican Americans and whites countered the council's notion that the project would be too expensive by arguing that the social cost of crime bred in areas of poor housing would eventually outweigh the initial expense of the program. In 1951, Mexican

American and white community leaders eventually convinced enough council members to reverse the decision and support the project proposal. The schism between Morales and López, however, led to a divisive campaign by leaders in the Mexican American community to oust Morales from his council seat. Although he narrowly won reelection in 1950, Morales would lose his position in 1954.

During the 1950s, the subject of fair housing continued to be an important topic for López. He engaged in several campaigns against housing discrimination, including a bitter fight with a construction firm, Carlton Corporation, over racial restrictive covenants in its new Upland tracts. Although the company refused to admit racial minorities in tracts they had already built, López wrote editorials and mobilized a grassroots protest that forced Carlton to integrate an adjacent community then under development.[63] López and the Mexican American community won nominal gains in battles such as the one in Upland, but continued to lose the larger war for residential integration throughout Southern California.[64]

The late 1940s and early 1950s constituted a period of limited desegregation on many fronts, though racial minorities had to fight for these gains. In 1947, the Ninth Circuit Federal Court of Appeals, in the case *Mendez v. Westminster*, dismantled de jure segregation of Mexican children in the California school system. By November 7, 1947, Los Angeles County superintendent of schools C. C. Trillingham reported that most schools in the San Gabriel Valley had eliminated segregation, and provided details of their actions in the towns of Claremont, El Monte, Puente, and La Verne.[65]

Similarly, under Executive Order 8802, Franklin Delano Roosevelt established the Committee on Fair Employment Practices (FEPC), which alleviated some occupational discrimination in the defense industry. Cletus Daniel has pointed out that the FEPC mostly ignored Mexican Americans' complaints of discrimination, due to the committee's singular focus on the plight of black workers and President Roosevelt's fear that revelations would injure diplomatic relations with Mexico and lead to the disruption of the *bracero* program.[66] Moreover, Proposition 11, a ballot initiative to institute fair employment practices in California, failed to gain voters' approval in 1947. Nevertheless, the creation of the FEPC and pressures from prominent Mexican American leaders such as Ignacio López created a climate of integration that benefited some Mexican Americans seeking industrial jobs. For example, in 1954 roughly 50 percent of Mexican American men in Ontario, California, reported working in industries and other nonfarm establishments. By the end of the 1940s, anthropologist Ruth Hallo Landman found "it possible for a Mexican man to obtain industrial employment if he so chooses." She added, however, "Mexicans are still at the bottom of the economic order, and are merely participating in the general prosperity by drawing higher wages for unskilled work."[67]

Residential integration remained even more elusive than occupational and educational equality during the postwar period. In 1948, African American plaintiffs challenged de jure residential segregation in Los Angeles County in the case *Shelley v. Kraemer*. The plaintiffs sought to invalidate racial restrictive covenants that had prevented racial minorities from buying homes in exclusively white neighborhoods. Judge Thurmond Clarke of the Los Angeles Superior Court ruled that restrictive covenants violated the Fourteenth Amendment, becoming the first judge in the United States ever to strike down segregationist policies in housing. Three years later the U.S. Supreme Court upheld this decision.[68]

In spite of these advances, meaningful residential integration failed to occur throughout the Southland in the wake of these decisions. In 1934 the federal government established the Federal Housing Administration, an agency designed to make home loans more affordable for most Americans. In practice, however, federally subsidized private lenders and FHA's "confidential" city surveys discriminated against communities of color and channeled most loan money toward white applicants.[69] From the 1970s to the present, white politicians and homeowners' associations have rebuffed housing integration efforts by manipulating voting districts and incorporating all-white suburbs. These practices have resulted in a return to educational segregation, this time de facto style.[70]

Yet residential segregation was not a fait accompli for citrus belt communities at the end of the 1940s, nor did all whites advocate the complete separation of the "races" in the postwar period. Many Euroamericans championed the accomplishments of Ignacio López and the Mexican American community and supported their goal of integration. Interest in residential integration grew among progressive-minded whites even as López's conflict with Morales and his increasing involvement in electoral politics led him away from the frontline of the battle to desegregate housing in the San Gabriel Valley. Informal and formal contact between Mexican Americans and whites in such organizations and institutions as Friends of the Mexicans, Su Casa, the Claremont Colleges, and the Padua Hills Institute created a foundation for "intercultural understanding" that some hoped to translate into social action.

The formation of the Intercultural Council (ICC) in Claremont, California, represented the most earnest attempt by progressive-minded whites to achieve residential integration in Los Angeles County during the 1950s and 1960s. Led by a cadre of white artists, community philanthropists, and college professors, the ICC's idealistic prescription for intercultural relations provided an alternative vision to the de facto segregation that came to dominate the cultural landscape of Southern California from 1950 to the present.

The Intercultural Council

In Claremont, the presence of the Claremont Colleges significantly influenced local thinking on segregation and the separation of the "races."[71] Social scientists at the colleges interested in researching social relations frequently used the Arbol Verde community as a laboratory for understanding the conditions of Mexican Americans. Although these scholars and students sometimes approached their subjects with an attitude of sympathy, their studies often objectified Mexican residents by portraying them as impressionable, ignorant, and unorganized. For example, in her 1932 study, Helen O'Brien concluded, "the Claremont group is not organized" and found them "to be highly susceptible to social attitudes (in this sense, the attitudes which members of another race have toward [them])."[72] Studies conducted by students and scholars did little to alleviate the social inequalities extant between Mexican Americans and whites in the community, while occasionally actions by college-sponsored organizations such as the Friends of the Mexicans generated distrust and resentment among local Mexican Americans.

During the late 1940s, however, a new attitude among a few scholars began to change the exploitative relationship that existed between the Mexican American and white communities in Claremont. First, the Padua Hills Theatre, an institution that depended on the support of many college professors and administrators, facilitated the development of friendships and mutual interest between some Euroamericans and Mexican Americans in the community. Although the institution and its plays often reinforced historical myths and Mexican stereotypes, the goal of "intercultural understanding" articulated by theater owners Herman and Bess Garner manifested itself in exchanges between audiences, managers, and players before and after the productions. These exchanges generated a general interest in Mexico and Mexican people among many faculty members working at the Claremont Colleges, including nationally renowned artists Millard Sheets, Milford Zornes, and Albert Stewart, who donated their time, work, and money to promote the Mexican Players.[73] Equally important, the increased activism of Mexican Americans throughout the citrus belt during the late 1930s and 1940s inspired some white scholars to become involved in organizations invested in the improvement of intercultural relations.

Among these scholars, Dr. W. Henry Cooke was recognized as the leader of intercultural studies at the Claremont Colleges. In 1918, an unspecified health problem forced Cooke to leave Lawrence College in Wisconsin for the promise of better weather and the chance to finish his degree at Pomona College. Under the direction of Dr. Sumner, Cooke successfully completed his Bachelor of Arts and stayed in California to earn a doctorate in history at Stanford University. Following the completion of his Ph.D. in 1925, Cooke returned to Pomona College where he became the secretary of the Honors Committee and eventually became a director of graduate studies at Claremont Graduate School in 1938.

Soon after assuming the position at Claremont Graduate School, Cooke attended a UNESCO Conference in San Francisco. In his graduate studies and the early part of his career, Cooke researched the history of diplomatic relations, or what he described as "world understanding, international understanding, and international relations." The San Francisco experience, however, significantly altered his perspectives. Cooke explained: "The strict international relations, in an academic sense, that I had been following, in connection with history, gave way in my mind to a study of the relation of peoples rather than governments." Cooke continued, "the relation of peoples to each other, in a formal sense, seemed to be almost completely based upon the cultural pattern of each people, and not upon the governmental, diplomatic maneuverings." [74] At the conference, he drafted a pamphlet outlining his new understanding of international relations that organizers copied and distributed to all registrants. In it, Cooke argued that meaningful peace had eluded nations primarily because understanding amongst people of various cultures had not first been achieved within the nations. Therefore, Cooke concluded, peace between nations could not be reached without first securing "cultural integration at home." [75]

This new understanding led Cooke to focus on the problem of segregation of Mexican Americans in Southern California. Initially, upon first arriving in Claremont, Cooke paid little attention to the Mexican *colonia* of Arbol Verde during his undergraduate studies. His only contact with Mexican people was through his wife, Mary Miller Cooke, who held a position teaching at Sycamore School in Claremont in 1919. At that time, the Claremont school district did not practice segregation, and seven of her twenty-eight first grade students came from the Arbol Verde community. Informally monitoring the progress of these seven children, Henry Cooke noted, "these children went right into the grades with everybody else and were taught the same as everybody else." He added, "while they were weak on language, they took hold in no time; nobody knew a different way." [76]

This early exposure to integrated education informed his criticisms of educational segregation during the 1940s. Cooke watched segregation in Claremont develop, as a local educator, Charlotte Merrill, first established what she called an "opportunity room" for Mexican children in a separate building on Sycamore's school grounds. Although he saw Merrill's actions as well-intentioned and "not real segregation," Cooke nevertheless disagreed with the practice of separating Mexicans from whites.[77]

During the late 1940s, Cooke became active in countywide organizations and wrote articles that articulated his opposition to segregation and discrimination. In 1948, for example, Cooke published an article entitled "The Segregation of Mexican-American School Children in Southern California," in which he championed the recent decision in the *Mendez* case and implored Southland school districts to comply with the court ruling. Cooke acknowledged the importance of an educated and organized second and third generation of Mexican Americans. "They are now in large numbers 'Americans' in every sense of the word," wrote Cooke, and have "organizations for their own improvement and integration."[78] Cooke also recommended action against discrimination in housing and all other public facilities, and advocated "break[ing] down the superiority doctrine of the white race and . . . replac[ing] it with the idea of racial equality." In an article entitled "The Continuing American Revolution," Cooke assessed U.S. society, arguing that "our whole social pattern, be it relative to the armed services, the churches, the composition of our cities, or our universities, seems out of joint when considered in the light of full acceptance of racial differences." He therefore called to action "all fearless souls who organize to combat injustice in inter-group or inter-racial relations."[79]

Following his own advice, Cooke founded a group in Southern California called the Committee on Community Relations of the Los Angeles Welfare Council. Meeting in the Chamber of Commerce Building in Los Angeles, the organization discussed incidents of ethnic and racial conflict in the county and strategies on how to resolve them. The council began by addressing a dispute in Los Angeles between African American residents and returning Japanese American internees. Before World War II, Japanese Americans had created a distinctive ethnic neighborhood in south Los Angeles known as "Little Tokyo." Due to the internment of Japanese families and the migration of African Americans for defense industry jobs, the area became a predominantly black community referred to as "Brownsville." When the war ended, Japanese Americans returned to the neighborhood intent on reclaiming their homes and businesses. The two groups clashed over control of the local economy and culture.[80]

African American entrepreneurs and musicians fostered the development of a lively jazz and art scene within the neighborhood. The Japanese, on the other hand, objected to black investments in liquor stores and nightclubs, which they believed caused a proliferation of crime and "vice" in the area. The Committee on Community Relations attempted to defuse the conflict by stopping new liquor licenses, controlling the spread of the "red-light district," and holding public meetings to discuss legal matters and religious differences. According to Cooke, the committee succeeded in resolving many differences fairly and peacefully by listening to both sides in the dispute. This even-handed approach, however, conflicted with the interests of the committee's supervising department, the Los Angeles Welfare Council, as Cooke explained: "[We] got so liberal eventually that the benefactors of the Los Angeles Welfare Council decided that we were too liberal for their support." He added, "they weren't so strong about settling the question with the Negroes; they were for kicking them out." [81] The rift with the Welfare Council led the committee to disband and reorganize as a private, nonprofit organization known as the Los Angeles County Conference on Community Relations. Cooke helped write the constitution for the group and served as president for the first two years beginning in 1947.[82]

Cooke assumed this position at a time of increased social action among a handful of liberal whites in Claremont. Two community residents in particular, Ruth Ordway and Harland Hogue, took the lead in renewing efforts to improve local white and Mexican American relations. During the 1920s, the Claremont Congregational Church contributed to the formation of Su Casa, a medical and hygiene program for Mexican women, and the Friends of the Mexicans.[83] Although the repatriations disrupted the relationship established between the church and the Arbol Verde residents, Ordway, a member of the Claremont Congregational Church, and Hogue, a Congregationalist minister and professor of religion at Scripps College, maintained an interest in improving the standard of living in the local *colonias*. Civic neglect, the discriminatory layout of county and city dividing lines, and depressed economic conditions among barrio residents allowed many of the structural problems to persist in Arbol Verde. The housing stock remained substandard in quality, while local discrimination and geographical separation kept Mexican American families segregated from the larger community in Claremont.

Around 1948, Hogue and Ordway had an informal discussion about how to remedy the situation in a meaningful way. During the conversation, Ordway mentioned to Hogue, "I understand that there is a tract of ground near the Mexican area of Claremont that is being sold for taxes. Why don't we see if we can buy it?" Both had faith that they could raise the necessary funds due to their significant connections in the community. Ordway served as chair for the Social Action Committee in the Women's Fellowship of the Claremont Church, while Hogue directed the Congregational Church Social Action Committee. Together, they developed the plan to purchase the land and provide affordable home loans to Mexican American families interested in settling in the area.

Ordway and Hogue decided to first consult Henry Cooke for guidance on the project. Cooke, a member of the Social Action Committee, also had been planning ways to unite his countywide organization with the local group in an effort to desegregate Claremont. Cooke first thought of trying to move the county lines that divided Arbol Verde, so as to bring all the local Mexican households within Los Angeles County and Claremont city boundaries. The plan proved to be impossible due to the excessive cost of redrawing government maps. Ordway and Hogue's idea provided a useful alternative; however, Cooke suggested one major alteration in the plans.

Cooke recommended that they change their focus. Instead of helping just Mexican Americans, the project would create an integrated neighborhood of Mexican and white families. In addition, the project would be governed by an association of concerned white citizens and serve as an exercise in intercultural cooperation. First, the governing body, known as the Intercultural Council (ICC), would not only raise the money for the purchase of land and help secure the promise of loans from local banks, but would also hold seminars and banquets to discuss strategies for integration and the improvement of race relations in Southern California. Second, Hogue, Ordway, and Cooke envisioned the actual construction of the houses as a cooperative effort, whereby future residents would join in the building of their own homes and get to know one another as the community took shape. Cooke explained the original plan: "The whole plan was to establish private homes in a tract with a uniform pattern of houses with a central space in the middle of the block for a common park area in which there was a big fireplace. The thought was that the Anglo families would help each other and the Mexican-Americans build their houses, decorate their houses, take care of each other's kids when there were some, and so forth—which they did—and that the Mexican-Americans would do the same."[84] Agreed on the plans, Ordway, Hogue, and Cooke returned to their respective groups intent on making the ICC and the intercultural community a reality.

The first step involved securing the land. Ordway and Hogue successfully persuaded the owner of the property, Realtor Claude Bradley, not to sell the land until the Social Action Committee could raise the money to buy it. Courting wealthy and influential members of the community, they got ten people to loan the committee $300 a piece at 3 percent interest, which enabled them to buy a square block adjacent to the Arbol Verde neighborhood. Ordway convinced the Women's Fellowship of the Claremont Church to put up an additional $200 to plant street trees, while the newly formed ICC paid a local surveyor to survey the tract and put in lot lines. The survey resulted in twelve lots to be parceled out to potential buyers by the Intercultural Council.[85]

In order to make the houses as affordable as possible, Ordway, Hogue, and Cooke sought out private funding to subsidize the construction plans. Cooke also enlisted the support of an interested and willing Millard Sheets, who joined the ICC and drew up architectural plans with a group of graduate students at the Claremont Graduate School (CGS).[86] Based on these plans, the ICC secured a grant of $5,000 from the Columbia Foundation of San Francisco, and later received $3,000 more. In addition, the ICC got an agreement from the local Citizens-National Bank and Security First National Bank to grant loans of between $3,000 and $6,000 at a low 4 percent interest to potential buyers considered "high-risk" by the Federal Housing Administration.[87] The entire ICC Board of Trustees served as cosigners to these loans, as did individual members including Bess Garner, Ruth Ordway, and a local nurse, Margaret Goff, who ran a health clinic for mothers and babies in the Arbol Verde *colonia*.[88]

Cooke worked to secure the intellectual foundations of the project by eliciting the support of renowned urban theorist and cultural historian Lewis Mumford. Cooke offered Mumford $1,000 to come to Claremont and produce a report that would "transmit the vision of what the project might mean to American life."[89] Although no record of Mumford's response exists, Cooke's letter to the fellow historian articulated his ambitious plans for the ICC. Cooke clearly expressed his intentions when he wrote:

> We have organized an Intercultural Council to work at the question of making it possible for Mexican Americans to improve their living conditions and to spread out into the residential areas from which they are now largely restricted [by racial restrictive covenants]. Our larger purpose is to start a change in the attitude of the community toward any or all outsiders of non-caucasian culture. We should be able to use our college-community character to take the lead in intercultural social and residential patterns for this whole area [of Southern California].[90]

Cooke thought of the ICC as a regional think tank and action committee for Greater Los Angeles, and hoped to produce in Claremont a model in intercultural living that other Southland communities could follow.[91] He spread the news of the project throughout the county through his position with the Conference on Community Relations. By 1948, the Los Angeles County Board of

Supervisors took special notice of the project and expressed their sincere interest in the ICC plans. In a letter of congratulations, a consortium of community organizations organized by the Board of Supervisors wrote: "It is hoped that your undertaking may serve as the pilot project to guide other communities in solving their problems."[92] Sheets shared this optimism, which he expressed in the community blueprints. Sheets wrote, "We want to prove that something can be done about segregative living in our area and in our own day." He concluded, "It is time people in America learn to live together without respect to color, race, nationality and creed—we hope our efforts may help to bring about this fundamental achievement."[93]

In practice, however, the community and the council's efforts exhibited both the problems and the promise of intercultural relations in Southern California. To fill houses designated for white residents, the ICC invited graduate students studying at the Claremont Graduate School to join the new community. Paul Darrow, an artist and resident of the ICC community, remembered, "all the caucasian families were graduate students on G.I. Bills [studying] Psychology, Political Science, history and Fine Arts."[94] Most were newlyweds and in their mid-twenties, and active in liberal politics on a local level. Darrow believed that most whites bought into the community "because it was a good deal and part of the deal was the inter-cultural situation."[95]

Mexican Americans, however, joined the ICC community with greater hesitation. Their experiences with Friends of the Mexicans, the repatriations and deportations, educational segregation, and general discrimination cast shadows of doubt over the project. Mary Palos, a resident of the ICC community recalled, "there were [Mexican] people who didn't trust those gringos, gabachos, or Americanos because of what they had done."[96] She also recounted an offense committed by the Intercultural Council against her brother when he tried to buy the land set aside for the community: "He had put in money, not the whole thing but he was already buying [the property]. . . . And then came these people [ICC], and they told him that they were buying it and that he should just as well get his money back."[97]

Paul Darrow also remembered that the ICC had difficulty persuading Mexican families to join the community and heard that some council members "semi-leaned on" potential Mexican American residents by threatening not to hire them for local jobs.[98] In spite of Mexican American distrust and allegations of white coercion, the Intercultural Council finally settled Mexican families in half the homes in the tract.

In addition to the six Mexican and five Caucasian families, the original settlement included the first African American homeowners in Claremont.[99] Isaac and Ann Livingston, graduate students in the Education Department at CGS, lived next door to the Palos family. Mary Palos commented that "bring[ing] blacks [into the neighborhood] was important to me and for us to live close together and learn about one another." [100] Although the Livingstons stayed only two years in the community, Bruno and Mary Palos forged a meaningful relationship with the couple. In later years, the Paloses visited the Livingstons in San Francisco where the two Claremont graduates found jobs teaching in public schools.

Once settled, community relations functioned like most suburban neighborhoods in postwar America. "We were just a bunch of young families in a unique social situation," commented Paul Darrow. He added, "like all neighborhoods there are several you relate to, more you chat with and most you nod to." [101] Mary Palos recalled having "potluck" parties and hosting neighborhood meetings at her house. Since the community shared washing machines, barbecues, and a park known as Neighbors Park, the residents conducted monthly meetings to regulate use and maintenance of these facilities. Mary recalled only one dispute among the residents. "The Felixes didn't want to participate in paying to keep up the park, [and] I had to go up there and speak to them." [102] Darrow remembered these meetings as some of the "rough" but "most successful times," commenting, "we argued as equals and most often sides on issues were mixed racially (terrible word)." [103]

Although disagreements arose between families, new understanding and genuine friendship also evolved. Paul Darrow commented that relationships "were not artificial," and believed that the personal and cultural exchanges within the neighborhood benefited his family. "My kids spoke Spanish as a result of growing up there," Darrow remembered. In addition, Darrow's son Chris forged a lifelong friendship with Roger ("Rogie") Palos. The experience also contributed to Darrow's development as an artist. Darrow recalled, "My first series of acceptable non-student work was the result of abstracted paintings of the gravel pits, the abandoned machinery, railroad cars and broken trucks behind El Chisme [the local market]."

Painting the *colonia* sensitized Darrow to the problems facing Mexican Americans. Occasionally, Darrow would invite students to his house to paint the community. "They would say 'hello' to Mary, and she would ignore them," remembered Darrow. Later, she explained to Darrow that their paintings "embarrassed her" and that she felt "condescended to" by their actions. Darrow discovered that this created a "strange kind of feeling of resentment," which he then respected after the exchange with Palos.[104]

Living together also shaped Mexican Americans' perceptions of whites, as

Mary Palos explained: "In my thinking before I started mixing with them and living with them . . . I had in my mind that over there [downtown Claremont] they were so clean because they were so white. [Shakes her head 'no,' and laughs] And then I learned that some of us are not as clean as others! I learned that it's not true."[105]

The experience of intercultural living dispelled some popular myths about whites and allowed Mexican Americans to counter white popular notions concerning Mexicans. Mary Palos remembered, "I thought it helped to show that we were not as ignorant as I thought that they thought we were." She also revealed, "I learned that the Caucasians get more opportunities . . . like the professors we were dealing with in the Intercultural Council . . . that was the *big* difference—and the money—you know, they had more money."[106]

These differences also manifested themselves among the twelve families. As the white (and black) graduate students finished their studies and moved out of the *colonia*, the ICC found it difficult to maintain the racial "mix" originally established in the community. Cooke explained: "We got graduate students who were interested in Spanish, in art, and in city planning courses and so forth, to buy some of the places, and Mexican-Americans of what I would call laboring class to buy the others. This made a little community that was bifurcated and never quite wholesome because there were two kinds of people in it, some with a temporary interest as they went through college, others with a more permanent interest."[107]

Paul Darrow recalled a conversation with Bruno Palos that illustrated this fact. "Bruno told me, 'for you, this is temporary, but for me, this is as good as I'm going to get.'" Palos added, "You're not going to stay here." Like many of the graduate students, Darrow fulfilled Palos's prediction, as his art career took off and his need for space increased. Although Darrow lived in the ICC house for a few years after graduation, he eventually moved to a larger home in a white neighborhood in north Claremont during the late 1950s.[108]

Throughout the 1950s and 1960s, the Intercultural Council labored to maintain the mixed-race community and to keep alive the dream of intercultural understanding. Private ownership complicated this ambition, as most white but few Mexican American families sold their property. Frequently, the ICC would locate new families, replacing Mexican Americans with Mexican Americans, and whites with whites. After the Livingstons moved, no African Americans lived in the community until the late 1950s. Finding replacement families proved to be extremely difficult and taxing for the ICC. As Darrow recalled, "capitalism took over," as residents sold their properties for much higher prices than they originally paid.

For the families who stayed in the community, privacy within and around individual homes became increasingly important. The washing facilities became obsolete as families attained better incomes and bought their own washers and dryers. Moreover, the upkeep of Neighbors Park, an issue that troubled the Felix family from the beginning, came to be viewed as a burden by other families as well. Cooke recalled: "They didn't want the rest of the neighborhood—even their friends—using that park. The 'neighbors' did not want the park open to the public right at their back doors. . . . You could have a small golf course there and everything else, but they didn't want that." [109]

Maintenance and the shared expense of the park troubled many poor Mexican American families who refused to pay the $2.00 per month to water the area. In 1957, Paul Darrow sold his house to a gay couple, which he remembered "upset" many residents who refused to share facilities with them. [110] The couple, on the other hand, complained, "the 'Mexicans' would come [to the park] right at the back of [our] holding, beyond [our] fence, and make love." [111] Eventually, the two men went to the ICC attorney and had the park surveyed and divided up amongst the residents. No residents raised meaningful objections to their actions and Neighbors Park vanished by 1960.

For Cooke and the ICC, arguments among the residents shattered their idealistic vision of community relations. Cooke found the community irritatingly "clique-y" and not as united as he had hoped them to be. However, Claremont elites associated with the Intercultural Council required community residents to bear the unrealistic burden of representing positive intercultural relations. Cooke invited county officials and members of the Conference on Community Relations to the neighborhood, while Ordway often conducted weekend tours with college visitors to highlight the ICC's accomplishments. Paul Darrow, for example, recalled one Saturday when Mrs. Ordway called and asked if he would go outside and talk with Bruno Palos while she brought by a group of visiting scholars from the colleges. "When she arrived," Darrow explained, "she got out of an expensive car wearing a fur, and asked, 'Are we being intercultural today?!'" [112]

Material issues and class differences affected the community, while the attitude of white elites in the ICC further complicated relations between the council and the residents of the *colonia*. The council expanded its activities in the 1960s by offering college scholarships to Mexican American high school students, creating a "well-baby clinic" for Mexican American infants and their mothers, and contributing funding to a "Children's Center" and "Teen Post" for Mexican American youth. Within each of these projects, Intercultural Council members contributed much personal time and money to the venture;

however, their focus began to shift from integration and community interaction to voluntarism.[113]

Although Mexican Americans appreciated these efforts, some also despised the condescension that often accompanied these programs. For example, Daniel Martínez Jr., a recipient of the Intercultural Council Scholarship in the 1950s, thankfully accepted the funding, but found some of the benefactors "more interested in clearing their own consciences, rather than helping the Mexican people."[114] During the late 1960s and early 1970s, the Chicano Movement intensified Mexican American criticisms of white paternalism in the barrio. For example, at the Children's Center, controversy erupted in 1970 when the director, Albert Gutiérrez, resigned his position due to "the intrusion of what he considered alien values."[115] Blaming the Intercultural Council and Mexican Americans sympathetic to the organization, Gutiérrez complained, "[the center] had become a white middle class charity house rather than a beacon of identity for the Chicano community."[116] In the wake of this conflict, ICC community resident Rey Contreras explained the problem with the Intercultural Council: "They were good people with good intentions. They were honest people but there is always a hazard trying to be the mind and body of someone else. It develops a kind of dependency. . . . Some times the social differences are too great."[117]

From the ICC's inception in 1948 to the Children's Center controversy in 1970, social and class differences between Mexican Americans in Arbol Verde and white elites in the Intercultural Council manifested themselves in very obvious ways. First, not one leading member of the Intercultural Council chose to make Arbol Verde their home. Second, though the purchase of available land in the Arbol Verde tract made it a target area for the project, the council did not consider other neighborhoods as potential sites, before, during, or after the formation of the community. The idea of integration appealed to white Claremonters, but only in areas inhabited by Mexican Americans. An attempt by a Mexican American family to move into an all-white neighborhood in the early 1960s illustrated this point. Cooke remembered: "Now, there was a time when one [Mexican American] family wanted to move over here on 12th and Indian Hill and there was trouble. Even Dr. Blaisdell [ex-President of Pomona College] told me that the neighbors didn't want them. He said, 'They wouldn't fit in there. They will be different. They'll have a road full of cars and everything else.'"[118]

Like Claremont neighborhoods outside of Arbol Verde, the Intercultural Council remained predominantly a white organization, with token participation granted to a few Mexican Americans. During the founding of the council and the construction of the community, Henry Cooke commented, "there was no Mexican in on the planning of his own original house."[119] This pattern continued after the establishment of the community, when Intercultural Council conferences and neighborhood meetings took place separately. Although Mexican American residents attended the annual banquet and paid their dues, few went to the regular monthly meetings of the council. Occasionally, Mexican American representatives from the neighborhood attended these larger gatherings only to report on conditions within the community. As Cooke recalled, "the backbone of the Intercultural Council was obviously Anglo."[120]

During the 1950s, the council made efforts to include Mexican Americans, but the general attitudes of many members offended Mexican participants. Former Paduano and post office worker José O'Beso remembered joining the council briefly during the late 1950s. O'Beso believed "they want[ed] a Mexican on their council so that they could show they were not prejudiced." At his first meeting, a white council member asked O'Beso, "you work in the post office and you're Mexican. I want you to tell me why the Mexican people don't open their letters." O'Beso responded, "I don't know what you are talking about, or why you would say that." "Well," the man answered, "this [Mexican] guy owes us so much money. And every month we mail him the bill and he never answers. Evidently, he doesn't open the letter." O'Beso, angered by the interrogation, responded, "Well, that shows you that the Mexican people are very smart. They know what's in the letter, so why bother to open it?" At the conclusion of the meeting, O'Beso resigned his position, announcing, "I'm sorry, but I don't want to be part of your entertainment and I don't like this group."[121]

The Intercultural Council represents in a microcosm an intriguing and illustrative example of race relations in Southern California after World War II. During the late 1960s and early 1970s, a shift in the ICC's focus from integrated living to social services troubled many Mexican American participants. Moreover, the emergence of the Chicano Movement generated a backlash among younger Mexican Americans who believed self-determination was paramount. Commenting on the fight over the Children's Center, Mrs. Donald Bray, a member of the ICC, admitted, "there seemed to be an isolation of the policy board from the community—there seemed to be a rift developing—a failure of communication." According to Albert Gutiérrez, "the policy board wanted a white middle class thing—they wanted to make middle class kids from Mexican kids."[122]

Events surrounding the Children's Center reflected larger problems with white philanthropy in Claremont. Although Cooke had originally hoped "to start a change in the attitude of the community toward any or all outsiders of non-Caucasian culture," the Intercultural Council (and its many satellite organizations like the Children's Center policy board) defeated this purpose by focusing their attentions on the transformation of Mexican Americans.[123] Ruth Ordway demonstrated this attitude when she considered the legacy of the Intercultural Council in a 1978 interview: "[ICC] changed the attitude of the Mexican-Americans about the kind of housing they should have. When we went in there, I think there weren't any houses with running water and there were no bathrooms. Sometimes three or four houses used one outside toilet. I think the Organization changed the attitude of Mexicans about what housing should be."[124]

Ordway's comments reveal a common belief among many white philanthropists that Mexican "attitudes" caused the material deprivations suffered by Mexican Americans living in the citrus belt of Southern California. Although Ordway and other Claremont philanthropists mentioned "intercultural understanding" as an objective of the Intercultural Council, few whites involved in this and other similar ventures changed their subjective positions to see the world from the point of view of Mexican Americans. Even fewer altered their geographic and social positions to join the Arbol Verde neighborhood and live the dream of "intercultural living." Still others, such as Dr. James Blaisdell, endorsed "intercultural understanding" and integration as long as it happened in prescribed locations such as the Padua Hills Theatre, or in marginalized neighborhoods such as Arbol Verde.

The shortcomings of the Intercultural Council also provide some insight into why Ignacio López stressed self-help and political empowerment for the Mexican American community. Although López came from a relatively privileged background, he used this position to foster a civil rights movement among Mexican Americans. Operating between the white world and the Mexican *colonia*, López attempted to shape both communities into compatible entities within a pluralistic society. Ultimately, neither one conformed. Whites, by and large, eventually accepted Mexican American civil rights; however, the majority of Euroamericans resisted López's call for residential integration. Mexican Americans, on the other hand, mobilized behind López's movements; however, not all shared his enthusiasm for discipline. López's battles with Andrés Morales demonstrated that political factions existed within the Mexican American community during the 1940s and 1950s. In the 1960s, a generation of Chicano activists rejected López's accommodationist politics in favor of a more aggressive, antiestablishment message.

The limitations of the Mexican American civil rights movement in the San

Gabriel Valley, and the defects of the Intercultural Council, demonstrated the persistence of social and economic inequalities in Southern California after World War II. Although individual and collective efforts by Mexican Americans and whites successfully desegregated public and private institutions, those serious about improving race relations discovered residential integration to be an impossible dream. Ignacio López, for example, died while serving as the Spanish-Speaking Coordinator for the Department of Housing and Urban Development (HUD) under President Richard Nixon in 1973.[125] The mixed results of the Intercultural Council sobered the once idealistic Cooke, who found the goal of transforming white attitudes in Claremont, let alone Los Angeles County, a daunting task. In 1968, a beleaguered Cooke conceded, "I don't believe that Claremont as a whole has yet learned anything about integration."[126]

Yet, in spite of the ICC's limited vision of fair housing, and the inability of the Unity Leagues to achieve an equal place at the table for Mexican Americans, both their efforts contributed to the improvement of intercultural relations in post–World War II Southern California. Mexican Americans, more than any group, forced the transformations in citrus belt race relations. The maintenance of independent *colonias*, the creation of social spaces within society such as Rainbow Gardens, and the development of political groups and movements such as the Unity Leagues, boycotts, and protests all led to the advancement of Mexican American civil rights. Moreover, some Mexican Americans, such as Ignacio López and the Mexican Players of Padua Hills Theatre, successfully identified and collaborated with white allies to create "intercultural understanding" and promote cultural pluralism.[127] Through their own actions, Mexican Americans gained the attention and the respect of many whites who formerly ignored issues of social justice and equality.

The persistence of discrimination against Mexican Americans required a more forceful and less cooperative movement of Chicano students, laborers, and community groups during the 1960s and 1970s. Nevertheless, the advance of Mexican American civil rights in the name of cultural pluralism, integration, and intercultural understanding prior to the dawn of the Chicano Movement must be remembered. Following the repatriations and deportations of the early 1930s, Mexican Americans and progressive-minded whites worked together and separately for the improvement of race relations in Southern California. As a result of their efforts, citrus belt society moved from an era of Jim Crow and strict segregation in the 1920s, to modest but substantial gains in Mexican American civil rights by 1960.

Epilogue

In the three decades since the 1960s, Southern California has experienced demographic changes that have contributed to the transformation of the citrus belt. Both Asian and Latino populations have expanded largely due to the significant increases in immigration as a result of alterations in U.S. immigration laws and severe economic and political crises abroad. The Immigration Act of 1965 eliminated race as a consideration in immigration and dispensed with an old system of quotas favoring Western European countries. By establishing a single limit of 20,000 immigrants a year for each country in the Eastern Hemisphere, Congress intended to eliminate the low quotas set for Italy and other southern and eastern European countries, but its actions had the unintended consequence of opening up immigration from Asian countries. In the case of immigration from Mexico and other Latin American countries, numbers increased *in spite* of changes in the U.S. immigration law. Although Congress extended the annual 20,000 quota to the Western Hemisphere in 1976, thereby reducing the number of eligible Latino immigrants previously allowed into the United States, those totals have risen. Latinos increased at a rate far greater than any other minority group, increasing from just below 7 million persons in 1960 to approximately 10.5 million in 1970, 14.6 million in 1980, and an estimated 20 million in 1990.[1] Displaced by civil wars precipitated by U.S. counterinsurgency operations in Central America and neoliberal economic policies in Mexico, many people no longer feel "at home" in their homelands and have crossed the border as undocumented immigrants despite the passage of anti-immigrant legislation like California's Proposition 187 and the intensification of immigrant scapegoating by desperate politicians like the former governor of California, Pete Wilson. No one knows exactly how many people are living "illegally" in the United States, but a recent study by geographers James P. Allen and Eugene Turner estimate that during the 1980s at least 1.3 million resided in Southern California alone. Among these immigrants, Mexicans by far constituted the largest group, but Salvadorans, Guatemalans, Iranians, Chinese, and Filipinos also figured prominently.[2]

Many of these immigrants have made the San Gabriel, Pomona, and San Bernardino Valleys their home and have changed the face of the communities

I knew as a child. During the 1960s and 1970s, it was novel for my father, a second-generation Mexican American, to marry my Anglo mother and to purchase a home in neighborhoods not dominated by Mexican Americans. Today, my parents' neighbors are first-generation Colombian immigrants, while the businesses in downtown Ontario and Pomona are just as likely to advertise in Spanish as they are in English. In the citrus belt city of Azusa where my father owned a *carniceria* (meat market), changes in the ethnic and racial make-up of the clientele reflected the demographic changes going on in Southern California. When my father purchased "Frontier Meats" during the late 1980s, most of the customers and employees came from the white, African American, and Chicano working-class communities surrounding the market. By the mid-1990s, recent Latino and Asian immigrants constituted at least half our clientele, precipitating changes in our marketing strategies, products, and staff. To her surprise, my grandmother's homemade salsas, tacos, and *menudo* became customer favorites, while from the meat counter we sold more pounds of "flap" meat and skirt steak "para carne asada" than t-bone or porterhouse steaks. My father who had been socialized not to speak Spanish in public by Claremont and Upland schoolteachers, now found himself speaking his first language on a daily basis to customers hailing from places such as Tegulcigalpa, Honduras, Oaxaca, Mexico, and Managua, Nicaragua.

While we at the market adjusted to and even profited from these changes, others have reacted with hostility. The passage of Proposition 187, the California initiative that denies public services such as medical care and education to undocumented immigrants, and the successful 1994 reelection campaign of Governor Pete Wilson revealed the considerable white voter resentment toward immigrants in California. Motivated by the fear that all Mexicans wanted to take advantage of state welfare, proponents of Proposition 187 conducted a media campaign that characterized Latino immigrants as sexually unrestrained deviants intent on reaping benefits for their growing families.[3] Drawing on the groundswell of support among white voters for the initiative, Pete Wilson linked his 1994 bid for reelection to the pro-187 forces and erased the seemingly insurmountable lead of his Democratic challenger Kathleen Brown. During the campaign, syndicated columnist and presidential candidate Pat Buchanan captured the sentiments of many white Californians in a *Los Angeles Times* commentary entitled, "What will America Be in 2050?" Answering, "a nonwhite majority is envisioned if today's immigration continues," Buchanan called for a "timeout on immigration to assimilate the tens of millions who have recently arrived." In an appeal to the anti-immigrant and racist attitudes of many white voters, Buchanan ended his article with the ominous warning: "If we lack the courage to make the decisions as to what our country will look like in 2050, others will make those decisions for us, not all of whom share our love of the America that seems to be fading away." [4] Although in 1946 Carey McWilliams predicted that "political truculence, adolescent social noisiness, and strident cultural nativism in California" was nearing its end, California voters and politicians have demonstrated that immigrant scapegoating is alive and well in the golden state. [5]

Today Latinos are among the poorest of the poor in the United States and have not benefited from California's welfare system as critics of immigration have charged. Rather, the politics of hate and resentment expressed by Buchanan and Wilson and supported by the majority of California voters have encouraged many immigrants to withdraw from the use of public aid. Recent studies of immigration demonstrate that undocumented workers pay far more in taxes than they receive in social services, while most do not qualify for direct welfare assistance. [6] Moreover, a 1997 study published by the Ethnic and Hispanic Statistics Branch at the Census Bureau found that anti-immigrant attitudes have affected the opportunities of all Latinos, including those born in the United States. "When Census analysts separated out United States–born Hispanic people," reported the New York Times, "they found their income levels declining as well." This report contributes supporting evidence to historian David Gutiérrez's findings in his book, Walls and Mirrors: Mexican Americans, Mexican Immigrants, and the Politics of Ethnicity, that politics designed to limit the opportunities of undocumented immigrants adversely affects the social and economic mobility of Latinos born in the United States.

How have Latinos reacted to this dire situation? Like those who have come before them, Latinos have responded in various ways, from outright resistance to the more accommodating but equally important creation of community and entertainment spaces where alternative and more inclusive definitions of citizenship have been articulated. The historic march on Los Angeles on October 16, 1997, in which 70,000 Latinos protested against Proposition 187, did not alter the eventual outcome of the vote, but it manifested the outrage shared by all Latinos, undocumented and citizen alike, and demonstrated their organizing potential in Greater Los Angeles. Exhibiting the same determination demonstrated by Arbol Verde residents during repatriation in the 1930s, Rafael, an undocumented immigrant who marched at the 1997 Los Angeles rally, explained "our lives are here now, and we're not going back to Mexico no matter what happens." He added, "I work hard, and I don't think it's fair that my son should be thrown out of school." [7]

The appropriation of public space for the creation and celebration of alternative cultural practices constitutes yet another way in which Latinos have re-fused to accept their fate as marginalized and invisible members of Southern California society. Reminiscent of Cande Mendoza's foresight and ingenuity in creating radio programs and music concerts for Mexican Americans in the citrus belt during the 1950s and 1960s, Latino deejays in the 1990s have taken over the airwaves to criticize nativist politics and to promote *banda* music en-joyed by Mexicans living throughout the region. The Spanish-language station KLAX 97.9 has consistently ranked among the top radio stations in Los Angeles since 1992, attracting an average of 1,114,500 listeners at any given time.[8] As his-torian George Lipsitz and poet/journalist Rubén Martínez have demonstrated, the music played on KLAX has inspired a florescent working-class dance hall cul-ture throughout Southern California where lovers of *banda* dressed as *vaqueros* and *vaqueras* dance the *quebradita* to live music. Producing a social world that rejects assimilation, or at least recognizes the need for solidarity among Mexi-cans in the face of discrimination, this new generation of Mexican Americans evokes the memory of another era when youths congregated in dance halls and engaged in social relations that challenged their society.[9]

A crucial difference between then and now, however, has been the decline of cross-cultural exchange and meaningful intercultural contact. In answer-ing their own question, "is Southern California a multiethnic society?" geog-raphers James P. Allen and Eugene Turner concluded that while many ethnic communities exist in Southern California today, rarely do these groups overlap to create a multiethnic society in which people from different cultural back-grounds share the same living spaces and engage in meaningful relationships. Over the last thirty years, Asian and Mexican neighborhoods have become more concentrated, and thus have become more ethnically homogeneous over time. Studying trends and spatial patterns of intermarriage as one indicator of integration, Allen and Turner have discovered that despite increasing di-versity within Southern California, people are choosing to marry within their own ethnic group. The persistence of residential segregation and the growth of ethnic neighborhoods have resulted in low rates of intermarriage and fewer sites of interethnic contact.[10]

These social trends have continued to reshape and redefine Greater Los Angeles, just as the introduction of citrus and the immigration and employ-ment of many Mexican and Asian workers did a century ago. Rather than move toward a more pluricultural and integrated metropolis, the walls (both literal and figurative) separating Latinos, Asians, African Americans, and Euroameri-cans have grown taller. As Mike Davis illustrates, the persistence of de facto segregation has produced a unique urban model in the United States in which

"Latino Los Angeles" has grown so large—4.5 million in the Los Angeles–Orange County SMSA (Standard Metropolitan Statistical Area)—that a nervous and dwindling Anglo majority has constructed gilded *barrios* near the beaches or in the foothills to separate themselves from the bustling Latino metropolis happening all around them.[11] These developments demonstrate both the complete failure and persistent dreams of many Euroamericans throughout the twentieth century to control the growth of racial minority communities in the Southland. Unfortunately, the success of minorities in expanding the space of their lives has not resulted in significant Anglo concessions of power, and has, for now, postponed the realization of a more equitable and shared society.

Evolving from a period of de jure racial segregation to the formation of interethnic political coalitions and multiracial neighborhoods, the history of the citrus belt offers models of desegregation and integration useful to today's residents of Greater Los Angeles. Although not without their shortcomings, the Padua Institute, the Unity Leagues, and the Intercultural Council represent organizations in which individuals from different ethnic backgrounds collaborated in an effort to improve the world adopted by their respective generations. Today, the backlash against immigration has divided immigrant communities and facilitated distrust among nonwhites and whites. As we move into the twenty-first century, this increasingly diverse society will have to discover new ways of relating to one another that encourage a sense of community. The lessons of the California citrus belt during the first half of the twentieth century provide evidence of how intercultural communication and cooperation can lead to more meaningful relations across ethnic, racial, and class lines, and how today's Angelenos can realize a new "world of its own."

Appendix

TABLE 1. Nonwhite Population in Selected California Cities, 1890–1920

City	1890	1900	1910	1920
Pasadena	159	336	1,101	1,592
Pomona	87	44	90	74
Redlands	—	123	398	168
Riverside	258	614	1,706	1,898
San Bernardino	219	166	341	414

Source: California Cities Database, U.S. Census.
Note: Nonwhite population includes Chinese, Japanese, Native Americans, African Americans, and "non-black others."

TABLE 2. Percentage of Nonwhite Population in Selected California Cities, 1890–1920

City	1890	1900	1910	1920
Pasadena	3.25%	3.68%	3.63%	3.51%
Pomona	2.39	0.79	0.88	0.54
Redlands	—	2.56	3.80	1.75
Riverside	5.50	7.70	11.21	9.81
San Bernardino	5.45	2.69	2.66	2.21

Source: California Cities Database, U.S. Census.
Note: Nonwhite population includes Chinese, Japanese, Native Americans, African Americans, and "non-black others."

TABLE 3. Total Mexican Population in Selected California Cities, 1910–1930

City	1910	1920	1930
Pasadena	277	487	2,753
Pomona	116	638	—
Redlands	208	—	—
Riverside	436	1,050	3,942
San Bernardino	888	1,989	6,839

Source: Broadbent, "Distribution of Mexican Population in the United States."
Note: Total population includes all Mexicans, native and Mexican-born.

TABLE 4. Sex Ratios of Chinese and Japanese Populations in Selected California Cities, 1930 and 1940

| | 1930 | | | |
| | Chinese | | Japanese | |
	Males	Females	Males	Females
Alhambra	6	1	52	27
Monrovia	3	0	29	20
Pasadena	70	10	526	316
Pomona	0	0	20	22
Redlands	3	0	18	17
Riverside	21	1	150	127
San Bernardino	86	7	73	51

| | 1940 | | | |
| | Chinese | | Japanese | |
	Males	Females	Males	Females
Alhambra	10	0	34	29
Monrovia	1	0	46	29
Pasadena	54	19	455	340
Pomona	4	0	27	19
Redlands	6	0	20	15
Riverside	5	0	111	109
San Bernardino	55	20	44	35

Source: California Cities Database, U.S. Census.

TABLE 5. Mexican-Born Population in Selected California Cities, 1930–1940

City	1930	1940	1940 Population as Percentage of 1930 Population
Alhambra	190	137	72.1%
Monrovia	242	141	58.3
Ontario	579	429	74.1
Pasadena	1,247	695	55.7
Pomona	752	539	71.7
Redlands	763	494	64.7
Riverside	1,990	1,355	68.1
San Bernardino	3,172	2,244	70.7

Source: California Cities Database, U.S. Census.
Note: In spite of repatriation, the majority of Mexican-born Mexicans remained in these citrus belt cities.

TABLE 6. Percentage of Foreign-Born Population from Mexico in Selected California Cities, 1930–1940

City	1930	1940
Alhambra	5.98%	4.18%
Monrovia	19.48	14.57
Ontario	38.14	36.48
Pasadena	11.21	7.61
Pomona	37.21	34.38
Redlands	37.90	37.00
Riverside	48.52	42.74
San Bernardino	58.57	52.89

Source: California Cities Database, U.S. Census.

TABLE 7. Native-Born Mexican Population in Selected California Cities, 1930

City	Number of Mexicans	Percentage Native-Born Mexicans
Alhambra	456	58.33
Monrovia	727	66.71
Ontario	1,153	49.78
Pasadena	2,753	54.70
Pomona	1,576	52.28
Redlands	1,767	56.82
Riverside	3,942	49.52
San Bernardino	6,839	53.62

Source: California Cities Database, U.S. Census.
Note: In most citrus belt cities, the majority of the 1930 Mexican population had been born in the United States.

Notes

Abbreviations

The following are abbreviations for frequently cited archival sources in the notes.

Azusa-Foothill
  Azusa-Foothill Citrus Company Collection. Huntington Library, San Marino, Calif.
Clements Papers
  George Clements Collection, MS 118. Special Collections, University of California, Los Angeles, Calif.
DIR
  California Department of Industrial Relations. Division of Immigration and Housing. C-A 194. Bancroft Library, University of California, Berkeley, Calif.
LACC
  Los Angeles Chamber of Commerce Archives. Regional History Center of the University of Southern California, Los Angeles.
López Papers
  Ignacio López Collection. Special Collections, Green Library, Stanford University, Palo Alto, Calif.
McWilliams Papers
  Carey McWilliams Collection. Department of Special Collections, University of California, Los Angeles.
MOD
  La Verne M.O.D. Citrus Packinghouse Oral History Project. City Hall, La Verne, Calif.
Mumford Collection
  Mumford Collection. Van Pelt-Dietrich Library, University of Pennsylvania, Philadelphia.
National Archives
  National Archives. Washington, D.C.
Packinghouse Collection, CHF
  Packinghouse Collection. Claremont Heritage Foundation, Claremont, Calif.
Packinghouse Collection, PPL
  Packinghouse Collection. Pomona Public Library, Pomona, Calif.
Pasadena Playhouse Collection
  Pasadena Playhouse Collection. Huntington Library, San Marino, Calif.
PHC/Honnold
  Padua Hills Theatre Collection. Special Collections, Honnold Library, Claremont, Calif.

PHC/PPL
  Padua Hills Theatre Collection. Special Collections, Pomona Public Library, Pomona, Calif.
POGA
  Pasadena Orange Growers Association Collection. Huntington Library, San Marino, Calif.
Ross Papers
  Fred Ross Papers. Special Collections, Green Library, Stanford University, Palo Alto, Calif.
Ruiz Papers
  Manuel Ruiz, Jr. Papers. Special Collections, Green Library, Stanford Library, Palo Alto, Calif.
SGFLA Records
  San Gabriel Farm Labor Association Records, 1921–1922. Huntington Library, San Marino, Calif.
Sheets Collection
  Millard Sheets Collection. Archives of American Art, Washington, D.C.
Taylor Collection
  Paul Taylor Collection, 74/187c. Bancroft Library, University of California, Berkeley, Calif.
Teague Papers
  Charles C. Teague Papers, C-B 760. Bancroft Library, University of California, Berkeley.
UPL
  Oral History Collection. Upland Public Library, Upland, Calif.
Warren Collection
  Warren Collection. Huntington Library, San Marino, Calif.

Introduction

1. "Tierra de Nadie en Upland Discuten el Caso de la," *El Espectador*, June 5, 1948, 1. "Colonias" refers not only to the many citrus worker colonies established by employers, but also to independent Mexican communities that developed throughout the Southland. "Barrio" is an alternate term used by some residents, though it has an urban connotation that does not accurately represent the suburban/rural environment of these settlements prior to World War II. Both terms will be used.

2. Starr, *Material Dreams*, 68–69.

3. The San Gabriel Valley sits at the foot of the San Gabriel/San Bernardino Mountains, which frame the northeastern boundaries of the Los Angeles basin. The valley extends from Pasadena eastward toward San Bernardino and composes a portion of the expansive Los Angeles metropolis (referred to here as "Greater Los Angeles"). Although Pomona, San Bernardino, and Riverside geographically lie in separate (though connected) valleys of their own, culturally, politically, and economically they constitute the eastern "fringe" of Greater Los Angeles, and the gateway to the "Inland Empire" that extends to the Mojave Desert. These and other smaller cities like Azusa, Claremont, and Ontario constitute urban

"nuclei" that fall within the Los Angeles metropolitan district. For a discussion of this concept of "polynuclear Greater Los Angeles," see Preston, "The Changing Form and Structure of the Southern California Metropolis."

4. George Clements, "How the Back Country of Los Angeles Offers Many Favorable Conditions for Agriculturist," *Los Angeles Examiner*, December 25, 1924, A10. Only Carey McWilliams captured the importance of citrus to the political economy of greater Los Angeles, and laid the foundation for more thorough studies of this region's history. See McWilliams, *Southern California Country*. For a discussion of the importance of citrus to the regional economy, see Tobey and Wetherell, "The Citrus Industry."

5. Sánchez, *Becoming Mexican American*; Camarillo, *Chicanos in a Changing Society*. For other important studies of Mexicans in Los Angeles see Griswold del Castillo, *The Los Angeles Barrio*, and Romo, *History of a Barrio*.

6. González, *Labor and Community*, 3. See also his article co-authored with Raúl Fernández, "Chicano History: Transcending Cultural Models." McWilliams, *Southern California Country*, 216.

7. Soja, *Postmodern Geographies*.

8. Sassoon, *Gramsci's Politics*, 193–204.

9. Spivak, "Subaltern Studies"; Kelley, *Race Rebels*, 7–8.

10. Kelley, *Race Rebels*, 8.

11. Lipsitz, *Dangerous Crossroads*, 35; Sánchez, "Familiar Sounds of Change: Music and the Growth of Mass Culture," chapter 8 in *Becoming Mexican American*, 171–87. The term "Ambivalent Americanism" is from Sánchez. Ruiz refers to the shaping of Mexican American culture as "cultural coalescence." See Ruiz, " 'Star Struck' " and *From Out of the Shadows*, xvi, 49–50.

12. Paredes, *Folklore and Culture*; Saldívar, *Border Matters*; Haas, *Conquests and Historical Identities*; Rubén Martínez, *El Otro Lado*.

13. Robin D. G. Kelley made this similar point when he wrote: "Politics comprises the many battles to roll back constraints and exercise some power over, or *create some space within*, the institutions and social relationships that dominate our lives." See Kelley, *Race Rebels*, 9–10.

14. Ibid., 13.

15. McCarthy, *The Uses of Culture*, 24; Saldívar, *Border Matters*, 26–27; Johnson, "What Is Cultural Studies Anyway?" 44; Gilroy, *The Black Atlantic*, 39.

16. Stowe, "The Politics of Café Society," 1385–86.

17. Deverell and Sitton, *California Progressivism Revisited*.

18. Foley, *The White Scourge*, 7–9.

Chapter 1

1. McWilliams, *Southern California Country*, 207.

2. Ibid., 208.

3. Starr, *Inventing the Dream*, 140. For a classic debunker perspective, see Lillard, *Eden in Jeopardy*, 47–89.

4. Sackman, " 'By Their Fruits Ye Shall Know Them,' " 86; see also Starrs, "The Navel of California."

5. Coit, *Citrus Fruits*, 28–29. See also Zierer, "The Citrus Fruit Industry," 53–73.

6. McWilliams, *Southern California Country*, 205.

7. A. J. Cook, *California Citrus Culture*, 5.

8. Ibid., 6.

9. Fogelson, *The Fragmented Metropolis*, 72.

10. Jefferson, *Notes on Virginia*, Query XIX, as quoted in Marx, *The Machine in the Garden*, 124–25. See also Daniel, *Bitter Harvest*, 15.

11. Thomas Jefferson's plan for Virginia called for the end of primogeniture and the distribution of fifty acres to every landless adult. Henry Nash Smith, *Virgin Land*, 10, 128. The University of Virginia was not the first public university, being preceded by Miami University on the Ohio frontier and University of North Carolina to the south.

12. Henry Nash Smith, *Virgin Land*, 215.

13. Henry Nash Smith cited in Neil Smith, *Uneven Development*, 7.

14. For a critical treatment of Jefferson's political philosophy see Kirby, "Rural Culture in the American Middle West."

15. Leo Marx, as quoted in Neil Smith, *Uneven Development*, 12.

16. Southern Pacific Company, *The Inside Track*.

17. Tobey and Wetherell, "The Citrus Industry," 12–16.

18. Preston, "The Changing Form and Structure," 5.

19. The citrus towns of Orange and Ventura Counties also expanded the metropolis south and north, though to a lesser extent due to the type of citrus produced in those areas.

20. Banham, *Los Angeles*, 21.

21. Hise, *Magnetic Los Angeles*, 4; Scharf, *Taking the Wheel*, 151.

22. Book, *Los Angeles*, 37.

23. George Clements, "How the Back Country of Los Angeles Offers Many Favorable Conditions for Agriculturist," *Los Angeles Examiner*, December 25, 1924, A10.

24. Zierer, "The Citrus Fruit Industry," 57, 70.

25. McWilliams, *Southern California Country*, 206.

26. Ibid., 217. See also Zierer, "The Citrus Fruit Industry," 57.

27. Winther, "The Colony System of Southern California"; White, *"It's Your Misfortune and None of My Own,"* 425–29.

28. Alexander, *The Life of George Chaffey*, 55.

29. Ibid., 47. The reversionary clause meant that the future interest of the property would be left in the control of the grantor, in this case Chaffey's land company. This would ensure the continuation of his scheme even after an owner would pass on or move.

30. Ibid., 48.

31. Banham, *Los Angeles*, 168.

32. Roediger, *The Wages of Whiteness*, 23.

33. Ibid., 21–23; Haas, *Conquests and Historical Identities*, 65.

34. Alexander, *The Life of George Chaffey*, 32–33, 43.

35. White, *Roots of Dependency*, 263.

36. Saxton, *Rise and Fall of the White Republic*, 362–64.

37. Alexander, *The Life of George Chaffey*, 38, 86.

38. A. J. Cook, *California Citrus Culture*, 5.

39. Moses, "'The Orange-Grower is not a Farmer,'" 24–25; Starrs, "The Navel of California," 3.

40. Hartig, "'In a World He Has Created,'" 106; see also Williams, *The Country and the City*, 149.

41. Bowers, *The Country-Life Movement*; Hahamovitch, *The Fruits of Their Labor*.

42. Charles Galton, as quoted in Dreyer, *A Gardener Touched With Genius*, 156–57.

43. Burbank, *The Training of the Human Plant*, 68, 82; also reprinted in Dreyer, *A Gardener Touched With Genius*, 158, 236–64.

44. For an excellent discussion of the intellectual divisions within the American eugenics movement and an explanation of Burbank's theories, see Gould, "Does the Stoneless Plum Instruct the Thinking Reed?" in *Dinosaur in a Haystack*, 291. Such ideas continue to have currency among some social theorists. For an example, see Herrnstein and Murray, *The Bell Curve*, as well as a brilliant analysis of the impact of these ideas on social policy in McCarthy, *The Uses of Culture*, 123–24.

45. Hofstadter, *Social Darwinism in American Thought*, 161. Also quoted in Dreyer, *A Gardener Touched With Genius*, 157.

46. O. F. Cook, U.S. Department of Agriculture, "Eugenics and Agriculture. Extracts from an article in Journal of Heredity (June 1916)," *California Citrograph* (September 1916): 9.

47. Ibid.

48. Ibid., 10.

49. Ibid.

50. Ibid.

51. McWilliams, *Southern California Country*, 217.

52. George H. Whitney interview, 49; Russell Pitzer interview; Paul Naftel interview.

53. Hahamovitch, *The Fruits of Their Labor*; Clifford Pitzer interview.

54. Mitchell, *The Lie of the Land*.

55. J. B. Culbertson, "Housing of Ranch Labor," *California Citrograph* (May 1920): 212.

56. McWilliams, *Southern California Country*, 218.

57. Russell Pitzer interview.

58. Clifford Pitzer interview.

59. Devra Weber, *Dark Sweat, White Gold*, 37–38. George Clements writes of his cooperation with Parker Friselle, the head of a labor bureau which he identifies as the Farm Bureau, 1926 (probably the Agricultural Labor Bureau). According to Clements, representatives of Chambers of Commerce throughout California attended an annual meeting in Fresno. Although never completely successful, industry leaders made numerous attempts to organize a labor clearinghouse for farm labor for the entire state during the 1920s and 1930s. See Clements Papers, Box 62 and 63.

60. SGFLA Records. Bonuses also varied according to the type and quality of fruit picked. The SGFLA included: the Pasadena Orange Growers Association, the Sierra Madre–Lamanda Citrus Association, the San Marino Orange Growers Association, the Bradbury Estate Company and the Duarte-Monrovia Fruit Exchange.

61. González, *Labor and Community*, 30–31.

62. "What System of Paying Pickers Results in the Least Fruit Injury," *California Citrograph* (July 1921): 310.

63. POGA payroll records.

64. Fisher, *The Harvest Labor Market*, 11–14; White, *"It's Your Misfortune and None of My Own,"* 282–84. On the construction of "race-consciousness" and "whiteness" see Ian Haney López, *White by Law*, 22–33, and Foley, *The White Scourge*, 40–91.

65. Wiley W. Mathers interview, 47.

66. George H. Whitney interview, 45–46.

67. Black, "Story Twenty-five, A Kiss on the Hand."

68. "Machinery and Women May Solve Serious Labor Problem," *California Citrograph* (May 1918): 164.

69. Jensen, *With These Hands*, 150, 165–67. Jensen includes excerpts from the writings of Mabel Carney, the best known woman advocate for the Country Life Movement.

70. "Machinery and Women May Solve Serious Labor Problem," *California Citrograph* (May 1918): 164. See McBane, "The Role of Gender in Citrus Employment," 75–76.

71. McBane, "The Role of Gender," 75. See also "Send in for Women Workers, Says Land Army," *California Citrograph* (July 1918): 212; and "Overtime Rate for Women Packing House Employees," *California Citrograph* (May 1918): 167.

72. McBane, "The Role of Gender," 75.

73. Peggy Jeans, "At Home with the Citrus Grower," *California Citrograph* (May 1919): 196–97.

74. Peggy Jeans, "At Home with the Citrus Grower," *California Citrograph* (August 1919): 280–81.

75. Joan Jensen named Mabel Carney as a prominent example of a feminist who advocated the Country Life Movement. See Jensen, *With These Hands*, 165–67.

76. O. F. Cook, "Eugenics and Agriculture," 9.

77. Ibid.

78. Paul Taylor discovered this to be the case with sugar beet farmers as well. Although most sugar beet labor is highly seasonal, growers, when they wanted to settle a small number of resident Mexican workers, sought out Mexican families for permanent settlement rather than single male workers. Families provided more laborers (women and children), and growers regarded them as more dependable. See Taylor, *Mexican Labor in the United States*, vol. 1, 135–40.

79. Charles C. Teague, "How to House and Treat Citrus Ranch Employees," *California Citrograph* (November 1919): 12.

80. J. B. Culbertson, "Housing of Ranch Labor," *California Citrograph* (May 1920): 212.

81. O. F. Cook, "Eugenics and Agriculture," 9.

82. Taylor, *Mexican Labor in the United States*, 139.

83. "Mexicans Quit Jobs," *Claremont Courier*, April 12, 1917; "Mexican Strike," *Claremont Courier*, April 15, 1917.

84. "Agitators Causing Trouble Among Orange Pickers in South," *California Citrograph* (March 1919): 129.

85. Ibid.

86. McWilliams, *Southern California Country*, 220.

87. "Agitators Causing Trouble," *California Citrograph* (March 1919): 130.

88. Anthea Hartig brilliantly explains how growers transformed the social and physical

space to reflect the "class collectivity" of citrus belt elites in her article, "'In a World He Has Created.'"

89. V. V. Leroy, "Why Citrus Growers Should Organize Clubs," *California Citrograph* (March 1916): 4.

90. Cletus Daniel argues that the "erosion of the agrarian ideal" in California began with the farmers' dependence on Chinese farmworkers. See Daniel, *Bitter Harvest*, 26–39. See also Guerin-Gonzales, *Mexican Workers and American Dreams*, 12–14, 25.

91. González, *Labor and Community*, 1.

92. Williams, *The Country and the City*, 32.

Chapter 2

1. McWilliams, *Southern California Country*, 218.

2. Ibid., 219.

3. See Tomás Almaguer's *Racial Fault Lines* for nineteenth-century California labor history. Almaguer explains the rationale used by white farm owners to exclude and include various ethnic/racial groups from the workforce, namely Native American, Chinese, Japanese, and Mexican.

4. Kelley, *Race Rebels*, 9–10; Saldívar, *Border Matters*, 72, 90. See also Haas, *Conquests and Historical Identities*; Ruiz, "Claiming Public Space," chapter 6 in *From Out of the Shadows*; and Villa, *Barrio-Logos*. Regarding Kelley's challenge of labor historians to focus on why rather than how people engaged in working-class politics, some would argue that the two are the same. See Fischer, *Historians' Fallacies*. Kelley's point (and mine) is not that there is a difference between the two; in fact, I agree that there should not be a distinction made. However, in interpreting labor history, many traditionalists have unconsciously made such a distinction by favoring a focus on the work environment and ignoring other realms in which labor politics play out (for example, community, dance halls, etc.).

5. McWilliams, *Factories in the Field*.

6. Baudelio Sandoval interview. Most residents inaccurately referred to this last group of laborers as "Hindu." The complex history of Sikh immigrants in California and the "Hindu" identity is masterfully told by Karen Leonard, *Making Ethnic Choices*.

7. Sandoval interview.

8. Cheva García interview. For an understanding of the complex relationship between immigrant laborers and their contractors, see Peck, "Reinventing Free Labor." For another example of a local Mexican foreman, see the story of Emilio Valadez, found in Black, "Story Twenty-five, A Kiss on the Hand."

9. Sandoval interview; John Bice interview.

10. Sandoval interview. See also Nick Fuentes interview.

11. A. D. Shamel, "Housing Employees of California's Citrus Ranches," *California Citrograph* (June 1918): 177. Anthea Hartig also provides a thorough interpretation of segregation on the Leffingwell Ranch in an unpublished paper "Communities in Transition." See also Alamillo, "Bitter-Sweet Communities," for the history of another "ranch" setting, the Chase Plantation in Corona, Calif.

12. J. B. Culbertson, "Housing of Ranch Labor," *California Citrograph* (May 1920): 212.

For an insightful history of the Limoneira Rancho, see McBane, "The Role of Gender in Citrus Employment."

13. Bice interview; Sandoval interview.

14. Almaguer, *Racial Fault Lines*, 129–30.

15. "Editorial, Labor," *California Citrograph* (May 1917): 1.

16. A substantial amount of historical literature exists on the treatment of Asian immigrants in California, including Saxton, *The Indispensable Enemy*; Chan, *This Bitter-Sweet Soil* and *Asian Americans*; Takaki, *Strangers from a Different Shore*; Almaguer, *Racial Fault Lines*; Leonard, *Making Ethnic Choices*; and Matsumoto, *Farming the Home Place*.

17. Chan, *Asian Americans*, 45.

18. Ruth Milliken interview. Spadra was incorporated into Pomona and no longer exists.

19. Ibid.

20. *Pomona Weekly Times*, 28 October 1882; *Pomona Weekly Progress*, 4 March 1886; *Pomona Daily Times*, 14 March 1889. See Echeverri, "Pomona, California: The Early Years," 74–75. See also Stuart Wheeler interview.

21. Chan, *Asian Americans*, 51.

22. Ibid., 54–55. Politicians responded by blaming the victims. In 1880 the United States government negotiated a treaty with China that gave the United States the right to unilaterally limit Chinese immigration. In 1882 Congress went a step further with the Chinese Exclusion Law that suspended entry of Chinese laborers for ten years but exempted merchants, students and teachers, diplomats, and travelers from its provisions. An amendment to this law in 1888 disallowed the return of Chinese laborers who left the country unless they could prove that they owned at least $1,000 in property or that they had a wife in the United States. Congress closed this final loophole three weeks later with the Scott Act—legislation that denied reentry rights to any Chinese laborer, regardless of their marital status.

23. McWilliams, *Factories in the Field*, 74–77; Chan, *This Bitter-Sweet Soil*, 378–81.

24. Quote from Takaki, *Strangers From a Different Shore*, 130.

25. Milliken interview.

26. Takaki, *Strangers*, 188–89. Japanese immigrants used four methods to obtain farmland—contract, share, lease, and ownership. In 1910 Japanese ownership of agricultural land accounted for 16,980 acres. Most entered into contractual agreements with white landowners: 37,898 acres were under contract, 50,400 under share, and 89,464 under lease. Under the contract system, Japanese farmers agreed to plant and harvest a crop for a set amount to be paid by the landowner when the crop was sold. The share system involved greater risk since the farmer received a percentage of the crop's profit and not a prearranged sum of money. Under the lease system, Japanese farmers rented the land and were responsible for all the supplies and equipment used on the farm. In each case, farmers aspired to accumulate enough capital to purchase land and achieve independence from wage labor.

27. Ibid., 189–90.

28. "Growing Menace of Tenant Farming," *California Citrograph* (January–February 1917).

29. J. B. Culbertson, "Housing of Ranch Labor," *California Citrograph* (May 1920): 212; A. D. Shamel, "Housing Employees of California's Citrus Ranches," *California Citrograph* (June 1918): 177; McBane, "The Role of Gender," 74.

30. Ronald Takaki claims that this process of stabilizing the sex ratio of Japanese immigration was by the design of the Japanese government. In fact, the "Gentlemen's Agreement" of 1907 slowed the flow of common male laborers to the United States, but allowed for greater emigration of women. Japanese sought to avoid the "image" problems of prostitution, gambling, and drunkenness often associated with Chinese laborers (and thus "Asians") by providing the foundations for the establishment of family life in America. See Takaki, *Strangers*, 46–47.

31. Ibid., 190; Matsumoto, *Farming the Home Place*.

32. Takaki, *Strangers*, 191.

33. Frank Wheeler, minutes from the Chamber of Commerce of the San Gabriel Valley Board of Directors meeting, September 2, 1919, LACC.

34. Chan, *Asian Americans* 55; Takaki, *Strangers*, 203–5. In 1920, the United States government passed a law denying passports to picture brides from Japan. The Immigration Act of 1924 barred entry of "aliens ineligible to citizenship," virtually ending Japanese immigration. In response to the alien land laws in California, Issei parents circumvented the legislation by placing the land under the names of their Nisei (second generation, and therefore, citizen) children.

35. "Memories from the Courier Files: 25 Years Ago, Hindus Leave," *Claremont Courier*, November 1, 1935, 6.

36. Chan, *Asian Americans*, 55.

37. George Clements, "Mexican Immigration and Its Bearing on California's Agriculture, speech delivered before Lemon Men's Club, October 2, 1929," *California Citrograph* (November 1929): 3, 28.

38. Ibid., 28.

39. Facts About Filipino Immigration into California. Special Bulletin, No. 3. April 1930. Clements Papers, Box 62.

40. "Editorial, Labor," *California Citrograph* (May 1917): 1.

41. Sánchez, *Becoming Mexican American*, 36.

42. George J. Sánchez discusses these "push" factors in his book, *Becoming Mexican American*; see chapter 1, "Farewell Homeland," 17–37.

43. *Fourteenth Census of the United States: State Compendium California* (Washington, D.C.: Government Printing Office, 1924); González, *Labor and Community*, 7. Only Italians numbered more, totaling 88,502 of the foreign-born.

44. "Growth of Mexican Labor," *California Citrograph*, December 1919, 1.

45. Williamson, "Labor in the California Citrus Industry," 44, cited in González, *Labor and Community*, 7.

46. González, *Labor and Community*, 7.

47. Almaguer, *Racial Fault Lines*, 8.

48. Ibid.

49. Sánchez, *Becoming Mexican American*, 30. See also Foley, *The White Scourge*, 60–61.

50. A. D. Shamel, "Housing the Employees of California's Citrus Ranches," *California Citrograph* (February 1918): 70.

51. "The Well Housed Employee," *California Citrograph* (September 1918): 1.

52. Ibid.

53. George B. Hodgkin, "Survey of the Labor Situation," *California Citrograph* (August 1920): 314.

54. "History of Division of Immigration and Housing," Inventory of the State Archives of the California Division of Immigration and Housing, 1941, 16, DIR.

55. Gullett, "Women Progressives," 79, 94.

56. Letter from Director Edward Brown to Fred Rugg, May 3, 1926, DIR.

57. Leo Mott, "Address at the Fifth Conference of the Friends of the Mexicans" (Pomona College, Claremont, California, December 5 and 6, 1925), 1, DIR.

58. Joseph Timmons, "Citrus Workers in Model Homes," *Los Angeles Examiner*, September 2, 1920, 1. In addition to the housing projects built in the San Gabriel Valley, citrus ranchers in nearby Arlington, Fillmore, La Habra, Villa Park, and Santa Paula contributed to the boom in construction of worker housing.

59. Ibid., 7. Plans for the housing project at the Covina Orange Growers Association, letter from C. E. Crawford, Manager, to Pacific Portable Construction Co., Inc., August 14, 1920; letter from Pacific Portable to Crawford, August 27, 1920; letter from Karl Martin & Co. to Crawford, February 11, 1921, DIR. Pacific Portable Construction Co. Blueprints for Covina project (No Date), Packinghouse Collection, CHF. Leo Mott to R. W. Kearney, Attorney and Executive Officer of the DIR, May 9, 1925, DIR. For more information concerning Pacific Portable Construction Company and industrial housing in Southern California, see Hise, *Magnetic Los Angeles*, 59, 93–95.

60. Timmons, "Citrus Workers in Model Homes," *Los Angeles Examiner*, September 2, 1920, 1.

61. George B. Hodgkin, "Survey of the Labor Situation," *California Citrograph* (August 1920): 314, 330.

62. Timmons, *Los Angeles Examiner*, September 2, 1920, 3; "Bungalow Court" plans by "The Pacific Portable Construction Co." and Sanborn Map of Claremont, Packinghouse Collection, CHF; Julia Salazar interview by Ginger Elliot, 7.

63. Nick Fuentes interview by Margo McBane and author, March 15, 1995.

64. González, *Chicano Education*; Ruiz, "'La Malinche Tortilla Factory'"; Sánchez, *Becoming Mexican American*; Gullett, "Women Progressives"; and Raftery, *Land of Fair Promise*.

65. Gullett, "Women Progressives," 81, 94.

66. Gibson as quoted in Gullett, "Women Progressives," 83.

67. Chase as quoted in Gullett, "Women Progressives," 83, and Raftery, *Land of Fair Promise*, 75.

68. George B. Hodgkin, "Making the Labor Camp Pay," *California Citrograph* (August 1921): 354.

69. Tobias Larson, "Singing in the Rain," *Claremont Courier*, January 15, 1931.

70. Joseph Timmons, "Citrus Workers in Model Homes," *Los Angeles Examiner*, September 2, 1920, 1; George B. Hodgkin, "Survey of the Labor Situation," *California Citrograph* (August 1920): 314; A. D. Shamel, "Housing the Employees of California's Citrus Ranches," *California Citrograph* (February 1918): 70; O'Brien, "The Mexican Colony," 6.

71. A. D. Shamel, "Housing the Employees of California's Citrus Ranches," *California Citrograph* (February 1918): 71.

72. George B. Hodgkin, "Survey of the Labor Situation," *California Citrograph* (August 1920): 314, 330.

73. Pearl Idella Ellis, *Americanization Through Homemaking*, as quoted in Ruiz, *From Out of the Shadows*, 33. See also Ruiz, "'La Malinche Tortilla Factory'"; Sánchez, "'Go After the Women.'"

74. Hodgkin, "Making the Labor Camp Pay," 354.

75. Sánchez, "'Go After the Women.'"

76. R. S. Vaile, "Mexican Labor," *California Citrograph* (March 1918):97.

77. "How to House and Treat Citrus Ranch Employees," *California Citrograph* (November 1919): 12.

78. George B. Hodgkin, "Interesting the Mexican," *California Citrograph* (August 1920): 1.

79. González, *Labor and Community*, 97.

80. Vicki Ruiz discusses the difficulties of using ethnocentric literature for documenting Mexican American history. See Ruiz, "Dead Ends or Gold Mines?"

81. O'Brien, "The Mexican Colony."

82. Ibid., 1–2.

83. The camp was known as "West Barrio," also near the tracks and away from the downtown districts.

84. O'Brien, "The Mexican Colony," 6.

85. Monsignor Donald Strange interview.

86. Mary Palos interview.

87. Cheva García interview.

88. O'Brien, "The Mexican Colony," 17; Daniel Martínez, Jr. interview; Cheva García interview; Mary Palos interview.

89. O'Brien, "The Mexican Colony," 17.

90. For a history of cannery workers in California, see Ruiz, *Cannery Women*. Cheva's grandmother, Silveria Miranda, blazed a trail for her, finding work in the Starkist canning factory in San Pedro harbor soon after her arrival there in 1915.

91. Candalario José Mendoza interview; see also Alamillo, "Mexican American Baseball."

92. Mary Sevilla interview.

93. Taylor Collection, 84/38c, Carton 10, Folder 25 and 26.

94. Echeverri, "Pomona, California," 84.

95. For information concerning discrimination against Italian immigrants, See Kraut, "'That Is the American Way. And in America You Should Do as Americans Do': Italian Customs, American Standards," in *Silent Travelers*. For information concerning the WCTU activities in the citrus belt, See Lothrop-Ricci, *Pomona: A Centennial History*, 73; Wilhoite, *The Hatchet Crusade*. Pomona hosted the famed prohibitionist Susan B. Anthony in 1895, and held WCTU annual meetings for Southern California in 1896, 1909, and 1921. These strong prohibitionist sentiments inspired local Temperance Laws from 1911 to 1933, seven years prior to the National Temperance Law.

96. The "fiery cross" was the symbol often associated with the Ku Klux Klan, and served as the title of its main publication. See Wade, *The Fiery Cross*. The Women's Christian Temperance Union earned the nickname "Hatchet Crusade" by members traveling around with hatchets hacking wooden kegs full of alcohol.

97. "Klan Initiates 150 Candidates: Lavish Parade Precedes Initiatory Ceremonies at Chaffey Stadium," *Daily Report*, September 9, 1924.

98. Pomona Klan roster, located at the Pomona Public Library.

99. Lay, "Introduction: The Second Invisible Empire," in *The Invisible Empire in the West*, 9.

100. Helen O'Brien, the author of a 1932 study of the Claremont *colonia*, Arbol Verde, wrote "The pool hall, once a rooming house belonging to El Camino [citrus] packing house, is also located south of the tracks and is frequented by Mexican men and college students from Claremont." O'Brien, "The Mexican Colony," 4.

101. Nick Fuentes interview with Margo McBane.

102. Victor Murillo Ruiz interview, 7.

103. Sánchez, *Becoming Mexican American*, 57.

104. McWilliams, *North From Mexico*, 197.

Chapter 3

1. John Box quoted in Kenneth L. Roberts, "The Docile Mexican," *The Saturday Evening Post*, March 10, 1928, 41.

2. House of Representatives, Committee on Immigration, *Immigration from Countries of the Western Hemisphere*, 71st Cong., 2d sess., 1930, Report 898, to accompany HR 103433, 1–13, as quoted in Reisler, *By The Sweat of Their Brow*, 216.

3. Although sensitive to criticism from restrictionists and reformers alike, the agency followed a middle ground, favoring the improvement of work camp conditions, controls on the flow of Mexican immigrants, and the stabilization of Mexican immigrant communities in California.

4. For the history of Progressive-Era women reformers, see Deutsch, *No Separate Refuge*; Gullett, "Women Progressives"; Pascoe, *Relations of Rescue*; Raftery, *Land of Fair Promise*; Ruiz, *From Out of the Shadows*, and "'La Malinche Tortilla Factory.'"

5. Higham, *Strangers in the Land*, 300.

6. House of Representatives, Congressional Record, 68th Cong., 1st sess., 1923–1924, 65, pt. 6:6129; see Gutiérrez, *Walls and Mirrors*, 53, n32:230.

7. Albert Johnson, quoted by Reverend George L. Cady, "Report of Commission on International and Interracial Factors in the Problem of Mexicans in the United States," date unknown, 24–25, National Archives.

8. Roberts, "The Docile Mexican," 41.

9. Foley, *The White Scourge*, 41–42; Tuck, *Not With the Fist*, 14–19.

10. Harry H. Laughlin, House of Representatives, Committee on Immigration and Naturalization, *Immigration from Countries of the Western Hemisphere*, 70th Cong., 1st sess., 1928, Hearing No. 70.1.5, 711, 712.

11. George Horace Lorimer, "The Old Mistake," *Saturday Evening Post*, June 20, 1931.

12. Bob Shuler, *Bob Shuler's Magazine* (January 1928): 253, as quoted in House, Congres-

sional Record, 70th Cong., 1st sess., 1928, 27–28. For more on Shuler's connection to the local KKK, see Cocoltchos, "The Invisible Empire"; and Salley, "Activities of the Knights of the Ku Klux Klan."

13. William C. Hushings, House, Committee on Immigration and Naturalization, *Western Hemisphere Immigration*, 71st Cong., 2nd sess., 1930, 366, 368.

14. Kenneth L. Roberts, "Mexicans or Ruin," *Saturday Evening Post*, February 18, 1928, 15.

15. S. P. Frisselle, Chairman of the Agricultural Committee of the Fresno County Chamber of Commerce, representing the interest of California farmers, U.S. House of Representatives, *Seasonal Agricultural Laborers from Mexico: Hearings Before the Committee on Immigration and Naturalization*, 69th Cong., 1st sess., 1926, 6. See also Clements Papers, Box 63.

16. Charles C. Teague, "A Statement on Mexican Immigration," *Saturday Evening Post*, March 10, 1928, 169, 171.

17. Charles P. Bayer, U.S. House of Representatives, *Seasonal Agricultural Laborers from Mexico: Hearings Before the Committee on Immigration and Naturalization*, 69th Cong., 1st sess., 1926, 131.

18. U.S. House of Representatives, *Immigration from Countries of Western Hemisphere: Hearings Before the Committee on Immigration and Naturalization*, 70th Cong., 1st sess., 1928, 638–39.

19. Paul Taylor, handwritten footnote on his report on labor conditions in Orange County, 1928. Taylor Collection, folder 1:5.

20. Guerin-Gonzales, *Mexican Workers and American Dreams*, 45.

21. McWilliams, *Southern California Country*, 218.

22. Ruiz, *From Out of the Shadows*, 22.

23. O'Brien, "The Mexican Colony," 44–45.

24. Ibid., 1.

25. "Survey Conditions in Mexican Homes," *Claremontonia* (1925):1, 5; "Mexicans Develop Real Oasis at 'Arbol Verde,'" *Claremont Courier* (date unknown); O'Brien, "The Mexican Colony," 1.

26. Carmen Armendarez, unpublished and untitled family history, 2–3; Carmen Armendarez interview.

27. Leo T. Mott, "Address to the Fifth Conference of the Friends of the Mexicans" (Pomona College, Claremont, California, December 5 and 6, 1926), 5; Mott to Edward Glass, State Director of Housing, January 28, 1922, DIR.

28. O'Brien, "The Mexican Colony," 3.

29. Mott, "Friends of the Mexicans," 3.

30. "Mexican Situation Is Considered Here," *Riverside Enterprise*, June 17, 1924.

31. Author unnamed, "The Mexican in the United States," report to the Immigration and Housing Division, 1925, 1–4, DIR.

32. "Archbishop Asks Ban on Mexicans," *Daily Herald*, March 11, 1926; "Hanna Tells Problems of Immigration," *Los Angeles Examiner*, May 25, 1926. DIR, "Mexican Data" file.

33. "The Catholic Mexicans" of San Antonio, Texas to Archbishop Edward J. Hanna, March 10, 1926; signed RILD to Monsignor [*sic*] Edward J. Hanna, from Houston, Texas, March 20, 1926. DIR, "Mexican Data" file.

34. Anonymous letter from "a Mexican woman" to Hanna, from Los Angeles, March 1926, DIR, "Mexican Data" file.

35. Gutiérrez, *Walls and Mirrors*, 31–35; Foley, "Becoming Hispanic"; Lipsitz, *The Possessive Investment in Whiteness.*

36. "Conference in the Los Angeles Chamber of Commerce Board Room, October 5, 1927, re: proposed Bill to include Mexico in the immigration quota law," 17, Clements Papers.

37. George P. Clements, "Mexican Indian or Porto Rican Indian Casual Labor?—The Box Bill," speech to the Ladies of the Pasadena Women's Civic League, February 6, 1928, Clements Papers.

38. Clements, "Should the Quota be Applied to Mexico?" speech to the Seventh Annual Meeting of the Interdenominational Council on Spanish-Speaking Work, Pomona College, California, November 14–16, 1928, Clements Papers.

39. George Clements, "Mexican Immigration and Its Bearing on California's Agriculture, delivered before Lemon Men's Club, October 2, 1929," *California Citrograph* (November 1929): 3, 28, 29, Clements Papers.

40. Clements to unknown, Los Angeles, California, December 2, 1927, 2, Clements Papers.

41. Clements, "Mexican Immigration and Its Bearing on California's Agriculture," 29.

42. Pascoe, "Miscegenation Law."

43. R. S. Vaile, "Mexican Labor," *California Citrograph* (March 1918): 97.

44. Howard F. Pressey, "The Housing and Handling of Mexican Labor at Rancho Sespe. Delivered at Lemon Men's Club, November 6, 1929," *California Citrograph* (December 1929): 51.

45. Clements, "Mexican Immigration and Its Bearing on California's Agriculture," 29.

46. Cohen, *Making a New Deal*, 181.

47. Gullett, "Women Progressives," 83.

48. Clements, "Mexican Indian or Porto Rican Indian Casual Labor?—The Box Bill"; Clements to unknown, Los Angeles, California, December 2, 1927, 3; Kenneth L. Roberts, "Mexicans or Ruin," *Saturday Evening Post*, February 18, 1928, 15.

49. Clements to unknown, Los Angeles, California, December 2, 1927, Clements Papers.

50. McDowell, "A Study of Social and Economic Factors."

51. Ibid.

52. Ibid.

53. Ibid.

54. Reisler, *By The Sweat of Their Brow*, 217–18.

55. Report from Brice W. Hoskins, Director of the Department of Public Relations of the L.A. Community Chest, Clements Papers, #118, Box 62.

56. C. P. Visel to Crime and Unemployment Committee, January 7, 1931, LACC; "Illegal-Alien Bar Sought—Supervisors Indorse Bill to Forbid Residence and Employment to Such Individuals," *Los Angeles Times*, January 13, 1931.

57. "Chamber Gives Mexico Pledge—Kerr Letter Seeks to Block Tremendous Exodus—Ousting of Illegal Aliens Aim of Government—Forty Thousand Quit City Since First of Year," *Los Angeles Times*, June 1931, Clements Papers, Box 62.

58. Clements to Mrs. Robert A. Woods of the Neighborhood Settlement Association,

February 2, 1931, Clements Papers. Interestingly, Clements's ideas foreshadow the *bracero* program implemented in 1942 to manage Mexican agricultural labor during and after World War II.

59. "Editorial, Let's Have the Facts First," *California Citrograph* (March 1930): 1.

60. "Editorial, Mexican Boy Won," *California Citrograph* (August 1930): 1.

61. Guerin-Gonzales, *Mexican Workers and American Dreams*, 85.

62. Ibid. See González, *Labor and Community*, 7–8, for numbers of Mexican workers and repatriates from Orange County.

63. Because this area includes highly industrial districts of Los Angeles, including East Los Angeles, this number *does not* reflect the total number of Mexican citrus workers deported. Also, this number does not include the citrus growing regions of Ventura County. Calculations based on the numbers presented in Guerin-Gonzales, 85.

64. This percentage is probably inordinately high, since it is derived from the total number repatriated from Los Angeles, Riverside, and San Bernardino Counties (18,824—of which not all were citrus workers) divided by the lowest approximate total of Mexican residents in the citrus belt (75,000). According to Gilbert González, 75,000 to 100,000 lived in the citrus belt at the height of the industry. The industry employed 50,000 pickers, field hands, packers, and packinghouse employees, of which the overwhelming majority were Mexican men and women. See González, *Labor and Community*, 8.

65. McBane, "The Role of Gender," 78.

66. Ibid. Raymond Soper interview; MOD. In this last project, Margo McBane uncovers the history of Okie and Arkie labor in the citrus belt during the 1930s, and the relationship of these laborers with Mexican laborers.

67. *Claremont Courier*, February 13, 1930.

68. "To Promote Friendly Mexican Relations: Part of Purpose of Conference at Claremont College Saturday," November 8, 1923, and "Friends of Mexicans Hold Annual Meeting," *Claremont Courier*, November 20, 1924.

69. Raftery, *Land of Fair Promise*, 82–84; Gullett, "Women Progressives," 80–81; "Conference is Praised," *Claremont Courier*, November 20, 1930; "Report of the Seventh Annual Conference of the Friends of the Mexicans," November 11 and 12, 1927, DIR.

70. Raftery, *Land of Fair Promise*, 48; "500 Attend Friends of Mexicans Conclave Here," *Claremont Courier*, November 21, 1929.

71. "'Friends of Mexicans' Conference Ends Seventh Successful Session," *Claremont Courier*, November 17, 1927.

72. "To Promote Friendly Mexican Relations: Part of Purpose of Conference at Claremont College Saturday," *Claremont Courier*, November 8, 1923.

73. "Conference of 'Friends of the Mexicans' December 5 and 6," *Pomona College Quarterly Magazine* (December 1925): 75. This was the only year in which the conference convened in December.

74. Leavitt O. Wright, "Pomona College and the Mexicans," *Pomona College Quarterly Magazine*, December 1923, 107.

75. "Conference of 'Friends of the Mexicans,' December 5 and 6," *Pomona College Quarterly Magazine* (December 1925): 76.

76. Balderrama and Rodríguez, *Decade of Betrayal*; and Balderrama, *In Defense of La Raza*.

77. Both George Sánchez and Gilbert González have significantly revised Balderrama's favorable image of the Mexican consulate in California by pointing out that Mexican officials played a crucial role in aiding the repatriation and deportation movement during the 1930s. See Sánchez, *Becoming Mexican American*, 216; and González, *Labor and Community*, 133. See also González, *Mexican Consuls and Labor Organizing*; and Camille Guerin-Gonzales, *Mexican Workers and American Dreams*, chapters 4 and 5.

78. "'Friends of the Mexicans' Conference," *Pomona College Quarterly* (December 1927): 56.

79. Ibid.

80. "500 Attend Friends of Mexicans Conclave Here: Important Viewpoints on Labor and Educational Problems; Four Resolutions Passed by Conference," *Claremont Courier*, November 21, 1929, 1.

81. Ibid. The following year, delegates passed a resolution to oppose segregation of Mexican children in American schools, except while learning English. See "Conference is Praised: Friends of Mexicans Hear Many Notables Speak," *Claremont Courier*, November 20, 1930, 7. For more on Sterry and the role of school principals, see Raftery, 97–100, 122, 124–25.

82. *Claremont Courier*, November 21, 1929, 1.

83. "Conference Attendance Largest in Eleven Years: More Than 500 Registered at Friends of Mexican Conclave; New Committee Is Appointed," *Claremont Courier*, November 20, 1931, 1.

84. "Conference Assembles Tomorrow: College Campus Will Be Mecca for Large Gathering," *Claremont Courier*, November 13, 1931, 1; "Conference Meets Here Tomorrow," *Claremont Courier*, December 2, 1932, 1.

85. O'Brien, "The Mexican Colony," 1.

86. "Mexicans' Friends Postpone Meeting Date Until 1934," *Claremont Courier*, December 8, 1933.

87. López, "The El Monte Berry Strike of 1933," 101–5; Devra Weber, *Dark Sweat, White Gold*, 79–111, and "The Organizing of Mexicano Agricultural Workers," 326–28; González, *Labor and Community*, 135–60; "Dairy Strike, January 1934," confidential report from Agricultural Department, LACC, Clements Papers, Box 64.

88. Enrique Vasquez, interviewed by Jorge Castañeda; "Enrique Vasquez . . . he fights the good fight," *The Daily Report*, April 16, 1972; Donald J. Newman, "R.C. Man Organized Farm Labor Strike in 1933," *The Daily Report*, 13 August 1979; Gina Vasquez Cabral, "Pair Worked Hard For a Better Life," *Inland Valley Daily Bulletin*, December 5, 1990.

89. Candelario José Mendoza interview, May 6, 1994, 7–8.

90. Mr. F. R. interviewed by Helen O'Brien, March 30, 1932, in O'Brien, "The Mexican Colony," 98.

91. For an account of the 1933 cotton strike see Devra Weber, *Dark Sweat, White Gold*.

92. George Clements to Hon. Harry M. Baine of the Los Angeles County Board of Supervisors, December 7, 1933, Clements Papers. For a history of the 1936 Citrus Strike, see González, *Labor and Community*, 135–60.

93. González, *Labor and Community*, 178–79; For information concerning this tranformation in the Pomona/San Gabriel Valley, see Landman, "Some Aspects of the Acculturation of Mexican Immigrants," 36, 56.

94. González, *Labor and Community*, 177. *Braceros* also blended into existing Mexican *colonias* in the San Gabriel Valley. Donato and Alfonsa Bustos interview. Sometimes, however, competition between *braceros* and Mexican American workers resulted in conflicts between the two groups. See Mario T. García, *Mexican Americans*, 97–98; Gutiérrez, *Walls and Mirrors*, 133–46.

95. Sánchez, *Becoming Mexican American*, 87–107; Ruiz, *From Out of the Shadows*, 51–71, and "'Star Struck,'" 109–29; O'Brien, "The Mexican Colony," 29, 78.

96. Rosaldo, "Cultural Citizenship," 27–38.

Chapter 4

1. I am using the general term "performance" to talk about the distinct, though related phenomena of parades, pageants, and plays. In another article, I elaborate on the differences between pageants and little theater. See my article, "'Just Put on that Padua Hills Smile,'" 248. For an example of this type of performance, see McGroarty, *The Mission Play*, based on his book, *California: Its History and Romance*.

2. McWilliams, *Southern California Country*, 82. For an analysis of these types of performances, see Monroy, *Thrown Among Strangers*, 258–71. Monroy refers to parades and plays like these as the "California Pastoral" and a product of the "cultural narcissism" of Anglo Angelenos. See also Rosaldo, *Culture and Truth*, 68–87. Rosaldo refers to these practices in a postcolonial context as "imperialist nostalgia . . . a particular kind of nostalgia, often found under imperialism, where people mourn the passing of what they themselves have transformed."

3. Kanellos, *Mexican American Theatre: Legacy and Reality*; Kanellos, "The Mexican Stage in the Southwest," in Kanellos, *Mexican American Theatre: Then and Now*, 117–25; and Haas, "Regional Culture," chapter 4 in *Conquests and Historical Identities*, 138–60.

4. Undated Padua Institute booklet, PHC/PPL. For more on inter-American relations, see Delpar, *The Enormous Vogue of Things Mexican*.

5. Pascoe, *Relations of Rescue*, xvii–xxii.

6. Grossberg, *We Gotta Get Out of This Place*, 21–23. Grossberg recognizes the "polysemy of culture" without romanticizing the agency and intent of participants in the making of culture. His concept of a "double articulation" is useful here to subvert the notion that the Garners, the creators of the concept of intercultural understanding, had complete control over its definition. I want to thank my friend and colleague, Angharad Valdivia, for introducing me to this book.

7. Garza, *Contemporary Chicano Theatre*, 5.

8. Arrízon, "Contemporizing Performance"; Lott, *Love and Theft*, 8. Lott makes the valuable argument that, although somewhat "essentialist," the projection of "positive" ethnic images is a strategy that has its time and place.

9. Lott, *Love and Theft*, 7–8, 37; Matt García, "'Just Put on that Padua Hills Smile,'" 260. Although I tried to move beyond such binary interpretations in my first article on this subject, I also made the unfortunate error of dividing perspectives into "Mexican" and "non-Mexican." Eric Lott, in his book *Love and Theft*, offers a useful, poststructuralist analysis of cultural representation in performance and art that is applicable to interpretations of Padua Hills Theatre. Lott recommends that we acknowledge the antinomic and dualistic quali-

ties present in cultural performances such as blackface minstrelsy, and to avoid reducing our analysis to a search for the "authentic" and "counterfeit" in these expressions. Although unique in its own right, the history of Padua Hills and the few studies of the theater by Chicano theater scholars closely resemble the changing interpretations of blackface minstrelsy described by Lott.

10. Kelley, "Notes on Deconstructing 'The Folk,'" 1,405.

11. MacKay, *The Little Theatre in the United States*, 1.

12. Ibid., 1.

13. Herman H. Garner. Details of Syndicate Being Formed by R. W. Purpus Inc., #875–895, Subway Terminal Building, on Evey Canyon Property, May 11, 1928, PHC/PPL. Restrictions barring "undesirables" (non-whites) from owning homes in the Pomona Valley were extensive. The following restrictive covenant, taken from the original Padua Hills housing contract, was standard for many exclusive communities: "(a) No part of said property shall be sold, conveyed, rented or leased in whole or in part to any persons of African or Asiatic descent or to any person not of the white or Caucasian race." Such agreements contributed to the "barrioization" or "ghettoization" of racial minorities living in the valley.

14. Blakeslee, "History of Padua Hills Theatre," 49.

15. Undated Padua Institute booklet, PHC/PPL.

16. Camilla Romo Wolfe interview.

17. Blakeslee, "History of Padua Hills Theatre," 49.

18. Casilda Amador Thoreson interview.

19. Wolfe interview.

20. Many of these festivals and ceremonies originated at "Escuela Mexicana de Claremont, Leona Viscario," the school started by Arbol Verde residents discussed in Chapter 1. The school was founded to address and correct the academically inadequate and culturally insensitive education Mexican children were receiving at segregated schools. Cheva García interview; Christina Pérez interview; Daniel Martínez Jr. interview.

21. Cheva García interview; Candelario "Cande" Mendoza interview, May 6, 1994. Many barrio residents recall Spanish-language, Mexican music programming during the early morning hours when many Mexican citrus workers began their day working in the groves. "Cande" was one of the better known disc jockeys on KPMO broadcasting from Pomona in the 1940s and 1950s. He replaced Eddie Rodríguez, who went on to host radio programs in Los Angeles. Cheva García remembers that she, her sisters, and other local artists performed at a valley radio station in the 1930s. I want to thank Cheva García (my grandmother) for her insights on the history of Arbol Verde.

22. Fernanda Cruz Contreras interview.

23. July 2, 1932, marked the date of *Serenata Mexicana* and the arrival of the Mexican Players to the Padua Hills stage. Blakeslee, "History of Padua Hills Theatre," 50.

24. Padua Players file, Pasadena Playhouse Collection. At the conclusion of the season, the Claremont Community Players decided to finally give up their expensive venture. The Garners responded by contracting a small contingent from the Pasadena Playhouse known as the Padua Players to perform their most successful plays until the Mexican Players were ready to expand their Friday and Saturday night appearances to a full schedule. For a while, the Mexican Players shared the stage with the Padua Players; however, over the next few seasons the management cultivated the idea of producing exclusively Mexican plays.

25. Padua Institute Booklet: "A Non-profit Institution Dedicated to Inter-American Friendship," PHC/PPL. "The Story—A Very Important Discovery."

26. *Padua Hills News Notes*, February 5, 1944; Deuel, *Mexican Serenade*, 31, 40.

27. *Padua Hills News Notes*, March 21, 1947. I would like to thank Marian Perales for bringing this quote to my attention. See also Perales and Rodriquez, "Directing the Inter-cultural Experience."

28. Deuel, *Mexican Serenade*, 55.

29. Bess Garner, *Las Posadas*, 1.

30. Camilla Romo Wolfe interview; Casilda Amador Thoreson interview, May 19, 1995.

31. On *commedia dell'arte* at Padua, see Deuel, *Mexican Serenade*, 46–47. Fernanda Cruz Contreras interview; Camilla Romo Wolfe interview.

32. Casilda Amador Thoreson interview, May 19, 1995; Wright, *Claremont: A Pictorial History*, 284. Ramirez-Jara was a descendent of the Palomares, the Californio family who once owned the land on which Padua Hills was built.

33. *Pilgrimage Diary of Mexican Players of Padua Hills*, PHC/PPL.

34. Camilla Romo Wolfe interview; archival photos and letters documenting the trip in PHC/PPL.

35. Deuel, *Mexican Serenade*, 55. Undated document, written by Herman Garner, PHC/PPL. Herman Garner was probably wary of plays featuring "love triangles" since he, at the time, was engaged in an extramarital affair with his secretary and theater photographer, Irene Garner (her married name after she and Herman later married). Even when Paduanos introduced the ideas for plays, such as in the case of Miguel Vera introducing *Las Posadas*, the story lines were written by Bess Garner and Charles Dickinson and reviewed by Herman Garner. Casilda Amador Thoreson interview, May 19, 1995.

36. Undocumented scrapbook put together by Bess Garner in the 1940s, PHC/PPL. See also Perales and Rodriquez, "Directing the Intercultural Experience," 6.

37. Weber, *Foreigners in Their Native Land*, 98–99.

38. The primary weaver of this illusory history of Californios, and the California invasion was Hubert Howe Bancroft; see Bancroft, *California Pastoral, 1769–1848*. Among the first, if not the best known critics of this interpretation of California history was Carey McWilliams; see McWilliams, *Southern California Country*. Among the most recent historians presenting a revised vision of California history, see Haas, *Conquests and Historical Identities*; Monroy, *Thrown Among Strangers*; and Castañeda, "Comparative Frontiers."

39. *Padua Hills News Notes*, March 19, 1943. Marian Perales provides an in-depth focus on the effects of World War II on Paduanas in a brilliant untitled and unpublished paper, presented October 22, 1993.

40. Ibid.

41. Covarrubias, *Mexico South*; Herrera, *Frida Kahlo*, 2, 167–68. Although instructive, Covarrubias's observations tend to exoticize Tehuanas for his non-Zapotec readers. Moreover, his accounts do not fully explore the deep religious and political divisions within the regions, or the social movements that arose before, during, and especially after the publication of his book. For more recent treatments, see de la Cruz, *El General Charis*; and Muro, *Iglesia y Movimientos Sociales en Mexico*.

42. Perales and Rodriquez, "Directing the Intercultural Experience," 34; Casilda Amador Thoreson interview; *Padua Hills News Notes*, March 19, 1943. Juan Matute, a Paduano

who was not drafted into military service, also helped manage the theater during World War II. According to Camilla Romo Wolfe, a few players were employed in the front office at the theater, Wolfe interview. Another woman, Isabel López de Fages, accepted a management position during the late 1940s. See *Padua Hills News Notes*, October 11, 1949.

43. Covarrubias, *Mexico South*, 338–54. The Huave villages near Tehuantepec today continue the matriarchy they practiced a few centuries before the invasion of Spanish troops in the Mexican isthmus though with significant alterations due to contact with non-Zapotecs. Comprising a variety of communities living around Lagunas Superior and Inferior, men take care of most domestic affairs, while women control the economic and political operations among the villagers. Another matriarchal society thrives in Juchitan, Oaxaca, Mexico, also in the isthmus area. For more information see Darling, "The Women Who Run Juchitan," *Los Angeles Times*, March 31, 1995, sec. A, p. 1; and Iturbide, "Juchitan's Heart," *Mother Jones* 15, no. 2 (February–March 1990): 39.

44. Flyer, PHC/PPL.

45. Kelley, "Notes on Deconstructing 'The Folk,'" 1,402.

46. Lott, *Love and Theft*.

47. Oles, *South of the Border*, 5. Similarly, art historian James Oles, in his exploration of American expatriate artists in Mexico, found that "many American artists emphasized an idyllic and timeless rural world, often to the exclusion of images that offered any clue of modernity, mechanization, or industry."

48. Bess Garner, *Mexico: Notes in the Margin*, 164.

49. Huggins, *Harlem Renaissance*; Baker, *Modernism and the Harlem Renaissance*; Torgovnick, *Savage Intellects, Modern Lives*; Quirarte, "Mexican and Mexican American Artists in the United States: 1920–1970"; Oles, *South of the Border*; Jacobs, *Engendered Encounters*.

50. Bess Garner, *Windows in an Old Adobe*.

51. Garner and Post, *The Story of the Adobe de Palomares*, 6.

52. Esther Davis to Micaela Velázquez, March 31, 1955; Donald MacDonald to the artists of Padua Hills, March 26, 1955; Carl Spaulding to Padua Hills, November 6, 1956, PHC/PPL.

53. 4. Esther Davis to Micaela Velázquez, March 31, 1955, PHC/PPL.

54. 5. Marie Harrington to Mrs. Garner, October 8, year unknown, PHC/PPL.

55. Juan Matute's speech for Mr. Garner's Testimonial Dinner, May 9, 1973, PHC/PPL.

56. *Padua Hills News Notes*, August 22, 1942, PHC/PPL.

57. Shippey, "The Lee Side o' L-A," *Los Angeles Times*, [date?], 4.

58. Undated Padua Institute booklet, PHC/PPL.

59. Bess Garner, undated document, PHC/PPL. Also in Perales and Rodriquez, "Directing The Intercultural Experience."

60. Michele Martínez interview.

61. Christina Pérez interview.

62. *Padua Hills News Notes*, November 14, 1941, PHC/PPL.

63. Wolfe interview.

64. Ibid.

65. Contreras interview.

66. Camilla Romo Wolfe interview.

67. Bess Garner, undated document, PHC/PPL. Bess wrote: "Compensation for participation in the plays is not provided beyond board and room and an allowance for small personal expenses, but opportunities are afforded for earning money by working in the dining room, entertaining, or other work."

68. Ibid. Rosa Torrez interview. In the late 1940s, forty cents was minimum wage for one hour's labor. Alicia Rodriquez conducted oral histories that contributed to this chapter.

69. Irene Garner interview; Casilda Amador Thoreson interview. After their bitter divorce, Herman married Irene Garner, who had been an employee of the Vortox Company, and a photographer and assistant to the Mexican Players.

70. José O'Beso interview. Camilla Romo Wolfe corroborates this story stating, "[our living situation] was part of our salary." Wolfe interview.

71. Bess Garner, *Mexico: Notes in the Margin*. Her reference to "blondes and brunettes" was a popular expression used during the period to distinguish whites from nonwhites.

72. Romo Wolfe interview.

73. Amador Thoreson interview.

74. *Padua Institute Booklet*, "The Educational Phase."

75. Wolfe interview; Thoreson interview, May 19, 1995; evidence of film moguls from RKO and other Hollywood film companies visiting Padua Hills is present in the guest lists, PHC/PPL. Walt Disney was one of the few Hollywood figures that integrated the players into a film, *The Three Caballeros*, a Latin American theme movie that combined animated characters with live actors. The Garners trusted Disney because of his regular attendance at the theater, his friendship with Herman Garner and artists of the Claremont community, namely Millard Sheets and Phil Dike, and his willingness not to violate the integrity of the Mexican Player concept on screen. In spite of the Garners' trepidations, Padua Hills produced some of the first "Mexican American" film actors and radio performers, including Mauricio Jara, Natividad Vacio, Manuel Diaz, and Camilla Romo Wolfe. For the most part, however, persistent stereotyping of and discrimination against ethnic minorities in film and radio, and the Garners' interest in keeping the players away from Hollywood, denied most Paduanos advancement opportunities in the entertainment industry.

76. O'Beso interview.

77. In addition to Camilla Romo Wolfe's success on radio, Paduanos Mauricio Jara, Natividad Vacio, and Manuel Diaz went on to experience varying degrees of success in Hollywood. Jara acted in numerous films including the critically acclaimed *Giant*, and later became co-director of the Ramona Pageant with his wife, Hilda Ramirez-Jara. Natividad Vacio also enjoyed a long acting career and distinguished himself in Robert Redford's directorial debut, *The Milagro Beanfield War*. The author's aunt, Isabel Alba, turned down an opportunity to appear in the classic film *Westside Story* in 1961 for "family reasons." Isabel Alba interview. However, her granddaughter, Jessica Alba, is continuing the family legacy as an emerging television and film star.

78. José Alba Jr. interview.

79. Amador Thoreson interview; Stan Book, "Biographical Sketch," in the catalogue for an art exhibit organized by The Chaffey Community Art Association, *Lícon: A Memorial Retrospective*, at the Museum of History and Art, Ontario, Calif., April 14–May 16, 1985; Robert George interview.

80. Millard Sheets, "Carlos Lícon: A Personal Statement," in *Lícon* (see preceding note).

81. *The Scripture*, Scripps College Student Newsletter, 16, no. 21 (March 8, 1946). For a description of the project, including a photograph of Lícon and Ramos Martínez working side-by-side on the mural, see Nieto, "Mexican Art and Los Angeles, 1920–1940."

82. Book, "Biographical Sketch."

83. A Paduano and personal friend of Lícon who wishes to remain anonymous on this subject, interviewed by the author, September 9, 1995.

84. *Padua Hills News Notes*, April 28, 1944; Book, "Biographical Sketch"; also an anonymous Paduano interviewed by the author, September 9, 1995.

85. Book, *Biographical Sketch*. See also Marciano Martínez interview, May 27, 1995.

86. Cruz Contreras interview.

87. A collection of the special commendations granted Mr. Garner from Governor Reagan, U.S. senator Allan Cranston, and the Los Angeles County Supervisors, to name a few, exists at the Pomona Public Library.

88. This has begun to change due largely to the efforts of Ginger Elliot and Claremont Heritage who have recently hosted reunions that honor the contributions of the Paduanos. Claremont Heritage has successfully acquired national landmark status for the theater facility from the federal government.

89. Juan Matute, speech for Herman Garner's Testimonial Dinner, May 19, 1973, PHC/PPL.

90. Rebecca (Camilla) Romo Wolfe to planners of Herman Garner's Testimonial Dinner, May 5, 1973, PHC/PPL.

91. Many Paduanos met and got married as a result of working at Padua Hills. Some of these people include Alfonso and Conchita Gallardo, Hilda and Mauricio Jara, Porfilia and Enrique Lerma, Juan and Manuela Matute, and José and Isabel Alba, just to name a few.

92. Taken from a former Mexican Player who refused both the author and Dr. Vicki L. Ruiz an interview. Her name has not been included out of respect for the player's wish not to be identified. In addition to some former players and community members that have been cited above, Monsignor Donald Strange, formerly of Our Lady of Assumption Catholic Church and now deceased, mentioned that the Garners could have provided better housing and pay for the players, and that Herman Garner was thrifty when it came to investing money for the improvement of the theater. Monsignor Donald Strange interview.

93. Crispin González interview.

94. Correspondence from Manuela Huerta-Matute, May 20, 1996.

95. White, *Remembering Ahanagran*, 4.

96. Vicki Ruiz writes of the dialectic between reminiscence and reticence, noting a process by which "the past becomes memory and then memory becomes history." Ruiz and DuBois, *Unequal Sisters*, xv.

97. White, *Remembering Ahanagran*, 4.

98. Arrízon, "Contemporizing Performance."

99. Spivak, *Outside in the Teaching Machine*, 3–4; and Lipsitz, *Dangerous Crossroads*, 62.

100. Juan Matute, for example, went on to have a very successful career as an executive for Pan American Airlines. After their tenures at Padua Hills, some Paduanos maintained levels of income that would classify them as part of the "Mexican American middle class." Amador Thoreson interview.

101. Lott, *Love and Theft*, 36–37. Frederick Douglass, as quoted by Lott, reinforces this point: "It is something gained when the colored man in any form can appear before a white audience; and we think that even this company, with industry, application, and a proper cultivation of their taste, may yet be instrumental in removing the prejudice against our race." Although Douglass was speaking to the potential of whites performing in blackface during the mid-1800s, this argument is applicable (and perhaps stronger) in the case of Mexican youth performing before white audiences in California during the 1930s.

102. Candelario José Mendoza interview; O'Beso interview. For example, two former players, Candelario Mendoza and José O'Beso became active in community politics; Mendoza in the Unity Leagues, and O'Beso in the Intercultural Council (both discussed in Chapter 7). As well, Juan Matute established the Mexican school, Leona Viscario, while performing at the theater.

103. Huerta, *Chicano Theater*; Kanellos, *Mexican American Theatre: Legacy and Reality* and Kanellos, *Mexican American Theatre: Then and Now*. For the strongest condemnation of the Mexican Players, see Garza, *Contemporary Chicano Theatre*, 5. For the most recent example of this phenomenon, see Arrizón, "Contemporizing Performance."

Chapter 5

1. Tobey and Wetherell, "The Citrus Industry," 12–14.
2. Williamson, "Labor in the California Citrus Industry," 105.
3. Ibid., 153–56.
4. Ibid., 135, 150–51. McBane, "The Role of Gender," 80–81.
5. Daniel, *Chicano Workers*.
6. This figure of 4.6 million is the total number of contracts issued during the life of the program. See García y Griego, "The Importation of Mexican Contract Laborers," 49.
7. The idea of a "packinghouse culture" is a reference to Vicki Ruiz's concept of a "cannery culture" described in her groundbreaking book, *Cannery Women, Cannery Lives*. Ruiz demonstrates the development of a "cannery culture" among women workers in California canneries and packinghouses before, during, and after World War II. See pp. 31–39.
8. Thomas, *Citizenship, Gender, and Work*, 26–27. See also Schuck, "The Treatment of Aliens in the United States," and Smith, *Civic Ideals*. Smith argues that "inegalitarian ascriptive" principles limiting citizenship based on gender and race have stood alongside liberalism and republicanism to shape American concepts of civic identity since the founding of the United States.
9. Kessler-Harris, *Out to Work*; May, "The Historical Problem of the Family Wage"; Amott and Matthaei, *Race, Gender, and Work*, 63–94; Ruiz, *From Out of the Shadows*, 63.
10. Gilroy, *The Black Atlantic*, 85.
11. Williamson, "Labor in the California Citrus Industry," 7–8. Williamson argues: "The packing house does not take orders from the grower. On the contrary, it is the packinghouse which gives orders to the grower, and tells him when and how the crops will be harvested and processed." Williamson incorrectly reduces the relationship of growers and packinghouses to two separate businesses dependent on one another, and fails to examine who governs packinghouses and how. While it is plausible that small growers felt alienated from the processes of the packinghouse, owners of large farms did not share this experience. In

packinghouse records covering Covina, San Dimas, Glendora, Claremont, Pomona, and Upland, prominent men in the industry served as board members for most of these packinghouses from their inception, and significantly influenced employment policies that had a direct impact on who picked and packed their fruit and at what rate. See the College Heights Packing House records, the San Dimas Lemon Association records, and the Indian Hill Packing House records for examples, Packinghouse Collection, PPL.

12. The California Citrus Institute, billed as "a growers' educational organization," published an annual report advising growers and packinghouse managers on ranch management including labor policies. See "Third and Fourth Annual Report, 1921–1922 and 1922–1923," and "Holding Production Costs Down," by George Hodgkin, Packing House Collection, PPL. Julia Salazar, packinghouse employee at College Heights Packing House in Claremont and wife of picking crew foreman, Roman Salazar, confirmed the existence of this "loose chain-of-command." She mentioned that her husband owned his own truck and was responsible for most hiring decisions. The citrus association insured the truck, but they did not insure workers. Although workers picked fruit for the growers affiliated with the association, Salazar accepted full liability for his employees' on-the-job injuries.

13. Frank Hernández interview; Modesto López interview.

14. López interview.

15. All quotes from the documentary film, *The Claremont Citrus Industry: Then and Now* by Geoff Cook, 1992. A special thank you to Ginger Elliot of Claremont Heritage for loaning me a copy of this film.

16. For details regarding technological advances in the citrus industry, especially those invented for packinghouses by Fred Stebler and George Parker, see Moses, "The Flying Wedge of Cooperation," 104–8.

17. Glen Tompkins interview.

18. Ruiz, *Cannery Women*, 29.

19. Tompkins interview. Annual totals for packers also varied since workers did not maintain a consistent eight-hour day throughout the year, but rather came in when they were needed. Moreover, packers never received overtime or compensation during the low season.

20. Tompkins interview; Julia Salazar interview by author, April 23, 1998; documentary film, *The Claremont Citrus Industry: Then and Now*, by Geoff Cook, 1992.

21. Minutes of the San Dimas Lemon Association board meeting, January 5, 1918, PPL; Minutes, San Dimas Lemon Association, December 5, 1921, PPL.

22. Salazar interview.

23. Salud ("Sally") Pérez interview.

24. Salud Pérez interview; Salazar interview.

25. Vicki Ruiz, *Cannery Women*, 28–29.

26. Salud Pérez interview.

27. Tompkins interview.

28. Salazar interview. Those that could limit their motions and pack rapidly attained legendary status among packinghouse employees. Both Salazar and Tompkins fondly remembered Helen Ruiz from Pomona, a woman that Salazar described as "a real slim little girl who was one of the fastest packers they had there." She added, "[Helen] didn't even move [when she packed]!"

29. Salazar interview.

30. Ibid.

31. Ruiz, *Cannery Women*, 31–32. See also Benson, "'The Customers Ain't God'"; Lamphere, "Bringing the Family to Work"; Zavella, "'Abnormal Intimacy.'"

32. Lorraine Campos (Salazar) interview.

33. Ibid.

34. Salud Pérez interview.

35. Salazar interview; Carmen Bañales interview. After retiring from the packinghouse, Carmen, Amparo, and Maria worked as volunteers at the local Catholic Church, Our Lady of Assumption (OLA). Amparo and Carmen live in a house two blocks from the old College Heights Packing House and across the street from OLA. They have willed the house to the church.

36. Carmen Bañales interview. Tompkins interview. For the significance of kinship and marriage in Mexican families, see Alvarez, *Familia*.

37. Carmen Bañales interview.

38. Salazar interview.

39. Ruiz, *Cannery Women*, 32.

40. Salazar interview.

41. Devra Weber, *Dark Sweat, White Gold*, 123–25.

42. "Lemon Men's Club Hears of Various Aspects of Agricultural Labor," *California Citrograph* (November 1937): 32; "Picking a Poor Time," *Los Angeles Times*, January 9, 1938, Taylor Collection, 84/38c, Carton 46:3. See also Williamson, "Labor in the California Citrus Industry," 159–62. According to Williamson, the Exchange unsuccessfully appealed the rulings all the way to the Ninth Circuit Court of Appeals in 1940.

43. Tompkins interview.

44. Salazar interview.

45. A. D. Shamel, "Housing the Employes of California's Citrus Ranches," *California Citrograph* (March 1918):96.

46. Williamson, "Labor in the California Citrus Industry," 150–51. This is exactly what happened in the 1941 Strike at Limoneira Company in Ventura County. Charles C. Teague evicted striking workers and replaced them with Okies and Arkies. Also, Julia Salazar explained that she and her family were asked to leave the association-owned housing in 1951 when she stopped working for a short time, though her husband Roman continued to work as a foreman for College Heights Lemon House. Rather than fight management, the Salazares built their own home in nearby Arbol Verde. Salazar interview.

47. Williamson, "Labor in the California Citrus Industry," 21.

48. Ruiz, *Cannery Women*, 28.

49. Campos interview.

50. Salazar interview.

51. "Report Submitted by Neil Haggerty, Secretary L.A. Building Trades Council, Strikes—Citrus," Taylor Collection, 84/38c, Carton 46:3. For more on the anti-union, anti–civil rights actions of the Associated Farmers, see González, *Labor and Community*, 135–36, 173–74; and Williamson, "Labor in the California Citrus Industry," 156.

52. Donato and Alfonsa Bustos interview.

53. McWilliams, "They Saved the Crops," 12, as cited in Williamson, "Labor in the California Citrus Industry," 59.

54. García y Griego, "The Importation of Mexican Contract Laborers," 45–85; and Galarza, *Merchants of Labor*.

55. Report of the President's Commission of Migratory Labor, *Migratory Labor in American Agriculture* (Washington, D.C.: U.S. Government Printing Office, 1951), 226; and Wayne D. Rasmussen, *A History of the Emergency Farm Labor Program, 1943–1947*, U.S. Department of Agriculture, Bureau of Agriculture Economics (Washington, D.C.: Government Printing Office, 1951), 200–204, as cited in Daniel Martínez Jr., "The Impact of the Bracero Program," 17.

56. Daniel Martínez, "The Impact of the Bracero Program," 24.

57. Williamson, "Labor in the California Citrus Industry," 51–52; "Mexican National Program to Continue," The Sunkist Courier Department, *California Citrograph* (February 1946): 114.

58. Daniel Martínez, "The Impact of the Bracero Program," 34–35, 49.

59. Bustos interview; Daniel Martínez, "The Impact of the Bracero Program," 35. Many men like Donato Bustos lost this money when they "skipped" their contracts.

60. Daniel Martínez, "The Impact of the Bracero Program," 36–37.

61. Ibid., 44.

62. Bustos interview; Salazar interview; Hernández interview.

63. Bustos interview.

64. Most *bracero* strikes were over work camp conditions, especially the poor quality of food, not wages. See Mario T. García, *Mexican Americans*, 95, and Bustos interview. For evidence of wage differentials between Mexican Americans and *braceros* in California agricultural labor, see Daniel Martínez, "The Impact of the Bracero Program," 49; and Thomas, *Citizenship, Gender, and Work*, 62–73.

65. Bustos interview.

66. Daniel Martínez, "The Impact of the Bracero Program," 55, 67.

67. Ibid., 55.

68. Salazar interview.

69. Although *braceros* had camps, they were permitted to live outside these prescribed areas if they could find a host or provide for themselves. Bustos interview.

70. Candelario Mendoza interview, April 22, 1998.

71. Salazar interview.

72. Mendoza interview. Salazar also acknowledged that some of her coworkers and barrio neighbors dated and married *braceros*.

73. Bustos interview.

74. Monroy, "An Essay on Understanding the Work Experiences," 70; Ruiz, *From Out of the Shadows*, 63. See also Odem, "Teenage Girls, Sexuality, and Working-Class Parents."

75. Daniel Martínez, "The Impact of the Bracero Program," 56–57. Discussing the problem of prostitution with one bar owner in the Cucamonga's Northtown, Martínez reported: "The proprietor was asked what type of woman has been hired at his bar and at the other bars. He said that some of them are women who were left behind by *braceros* who promised to marry them. Because most of them have children to support, they have to find some type of employment. Since they have become outcasts in the community for associating with *braceros*, this is the only type of work they can find."

76. Mendoza interview, April 22, 1998.

77. Daniel Martínez, "The Impact of the Bracero Program," 60–61, 70.

78. *El Espectador*, June 22, 1952.

79. Ignacio López, "Grist for the Mills of the Axis," *El Espectador*, June 11, 1943, reprinted in Ignacio López's FBI file, No. 100-200298, part 1.

80. Ibid. For an example of another Mexican American critic of juvenile delinquency, see Manuel Ruiz Jr. Papers. The career of Manuel Ruiz Jr. is discussed in Pagán, "Sleepy Lagoon."

81. *El Espectador*, June 22, 1952, 1.

82. *El Espectador*, May 2, 1952, 1.

83. *El Espectador*, May 9, 1952, 1, 2, 7; Daniel Martínez, "The Impact of the Bracero Program," 73. Martínez reported, "The 200 residents of Northtown interviewed, with the exception of the businessmen, all believe that their problems have been aggravated by the presence of the Braceros." He concluded, "They feel very strongly against the Bracero Programs and if a solution is not found soon, additional complications will result."

84. *El Espectador*, May 9, 1952, 7. López said of local growers: "All these men, will use their political prestige and force for the general benefit of the entire community."

85. *El Espectador*, June 22, 1952. For recent interpretations of the connections between the *bracero* program and undocumented immigration, see García y Griego, "The Importation of Mexican Contract Laborers," 73–75; and Gutiérrez, *Walls and Mirrors*, 142. Although López only mentioned the AFL, the CIO also opposed the *bracero* program. See testimony of Elizabeth Sasuly, U.S. Congress, Senate Committee on Agriculture and Forestry, *Hearings on Farm-Labor Supply Program*, 80th Cong., 1st sess., 1947.

86. *El Espectador*, October 6, 1950.

87. *El Espectador*, June 22, 1952; Daniel Martínez, "The Impact of the Bracero Program," 44.

88. *El Espectador*, March 29, 1957; *El Espectador*, April 1, 1960.

89. Gutiérrez, *Walls and Mirrors*, 142.

90. Galarza, *Merchants of Labor*, 30, 59. See also Thomas, 68.

91. Daniel Martínez, "The Impact of the Bracero Program," 39.

92. Thomas, *Citizenship, Gender, and Work*, 67.

93. Ibid., 71, 75, 206.

94. Lillard, *Eden in Jeopardy*, 71–89; Davis, *Ecology of Fear*, 59–91.

95. Southern California Crop Reports, Agricultural Department of the Los Angeles Chamber of Commerce, 1958, LACC. The LACC reported that total crop acreage in the Los Angeles metropolitan area declined approximately 54 percent from a high of 318,380 in 1942 to 172,435 in 1958. See also Daniel Martínez, "The Impact of the Bracero Program," 85.

96. Salazar interview. Julia Salazar's job in Covina was with a company that assembled electronics.

97. Salazar interview; Campos interview.

98. Ruiz, *From Out of the Shadows*, 61.

Chapter 6

1. Candelario Mendoza interview, February 17, 1995.

2. What I call "Latin American music" in this chapter actually includes Latina/Latino

artists from the United States as well as those from Latin America. Although I understand the differences between these two groups, my purpose is to evoke Américo Paredes' concept of "Greater Mexico" and extend it to a concept of "Greater Latin America" so as to include Puerto Rican and Cuban artists that appealed to Mexican American audiences in Southern California. The emergence of a Latin American/Spanish-language music market in places like the Pomona Valley powerfully demonstrates the permeable nature of the cultural borders separating U.S.-based Latino communities and Latin America. See Paredes, *Folklore and Culture*.

3. Mendoza interview.

4. Lipsitz, "Land of a Thousand Dances"; and Loza, *Barrio Rhythm*.

5. Avila, "The Folklore of the Freeway"; and Villa, *Barrio-Logos*. Both authors tend to focus on urban barrios.

6. Mendoza interview, February 17, 1995. Also see Loza, *Barrio Rhythm*.

7. For an understanding of the significant development of Latin American music in the 1940s see Roberts, "The 1940s: The Watershed," in *The Latin Tinge*, 100–126.

8. Mendoza interview, February 17, 1995.

9. For distinctions among Latin American musical forms, see Roberts, *The Latin Tinge*. Also, Loza in his book, *Barrio Rhythms*, lists the various Latin American influences on music of Los Angeles during the twentieth century. Manuel Peña has written the most thorough analysis of Latin American music in the American Southwest. *Norteño* was a type of music developed in Monterrey, Mexico, during the nineteenth century, which consisted of the accordion-based sound brought to the country by eastern European immigrants and the indigenous music of Mexico. Later, this music migrated with Mexican immigrants to Texas, and became known as *conjunto*, a working-class music reflective of the socioeconomic status of Tejanos (Mexican Texans). *Orquesta* was a merging of the big band sounds popular in the United States during the 1930s and 1940s with the Latin American rhythms of Puerto Rico, Cuba, Mexico, and the American Southwest. Peña argues that this was a "status" music created for the Mexican middle class to differentiate themselves and their tastes from the Mexican working class. See Peña, *The Texas-Mexican Conjunto*.

10. Quotes taken from an article covering the MOD, Margo McBane, director. See Ruby Gonzáles, "The fruits of their labors: Historians preserve slice of life of Valley's citrus workers," *San Gabriel Valley Tribune*, March 16, 1995, A1, A4.

11. Paco Castellano interview.

12. Mendoza interview, February 17, 1995.

13. Ibid.

14. Although Manuel Peña argues that *orquesta* and *conjunto* music appealed to two different classes of Mexican Americans, both forms were accepted and appreciated by Rainbow Garden audiences. According to Cande, however, patrons favored the *orquesta* style of music. See Mendoza interview, February 17, 1995.

15. Peter Grendysa, liner notes for the compact disc *Mondo Mambo: the Best of Pérez Prado and His Orchestra*, 11.

16. Mendoza interview, February 17, 1995, 7–8.

17. Ibid.

18. Jerry Castellano interview.

19. Ibid.

20. Lipsitz, "Land of a Thousand Dances," 267–68. Lipsitz explains African Americans' and Chicanos' break with the music of a past generation and their creation of a new rock 'n' roll aesthetic, particularly in Southern California.

21. Jerry Castellano interview.

22. Peter Grendysa, liner notes for *Mondo Mambo*, 13.

23. Jerry Castellano interview.

24. According to John and Peter Setlich, brothers, entrepreneurs, and musicians who converted the structure before the Thomases bought the building, the ballroom was designed specifically to house big band music. They used the latest in dance hall architecture, running up a bill that ultimately forced them out of business. John and Peter Setlich interview.

25. Lipsitz, *Dangerous Crossroads*, and Gilroy, *The Black Atlantic*, 57.

26. Art Laboe interview.

27. Ibid. Two other concert promoters, Johnny Otis and Eddie Davis, confirmed that laws were more lax in the county than in the city when it came to shows for youths. On a compact disc insert to *The East Side Sound, 1959–1968*, Davis recounted his troubles with the law: "I gave a dance at the Shrine Exposition Hall [in Los Angeles]. 80% of the attendance was under 18. The police stopped the dance. I paid a fine and nothing ever happened." As a result, Davis moved his concerts to Rainbow Gardens in 1962 to avoid the harassment. Similarly, Johnny Otis moved his R&B shows to El Monte's American Legion Stadium to avoid "ancient blue laws" enforced by Los Angeles police officers designed to breakup interracial, youth-oriented concerts. Otis claims he eventually had to pay off "El Monte city fathers" to allow him to continue his shows. See Eddie Davis, liner notes to *The East Side Sound, 1959–1968*; and Otis, *Upside Your Head! Rhythm and Blues on Central Avenue*, 61.

28. Art Laboe interview.

29. Richard Rodríguez interview. Mr. Rodríguez attended shows regularly at El Monte's American Legion Stadium throughout its existence, and helped Art Laboe with the production of El Monte's reissued compilation album entitled *Art Laboe's Memories of El Monte: The Roots of L.A.'s Rock and Roll*. Today, Mr. Rodríguez serves on the board of directors for the Doo Wop Society, and is a part time organizer of concerts and music events.

30. Rodríguez interview; Marta Maestas interview. Maestas explained that her peers called the shoes "bunnies" because "they had bunny tails in the back and in the front that looked like bunny ears."

31. Rodríguez interview.

32. Jerry Castellano interview.

33. Rodríguez interview.

34. Ibid.

35. George Lipsitz identifies the process of fashion and youth culture influencing the themes of rock 'n' roll music coming out of Southern California. The "pachuco" style and subculture in particular had an early effect on Southland music, manifested in Don Tosti's 1948 hit "Pachuco Boogie." Chuck Higgins's 1952 hit "Pachuko Hop" (popular with El Monte's audiences) demonstrated a continuing influence of the pachuco in the fifties. According to Rodríguez, Castellano, Mendoza, and Lipsitz, however, the pachuco subculture gave way to what Lipsitz called a "cholo" style in the 1950s. See Lipsitz, "Land of a Thousand Dances," 271–72. Also Rodríguez, Mendoza, and Jerry Castellano interviews.

36. Lipsitz, "Land of a Thousand Dances."

37. Jerry Castellano interview.

38. Ibid.

39. Delbert Franklin interview.

40. Dan Pollock interview.

41. Eddie Davis interview in the compact disc insert, *The East Side Sound*; Candelario Mendoza interview. Davis never mentions the role of Candelario Mendoza in signing The Mixtures as Rainbow Gardens' house band. Instead, Davis claims that he found Rainbow Gardens through his relationship with disk jockeys Bob Eubanks and Wink Martindale. It is possible that as the booking manager, Mendoza worked through Eubanks and/or Martindale who occasionally hosted Friday Night Dances at Rainbow Gardens.

42. Franklin interview.

43. Pollock interview.

44. Eddie Davis interview.

45. Dick Moreland, liner notes to The Mixtures' album, *Stompin' at the Rainbow*.

46. Ibid.

47. Rosalie Mendez Hamlin interview, June 26, 1997.

48. Maestas interview.

49. Ibid.

50. Hamlin interview.

51. Lipsitz, "Land of a Thousand Dances," 270. The experiences of such labor and community organizers as Bert Corona and Hope Mendoza Schechter, who married non-Mexicans, demonstrates the effect activism had on breaking down cultural barriers in courtship and dating of this period. See Bert Corona interviewed by Mario T. García in *Memories of Chicano History*; Rose, "Gender and Civic Activism in Mexican American Barrios," 188. For issues surrounding interracial marriage, see Pascoe, "Race, Gender, and Intercultural Relations."

52. Rodríguez interview. A switch was the popular term commonly used during the 1950s and 1960s for a tree branch.

53. Ibid.

54. Ibid.

55. Ibid. Maestas interview.

56. Castellano interview

57. Ibid.

58. Ibid.

59. Ibid.

60. Ibid.

61. Rubén Guevara, as quoted in Lipsitz, "Land of a Thousand Dances," 280.

62. For a description of the *corrido* and its importance in Mexican/Mexican immigrant culture see, Herrera-Sobek, *Northward Bound*, xxii–xxv, and *The Mexican Corrido*.

63. Jerry Castellano interview.

64. María Elena Adams-González interview.

65. Ibid.

66. Ibid. Adams-González chose to sing for her local Catholic church parish. She still participates in her church choir.

67. Jerry Castellano interview.

68. Ibid.

69. Ibid. Also Mendoza interview, February 17, 1995. Castellano mentioned that the appropriation of artists' material by record executives was a common occurrence in the 1950s and 1960s. For example, he composed a song entitled "Jerry's Jump" with his first group The Velveteens. After Castellano left the band, however, the agent had the bandleader record the song under a new title "Johnny's Jump."

70. Hamlin interview.

71. For a thorough analysis of how commercial motives transformed the rock "business" during the late 1960s and early 1970s, see Wicke, "'We're Only in It for the Money': the rock business," chapter 6 in Rock Music, 113–34; and Guevara, "The View from the Sixth Street Bridge."

72. Mike Davis explains how many corporations in the 1960s adopted General Electric's 1950s strategy of moving production to the "Sunbelt" (for example, Arizona) where labor organizing was discouraged and legislated against. Davis, Prisoners of the American Dream, 127–38. In his book, City of Quartz, Davis examines how the white Los Angeles power structure directed redevelopment money into ventures that benefited white Angelenos while abandoning black and Latino communities. The 1965 Watts Rebellion and the 1970 Chicano Moratorium in East Los Angeles represented just two climactic events in an ongoing struggle to act out against such civic neglect. See Davis, "Power Lines," chapter 2 in City of Quartz, 101–49.

73. For a history of how homeowners' associations helped sculpt the segregated landscape of Greater Los Angeles see Davis, "Homegrown Revolution," chapter 3 in City of Quartz, 152–219.

74. Mendoza served as the president of the Pomona Unified School District twice, and started his own bilingual (Spanish/English) newspaper, La Voz, in the 1980s. Mendoza interview, February 17, 1995.

75. Richard Rodríguez, "El Monte Legion Stadium," The Doo Wop Society Newsletter (1996). I want to thank Rosie Hamlin for providing me with this article.

76. Roberts, "The 1940s: The Watershed," in The Latin Tinge, 100–126.

77. Gilroy, The Black Atlantic, 39.

78. Both Edward Said and Cameron McCarthy make this same argument with regard to culture and art on a global scale. See Said, Culture and Imperialism, 48–49; McCarthy, The Uses of Culture, 5–6.

Chapter 7

1. Kelley, Race Rebels, 47.

2. Mario T. García, Mexican Americans; González, Labor and Community; Gutiérrez, Walls and Mirrors; Ruiz, Cannery Women; Sánchez's "The Rise of the Second Generation," chapter 12 in Becoming Mexican American, also fits into this group.

3. González, Labor and Community, 178.

4. Landman, "Some Aspects of the Acculturation of Mexican Immigrants," 36.

5. Ruth Hallo Landman made the following point regarding Mexican Americans' entry into the industrial labor force and upward occupational mobility: "As far as the larger com-

munity is concerned, the Mexicans [in Ontario] are still at the bottom of the economic order, and are merely participating in the general prosperity by drawing higher wages for unskilled work." Landman, "Some Aspects of the Acculturation of Mexican Immigrants," 56.

6. Ignacio López, for example, often complained that Mexican Americans had been excluded from defense industry jobs in Southern California due to discrimination. The Federal Bureau of Investigation identified López's comments as "un-American," and maintained an extensive file on him. See FBI file on Ignacio López, filed August 27, 1943, no. 100-200298-3; see also Haas, "The Bracero in Orange County," 31; González, *Labor and Community*, 179.

7. J. Frederic Blitstein charts these transformations in the Pomona Valley in his 1971 dissertation. Blitstein, "America's Turmoil."

8. Ibid., 22.

9. Landman, "Some Aspects of the Acculturation of Mexican Immigrants," 35.

10. Lillard, *Eden In Jeopardy*, 71–89; Davis, *Ecology of Fear*, 59–91.

11. El Congreso del Pueblo de Habla Española (El Congreso) is the best example of whites and Mexican Americans working together for the protection of Mexican American civil rights during the 1930s. See Mario T. García, "The Popular Front: Josefina Fierro de Bright and the Spanish-Speaking Congress," in *Mexican Americans*, 145–74; Gutiérrez, *Walls and Mirrors*, 110–16; and Ruiz, *Cannery Women*, 76.

12. Mario T. García most clearly articulates this connection between World War II and Mexican American civil rights when he writes: "As he [Bert Corona] and others rediscovered racial and cultural exclusion in their hometowns, this ignited various community and even regional efforts by Mexican-Americans to wage still another war, this time on the homefront." In the "Introduction" to Bert Corona, *Memories of Chicano History*, 9. See also García, "Americans All"; Alvárez, "Psycho-historical and Socioeconomic Development of the Chicano Community"; and Tirado, "Mexican American Community Political Organization."

13. O'Brien, "The Mexican Colony," 79; Sánchez, *Becoming Mexican American*, 256.

14. Vicki Ruiz also discusses the significance of generational difference in the pre–World War II era. See Ruiz, "'Star Struck.'"

15. For information on LAO, see González, *Labor and Community*, 172–75. For information pertaining to CSO, see Gutiérrez, *Walls and Mirrors*, 168–72; Griffith, "Viva Roybal." For information on the Unity Leagues, see Mario T. García, *Mexican Americans*, 101–6; Tuck, "Sprinkling the Grass Roots"; and Candelario José Mendoza interview, May 6, 1994.

16. Mendoza interview, May 6, 1994, and March 13, 1996.

17. López FBI file, nos. 100-200298 and 140-36569; also see Mario T. García, "Mexican-American Muckraker: Ignacio L. López and *El Espectador*," in *Mexican Americans*, 84–85. I want to thank Mario T. García for supplying me with a copy of López's FBI file. García's chapter concerning Ignacio L. López is the most thorough treatment of his life to date.

18. López married four times in his life. His first wife Beatriz, who helped establish *El Espectador*, died in 1951. The date of the first edition seems to be in question. García claims that it began in 1933; volume numbers in the collection at Stanford count back to 1935; FBI records suggest the weekly began in 1935; and Candelario Mendoza, López's protégé, does not remember the exact date of the first edition. I have accepted García's claim that

it began in 1933, though for the purpose of this chapter, the important fact is that it began well before World War II.

19. Mendoza interview, March 13, 1996. Stanford's Green Library does not contain the editions of *El Espectador* from 1933 to 1936; the collection does include newspapers from 1937 to 1960.

20. *El Espectador*, vol. 5, no. 29, May 19, 1939.

21. "Pedimos Justicia," *El Espectador*, February 5, 1937, 2.

22. López FBI file, no. 100-200298, part 1.

23. López, *El Espectador*, February 17, 1937.

24. *El Espectador*, October 22, 1937; November 12, 1937; and December 3, 1937.

25. For a detailed analysis of how cosmetic companies specifically targeted young Mexican American women consumers in their advertisements, see Ruiz, "'Star Struck.'" *La Opinion*, the primary Spanish-language newspaper in Los Angeles, appealed to women through similar columns concerning beauty, fashion, and diet.

26. Other Spanish-language newspapers, like *La Opinion*, criticized pachucos as well.

27. López FBI file, no. 100-200298, part 1.

28. Mendoza interview, May 6, 1994.

29. Ibid. Mendoza recalled his first encounter with López: "he [López] said 'I have a Spanish newspaper called *El Espectador* and I'd like to start at least one page in English featuring news about Mexican American kids at Chaffey [High School] and Pomona High and in the area . . . and I'd like to know if you'd like to come and work with me and edit that page.'" Similarly, Nisei (second generation) Japanese American women published English language pages in Japanese newspapers in California. See Matsumoto, "Desperately Seeking 'Deirdre.'"

30. Candelario Mendoza, "And So It Goes: Are We To Obey Regardless," *El Espectador*, November 18, 1938.

31. Eugenio Nogueras, "Donde Estan Los Lideres de la Colonia?" *El Espectador*, March 28, 1941; also in López's FBI file, no. 100-200298, part 1. The analogy of the Mexican American electorate as the "sleeping giant" has been a common one in Chicano politics.

32. López, *El Espectador*, March 29, 1940.

33. Victor Murillo Ruiz interview, 15.

34. López's FBI file, no. 100-200298, part 1.

35. Ibid.

36. Ruth D. Tuck, author of the book *Not With the Fist* and Redlands University professor, was one of his closest friends and most loyal allies. López delivered a convocation speech at the college, and wrote the foreword to Tuck's 1946 book.

37. López joined Carey McWilliams, Josephina Fierro de Bright, and other leftist activists in the Sleepy Lagoon Defense Committee in 1944. See López's FBI file, no. 100-200298, part 1.

38. Ibid.

39. Ibid.

40. Mario T. García discusses each one of these crusades in detail in his chapter "Mexican-American Muckraker: Ignacio L. López and *El Espectador*," in *Mexican Americans*, 84–112. See also Enrique M. López, "Community Resistance to Injustice and Inequality."

41. *The Ontario Daily Report*, March 3, 1939, 1.

42. For a history of the criminalization of Mexican American youth by Southern California media and law officers during the early and mid-1940s, see Mazón, *The Zoot-Suit Riots*. See also Escobar, *Race, Police, and the Making of a Political Identity*.

43. F. Moreno, "La Labor de Las Sociedades," *El Espectador*, February 19, 1937, 2.

44. Ross Papers, Box 20, folder 19, 83. More research is needed on multiracial Unity Leagues in Riverside and San Diego, California.

45. Mendoza interview, May 6, 1994.

46. Ibid.

47. Davis, *City of Quartz*, 399–401. The story of Ross's arrival is in his unpublished autobiographical notes, Ross Papers, Box 20, folders 4 (p. 1), 14, 17.

48. Acuña, *Occupied America*, 209; Enriquez López, "Community Resistance to Injustice and Inequality," 11; Tirado, "Mexican American Community Political Organization," 61–62. Until recently, historians believed Ross came to Southern California as a representative of the Industrial Areas Foundation. Ross explains that he came as a representative of the American Council on Race Relations. See Ross Papers, Box 20, folders 4, 82; Burt, "Latino Empowerment in Los Angeles," 13.

49. Ross Papers, Box 20, folder 4, p. 1, and Box 20, folder 19, p. 83. Ross credited López and Tuck with helping him discover effective organizing strategies among Mexican Americans and African Americans in Southern California. Tinged with narcissism or just humor, Ross explained their importance in his unpublished, unfinished autobiography. He wrote: "It begins with my acquaintance with Ruth Tuck and Ignacio López, how they and a long trip through the Citrus Belt help me convince myself I am doomed to become the New Messiah among California's Mexican-Americans, and how, by going into two Mexican-American-Negro communities and flailing about for a while I learn some of the rudiments of mass-organization."

50. Foley, Neil. "Becoming Hispanic," 55–56.

51. Candelario Mendoza stated: "the main objective was we wanted to unite the people by getting them to register to vote. And that was one of our main objectives, was registration of voters. And hopefully to get some Latinos to city council." Mendoza interview, May 6, 1994.

52. Ross Papers, Box 20, folder 19.

53. Ibid.

54. Mario T. García, *Mexican Americans*, 103; Enrique López, "Community Resistance to Injustice and Inequality," 22–25.

55. *The Ontario Daily Report*, April 10, 1946, 1.

56. Mario T. García, *Mexican Americans*, 104.

57. Following World War II, many politically liberal Americans depended on an "ideology of the liberal consensus" in order to focus on their own lives. See Hodgson, "The Ideology of the Liberal Consensus." Moreover, many sought the ambiguous goal of "normalcy," defined by the pressures of the Cold War and America's opposition to Soviet Communism. See Elaine Tyler May, *Homeward Bound*.

58. Mendoza interview, May 6, 1994.

59. López's FBI file, no. 100-200298.

60. *El Espectador*, August 11, 1950, 2–3.

61. Mario T. García, *Mexican Americans*, 93.

62. *El Espectador*, November 4, 1949, 1, 2, 4.

63. Mario T. García, *Mexican Americans*, 95.

64. Carlton Corporation continued to exclude the Mexican family from the particular tract they were attempting to move into, but agreed to integrate an adjacent tract scheduled for development in 1950. See Mario T. García, *Mexican Americans*, 95.

65. C. C. Trillingham, *Status of "Segregation" in School Districts*.

66. Daniel, *Chicano Workers*.

67. Landman, "Some Aspects of the Acculturation of Mexican Immigrants," 55–56; Tuck, *Not With the Fist*, 174–75. For experiences of Mexican American women in industrial labor positions, see Gluck, *Rosie the Riveter Revisited*.

68. McWilliams, "Los Angeles." For an insightful discussion of the *Shelley v. Kraemer* case, see Lipsitz, *The Possessive Investment in Whiteness*, 25–33.

69. Lipsitz, *The Possessive Investment in Whiteness*, 372.

70. For a history of de facto segregation in Southern California, see Davis, "Homegrown Revolution," in *City of Quartz*. For a history of educational segregation in Los Angeles County, see Raftery, *Land of Fair Promise*.

71. For a history of the transformation in racial ideology between World War I and World War II, see Barkan, *Retreat of Scientific Racism*. For an explanation of the "modernist racial ideology" which replaced scientific racism in the interwar period, see Pascoe, "Miscegenation Law,'" 46–48.

72. O'Brien, "The Mexican Colony," 8, 76.

73. Milford Zornes served as the art director at the theater during the mid-1950s and painted many of the posters advertising Mexican Players' plays, while sculptor Albert Stewart created an image of a Mexican Indian woman that still stands at the entrance of Padua Hills Theatre. Millard Sheets served as a trustee of the Padua Institute and introduced many of his friends, including Walt Disney, to the theater. Deuel, *Mexican Serenade*, 42–43.

74. W. Henry Cooke interview, 3.

75. Ibid., 4.

76. Ibid., 2.

77. Ibid.

78. W. Henry Cooke, "The Segregation of Mexican-American School Children," 418.

79. W. Henry Cooke, "The Continuing American Revolution," 8–10, 25.

80. Cooke interview, 4.

81. Ibid.

82. Ibid. See also "Obituaries: W. Henry Cooke," *Claremont Courier*, February 4, 1978; "Obituaries: W. Henry Cooke," *Progress Bulletin*, Sunday, February 5, 1978, 4.

83. Though little information exists about *Su Casa*, the activities of this group included providing "food baskets," medical and "hygiene" clinics, and Christmas parties for the Mexican American community. Operating out of the Claremont Congregational Church, the volunteers functioned as "missionaries" such as those that operated settlement houses for ethnic minorities in the United States during the first half of the twentieth century. For an example of this kind of institution in the Southwest, see Vicki Ruiz's discussion of the Rose Gregory Houchen Settlement House in El Paso, Texas. Ruiz, "'La Malinche Tortilla Factory.'"

84. Cooke interview, 6.

85. Ibid., 5.

86. Alfonso and Esther Sevilla interview. The Sevillas mentioned that Lou Crusher, a graduate student studying under Sheets, took a lead role in supervising the construction of the houses.

87. Ibid. See also Cooke interview, 5–6; W. Henry Cooke to Lewis Mumford, July 7, 1947, Mumford Collection. Thank you to Al and Esther Sevilla for sharing their original mortgage documents to confirm these numbers. Mortgage from the Security First National Bank in author's possession.

88. Cooke interview, 6–9.

89. Cooke to Mumford, July 7, 1947, Mumford Collection.

90. Ibid.

91. Ibid.

92. Stephen J. Keating, Executive Secretary of the Federation of Community Coordinating Councils, to Millard Sheets, author of the ICC plans, July 19, 1948, Sheets Collection.

93. Millard Sheets, "Long Term Goals," ICC plans, 1948.

94. Correspondence, Paul Darrow to the author, May 21, 1996.

95. Ibid.

96. Mary Palos interview.

97. Ibid.

98. Paul Darrow interview.

99. Palos interview. Prior to this discovery, Merle Evers, widow of slain civil rights activist Medgar Evers and former NAACP president, was believed to be Claremont's first African American homeowner in the early 1970s.

100. Ibid.

101. Darrow interview.

102. Palos interview.

103. Darrow interview.

104. Ibid.

105. Palos interview.

106. Ibid.

107. Cooke interview, 5.

108. Darrow interview.

109. Cooke interview, 14.

110. Darrow interview.

111. Cooke interview, 14.

112. Darrow interview.

113. For a history of women's voluntarism, see Evans, *Born For Liberty*.

114. Daniel Martínez Jr. interview.

115. Thelma O'Brien, "Pioneers," *Almanac*, date unknown, 23, CHF. In a conversation with Vicki Ruiz, Dr. Ruiz mentioned that a similar Chicano backlash against Americanization happened at the Rose Gregory Houchen Settlement House in El Paso. See Ruiz, "'La Malinche Tortilla Factory.'"

116. Ibid.

117. Ibid., 33.

118. Cooke interview, 32.

119. Cooke interview, 7. In an oral history with the author, former Arbol Verde resident, Alfonso Sevilla, explained that the blueprints were given to him, but that he constructed most of his home. Sevilla interview.

120. Ibid., 25.

121. José O'Beso interview.

122. "Working Things Out at the Center," *Claremont Courier*, February 21, 1970, 9.

123. Correspondence, Cooke to Mumford, July 7, 1947.

124. Ruth Ordway interview, 3.

125. Mario T. García, *Mexican Americans*, 111.

126. Cooke interview, 29.

127. Mario García characterized López as an advocate of "political integration" and "cultural pluralism." García, *Mexican Americans*, 106.

Epilogue

1. Gutiérrez, *Walls and Mirrors*, 1.

2. Allen and Turner, *The Ethnic Quilt*, 39–40.

3. Lipsitz, *The Possessive Investment in Whiteness*, 49.

4. Pat Buchanan, "What Will America Be in 2050?," *Los Angeles Times*, Friday, October 28, 1994.

5. McWilliams, *Southern California Country*, 373.

6. Patrick J. McDonnell, "Immigrants a Net Economic Plus, Study Says," *Los Angeles Times*, May 18, 1997, sec. A. See also Lipsitz, *The Possessive Investment in Whiteness*, 51.

7. Patrick J. McDonnell and Robert J. Lopez, "70,000 March Through L.A. Against Prop. 187," *Los Angeles Times*, October 17, 1994, A1, A14.

8. Lipsitz, "'Home is Where the Hatred Is,'" 197–98.

9. Ibid., 201–2; Rubén Martínez, "The Shock of the New," *Los Angeles Times Magazine*, January 30, 1994.

10. Allen and Turner, *The Ethnic Quilt*, 250–52.

11. Mike Davis, "Magical Urbanism," 20–23. For a fictional and ironic exploration of this trend, see T. Coraghessan Boyle, *The Tortilla Curtain*.

Bibliography

Archives and Collections

Azusa-Foothill Citrus Company Collection. Huntington Library, San Marino, Calif.

California Department of Industrial Relations. Division of Immigration and Housing. C-A 194. Bancroft Library, University of California, Berkeley, Calif.

George Clements Collection, MS 118. Special Collections, University of California, Los Angeles, Calif.

La Verne Mutual Orange Distributors Citrus Packinghouse Oral History Project. City Hall, La Verne, Calif.

Ignacio López Collection. Special Collections, Green Library, Stanford University, Palo Alto, Calif.

Los Angeles Chamber of Commerce Archives. Regional History Center of the University of Southern California, Los Angeles.

Carey McWilliams Collection. Special Collections, University of California, Los Angeles, Calif.

Mumford Collection. Van Pelt-Dietrich Library, University of Pennsylvania, Philadelphia.

National Archives. Washington, D.C.

Oral Histories, Claremont Local History. Special Collections, Honnold Library, Claremont Colleges, Claremont, Calif.

Oral Histories. Model Colony Room, Ontario City Library, Ontario, Calif.

Oral History Collection. Upland Public Library, Upland, Calif.

Packinghouse Collection. Claremont Heritage Foundation, Claremont, Calif.

Packinghouse Collection. Pomona Public Library, Pomona, Calif.

Padua Hills Theatre Collection. Special Collections, Honnold Library, Claremont Colleges, Claremont, Calif.

Padua Hills Theatre Collection. Special Collections, Pomona Public Library, Pomona, Calif.

Pasadena Orange Growers Association Collection. Huntington Library, San Marino, Calif.

Pasadena Playhouse Collection. Huntington Library, San Marino, Calif.

Fred Ross Papers, M 812. Special Collections, Green Library, Stanford University, Palo Alto, Calif.

Manuel Ruiz Jr. Papers. Special Collections, Green Library, Stanford University, Palo Alto, Calif.

San Gabriel Farm Labor Association Records, 1921–1922. Huntington Library, San Marino, Calif.

Millard Sheets Collection. Archives of American Art, Washington, D.C.

Paul Taylor Collection, 74/187c. Bancroft Library, University of California, Berkeley.

Charles C. Teague Papers, C-B 760. Bancroft Library, University of California, Berkeley.

Warren Collection. Huntington Library, San Marino, Calif.

Interviews

Alba, José, Jr. Interview by author, April 24, 1993.

Alba, José, Sr. Interview by author, September 9, 1995.

Amador Thoreson, Casilda. Interview by author, June 18, 1995.

Armendarez, Carmen. Interview by author, October 3, 1997.

Bañales, Carmen. Interview by author, June 16, 1998.

Benjamin, Karl. Interview by author, May 15, 1996.

Bice, John. Interview by Betty Maxie, date not given. Oral History Collection, Upland Public Library, Upland, Calif.

Bustos, Donato and Alfonsa. Interview by Margo McBane, December 23, 1994.

Campos (Salazar), Lorraine. Interview by author, June 18, 1998.

Castellano, Jerry. Interview by author, May 11, 1995.

Castellano, Paco. Interview by author, May 11, 1995.

Cruz Contreras, Fernanda. Interview by author, June 19, 1998.

Cooke, W. Henry. Interview by Georgenia Irwin, October 31, 1968. Transcript at Claremont Heritage Foundation, Claremont, Calif.

Darrow, Paul. Interview by author, May 20, 1996.

Franklin, Delbert. Interview by author, July 23, 1997.

Fuentes, Nick. Interview by Margo McBane, March 15, 1995. Video at La Verne Mutual Orange Distributors Citrus Packinghouse Oral History Project, City Hall, La Verne, Calif.

———. Interview by Margo McBane and author, March 15, 1995. La Verne Mutual Orange Distributors Citrus Packinghouse Oral History Project, City Hall, La Verne, Calif.

García, Cheva. Interview by author, February 10, 1993.

Garner, Irene. Interview by author, June 17, 1993.

George, Robert. Interview by author, May 21, 1996.

González, Crispin. Interview by author, July 17, 1995.

González-Adams, María Elena. Interview by author, August 28, 1995.

Hernández, Frank. Interview by Margo McBane, December 18, 1994. La Verne Mutual Orange Distributors Citrus Packinghouse Oral History Project, City Hall, La Verne, Calif.

Laboe, Art. Interview by author, May 15, 1995.

López, Modesto. Interview by Margo McBane, December 18, 1994. La Verne Mutual Orange Distributors Citrus Packinghouse Oral History Project, City Hall, La Verne, Calif.

Maestas, Marta. Interview by author, April 21, 1998.

Martínez, Daniel, Jr. Interview by author, May 16, 1995.

Martínez, Michele. Interview by author, March 22, 1993.

Martínez, Marciano. Interview by author, May 21 and May 27, 1995.

Martínez, Richard. Interview by author, February 21, 1995.

Mathers, Wiley W. Interview by Betty Maxie, April 24, 1975. Transcript at Oral History Collection, Upland Public Library, Upland, Calif.

Mendez-Hamlin, Rosalie ("Rosie"). Interview by author, June 26, 1997.

Mendoza, Candelario José. Interview by author, May 6, 1994; February 17, 1995; March 13, 1996; April 22, 1998. Transcript at Special Collections, Pomona Public Library.

Milliken, Ruth. Interview by Betty Maxie, date not given. Oral History Collection, Upland Public Library, Upland, Calif.

Naftel, Paul. Transcript in Oral Histories, Honnold Library, Claremont Colleges.

O'Beso, José. Interview by author, June 3, 1993.

Ordway, Ruth. Interview by Caroline Beatty, September 18, 1978. Transcript at Special Collections, Honnold Library, Claremont Colleges.

Palos, Mary. Interview by author, May 24, 1996.

Pérez, Christina. Interview by author, April 26, 1993.

Pérez, Salud ("Sally"). Interview by Betty Maxie, November 19, 1975. Oral History Collection, Upland Public Library, Upland, Calif.

Pitzer, Clifford. Transcript in Oral Histories, Honnold Library, Claremont Colleges.

Pitzer, Russell. Transcript in Oral Histories, Honnold Library, Claremont Colleges.

Pollock, Dan. Interview by author, July 23, 1997.

Rodríguez, Richard. Interview by author, May 26, 1995.

Ruiz, Victor Murillo. Interview by Robert Collins, June 16, 1978. Transcript at Model Colony Room, Ontario Public Library, Ontario, Calif.

Salazar, Julia. Interview by Ginger Elliot, February 17, 1997. Transcript at Claremont Heritage Foundation, Claremont, Calif.

———. Interview by author, April 23, 1998.

Sandoval, Baudelio. Interview by Carlos Arturo Castañeda, April 13, 1978. Transcript, Spanish with an English translation, at Oral History Collection, Upland Public Library, Upland, Calif.

Setlich, John and Peter. Interview by author, July 21, 1995.

Sevilla, Alfonso and Esther. Interview by author, October 3, 1997.

Sevilla, Mary. Interview by author, May 21, 1997.

Sheets, Millard. Interview by Paul Karlstrom for the Archives of American Art, Smithsonian Institution, the San Francisco Archives, October–July 1986–1988. Transcript at the Archives of American Art, San Marino, Calif., and Washington, D.C.

Soper, Raymond. Interview by James Stickels and Caroline Beatty, February 6, 1979. Transcript at Model Colony Room, Ontario City Library.

Stary-Sheets, David. Interview by author, March 14, 1996.

Strange, Monsignor Donald. Interview by author, July 2, 1993.

Tompkins, Glen. Interview by author, April 21, 1998.

Torrez, Rosa. Interview by Alicia Rodriquez, April 8, 1993.

Vasquez, Enrique. Interview by Jorge Castañeda, date unkown, 1978.

Wheeler, Stuart G. Transcript in Oral Histories, Honnold Library, Claremont Colleges.

Whitney, George H. Interview by Betty Maxie, date not given. Oral History Collection, Upland Public Library, Upland, Calif.

Wolfe, Camilla Romo. Interview by author, June 21, 1994.

Government Documents

Book, Harry Ellington. *Los Angeles: The City and County*. Los Angeles Chamber of Commerce Home Printing Company, June 1911, revised.

Cook, A. J. *California Citrus Culture*. Printed at the State Printing Office, Friend of Wm. Richardson, Superintendent, The State Commission of Horticulture, 1913.

Federal Bureau of Investigation File on Ignacio López. File No. 100-200298, part 1 and 2; File No. 140-36569, part 1 and 2.

Southern California Crop Reports. Agricultural Department of the Los Angeles Chamber of
    Commerce, 1958.

Trillingham, C. C., superintendent of schools. *Status of "Segregation" in School Districts
    Served by the Office of County Superintendent of Schools*. Office of County
    Superintendent of Schools, prepared by Division of Elementary Education, 1947.

U.S. Bureau of the Census. *Fourteenth Census of the United States: State Compendium
    California*. Washington, D.C.: Government Printing Office, 1924.

———. *Fifteenth Census of the United States: State Compendium California*. Washington,
    D.C.: Government Printing Office, 1931.

U.S. Congress. Senate Committee on Agriculture and Forestry. *Hearings on Farm-Labor
    Supply Program*, 80th Cong., 1st sess., 1947.

U.S. House of Representatives. Committee on Immigration. *Immigration from Countries of the
    Western Hemisphere*, 71st Cong., 2nd sess., 1930.

———. *Congressional Record*, 68th Cong., 1st sess., 1923–1924.

———. *Congressional Record*, 70th Cong., 1st sess., 1928.

———. *Hearings before the Committee on Immigration and Naturalization*, 69th Cong., 1st
    sess., 1926.

———. *Seasonal Agricultural Laborers from Mexico*, 69th Cong., 1st sess., 1926.

Newspapers and Magazines

Almanac (Claremont)
The California Citrograph
Claremont Courier
Claremontonia
Daily Herald
El Espectador (Pomona Valley)
Los Angeles Examiner
Los Angeles Times
Los Angeles Times Magazine
Mother Jones
The (Ontario) Daily Report
Pomona College Quarterly Magazine
Pomona Daily Times
(Pomona) Progress Bulletin
Pomona Weekly Progress
Pomona Weekly Times
Riverside Enterprise
San Gabriel Valley Tribune
The Saturday Evening Post
Scripps College Student Newsletter

Secondary Sources

Acuña, Rudolfo F. *Occupied America: A History of Chicanos*. 2d ed. New York: Harper and
    Row, 1981.

Alamillo, José. "Bitter-Sweet Communities: Mexican Workers and Citrus Growers on the California Landscape, 1880–1941." Ph.D. diss., University of California, Irvine, 2000.

———. "Mexican American Baseball, Masculinity and the Struggle for Leisure Space, 1920–1950." Paper presented at American Historical Association, Pacific Coast Branch Conference, Park City, Utah, 2000.

Alexander, J. A. *The Life of George Chaffey: A Story of Irrigation Beginnings in California and Australia.* London: Macmillan and Company, 1928.

Allen, James P., and Eugene Turner. *The Ethnic Quilt: Population Diversity in Southern California.* Northridge, Calif.: The Center for Geographical Studies, Department of Geography, California State University, Northridge, 1997.

Almaguer, Tomás. *Racial Fault Lines: The Historical Origins of White Supremacy in California.* Berkeley: University of California Press, 1994.

Alvarez, Robert, Jr. *Familia: Migration and Adaptation in Baja and Alta California, 1800–1975.* Berkeley: University of California Press, 1987.

Alvárez, Rodolfo. "Psycho-historical and Socioeconomic Development of the Chicano Community in the United States." *Social Science Quarterly* 52 (1973): 931–36.

Amott, Teresa, and J. Matthaei. *Race, Gender, and Work: A Multicultural Economic History of Women in the United States.* Boston: South End Press, 1991.

Anderson, Susan M. "Dream and Perspective: American Scene Painting in Southern California." In *American Scene Painting: California, 1930s and 1940s,* edited by Ruth Lilly Westphal and Janet Blake Dominik. Irvine, Calif.: Westphal Publishing, 1991.

Arrízon, Alicia. "Contemporizing Performance: Mexican California and the Padua Hills Theatre." *Mester* 22 and 23, nos. 1 and 2 (Special Double Issue, Chicana/o Discourse, Fall 1993/Spring 1994): 5–30.

Avila, Eric R. "The Folklore of the Freeway: Space, Culture, and Identity in Postwar Los Angeles." *Aztlán* 23, no. 1 (Spring): 15–31.

Baker, Houston A., Jr. *Modernism and the Harlem Renaissance.* Chicago: University of Chicago Press, 1987.

Balderrama, Francisco. *In Defense of La Raza.* Tucson: University of Arizona Press, 1982.

Balderrama, Francisco, and Raymond Rodríguez. *Decade of Betrayal: Mexican Repatriation in the 1930s.* Albuquerque: University of New Mexico Press, 1995.

Bancroft, Hubert H. *California Pastoral, 1769–1848.* San Francisco: 1888.

Banham, Reyner. *Los Angeles: The Architecture of Four Ecologies.* London: Penguin Books, 1971.

Barkan, Elazar. *Retreat of Scientific Racism: Changing Concepts of Race in Britain and the United States Between the World Wars.* Cambridge: Cambridge University Press, 1992.

Benson, Susan Porter. "'The Customers Ain't God': The Work Culture of Department Store Saleswomen, 1890–1940." In *Working Class America: Essays on Labor, Community, and American Society,* edited by Michael H. Frisch and Daniel J. Walkowitz. Urbana: University of Illinois Press, 1983.

Blakeslee, Norma Hopland. "History of Padua Hills Theatre." *Pomona Valley Historian* 9, no. 2 (Spring 1973).

Blitstein, Frederic J. "America's Turmoil: A View from the Suburbs." Ph.D. diss., The Claremont Graduate School, 1971.

Bowers, William L. *The Country-Life Movement in America, 1900–1920.* Port Washington, N.Y.: Kennikat Press, 1974.

Boyle, T. Coraghessan. *The Tortilla Curtain*. New York: Penguin Books, 1995.

Broadbent, Elizabeth. "The Distribution of Mexican Population in the United States." Ph.D. diss., University of Chicago, 1941.

Brodsly, David. *L. A. Freeway: An Appreciative Essay*. Berkeley: University of California Press, 1981.

Brokaw, John W. "A Mexican-American Acting Company, 1849–1939." *Educational Theatre Journal* 27 (March 1975): 23–29.

———. "Teatro Chicano: Some Reflections." *Educational Theatre Journal* 29 (December 1977).

Burbank, Luther. *The Training of the Human Plant*. New York: Century Co., 1907.

Burt, Kenneth. "Latino Empowerment in Los Angeles: Postwar Dreams and Cold War Fears, 1948–1952." *Labor's Heritage* 8, no. 1 (1996): 4–25.

Camarillo, Albert. *Chicanos in a Changing Society: From Mexican Pueblos to American Barrios in Santa Barbara and Southern California, 1848–1930*. Cambridge, Mass.: Harvard University Press, 1979.

Castañeda, Antonia I. "Comparative Frontiers: The Migration of Women to Alta California and New Zealand." In *Western Women: Their Land, Their Lives*, edited by Lillian Schlissel, Vicki Ruiz, and Janice J. Monk, 283–300. Albuquerque: University of New Mexico Press, 1988.

Chan, Sucheng. *Asian Americans: An Interpretive History*. Boston: Twayne Publishers, 1991.

———. *This Bitter-Sweet Soil: The Chinese in California Agriculture, 1860–1910*. Berkeley: University of California Press, 1986.

Chávez, Lydia. *The Color Bind: California's Battle to End Affirmative Action*. Berkeley: University of California Press, 1998.

Cocoltchos, Christopher N. "The Invisible Empire and the Search for the Orderly Community: The Ku Klux Klan in Orange County, California during the 1920s." Ph.D. diss., University of California, Los Angeles, 1979.

Cohen, Lizabeth. *Making a New Deal: Industrial Workers in Chicago, 1919–1939*. Cambridge: Cambridge University Press, 1990.

Coit, J. Eliot. *Citrus Fruits: An Account of the Citrus Fruit Industry with Special Reference to California Requirements and Practices and Similar Conditions*. New York: Macmillan Company, 1915.

Cooke, W. Henry. "The Continuing American Revolution." *Social Science Review* 24, no. 2 (April 20, 1948): 8–10, 25.

———. "The Segregation of Mexican-American School Children in Southern California." *School and Society* 67, no. 1745 (June 5, 1948): 418–21.

Corona, Bert. *Memories of Chicano History: The Life and Narrative of Bert Corona*. Interviewed and edited by Mario T. García. Berkeley: University of California Press, 1994.

Covarrubias, Miguel. *Mexico South: The Isthmus of Tehuantepec*. New York: Alfred A. Knopf, 1947.

Daniel, Cletus. *Bitter Harvest: A History of California Farmworkers*. Ithaca: Cornell University Press, 1981.

———. *Chicano Workers and the Politics of Fairness: The FEPC in the Southwest, 1941–1945*. Austin: University of Texas Press, 1991.

Davis, Mike. *City of Quartz: Excavating the Future of Los Angeles*. London: Verso, 1990.

———. *Ecology of Fear*. New York: Metropolitan Books, 1998.

————. "Magical Urbanism: Latinos Reinvent the US Big City." *New Left Review* April/March, no. 234 (1999): 3–43.

————. *Prisoners of the American Dream*. London: Verso, 1986.

De la Cruz, Victor. *El General Charis y la Pacificacion del Mexico Posrevolucionario*. Edited by La Casa Chata. Mexico, D.F.: Centro de Investigaciones y Estudios Superiores en Antropologia Social, 1993.

Delpar, Helen. *The Enormous Vogue of Things Mexican: Cultural Relations Between the United States and Mexico, 1920–1935*. Tuscaloosa: University of Alabama Press, 1992.

Deuel, Pauline B. *Mexican Serenade: The Story of the Mexican Players and the Padua Hills Theatre*. Claremont, Calif.: Padua Institute, 1961.

Deutsch, Sarah. *No Separate Refuge: Culture, Class, and Gender on an Anglo-Hispanic Frontier in the American Southwest, 1880–1940*. New York: Oxford University Press, 1987.

Deverell, William, and Tom Sitton, eds. *California Progressivism Revisited*. Berkeley: University of California Press, 1994.

Di Leonardo, Micaela, and Roger Lancaster, eds. *The Gender Sexuality Reader: Culture, History, Political Economy*. New York: Routledge, 1997.

Dreyer, Peter. *A Gardener Touched with Genius: The Life of Luther Burbank*. Berkeley: University of California Press, 1985.

Echeverri, Mark. "Pomona, California: The Early Years, 1875–1920." Ph.D. diss., The Claremont Graduate School, 1980.

Escobar, Edward J. *Race, Police, and the Making of a Political Identity: Mexican Americans and the Los Angeles Police Department, 1900–1945*. Berkeley: University of California Press, 1999.

Evans, Sara M. *Born for Liberty: A History of Women in America*. New York: Free Press, 1989.

Fischer, David Hackett. *Historians' Fallacies: Toward a Logic of Historical Thought*. New York: Harper and Row, 1970.

Fisher, Lloyd H. *The Harvest Labor Market in California*. Cambridge, Mass.: Harvard University Press, 1953.

Fogelson, Robert M. *The Fragmented Metropolis: Los Angeles, 1850–1930*. Berkeley: University of California Press, 1967.

Foley, Neil. "Becoming Hispanic: Mexican Americans and the Faustian Pact with Whiteness." In *Reflexiones 1997: New Directions in Mexican American Studies*, edited by Neil Foley, 53–70. Austin, Texas: Center for Mexican American Studies, 1998.

————. *The White Scourge: Mexicans, Blacks, and Poor Whites in Texas Cotton Culture*. Berkeley: University of California Press, 1997.

Galarza, Ernesto. *Merchants of Labor: The Mexican Bracero Story*. Charlotte, N.C.: McNally and Loftin, 1964.

García, Mario T. "Americans All: The Mexican American Generation and the Politics of Wartime Los Angeles, 1941–1945." In *The Mexican American Experience: An Interdisciplinary Anthology*, edited by Rodolfo de la Garza, 201–12. Austin: University of Texas Press, 1985.

————. *Desert Immigrants: The Mexicans of El Paso, 1880–1920*. New Haven: Yale University Press, 1981.

————. *Mexican Americans: Leadership, Ideology, and Identity, 1930–1960*. New Haven: Yale University Press, 1989.

Garcia, Matt. "'Just Put on that Padua Hills Smile': The Mexican Players and The Padua Hills Theatre, 1931–1974." *California History* 74, no. 3 (Fall 1995): 244–61.

García y Griego, Manuel. "The Importation of Mexican Contract Laborers to the United States, 1942–1964." In *Between Two Worlds: Mexican Immigrants in the United States*, edited by David Gutierrez. Wilmington, Del.: Jaguar/SR Books, 1996.

Garner, Bess Adams. *Las Posadas, The Songs of Christmas in Mexico*. Claremont: Vortox Printing Department, 1935.

———. *Mexico: Notes in the Margin*. Boston: Houghton Mifflin, 1937.

———. *Windows In An Old Adobe*. Claremont, Calif.: Saunders Press, 1939.

Garner, Bess Adams, and Miriam Colcord Post. *The Story of the Adobe de Palomares in Pomona California*. 1962 ed. 2 vols. Vol. 2. Pomona: Pomona First Federal Savings and Loan Association, 1962; 1940.

Garza, Roberto J., ed. *Contemporary Chicano Theatre*. Notre Dame: University of Notre Dame Press, 1976.

Gilroy, Paul. *The Black Atlantic: Modernity and Double Consciousness*. Cambridge, Mass.: Harvard University Press, 1993.

Gluck, Sherna Berger. *Rosie the Riveter Revisited: Women, The War, and Social Change*. Boston: Twayne Publishers, 1987.

González, Gilbert. *Chicano Education in the Era of Segregation*. Philadelphia: Balch Institute Press, 1990.

———. *Labor and Community: Mexican Citrus Worker Villages in a Southern California County, 1900–1950*. Urbana: University of Illinois Press, 1994.

———. *Mexican Consuls and Labor Organizing: Imperial Politics in the American West*. Austin: University of Texas Press, 1999.

González, Gilbert, and Raúl Fernández. "Chicano History: Transcending Cultural Models." *Pacific Historical Review* (1994): 490–92.

Gould, Stephen Jay. *Dinosaur in a Haystack: Reflections in Natural History*. New York: Harmony Books, 1995.

Griffith, Beatrice. "Viva Roybal." *Common Ground* 10, no. 1 (Autumn 1949): 61–70.

Griswold del Castillo, Richard. *The Los Angeles Barrio, 1850–1890: A Social History*. Berkeley: University of California Press, 1979.

Grossberg, Lawrence. *We Gotta Get Out of This Place: Popular Conservatism and Postmodern Culture*. New York: Routledge, 1992.

Guerin-Gonzales, Camille. *Mexican Workers and American Dreams: Immigration, Repatriation, and California Farm Labor, 1900–1939*. New Brunswick, N.J.: Rutgers University Press, 1994.

Guevara, Rubén. "The View from the Sixth Street Bridge: The History of Chicano Rock." In *The First Rock and Roll Confidential Report*, edited by David Marsh, 113–126. New York: Pantheon Books, 1985.

Gullett, Gayle. "Women Progressives and the Politics of Americanization in California, 1915–1920." *Pacific Historical Review* 64, no. 1 (1995 February).

Gutiérrez, David. *Walls and Mirrors: Mexican Americans, Mexican Immigrants, and the Politics of Ethnicity*. Berkeley: University of California Press, 1995.

———, ed. *Between Two Worlds: Mexican Immigrants in the United States*. Wilmington, Del.: SR Books, 1996.

Haas, Elizabeth. "The Bracero in Orange County, California: A Work Force for Economic

Transition." San Diego: University of California, Program in United States–Mexican Studies, Q-060, 1981.

———. *Conquests and Historical Identities in California, 1769–1936*. Berkeley: University of California Press, 1995.

Hahamovitch, Cindy. *The Fruits of Their Labor: Atlantic Coast Farmworkers and the Making of Migrant Poverty, 1870–1945*. Chapel Hill: University of North Carolina Press, 1997.

Hall, Stuart. "New Ethnicities." In *"Race," Culture, and Difference*, edited by James Donald and Ali Rattansi. London: Sage Publications, 1992.

Hartig, Anthea. "Communities in Transition: The Transformation of the San Gabriel Valley." Paper presented at the California Issues Conference, November 21, 1997.

———. "'In a World He Has Created': Class Collectivity and the Growers' Landscape of the Southern California Citrus Industry, 1890–1940." *California History* 74, no. 2 (Summer 1995): 100–111.

Herrera, Hayden. *Frida Kahlo: The Paintings*. New York: HarperPerennial, 1991.

Herrera-Sobek, Maria. *The Mexican Corrido: A Feminist Analysis*. Bloomington: Indiana University Press, 1990.

———. *Northward Bound: The Mexican Immigrant Experience in Ballad and Song*. Bloomington: Indiana University Press, 1993.

Herrnstein, R., and Charles Murray. *The Bell Curve*. New York: The Free Press, 1995.

Higham, John. *Strangers in the Land: Patterns of American Nativism, 1860–1925*. New Brunswick, N.J.: Rutgers University Press, 1955.

Hise, Greg. *Magnetic Los Angeles: Planning the Twentieth-Century Metropolis*. Baltimore: Johns Hopkins University Press, 1997.

Hodgson, Godfrey. "The Ideology of Liberal Consensus." In *A History of Our Time: Readings on Postwar America*, edited by William H. Chafe and Harvard Sitkoff, 97–119. New York: Oxford University Press, 1995.

Hofstadter, Richard. *Social Darwinism in American Social Thought*. Boston: Beacon Press, 1944.

Huerta, Jorge. *Chicano Theater: Themes and Forms*. Michigan: Bilingual Press, 1982.

Huggins, Nathan I. *Harlem Renaissance*. New York: Oxford University Press, 1971.

Jacobs, Margaret D. *Engendered Encounters: Feminism and Pueblo Cultures, 1879–1934*. Lincoln: University of Nebraska Press, 1999.

Jensen, Joan M. *With These Hands: Women Working on the Land*. Old Westbury, N.Y.: The Feminist Press, 1981.

Johnson, Richard. "What is Cultural Studies Anyway?" *Social Text* 6, no. 1 (1987).

Kanellos, Nicolás. *Mexican American Theatre: Legacy and Reality*. Pittsburgh: Latin American Literary Review Press, 1987.

———. *Mexican American Theatre: Then and Now*. Houston: Arte Publico Press, 1989.

Kelley, Robin D. G. "Notes on Deconstructing 'The Folk.'" *The American Historical Review* 97, no. 5 (December 1992): 1400–1408.

———. *Race Rebels: Culture, Politics, and the Black Working Class*. New York: The Free Press, 1994.

Kelly, Marcia Patricia Fernandez. "Maquiladoras: The View from the Inside." In *Everyday Trials and Triumphs of Women Workers*, edited by Karen Sacks and Dorothy Remy. New Brunswick, N.J.: Rutgers University Press, 1989.

Kessler-Harris, Alice. *Out to Work: A History of Wage-Earning Women in the United States.* New York: Oxford University Press, 1982.

Kirby, Jack Temple. "Rural Culture in the American Middle West: Jefferson to Jane Smiley." *Agricultural History* 70, no. 4 (1996): 281–97.

Kraut, Alan M. *Silent Travelers: Germs, Genes, and the "Immigrant Menace."* New York: Basic Books, 1994.

Lamphere, Louise. "Bringing the Family to Work: Women's Culture on the Shop Floor." *Feminist Studies* 11 (Fall 1985): 519–40.

Landman, Ruth Hallo. "Some Aspects of the Acculturation of Mexican Immigrants and their Descendants to American Culture." Ph.D. diss., Yale University, 1954.

Lay, Shawn, ed. *The Invisible Empire in the West.* Urbana: University of Illinois Press, 1992.

Leonard, Karen. *Making Ethnic Choices: California's Punjabi Mexican Americans.* Philadelphia: Temple University Press, 1992.

Lillard, Richard G. *Eden in Jeopardy.* New York: Knopf, 1966.

Lipsitz, George. *Dangerous Crossroads: Popular Music, Postmodernism, and the Poetics of Place.* London: Verso, 1995.

———. "'Home Is Where the Hatred Is': Work, Music, and the Transnational Economy." In *Home, Exile, Homeland: Film, Media and the Politics of Place,* edited by Hamid Naficy. New York: Routledge, 1999.

———. "Land of a Thousand Dances: Youth, Minorities, and the Rise of Rock and Roll." In *Recasting America: Culture and Politics in the Age of Cold War,* edited by Lary May. Chicago: University of Chicago Press, 1989.

———. *The Possessive Investment in Whiteness: How White People Profit from Identity Politics.* Philadelphia: Temple University Press, 1998.

———. "The Possessive Investment in Whiteness: Racialized Social Democracy and the 'White' Problem in American Studies." *American Quarterly* 47, no. 3 (September 1995): 369–87.

López, Enrique M. "Community Resistance to Injustice and Inequality: Ontario, California, 1937–1947." *Aztlán* (Fall 1986): 1–29.

López, Ian Haney F. *White By Law: The Legal Construction of Race.* New York: New York University Press, 1996.

López, Ronald W. "The El Monte Berry Strike of 1933." *Aztlán* 1, no. 1 (Spring 1970).

Lothrop-Ricci, Gloria. *Pomona: A Centennial History.* Northridge, Calif.: Windsor Publications, 1976.

Lott, Eric. *Love and Theft: Minstrelsy and the American Working Class.* New York: Oxford University Press, 1993.

Loza, Steven. *Barrio Rhythm: Mexican American Music in Los Angeles.* Urbana: University of Illinois Press, 1993.

McBane, Margo. "The Role of Gender in Citrus Employment: A Case Study of Recruitment, Labor, and Housing Patterns at the Limoneira Company, 1893 to 1940." *California History* 74, no. 2 (Summer 1995): 69–81.

McBane, Margo, and Anthea M. Hartig. "Oranges on the Plains of Id: The Influences of the Citrus Industry on San Gabriel Valley Communities." *California Politics and Policy* (1998): 9–17.

McCarthy, Cameron. *The Uses of Culture: Education and the Limits of Ethnic Affiliation.* New York: Routledge, 1998.

McGroarty, John Steven. *California: Its History and Romance*. Los Angeles: Grafton Publishing, 1911.

MacKay, Constance D. *The Little Theatre in the United States*. New York: Henry Holt and Company, 1917.

McWilliams, Carey. *Factories in the Field: The Story of Migratory Farm Labor in California*. Boston: Little, Brown, 1935.

————. "Los Angeles: An Emerging Pattern." *Common Ground* 9, no. 3 (Spring 1949): 3–10.

————. *North from Mexico: The Spanish-Speaking People of the United States*. 1948. Reprint (new ed.), New York: Praeger, 1990.

————. *Southern California Country: An Island in the Land*. 1946. Reprint, Salt Lake City, Utah: Gibbs-Smith Publisher, Peregrine Smith, 1973.

————. "They Saved the Crops." *The Inter-American* 2, no. 8 (1943 August): 10–14.

Martínez, Daniel, Jr. "The Impact of the Bracero Program on a Southern California Mexican-American Community: A Field Study of Cucamonga, California." M.A. thesis, The Claremont Graduate School, 1958.

Martínez, Rubén. *El Otro Lado, The Other Side*. London: Verso, 1993.

————. *The Other Side: Notes from the New L.A., Mexico City, and Beyond*. New York: Vintage Books, 1993.

————. "The Shock of the New." *Los Angeles Times Magazine*, January 30, 1994.

Marx, Leo. *The Machine in the Garden: Technology and the Pastoral Ideal in America*. New York: Oxford University Press, 1964.

Matsumoto, Valerie J. "Desperately Seeking 'Deidre': Gender Roles, Multicultural Relations, and Nisei Women Writers of the 1930s." *Frontiers: A Journal of Women Studies* 12, no. 1 (1991): 19–32.

————. *Farming the Home Place: A Japanese American Community in California, 1919–1982*. Ithaca, N.Y.: Cornell University Press, 1993.

May, Elaine Tyler. *Homeward Bound: American Families in the Cold War Era*. New York: Basic Books, 1988.

May, Martha. "The Historical Problem of the Family Wage: The Ford Motor Company and the Five Dollar Day." *Feminist Studies* 8, no. 2 (Summer 1982).

Mazón, Mauricio. *The Zoot-Suit Riots: The Psychology of Symbolic Annihilation*. Austin: University of Texas Press, 1984.

Merlo, Catherine. *Heritage of Gold: The First 100 Years of Sunkist Growers, Inc., 1893–1993*. Published by Sunkist, Inc., 1993.

Mitchell, Don. *The Lie of the Land: Migrant Workers and the California Landscape*. Minneapolis: University of Minnesota Press, 1996.

Monroy, Douglas. "An Essay on Understanding the Work Experiences of Mexicans in Southern California, 1900–1939." *Aztlán* 12 (Spring 1981).

————. *Thrown Among Strangers: The Making of Mexican Culture in Frontier California*. Berkeley: University of California Press, 1990.

Moses, Vincent. "The Flying Wedge of Cooperation: G. Harold Powell, California Orange Growers, and the Corporate Reconstruction of American Agriculture, 1904–1922." Ph.D. diss., University of California, Riverside, 1994.

————. "'The Orange-Grower is not a Farmer': G. Harold Powell, Riverside Orchardists and the Coming of Industrial Agriculture, 1893–1930." *California History* 74, no. 1 (Spring 1995).

Muro, Victor Gabriel. *Iglesia y Movimientos Sociales en Mexico, 1972–1987. Los Casos de Ciudad Juarez y el Istmo de Tehuantepec*. Puebla, Mexico: Red Nacional de Investigacion Urbana, 1994.

Nieto, Margarita. "Mexican Art and Los Angeles, 1920–1940." In *On the Edge of America: California Modernist Art, 1900–1950*, edited by Paul J. Karlstrom, 121–35. Berkeley: University of California Press, 1996.

O'Brien, Helen. "The Mexican Colony: A Study of Cultural Change." Senior thesis, Pomona College, 1932.

Odem, Mary E. "Teenage Girls, Sexuality, and Working-Class Parents in Early Twentieth-Century California." In *Generations of Youth: Youth Cultures and History in Twentieth-Century America*, edited by Joe Austin and Michael Nevin Willard. New York: New York University Press, 1998.

Oles, James, ed. *South of the Border: Mexico in the American Imagination, 1914–1947*. Washington, D.C.: Smithsonian Institution Press, 1993.

Otis, Johnny. *Upside Your Head! Rhythm and Blues on Central Avenue*. Hanover, N.H.: Wesleyan University Press, 1983.

Pagán, Eduardo Obregón. "Sleepy Lagoon: The Politics of Youth and Race in Wartime Los Angeles, 1940–1945." Ph.D. diss., Princeton University, 1996.

Paredes, Américo. *Folklore and Culture on the Texas-Mexican Border*. Edited by Richard Bauman. Austin: Center for Mexican American Studies, 1993.

Pascoe, Peggy. "Miscegenation Law, Court Cases, and Ideologies of 'Race' in Twentieth-Century America." *Journal of American History* 83, no. 1 (June 1996): 44–69.

———. "Race, Gender, and Intercultural Relations: The Case of Interracial Marriage." *Frontiers: A Journal of Women Studies* 12, no. 1 (1991): 5–18.

———. *Relations of Rescue: The Search for Female Moral Authority in the American West, 1874–1939*. New York: Oxford University Press, 1990.

Peck, Gunther. "Reinventing Free Labor: Immigrant Padrones and Contract Laborers in North America, 1885–1925." *Journal of American History* 83, no. 3 (December 1996): 848–71.

Pells, Richard H. *Radical Visions and American Dreams: Culture and Social Thought in the Depression Years*. Middletown, Conn.: Wesleyan University Press, 1973.

Peña, Manuel. *The Texas-Mexican Conjunto: History of a Working-Class Music*. Austin: University of Texas Press, 1985.

Perales, Marian, and Alicia Rodriquez. "Directing the Intercultural Experience: The Impact of World War II on Women at Padua Hills Theatre." Seminar Paper, The Claremont Graduate School, May 6, 1993.

Perales, Marian, and Alicia Rodriquez. "Untitled Paper." Delivered at Padua Hills Theatre, October 22, 1993.

Perry, Clarence A. *The Work of the Little Theatres*. New York: Russell Sage Foundation, 1933.

Pomona Centennial History. Pomona, Calif.: Pomona Centennial-Bicentennial Committee, August 1976.

Preston, Richard E. "The Changing Form and Structure of the Southern California Metropolis." *California Geographer* 12 and 13 (1971 and 1972).

Prevots, Naima. *American Pageantry: A Movement for Art and Democracy*. Ann Arbor, Mich.: UMI Research Press, 1990.

Quirarte, Jacinto. "Mexican and Mexican American Artists in the United States: 1920–1970."

In *The Latin American Spirit: Art and Artists in the United States, 1920–1970*, 14–71. New York: The Bronx Museum of the Arts with Harry N. Abrams, 1988.

Raftery, Judith. *Land of Fair Promise: Politics and Reform in Los Angeles Schools, 1885–1941.* Stanford, Calif.: Stanford University Press, 1992.

Reisler, Mark. *By the Sweat of Their Brow: Mexican Immigrant Labor in the United States, 1900–1940.* Westport, Conn.: Greenwood Press, 1976.

Roberts, John Storm. *The Latin Tinge: The Impact of Latin American Music on the United States.* New York: Oxford University Press, 1979.

Roediger, David R. *The Wages of Whiteness: Race and the Making of the American Working Class.* London: Verso, 1991.

Romo, Ricardo. *History of a Barrio: East Los Angeles.* Austin: University of Texas Press, 1983.

Rosaldo, Michelle Z. "The Use and Abuse of Anthropology: Reflections on Feminism and Cross-Cultural Understanding." *Signs: Journal of Women in Culture and Society* 5, no. 3 (1980).

Rosaldo, Renato. "Cultural Citizenship, Inequality, and Multiculturalism." In *Latino Cultural Citizenship: Claiming Identity, Space, and Rights*, edited by Willam V. Flores and Rina Benmayor. Boston: Beacon Press, 1997.

———. *Culture and Truth: The Remaking of Social Analysis.* Boston: Beacon Press, 1989.

Rose, Margaret. "Gender and Civic Activism in Mexican American Barrios in California, The Community Service Organization, 1947–1962." In *Not June Cleaver: Women and Gender in Postwar America, 1945–1960*, edited by Joanne Meyerowitz. Philadelphia: Temple University Press, 1994.

Ruiz, Vicki. *Cannery Women, Cannery Lives: Mexican Women, Unionization, and the California Food Processing Industry, 1930–1950.* Albuquerque: University of New Mexico Press, 1987.

———. "Dead Ends or Gold Mines? Using Missionary Records in Mexican American Women's History." In *Unequal Sisters: A Multicultural Reader in U.S. Women's History*, edited by Vicki Ruiz and Ellen Carol DuBois, 298–315. New York: Routledge, 1994.

———. *From Out of the Shadows: Mexican Women in Twentieth-Century America.* New York: Oxford University Press, 1998.

———. "'La Malinche Tortilla Factory': Negotiating the Iconography of Americanization, 1920–1950." In *Privileging Positions: The Sites of Asian American Studies*, edited by Gary Y. Okihiro et al., 201–15. Pullman: Washington State University Press, 1995.

———. "'Star Struck': Acculturation, Adolescence, and the Mexican American Woman, 1920–1940." In *Building With Our Hands: New Directions in Chicana Studies*, edited by Adela de la Torre and Beatríz Pesquera, 109–29. Berkeley: University of California Press, 1993.

Ruiz, Vicki, and Ellen DuBois, eds. *Unequal Sisters: A Multi-cultural Reader in U.S. Women's History.* 3rd ed. New York: Routledge, 2000.

Sackman, Douglas. "'By Their Fruits Ye Shall Know Them': 'Nature Cross Culture Hybridization' and the California Citrus Industry, 1893–1939." *California History* 74, no. 1 (Spring 1995).

Said, Edward. *Culture and Imperialism.* New York: Alfred A. Knopf, 1993.

Saldívar, José David. *Border Matters: Remapping American Cultural Studies.* Berkeley: University of California Press, 1997.

Salley, Robert Lee. "Activities of the Knights of the Ku Klux Klan in Southern California, 1921–1925." M.A. thesis, University of Southern California, 1963.

Sánchez, George. *Becoming Mexican American: Ethnicity, Culture and Identity in Chicano Los Angeles, 1900–1945*. New York: Oxford University Press, 1993.

———. " 'Go After the Women': Americanization and the Mexican Immigrant Woman, 1915–1929." In *Unequal Sisters: A Multi-Cultural Reader in U.S. Women's History*, edited by Vicki L. Ruiz and Ellen Carol DuBois, 284–97. New York: Routledge, 1994.

Sassoon, Anne S. *Gramsci's Politics*. Minneapolis: University of Minnesota Press, 1987.

Saxton, Alexander. *The Indispensable Enemy: Labor and the Anti-Chinese Movement in California*. Berkeley: University of California Press, 1971.

———. *The Rise and Fall of the White Republic: Class Politics and Mass Culture in Nineteenth-Century America*. New York: Verso, 1990.

Scharf, Virginia. *Taking the Wheel: Women and the Coming of the Motor Age*. New York: The Free Press, 1991.

Schuck, Peter H. "The Treatment of Aliens in the United States." In *Paths to Inclusion: The Integration of Migrants in The United States and Germany*, edited by Peter Schuck and Rainer Munz, 203–42. New York: Berghahn Books, 1998.

Sidran, Ben. *Black Talk*. 2d ed. New York: Da Capo Press, 1981.

Smith, Henry Nash. *Virgin Land: The American West as Symbol and Myth*. Cambridge, Mass.: Harvard University Press, 1950.

Smith, Neil. *Uneven Development: Nature, Capital, and the Production of Space*. New York: Blackwell, 1984.

Smith, Rogers M. *Civic Ideals: Conflicting Visions of Citizenship in U.S. History*, The Yale Institution for Social and Policy Studies Series. New Haven, Conn.: Yale University Press, 1997.

Soja, Edward. *Postmodern Geographies: The Reassertion of Space in Critical Social Theory*. London: Verso, 1989.

Southern Pacific Company. *The Inside Track: The Way through the Wonderful Fruit and Flower Gardens of Southern California*. San Francisco, Calif.: Southern Pacific Publishing, 1907.

Spivak, Gayatri Chakravorty. *Outside in the Teaching Machine*. New York: Routledge, 1993.

———. "Subaltern Studies: Deconstructing Historiography." In *Selected Subaltern Studies*, edited by R. Guha and Gayatri Spivak, 3–32. New York: Oxford University Press, 1988.

Starr, Kevin. *Inventing the Dream: California through the Progressive Era*. New York: Oxford University Press, 1985.

———. *Material Dreams: Southern California through the 1920s*. New York: Oxford University Press, 1990.

Starrs, Paul. "The Navel of California and Other Oranges: Images of California and the Orange Crate." *California Geographer* 28 (1988): 1–41.

Stoll, Steven. *The Fruits of Natural Advantage: Making the Industrial Countryside in California*. Berkeley: University of California Press, 1998.

Stowe, David W. "The Politics of Café Society." *Journal of American History* 84, no. 4 (March 1998).

Takaki, Ronald. *Strangers from a Different Shore: A History of Asian Americans*. New York: Penguin, 1990.

Taylor, Paul. *Mexican Labor in the United States*. Vols. 1 and 2. 1932. Reprint, New York: Arno Press and The New York Times, 1970.

Thomas, Robert J. *Citizenship, Gender, and Work: Social Organization of Industrial Agriculture*. Berkeley: University of California Press, 1985.

Tirado, Miguel David. "Mexican American Community Political Organization: The Key to Chicano Political Power." *Aztlán* 1–2 (1970): 53–78.

Tobey, Ronald, and Charles Wetherell. "The Citrus Industry and the Revolution of Corporate Capitalism in Southern California, 1887–1944." *California History* 74, no. 2 (Summer 1995): 6–19.

Torgovnick, Marianna. *Savage Intellects, Modern Lives*. Chicago: University of Chicago Press, 1990.

Tuck, Ruth D. *Not With the Fist: Mexican-Americans in a Southwest City*. 1946. Reprint, New York: Arno Press, 1974.

———. "Sprinkling the Grass Roots." *Common Ground* 7, no. 3 (Spring 1947): 80–83.

Villa, Raúl H. *Barrio-Logos: Space and Place in Urban Chicano Literature and Culture*. Austin: University of Texas Press, 2000.

Wade, Wyn Craig. *The Fiery Cross: The Ku Klux Klan in America*. New York: Simon and Schuster, 1987.

Weber, David J. *The Spanish Frontier in North America*. New Haven, Conn.: Yale University Press, 1992.

Weber, David J., ed. *Foreigners in Their Native Land: Historical Roots of the Mexican Americans*. Albuquerque: University of New Mexico Press, 1973.

Weber, Devra. *Dark Sweat, White Gold: California Farm Workers, Cotton, and the New Deal*. Berkeley: University of California Press, 1994.

———. "The Organizing of Mexicano Agricultural Workers: Imperial Valley and Los Angeles, 1928–1934, an Oral History Approach." *Aztlán* 3, no. 2 (Fall 1972).

White, Richard. "*It's Your Misfortune and None of My Own*": A New History of the American West. Norman: University of Oklahoma Press, 1991.

———. *Remembering Ahanagran: Storytelling in a Family's Past*. New York: Hill and Wang, 1998.

———. *The Roots of Dependency: Subsistence, Environment, and Social Change among the Choctaws, Pawnees, and Navajos*. Lincoln: University of Nebraska Press, 1983.

Wicke, Peter. *Rock Music: Culture, Aesthetics and Sociology*. Translated by Rachel Fogg. Cambridge: Cambridge University Press, 1987.

Wilhoite, Reverend Lucy D. *The Hatchet Crusade: "Women's Part in the Battle for Freedom."* Upland, Calif., 1928.

Williams, Raymond. *The Country and the City*. New York: Oxford University Press, 1973.

Williamson, Paul Garland. "Labor in the California Citrus Industry." M.A. thesis, University of California, Berkeley, 1946.

Winther, Oscar Osburn. "The Colony System of Southern California." *Agricultural History* 3 (1953).

Wright, Judy. *Claremont: A Pictorial History*. 2nd ed. Claremont, Calif.: The Claremont Historic Resources, 1999.

Zavella, Patricia. "'Abnormal Intimacy': The Varying Work Networks of Chicana Cannery Workers." *Feminist Studies* 11 (Fall 1985): 541–57.

————. *Women's Work and Chicano Families: Cannery Workers of the Santa Clara Valley.* Ithaca, N.Y.: Cornell University Press, 1987.

Zierer, Clifford M. "The Citrus Fruit Industry of the Los Angeles Basin." *Economic Geography* 10 (January 1934).

Miscellaneous

Armendarez, Carmen. Unpublished and untitled family history.

Black, Esther Boulton. "Story Twenty-Five, A Kiss on the Hand." A story based on an oral history with Joe Valadez (son of Emilio Valadez). Interview by Alexandra Morales, July 1967. Oral History Collection, Upland Public Library.

Chaffey Community Art Association. "Lícon: A Memorial Retrospective." Exhibit catalogue, Museum of History and Art, Ontario, Calif., 1985.

Cook, Geoff. *The Claremont Citrus Industry: Then and Now.* Documentary film, 1992.

Davis, Eddie. Interview in the compact disc insert, *The East Side Sound, 1959–1968.* Dionysus Records, 1996.

"Facts about Filipino Immigration into California." Special Bulletin, No. 3, April 1930. Clements Papers Box 62.

Garner, Bess. Padua Hills Newsletters. Padua Hills Theatre Collection, Special Collections, Pomona Public Library.

Garner, Herman H. "Details of Syndicate Being Formed by R. W. Purpus Inc., #875–895, Subway Terminal Building, on Evey Canyon Property, May 11, 1928." Padua Hills Theatre Collection, Special Collections, Pomona Public Library.

Grendysa, Peter. Liner notes for the compact disc *Mondo Mambo: The Best of Pérez Prado and His Orchestra.* Words on Music Ltd., RCA/Rhino Records, Inc., 1995. R2 71889/DRCI-1242.

Hoskins, Brice W. "Report, Director of the Department of Public Relations of the L.A. Community Chest."

Information Regarding Plays Suitable to Padua Hills Theatre for Allied Arts Contest. Padua Hills Collection, Special Collections, Pomona Public Library, date unknown.

McDowell, John. *A Study of Social and Economic Factors Relating to Spanish-Speaking People in the United States.* Home Mission Council, Commission on Social and Economic Factors, 1926.

McGroarty, John Steven. *The Mission Play.* San Gabriel, Calif.: The Mission Playhouse, 1912.

McNaughton, Mary Davis. "Art at Scripps: The Early Years." Exhibit catalogue, 1988.

Martínez, Rubén. "Tanda in L.A." Catalogue for Diva L.A., Mark Taper Forum, Los Angeles, Calif., 1995.

Moreland, Dick. Liner notes to *Stompin' at the Rainbow.* The Mixtures. Los Angeles: Linda Records, 1962.

Padua Hills Theatre playbills, flyers, and awards. Padua Hills Theatre Collection, Special Collections, Pomona Public Library.

Padua Institute Booklet: A Non-profit Institution Dedicated to Inter-American Friendship. Padua Hills, Claremont, Calif., 1936. Padua Hills Theatre Collection, Special Collections, Pomona Public Library.

Pilgrimage Diary of Mexican Players of Padua Hills. Claremont, Calif.: Vortox Company, Printing Department, 1934.

Pomona Ku Klux Klan roster, January 10, 1924. Special Collections, Pomona Public Library.

Sheets, Millard. "Long Term Goals, Intercultural Council Plans." Claremont, Calif.: Claremont Heritage, 1948.

Zornes, Millford. Posters and flyers. Padua Hills Theatre Collection, Special Collections, Pomona Public Library.

Index

Scripps College, 245. *See also* Claremont
  Colleges
Segregation: in local businesses, 52, 236; in
  housing, 204, 211, 238–42, 260–61, 284 (n.
  13), 301 (n. 64); and "jim-towns," 94, 233; in
  labor camps, 51, 71; in public facilities, 8–9,
  204, 233; in public schools, 72, 128, 243–44,
  282 (n. 81)
Sevilla, Mary, 73
Shamel, Archibald D., 52–53, 67
Sheets, Millard, 131, 147–49, 242, 247–48, 301
  (n. 73)
Shelley v. Kraemer, 241
Short, O'Day, 234
Shuler, Bob, 91–92
Sikhs. *See* Asian Americans
Smith, Henry Nash, 21
Soja, Edward, 4–5
Southwick, Grace Ruth, 110
Spaulding, Carl, 141
Spivak, Gayatri, 6, 152–53
Stanley, Grace C., 109
Sterry, Nora, 113–14
Stewart, Albert, 131, 242, 301 (n. 73)
Stowe, David, 9
Strangers in the Land (Higham), 89–90. *See
  also* Nativism
Strategic essentialism, 152–54
Suburbanization: cultural importance of, 214;
  "Greater Los Angeles" landscape and, 2, 24–
  25, 268 (n. 3); freeways/parkways and, 191,
  199–201; housing development and, 187, 241;
  industrialization and, 225–26, 297 (n. 72);
  settlement patterns of, 27–29, 35
Su Casa, 111, 124, 245, 301 (n. 83)
Sunkist. *See* California Fruit Growers Exchange
Swing, 198

Taylor, Paul, 69–70, 74–75, 94, 114
Teague, Charles C., 42, 93, 108–9, 159
Teatro Campesino, El, 154
Tehuantepec, Mexico, 136–38, 286 (n. 43)
Television, 191, 197
Theater/performance: California "pastoral pag-
  eants," 121–23; *commedia dell'arte*, 133; and
  definition of performance, 283 (n. 1); "ethnic
  theater," 122–23, 129; "imperialist nostalgia,"
  283 (n. 2); and Little theater movement, 125–
  27; and polysemy, 283 (n. 6). *See also* Padua
  Hills Theatre
Thomas, Gertie, 189–90, 195
Thomas, Ray, 190
Thunderbirds, The (Roller derby), 198

Tín Tan, 194–95
Tompkins, Glen, 163–64, 166, 169
Torres, Alejandrina, 167
Torrez, Rosa, 145
Touzet, Ray
Tuck, Ruth, 14, 225, 234–35
Turner, Ike, 206
Turner, Tina, 206

Unions/unionization. *See* Labor; Packinghouses
Unity Leagues: Chino, 237–40; electoral poli-
  tics in, 236–38; history of, 14, 214, 225, 227,
  234; housing desegregation and, 239–40;
  Ontario, 237–38; Pomona, 234; Riverside
  ("Casa Blanca"), 236–37
University of California, Los Angeles (UCLA),
  144
Uriburu, J. Z., 43, 68

Vaile, R. S., 68
Valadez, Emilio, 39–40
Valens, Ritchie, 8, 195, 197, 204
Vacio, Natividad, 147, 287 (nn. 75, 77)
Vásquez, Enrique
Vásquez de Buriel, Eusebia, 94
Velásquez, Micaela, 141
Velez, Lupe, 153
Velveteens, The, 195–96, 210
Vera, Miguel, 132–33
Victoria, María, 194–95
Vietnam War, 211
Villa, Beto, 8, 190, 193, 194
Villa, Raúl H., 191
Virginia's (dance hall), 212
Visel, C. P., 107

Washington, Booker T., 110, 132
Webber, Devra, 171
Weinberger, Martin, 163
Welfare capitalism, 103–4
Well-baby clinic (Arbol Verde), 251
White, Berry, 204
White, Richard, 152
Whiteness, 11. *See also* Race, categories of
Whitney, George, 35, 39
Williams, Bert, 152
Williams, Raymond, 32, 45
Wilson, Pete, 257–59
Windows in an Old Adobe (Garner), 140
Woman's Christian Temperance Union
  (WCTU), 75, 277 (n. 95)
Woman's Land Army, 40
Wood, Walter W., 178